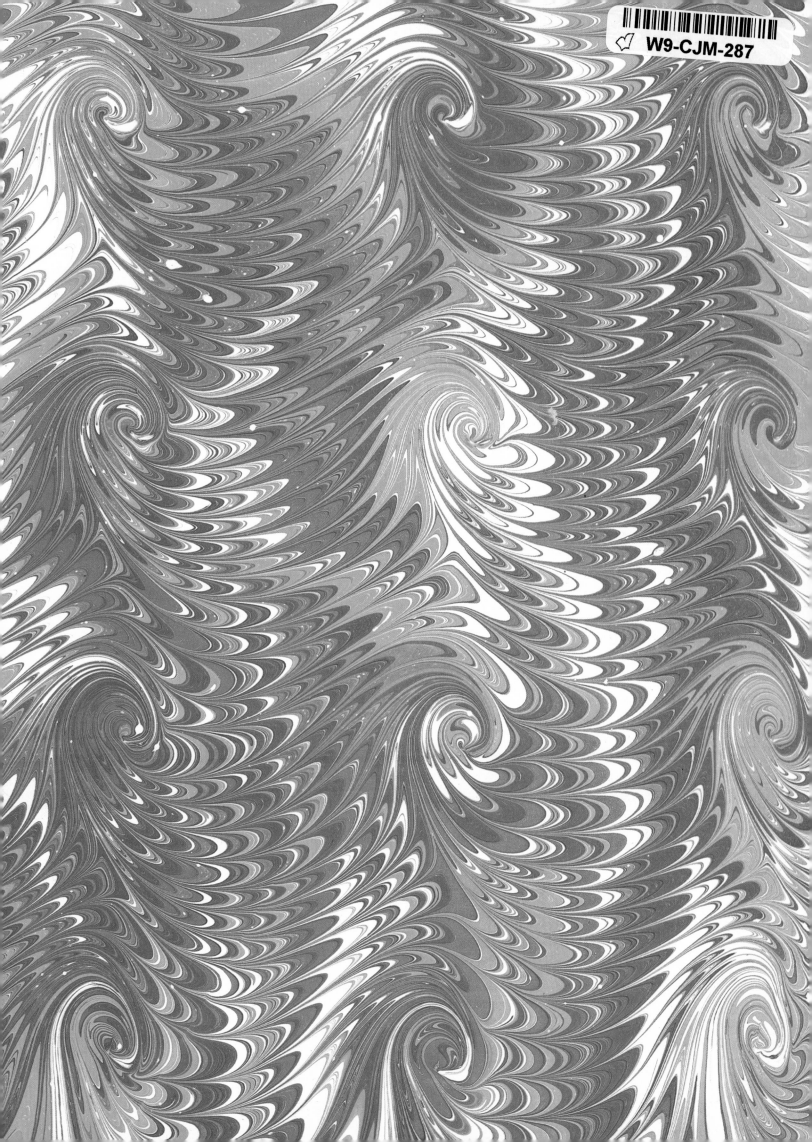

The Book Of
Meissen

by Robert E. Röntgen

Schiffer Publishing Ltd

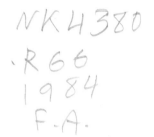

PHOTO CREDITS

The author thanks the following persons and institutions for their permission to reproduce photographs of objects in their collections in this book.

Germanisches Nationalmuseum, Nürnberg, FRG; Plates 21, 29. 217. Figs. 41, 76, 78, 86, 89, 91, 302, 363.

Reiner Grabowitz, Berlin, GDR; Fig. 539 and 637. Photos by Zentrale Fotoabteilung Berliner Verlag, Berlin, GDR and Peter Garbe, Berlin, GDR.

Internationaler Kunsthandel Schloss Ricklingen, Garbsen, FRG; Plate 54.

Iparművészeti Múzeum, Budapest, Hungary; Fig. 830. Photo by Imre Katona, Budapest, Hungary.

Kungl. Husgeradskammaren, Stockholm, Sweden; Fig. 171. Photo by museum.

Kunsthandel Edmund Joachim Kratz, Hamburg, FRG; Plate 222.

Collection of Delorés Beck Martin, U.S.A.; Fig. 77.

Reinhard Mields, Berlin, GDR; Figs. 334, 335, 633. Photos by Zentrale Fotoabteilung Berliner Verlag, Berlin, GDR.

Museen der Stadt Arnstadt, Schlossmuseum, Arnstadt, GDR; Plate 31. Figs. 35, 111, 294, 296. Photos by Jürgen Karpinski, Dresden, GDR.

Museum für Kunst und Gewerbe, Hamburg, FRG; Figs. 26, 38, 49, 54, 60, 62, 82, 85, 88, 112, 168, 170, 301, 307, 312, 313, 321, 344, 345.

National Museum of American History, Smithsonian Institution, Washington,, D.C., U.S.A.; Plates 67, 137, 246, Hans Syz Collection. Plate 271, gift of A.B. Meyer. Figs. 79, 87, 108, 169, 298-300, 304, 305, 309, 366-368, 384, 569, 586, 587, 596, 695, 696, Hans Syz Collection. Fig. 134, gift of Mr. Hanns Weinberg. Fig. 136, gift of Mrs. Jean Mauzé. Fig. 303, gift of Mr. Henry Arnhold. Fig. 352, gift of Mrs. Lyn Revson. Fig. 362, gift of Mr. & Mrs. H. Graves. Figs. 385, 602, 603, Adams-Clement Account.

Nikolai Church, Meissen, GDR; Fig. 167. Photo VEB Staatliche Porzellanmanufaktur Meissen, GDR.

Heinz Reichert, Kunsthandel, Freiburg i. Br., FRG; Plate 106.

Rijksmuseum Amsterdam, Netherlands; Fig. 677. Photo by museum.

Schlossmuseum Gotha, GDR; Fig. 103.

Staatliche Kunstsammlungen Dresden, Porzellansammlung, Dresden, GDR; Plates 19, 20, 250. Figs. 55, 308. Photos by Jürgen Karpinski, Dresden, GDR.

Staatliches Museum Schwerin, GDR; Plates 28, 48, 90, 91, 100-102, 104, 105, 130-132, 172, 174, 206, 209. 210, 216, 218-221, 223-227, 272. Fig. 663. Photos by Peter Garbe, Berlin, GDR.

Stiftung Preussischer Kulturbesitz, Staatliche Museen, Kunstgewerbemuseum Berlin (West); Figs. 52, 61, 84, 90, 110, 127-130, 295, 364, 365. Photos by Arne Psille and Hans-Joachim Bartsch.

Thüringer Museum in Eisenach, GDR; Figs. 24, 25, 429, 442. Photos by Ursula Holzapfel and Peter Jurtzig, Eisenach, GDR.

VEB Staatliche Porzellanmanufaktur Meissen, GRD; Plates 2-10, 12-18, 22-27, 30, 32-47, 49-53, 55-66, 68-89, 93, 94, 96-99, 107-128, 138-171, 173, 175-177, 179-186, 188-205, 207, 208, 211-215, 239, 253-256, 273-282. Figs. 1-5, 7, 9-23, 27-33, 36, 37, 43-48, 50, 51, 57-59, 64-72, 75, 80, 81, 92-102, 106, 107, 113-126, 131-133, 135-140, 142-166, 172, 261-265, 270, 271, 287-290, 292, 294, 297, 306, 314, 315, 319, 320, 322, 323, 328, 346-351, 354-361, 370, 540, 541, 566, 577, 668, 1001, 1002, 1004-1023. Photos by Helfried Kotte, Klaus Tänzer e.a.

Westfälisches Landesmuseum für Kunst und Kulturgeschichte, Münster, FRG; Plate 1. Photo by museum.

Private owners; Figs. 73, 74, 1003.

Author's collection; Plates 11, 92, 95, 178, 187, 228-238, 240, 242-245, 248, 249, 251, 252, 257-270. Figs. 8, 39, 40, 42, 104, 105, 141, 269, 273-284, 291, 310, 311, 316-318, 326, 327, 329-333, 336-343, 369, 371-375, 377-383, 387, 389, 392, 394, 396, 398, 404, 409, 421, 424, 427, 431, 433, 435, 436, 438, 440, 444, 446, 448, 450, 452, 454, 456, 458, 460, 462, 464, 465, 467, 469, 471, 472, 474, 476, 477, 479, 481, 483, 485, 487, 489, 491, 493, 495, 497, 499, 501, 503, 505, 507, 509, 511, 512, 514, 515, 517, 518, 520, 522, 523, 525, 537, 538, 615, 647, 671, 672, 679-681. Photos by Zentrale Fotoabteilung Berliner Verlag, Berlin, GDR and by author.

Front Cover: *One of the pulls of the original Clemens-August-Hunt-Goblet by Kaendler and Ehder, 1741, now at the Westphalian State Museum of Art and Cultural History in Münster, FRG.*
Back Cover: Tailor Astride a Goat, *larger version, modelled by Kaendler in 1737, later pull.*

Designed by Nancy N. Schiffer and Ellen J. Taylor

Printed in the United States of America.
ISBN: 0-88740-014-0
Published by Schiffer Publishing Limited, Box E, Exton, Pennsylvania 19341

This book may be purchased from the publisher.
Please include $1.50 postage.
Try your bookstore first.

Preface

A book about Meissen porcelain can approach its subject from many different points of view, and all approaches would yield a wealth of information and entertainment. Meissen's greatest period was in the 18th century, and it is not surprising that the first hundred years of the manufactory are fairly well researched and described in a large number of books. Most of them concern themselves with certain aspects of Meissen and its porcelain, some give a history of Meissen and its products, but only very few deem the period after 1814 interesting enough to be dealt with.

No doubt is possible that the Meissen manufactory has produced far more porcelain since 1814 than during the time before. These pieces are the bulk of Meissen porcelain offered on the market today. They are very important for a collector with limited means, who cannot expect to find 18th century Meissen porcelain at an affordable price. Most pieces available were made in the 19th and 20th centuries, and about this period precious little has been written. This lack is especially annoying since most imitations, copies and forgeries of Meissen porcelain were made in the last 150 years. Insufficient information about Meissen and its products during this century and a half makes it difficult to distinguish spurious Meissen from the real porcelain of the famous manufactory.

In addition, Meissen is still a very productive and innovative manufactory with a number of interesting new designs in the tradition of the manufactory and also with faithfully executed new pulls of old models and designs. And Meissen has remained a manufactory in the original sense of the Latin word *manufactus*, meaning handmade, and that applies to moulding, shaping and finishing as well as to painting.

This book intends to help collectors, connoisseurs and admirers of Meissen porcelain to appreciate the many facets of these products of human ingenuity, handicraft and love of beauty. But moreover this book is destined to be practical, usable and informative, a handy reference which gives assistance in the identification of Meissen porcelain, of its age, its marks and its importance. It therefore does not concentrate on the most beautiful Meissen pieces, it also deals with the most typical and includes even those products that changed tastes and aesthetic prejudices view as aberrations best to be hushed up.

American museums and collections possess a wealth of Meissen porcelain, and the American antiques market is surprisingly well supplied with Meissen. To help understand and enjoy these products of almost three hundred years of porcelain making by the oldest manufactory in the Western world is another goal of this book. It is devoted less to the expert but rather to the lover and admirer of Meissen porcelain, which remains unique in the history of ceramics.

Nevertheless all factual statements in this book are supported by reliable sources, mainly from the archive of the manufactory, by the files of the State's Archive in Dresden, GDR, and by other original documents. Footnotes refering to these sources are indicated within the text. But in order to make the book more readable for those who like to follow the presentation of the author, the footnotes have been changed to endnotes which can be found before the index.

In the course of the last 120 years and especially in this century a great number of books and articles about Meissen have been written. Most of them give invaluable help, information and opinions. But none of the information has been included in this book before it has been checked against original documents. If that was not possible, the sources from which the information was obtained were identified as secondary sources.

Not always did the author feel able to follow previously published interpretations, definitions or even factual statements, but he feels that his research justifies any deviation from representations which hitherto have been considered acceptable. Occasionally it was necessary to argue with other opinions, these discussions have been placed in the endnotes.

Any book about Meissen will be incomplete. Since a whole human life would not be sufficient to peruse all the files in the manufactory and in the other archives, many questions will remain unanswered, and even conclusions found in this book later may turn out to be erroneous. The author begs his readers' forgiveness in advance if more research should turn up information that contradicts him in one point or another. This would only confirm his feeling that the occupation with Meissen porcelain is a never ending adventure.

Berlin, GDR, January 1984

Table of Contents

Glossary

Arcanist   In Meissen: techonologist knowing the secret of porcelain making.

Arcanum   Alchemist's term for the great secret of nature, in Meissen: the term for the secret of porcelain making.

Biscuit firing   *(Schrühbrand)* First firing of air dried porcelain paste to 900°C (1650°F). The term is not used in Germany because there biscuit ware is fired a second time at higher temperatures in the sharp fire.

Biscuit ware   Porous, unglazed porcelain after the first firing, see biscuit firing.

Chemical and Technical Porcelain   Vessels, implements or parts made from porcelain for use in laboratories, electrical installations or in machines.

Copgen   Small cup without handle.

Flux   Alkaline oxides promoting ceramic fusion at lower temperatures.

Form   In Meissen: term for any tableware design.

Footring   Protruding ring on the bottom of plates, saucers, vessels or pots.

FRG   Federal Republic of Germany.

Garnish   *(staffieren)* to highlight edges, contours, faces or generally parts of porcelain pieces by painting.

GDR   German Democratic Republic.

Pull   *(Ausformung)* composed and finished figurine or group after their parts have been shaped in press moulds, pulled from them, pasted together, fired and garnished.

Repairer   *(Bossierer)* worker who composes the single parts of a figurine or group.

Saggar   Case or box of a fireproof clay compound to protect porcelain pieces during firing from direct flames and ash.

Sharp fire   *(Glattbrand)* also called glost fire, temperatures necessary for the vitrification of porcelain paste and the melting and fusing of the glaze, usually 1450°C (2730°F) for hard paste porcelain.

Shard   *(Scherben)* in Meissen: designation for a formed or modelled porcelain piece in all stages of production.

Thrower   worker throwing and shaping porcelain plates or vessels on a potter's wheel.

Chapter One
Meissen Today

On October 27th, 1739, the Prince-Elector of Cologne, Clemens August, set out for a hunt on horseback behind his dogs. Clemens August was not just Prince-Elector, one of the nine German Princes entitled to choose the German Emperor. He was also Archbishop of Cologne, Prince-Bishop of the regions of Münster, Paderborn, Osnabrück, and Hildesheim, and in addition, worldly ruler of those properties. At this time His Eminence was 39 years old. Despite his ecclesiastical vocation he had a very wordly hobby. He never missed a chance for coursing. (Fig. 1)

On this day, the nine dogs in front of the hunters stirred up a stag in the underbrush and chased it up a little hill. It was a twelve pointer, strong and powerful. Cornered, the stag had no way out and at last in despair it jumped on the thatched roof of a sheepfold. There the Prince-Elector "caught" it, as contemporary sources mercifully describe the end of the chase.[1] It was the eleventh stag the Prince had caught that season, but this episode must have impressed him more than the other ten, and he wanted to immortalize it. His architect, Johann Conrad Schlaun, sketched some designs for sculptures. One of them was intended to crown the chimney of Clemens August's castle Clemenswerth, but it was never executed because it would have been a fire-hazard.

Then the Prince-Elector's noble subjects, the estates of his realm, decided to present him with an elaborate covered hunt-goblet depicting the chase. They probably sent one of the sketches made by Schlaun to the Royal Porcelain Manufactory in Meissen. In 1741 the famous Meissen modeller J.J. Kaendler noted in his work reports that he worked on a goblet for Clemens August. He described it in the language of his time: "On the cover of the goblet a thatched cottage is presented on which the hunted stag sought refuge and nine coursing dogs pursuing it, everything very labouriously modelled."[2]

Fig. 2: Clemens-August-Hunt-Goblet reconstructed by Hösel in 1924

The Prince-Elector probably received the goblet with great pleasure. It was the first one made from porcelain. Until then these drinking vessels, very popular with the high nobility in those days, were made from gold or silver and used at festive occasions. The common man neither could afford them nor was he allowed to hunt at all, and only noblemen of high rank were allowed to chase stags.

Porcelain was exquisite and expensive, but also very breakable. Nothing is left from the goblet of Clemens August. For many years, a few broken pieces of porcelain were treasured as relics of the drinking vessel at Castle Brühl, south of Cologne.[3] Only a few years ago, closer scrutiny revealed that they were *not* pieces of the original, which seems to have perished less than 25 years after the Prince-Elector had received it.[4]

The hunt-goblet, one of the masterpieces of the Meissen sculptors Johann Joachim Kaendler and Johann Jacob Ehder[5], was not only lost, it was forgotten until 1924. Then the German art historian Edmund Renard recommended to the manufactory a reconstruction of the goblet, and the chief of the design department, Erich Hösel, took up the idea. A few of the 69 single moulds for the goblet could be found in Meissen. With their help, with old descriptions and some preserved small parts of the 1741 model, he re-designed the hunt-goblet as close to the original as was possible at that time (Fig. 2).

Fig. 1: Hunter on horseback, model by Kaendler, 1756-1753

In the following years, a number of pulls was made which now mainly stand in museums. It was not until 1957 that a goblet came into public view showing all signs of being much older, when the James A. de Rothschild collection at Waddesdon Manor, England, was given to the National Trust for Places of Historic Interest or National Beauty. Baron Ferdinand de Rothschild evidently had acquired the hunt-goblet before 1898, and kept it in his library.[6] The piece is damaged, especially the delicate racks on both stags, and some of the dogs' tails are broken off.

A second antique hunt-goblet appeared in 1974, when Lesley and Emma Sheafer bequeathed their collection to the Metropolitan Museum of Art in New York. A third one was sold at Sotheby, Parke-Bernet's auction in New York in March of 1979. At first it seemed to have been lost to the public again, until the State Museum of Art and Cultural History in Münster, Germany proudly announced that it had bought the the goblet. Now at least one old pull of the goblet came back to the region once ruled by Clemens August (Plate 1).

These three vessels have much in common. They all bear the impressed number 46 under the base. That is not the model number, because the records in Meissen show that the goblet was registered under the number 267. It might have been a work number or an aid for the assembly of the many parts.

There are slight variations between the three goblets in the positioning of the dogs and their markings. A nesting dove between the leaves of the oak tree appears on the right side of the Waddesdon Manor piece, while it is on the left side of the Münster goblet. The foot bases of the pieces in Münster and New York are higher than the one in Waddesdon Manor.

Despite these slight differences, there seems to be little doubt that the three goblets are pulls from the original moulds, and that they were probably made at the same time. Records in Meissen show that in most cases a difficult and elaborate piece (Fig. 3) was not made in only one copy. The risk was to high that the piece might crack in the fire or be damaged or deformed. So in this case several goblets could have been made to be on the safe side.

It is not known if the hunt-goblet was painted.[7] Only guesses are possible, because until now no records have been found telling of decorative work on the goblet. The three preserved pieces are painted. The one in the Metropolitan Museum of Art bears the coat-of-arms of August III, King of Poland and Prince-Elector of Saxony, who owned the Meissen manufactory and was also a fierce hunter. The huntsman standing by the oak tree blowing his horn is dressed in a coat showing the hunting colors of August III, yellow and blue. The prince-elector's hat, appearing in low relief on the cup, is painted over with the royal crown.[8]

Fig. 3: Moulding of the 69 single parts of the Clemens-August-Goblet with plaster moulds

Fig. 4: Application of oak leaves to the Clemens-August-Goblet. An earlier pull serves as model

The other two goblets seem to have been spares. They too, show the prince-elector's hat in low relief on the cup or cupola, as it is called. But the small cartouches below the hat are not filled with heraldic signs as on the goblet made for August III. Instead miniature hunting scenes are painted in the cartouches. The goblets probably were decorated without a specific order by a noblemen, who certainly would have wanted his own coat of arms put in the cartouches, and either sold or given as a gift by August III. The huntsmens' coats are green, the color of regular hunting clothes in Germany.

Today, the Meissen manufactory still produces the *Clemens-August-Goblet*, as it is called, from the re-designed moulds of 1924. At that time, no surviving goblet was known that could be used for comparison, and it is a small wonder that the 1924 goblet came out a little different than the original.[9] To the eyes of a hunter who rides behind a pack of hounds, some of the dogs on the goblet behave strangely, biting each other or quail. The face of the huntsman is hidden by leaves, and he puts his foot on the stag that lies skinned in front of him. That indeed would have been unpardonable, because only the hunter who fells the stag is allowed to do that, and even then, it is considered bad manners.

Erich Hösel, who re-designed the goblet, evidently was not a hunter, and that accounts for some of the mistakes. But the Meissen manufactory did not let it rest at that. With every new piece of information about the originals, it improved the goblet step by step. This is possible to a certain degree since the goblet is - as all things in Meissen are - made by hand (Fig. 4). The repairer who assembles the many parts can change the position of small pieces, bend them a little differently and thus improve the piece (Plate 2)

Fig. 5: Decoration of a Clemens-August-Goblet. An earlier decorated goblet is used as an example

On the pulls made in the late 1970s, the face of the huntsman is visible again, and his foot does not rest on the stag, but is lifted a little so as not to touch the animal (Fig. 5). These changes were possible without a complete overhaul of the moulds, but nevertheless, a new model of the goblet was begun. The modellers are still at work on it. When they are finished the pulls from these moulds will look exactly like the originals. The new pulls are painted mainly in the colors of the goblet made for August III, with the hunter's coat in yellow and blue.

Hunting motifs were always very popular in Meissen and other manufactories. They also adorn the table setting on Plate 3. But this festive dinner set and the table decorations are not antiques, they are from the current Meissen production. The design, *Large Cutout (Grosser Ausschnitt)*, was developed by chief designer Ludwig Zepner in 1973. The decoration, *Hunting Scenes*, a combination of underglaze and overglaze painting, is the collective work of chief painter Heinz Werner and leading painter Rudi Stolle.

With this table set, the manufactory feels that it successfully has found a design that combines tradition with modern taste and requirements. Even the name expresses this feeling. *Large Cutout* is reminiscent of one of the first - and evidently unbeatable - designs for a dinner set by J.J. Kaendler, called *New Cutout (Neuer Ausschnitt)*.

The manufactory has tried to revive the seemingly lost art of table decoration. Chief sculptor Peter Strang designed a number of candleholders with hunting scenes and other table adornments (Plate 4 and 5). The Meissen painters developed some imagination in decorating this table set. The dinner dishes are painted with hunting scenes of different

kind, the coffee set depicts fowling scenes and the pieces of the mocha set illustrate hunters yarns (Plate 6).

In the history of the Meissen manufactory, periods of productive porcelain designing have always alternated with times of a predominace of painting. In the field of tableware, painting is preponderant in Meissen today.

The large white areas of the design *Large Cutout* invite painting. This design was developed with the intention of offering large plain surfaces for painting without any plastic relief or pattern.[10] It was inspired basically by the shape of flowers and then sublimated to the essence of flowering blossoms. [11] The head of the painting department, Heinz Werner, and his collaborators Rudi Stolle and Volkmar Bretschneider have developed a number of decorations especially suited for the form *Large Cutout* (Plates 7 to 10). More decorations can be expected from them, since the manufactory at the present and for some time to come is in a period of predominance of painting. So much that there seems to be a feeling that it is not necessary to develop new forms for dinnerware.[12]

The form *Large Cutout* quickly found acceptance. Among the many forms the manufactory produces today, it has risen to be in the top ten sales leaders. Enough customers evidently feel that this form system, as it is called today, has an organic relation to the forms of the 18th and 19th centuries. But - as it was in earlier days - it did not come about as a stroke of genius one day. It was a special order by the government of the German Democratic Republic (GDR). Most famous dinner sets of the 18th century were created for a patron. In this case the government was the patron.

Until the order for a new festive and representative table set reached the manufactory in 1972, other forms had been developed in twenty-seven years after World War II without lasting success. The manufactory had to grope its way out of the ruins of the war and to adjust to the radically changed political and social conditions. Meissen's history shows many ups and downs, but it never was so close to a final down as in the years after that war.

People in Europe were struggling for survival in those years. They were more interested in putting something edible on a plate than in the plate itself, even if it was beautiful Meissen porcelain. They lived crowded in wrecked houses, glad to be alive after the terrible destruction. The war that had gone out from Germany had come back with a vengeance.

The victorious Allies had agreed to divide Germany into four zones of occupation. Each of the four powers, the United States, the Soviet Union, Great Britain, and France was to occupy one of them. The city of Meissen was within the territory assigned to the Soviet Union. The Allies also had concurred that Germany should pay at least for part of the damages it had inflicted upon her war enemies. One way of paying was to dismantle industrial equipment to be removed and reassembled in allied countries.

The Meissen manufactory was on the dismantling list. After most of the equipment had been shipped to the Soviet Union, the manufactory still was not dead. About three hundred former employees started anew, preparing the porcelain paste by hand as workers had done it more than 200 years before. The kilns, sturdy pieces of masonry, had been left behind, and they were important. Slowly production picked up again and by the fall of 1946, the manufactory participated in the first Saxonian Industry Fair in Dresden with its products.

There was not much to be shown. Raw materials were hard to come by, ingredients for paints were lacking, and the workers and painters had to do with what little they could find. During the war the paints had been made with substitutes. The so-called K-paints (K for Krieg=war) were duller and less intense. Red looked pale, and instead of gilding, yellow paint was used.

At first, not enough white porcelain was produced to occupy the painters fully. But in the stockrooms or even in private possession of the Meissen workers was some white porcelain from earlier periods and pieces that had been sorted out because of deformations or firecracks. These wares had been lying there in somes cases for more than half a century. They now were painted occasionally with decorations unusual for Meissen. Persian motifs which had been bought by the manufactory late in the 19th century, were applied (Plate 11). These pieces are bewildering even for experts. They bear old marks (Fig. 6) used in the second half of the 19th century until 1924. They are evidently rejected ware but the decoration still is painted meticulously and beautifully. Only the motifs do not match the usual and expected Meissen style and the paint does not show the accustomed Meissen quality. Nothing seems to fit together but these pieces are genuine Meissen.[13]

In 1946, the manufactory became part of a Soviet Joint Stock Company in Germany. These corporations, owned and directed by the Soviet Government, exclusively produced for reparations to the Soviet Union. In retrospect this might have saved the manufactory.

After 1945 everything had changed in Germany, especially in the part occupied by the Soviet Union. She had come to Germany with the intent to change the old political, economical and social systems, which she considered to have been the nutrient soil for German military agressiveness. And since the Soviet Union believed that her kind of socialism was the only way into the future for Germany, she began to lay the groundwork for a socialist society in her part of occupied Germany.

But the Germans had no experience with this new system. Some of the newly-appointed German administrators and managers thought it best to radically destroy and remove all the remains of the feudal and bourgeois periods in German history. The products of the Meissen manufactory mirrored these historical epochs, so many of them were destroyed by those who thought that destruction of the witnesses of history also would change past history. Many irreplacable pieces were lost in those days, but - whatever their reasons might have been - the Soviet administrators under general manager Nikotin intervened and put an end to this iconoclasm. They showed that they had a better feeling for the need for history. They knew that the new society could not be created without historical roots and a sound relation to its past.

During the five years the manufactory had to work for reparation payments, it delivered chemical and technical porcelain, but mainly dinner and coffee sets, figurines, groups and other decorative porcelain in the old styles (Fig. 7). The Soviet administrators considered these pieces to be typical Meissen, and their taste was the same as that of people in other countries.

Fig. 6: Mark on plate shown in color plate 7. An attempt to cover the firecrack by flux was unsuccessful

In 1950, the manufactory was handed over to the government of the newly created German Democratic Republic, founded in 1949 on the territory of the former Soviet zone of occupation in Germany. And now the search began for the future purpose of the Meissen manufactory. The wealthy burghers had disappeared. People salvaging usable building material from the ruins had little use for Meissen figurines. Workers and peasants, the new privileged classes, could not easily relate to elaborately gilded showplates. The newly emerging society semed to have no demand for porcelain pieces which only could be enjoyed.

And because it was necessary first to put dishes on the table, the manufactory had to produce simple tableware, plain white or with mechanically applied decorations. A considerable number of inexpensive and modest tableware was made in Meissen after 1950. The quality did not always match the usual standards, but these pieces nevertheless were marked with the crossed swords.

Not all of the white ware could be decorated at the manufactory. The stock of white porcelain grew to such proportions that the manufactory had to sell undecorated ware. In order to prevent outside painters from painting it and selling it as Meissen porcelain, the crossed swords marks were sandblasted out. Older employees of the manufactory still remember that it cost 7 pfennig (1 3/4 cents) to sandblast out one mark (Fig. 8).

Fig. 7: Coffee set form Neuer Ausschnitt *(New Cutout) with rose decoration*

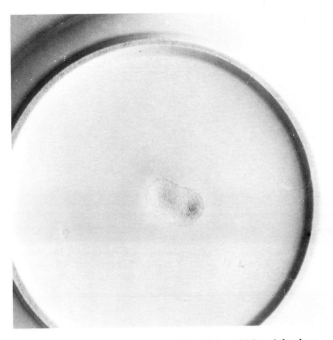

Fig. 8: Bottom of plate produced in 1953 with the crossed swords mark sandblasted out later

Fig. 10: Spring by Ullmann, 1948, Böttger stoneware

Fig. 9: Otter by Max Esser, model designed in 1931, Böttger stoneware

The porcelain without marks had to be sold, because the manufactory was, and still is, an enterprise that has to make a profit. Early in the 1950s, profit considerations were foremost in the thoughts of the government's central planning commission, to which the manufactory was subordinate. In 1957, the manufactory administration pointed out that a purely economic orientation brought about the danger of a permanent loss of values and abilities. This, so the administration warned, could lead to considerable damage to the worldwide reputation of the manufactory. [14]

The declining sales proved it right. Until 1955, the manufactory operated in the red, because foreign buyers stayed away. An artistic advisory board was charged with selecting designs for figurines and groups. Its judgement was not always certain, but in those years artists all over the world were searching for new means of expression and new forms. Many of the designs of the 1950s today only cause a shudder.

Meissen, too, was caught up in this search. The advisory board rejected models by famous sculptors like Paul Scheurich (Plate 12) and Max Esser (Fig. 9) as out of touch with the times and as failures. [15] Both sculptors had designed a number of very successful figurines and groups for the manufactory before World War II. Some of the figurines accepted in the 1950s still show their kinship with the artistic school preferred by the leaders of the Third Reich (Fig. 10). After some experiments without great success, the advisory board was not consulted any more. It might have had the right feeling for the new political demands made to the manufactory, but it had very little knowledge about the taste of the buying public abroad and the economic repercussions of its recommendations.

Unable to develop sufficient new ideas on its own the manufactory after 1950 bought about one hundred models for figurines and groups from outside artists. Among them were designs by the reputed sculptors Willi Münch-Khe (Fig. 11) and Erich Oehme (Fig. 12) who had worked for the manufactory before World War II and were especially famous for their animal sculptures. Models acquired by the manufactory already in the 1930s now were put into production for the first time (Fig. 13). A small number of new figurines came from modellers employed by the manufactory or from outside (Fig. 14).

The results were not bad. In 1959 the new models had conquered a substantial share of the sales abroad, outselling even some of the 18th century models. The manufactory and the government's central planning commission had learned the hard way the dangers of producing against the demands of the buying public.

Just when it thought it had found its new way the manufactory in 1960 was pointed in a different direction. It was instructed to produce for everyone in the German Democratic Republic, not only with new forms, but also with motifs representing the new meaning of life in a socialist society. The old traditional forms were not to be used as examples any more.[16]

The manufactory never in its history had produced for everybody, it could not offer wares for common use. All of its products were rare, exquisite, and of excellent quality. To abandon these standards meant converting the manufactory into one of the common porcelain factories, which show only slight differences in the quality of their products. At the end of this way the Meissen manufactory would have lost its personality, its reputation and its uniqueness.

Proof came soon when export sales, always the mainstay of the manufactory, went down, In 1959, eighty percent of the products were sold abroad. In 1969, foreign sales had gone down to fifty-eight percent of production because the manufactory had replaced many of the old forms with unsalable new designs.

It was not a comfortable and easy situation. The manufactory was supposed to offer porcelain for the members of the new socialistic society in the GDR, reflecting their lifestyle and their approach to life and work. But it was also obliged to export in order to stand on sound financial ground.

The new society in the GDR had done away with the wealthy classes which once were the main buyers and collectors of Meissen porcelain. Workers and peasant were supposed to be the ruling classes, and it was thought that they wanted porcelain in their homes depicting working life. They actually did not as manufactory officials found out later.

Meissen porcelain was supposed to represent the new times, but the ones who bought the bulk of Meissen products were the wealthy burghers abroad, who had no taste for socialistic themes. So the manufactory was caught in a double bind: They could either hold on to a style suited for the new society and go broke, or give in to the taste of the buyers abroad and survive.

For a few years, the manufactory tried a road in between. It was not passable because at the same time there was a great uncertainty about new styles. In Meissen, designers and artists groped for new and durable means of combining form and function (Fig. 15 to 17, Plate 13). Porcelain designed by Meissen in those years should be judged with the understanding that many designs from those years by artists all over the world did not survive either. When the manufactory in the early 1960s offered a newly designed dinner set at the Leipzig Fair, there were no buyers at all.

Fig. 11: Roe Buck by Willi Münch-Khe, designed 1938

Fig. 12: Head of stud Maestoso *by Erich Oehme, 1951*

Fig. 13: Shetland Pony *by Heinrich Drake, designed in 1935, first pull in 1957*

Fig. 14: Two Flamingoes *by Elfried Reichel-Drechsler, 1958*

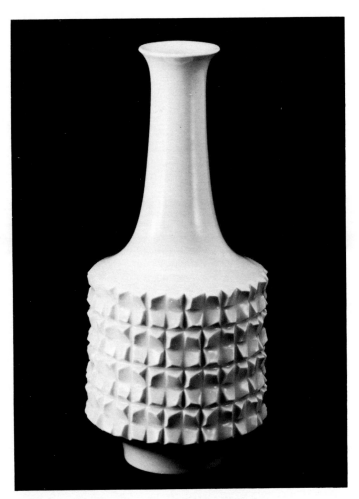

Fig. 16: Vase by Ludwig Zepner, 1966

Fig. 15: Vase by Ludwig Zepner, 1965

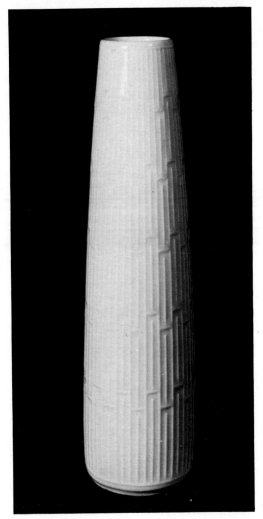

*Fig. 17: Vase by
Hans Merz, 1950*

Fig. 18: Work Break *by Wilfried Pfitzenreiter, 1967, Böttger stoneware*

Fig. 19: Liberated Africa *by Gerhard Geyer, 1967, Böttger stoneware*

Fig. 20: Girl member of the GDR youth organisation Young pioneers *by Manfred Wünsche, 1967*

The illustration of the new political philosophy and its manifestations was seen as the main requirement in Meissen at this time. The Russian October Revolution of 1917 was depicted, busts of Lenin and Karl Marx were representative of the new political course. Motifs of working life (Fig. 18) and political struggle against colonialism (Fig. 19) showed the future way the manufactory was supposed to go, not inspiring and joyful but simply reflecting everyday life like a photograph (Fig. 20).

But here an immanent law of porcelain modelling had been violated. Porcelain does not lend itself easily to the depiction of serious motifs, especially when they are conceived intellectually. After many dissatifying attempts, the sculptor Peter Strang came to the conclusion that porcelain is better suited for playful motifs. The properties of the porcelain itself taught him, and he was a quick and sensitive learner. He had always wanted to model serious themes, but most of the time they turned out to be cheerful.[17] And with this experience he found his way to an imaginative, fantastic style (Fig. 21 to 23, Plates 14 to 16).

Working with porcelain is quite different from working with wood or metal. Everything has to be slightly exaggerated, because the wet pull from the moulds shrinks about one sixth in drying and firing. In addition, the glaze softens the contours and profiles. Many famous sculptors have tried their hands at porcelain, but only a few succeeded. Most of them gave up in frustration.

Fig. 21: Group, Dragon, Elsa and Lancelot *by Peter Strang, 1967, after the play* The Dragon *by Jewgeni Schwarz*

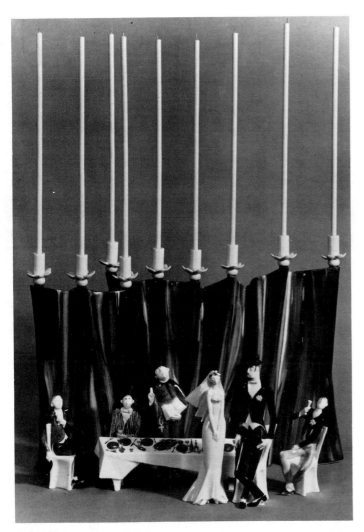

Fig. 22: Group Macheath' Wedding *by Peter Strang, 1970, inspired by the* Three Penny Opera *by Brecht and Weill*

In the 19th century, the manufactory had tried to win renowned artists and designers to work for Meissen. The same attempt was made again in 1967. First, models were bought which already had been executed in other materials. Most artists let the manufactory have their models, but at the same time left the clear impression that they did not consider porcelain the right material for their creations. Two years later, manufactory envoys visited a number of sculptors and tried to encourage them to work for Meissen, but nothing came of their attempts. The difficulties of modelling porcelain is one of the reasons why today mainly designers and artists trained at the manufactory became successful in the long run.

Ludwig Zepner, present head of the design department, and designer Gerhard Wronkowski grew up in the manufactory, as did the head of the painting department, Heinz Werner, and the leading painters Rudi Stolle and Volkmar Bretschneider. Peter Strang, the sculptor, was first a repairer in Meissen. He then studied art in Dresden before returning to the manufactory.

In the 1960s, the discussions in Meissen also centered around the question of whether the manufactory should remain a manufactory, or whether it should become a factory. If Meissen's future was seen in the mass production of consumer goods, then machines were necessary to produce rationally the large amount of porcelain required. If the manufactory decided to stick to its method of doing everything by hand, starting from moulding to the last stroke of the paint brush, then it could not mass produce, and Meissen porcelain would remain rare and expensive. It also would retain the charm and singular beauty of a handmade product of which even two pieces made one after the other are not exactly alike.

Fig. 23: Large Floor Vase with plastic decoration Zauberpferdchen *(Magic Horse) by Peter Strang, 1974*

15

The future of the Meissen manufactory was not decided before 1969. When Karl Petermann became director of the manufactory, he revived many unused capabilities in Meissen. Until then everything, even artistic experiments, had to be approved beforehand. That had put designers and artists in such a confining role that some of them worked as freelancers for the porcelain factory in Wallendorf in Thuringia, whose director offered them a chance to break out of the rut. (Fig. 24 and 25). With Petermann's arrival, all this changed. He encouraged the manufactory artists, but more importantly under his guidance the future course of the manufactory was charted.

Throughout its history, the Meissen manufactory survived the many struggles for its existence because it was able to preserve the old traditions and at the same time develop new creativity. That again became the principle for the manufactory after 1969, and it worked as well as it had during the two-and-a-half centuries before. This principle, combined with the flexibility described earlier in the paragraphs about the redesign of the Clemens-August-Goblet are the main reasons for the viability of the manufactory.

This can be seen in the new pulls the manufactory makes from 18th century models. The gypsum moulds, from which the pulls are taken, are carefully restored to their 18th century shape. In the 19th century Rococo figurines and groups, as well as other decorative porcelain, sometimes were drastically changed to suit contemporary tastes. But the new pulls are very close to the originals. They express the same feelings, and they are true to the intentions of their designers (Figs. 26 and 27). Small variations are not unusual, they even occur on several original pulls made from the same mould at the same time. An arm put on the body just a fraction of an inch differently changes the appearance of a figurine ever so slightly. As long as handwork dominates in Meissen, no two pulls from the same mould will be perfectly alike.

That is part of the charm of Meissen porcelain and this quality has made Meissen products most desirable. After it had revived the old virtues, the manufactory was able to survive. It has gone through many crises in its history, some of them as bad as the one after World War II. One of the reasons was the high goal set for the manufactory. From its beginning, the manufactory's purpose was twofold. Its founder, Augustus the Strong, King of Poland and Prince-Elector of Saxony, expressed it his way when he said, "the manufactory should serve the glory of the King as well as the commerce." Translated into today's language this means that the manufactory was expected to contribute to the art world, but at the same time, it had to be a profitmaking enterprise.

Fig. 24: Lovers, designed by Peter Strang for the porcelain factory in Wallendorf, garnished by Heinz Werner, 1964

Fig. 25: Honeymoon service designed by Ludwig Zepner for the porcelain factory in Wallendorf, decoration by Heinz Werner with silver and brass mounts and semi-precious stones on the knobs of the covers of coffee and sugar pots, 1964

Fig. 26: **Dancing Couple** *by Johann Gottlieb Ehder, original pull of 1742*

Today, eighty percent of the Meissen products find buyers abroad, and those buyers show increasing interest in the new designs and figurines. The Meissen artists benefit from this situation. They now have a considerable margin of freedom for experiments, and the manufactory also gives outside artists a chance to try their hands on porcelain.

An exhibition of those experimental pieces was shown in 1982 in Dresden, on the three-hundredth birthday of the inventor of European hardpaste porcelain, Johann Friedrich Böttger. Even if only few of these experimental pieces should survive, the manufactory can afford to finance, support and encourage the search for new forms of expression.

Böttger was honored on his anniversary with an elaborate series of festive and scientific events sponsored by the government of the German Democratic Republic, with many international guests participating. The manufactory issued a special memorial cup and saucer. The saucer was made from red stoneware, Böttger's first ceramic invention, the cup was made from porcelain (Fig. 28). In addition, the manufactory selected five pieces from the first years of porcelain making in Meissen to be remade as replicas for the Böttger-Jubilee, two in red stoneware (Fig. 29 and 30), and three in porcelain (Fig. 31 to 33). Added to the mark on these pieces (Fig. 34) are the letters CD, the Roman numerals for the number 400, because these replicas were only manufactured in a limited edition of four hundred each. Except for the paste, which was quite different in the first years of the manufactory, they are true replicas of the originals. Meticulously executed, they give an impression of the quick progress of porcelain designing during the nine years between the foundation of the manufactory and Böttger's death.

Böttger himself described the charm of porcelain with these words: "Three things arouse the desire of men to own something they ordinarily could do without. 1. Beauty, 2. Rarity and 3. Utility Value connected with them. These three qualities make a thing pleasant, valuable and necessary, so that everybody - if not for use or adornment - at least because of its Curiosity would want to own some of it."[18]

Fig. 27: Modern pull of the **Dancing Couple** *by Ehder in Fig. 26*

Fig. 28: Memorial cup and saucer made in a limited edition for the occasion of the 300th birthday of J.F. Böttger, 1981/82

Fig. 29: *Candlestick, replica after the original created about 1711 now at the Dresden Porcelain Collection, Böttger stoneware, height 14.1 cm (5 1/2 inches)*

Fig. 30: Head of Proserpina *by Benjamin Thomae after Bernini, replica after the original created about 1710-1712 now at the Schlossmuseum Arnstadt, GDR, Böttger stoneware*

Fig. 31: Covered Vase with two masks in relief, replica after the original created between 1714 and 1719 now at the Dresden Porcelain Collection, height 21.8 cm (8 19/32 inches)

Fig. 32: Covered Bowl with applied twigs and blossoms of wild roses, replica after the original created between 1714 and 1719 now at the Dresden Porcelain Collection, height 15.1 cm (5 15/16 inches)

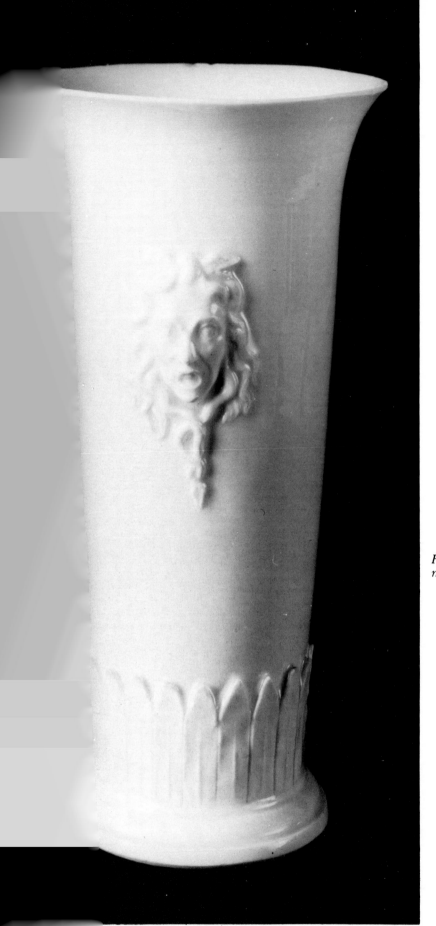

Fig. 34: Mark on replicas and memorial cup and saucer
manufactured for the occasion of Böttger's 300th birthday

Vase with two heads of Medusa, replica after the
reated between 1714 and 1718 now at the Dresden
Collection

Chapter Two
History of the Manufactory

Fig. 35: Pagoda *as an incense burner after Chinese models, Böttger porcelain, about 1715*

European porcelain is a child of medieval superstition and enlightment. Its godparents were cupidity and political prudence. Born to a royal court, it soon became a democratic household object. The historical setting is important, because it provided all the incentives for the invention of hard-paste porcelain and the quick rise of porcelain production. Inventions of this or any other kind don't just happen, two conditions are necessary: science and technology must be ripe, and there must be a demand for the product. If human ingenuity joins these two conditions, then inventions are not only possible, they are unavoidable.

Despite the fact that the Chinese and Japanese already had made porcelain for centuries, European hard-paste porcelain was an invention, not a re-invention or the discovery of a hitherto secret manufacturing process (Fig. 35). The Chinese did not invent porcelain, nor did the Japanese, who learned porcelain-making from China.

Historical sources about the beginning of porcelain-making in China have not yet been found, but the available informations point strongly to the presumption that the Chinese actually did not invent porcelain at all. At one point in their long history of making pottery, they seem to have found all the ingredients necessary for porcelain-making ready-mixed in the ground. Judging from the oldest preserved porcelain pieces, this must have been around the year 900 A.D. Chinese potters improved the mixture, added or reduced some of the ingredients, and by trial and error found the best way to make porcelain.

When Portuguese ships began trade with China in the 16th century, the Chinese had mastered porcelain produc-

tion for a long time. In Europe, porcelain soon became desirable, because it was much better suited for food and beverages than the metal dishes and vessels used until then. Impervious to acids and other aggressive chemicals, and resistant to heat, porcelain had many advantages over silver and pewter. Several attempts at producing porcelain in Europe were made without usable results.

Early in the 17th century, the newly founded Dutch United East India Company organized the China-trade and brought back large cargoes of Chinese and Japanese porcelain to Europe. The Dutch even had porcelain wares made to order, including copies of old Chinese porcelain. Even though the British joined the trade, the Dutch remained the main importer of Chinese and Japanese porcelain for continental Europe. At their porcelain auction sales, anyone could buy the wares from the Far East, but only the wealthy could afford the extraordinary products of the potters in China and Japan. Because they were so expensive, they came to represent wealth, importance and refined taste.

Late in the 17th century, Europe was under the spell of Louis XIV of France, the "Sun King". His court in Versailles, with its splendor and extravaganzas, its breath-taking pomp and riches, nourished the ardent desire for at least a small copy of Versailles in every ruler and princeling in the old World. But Louis XIV could rely on the ingenuity and skills of his economic adviser Jean Baptiste Colbert to provide the necessary revenues for the lavish exposition of royal grandeur. Most of the other potentates in Europe lived on limited budgets compared to *"le Roi soleil"*.

One of the few exceptions was the Prince-Elector of Saxony, Friedrich August I, who converted the city of Dresden into an impressive residence (Fig. 36). By promoting economy and trade in Saxony in the mercantile fashion, he increased his revenues and brought Saxony on becoming the economically most progressive state in Germany. The Prince-Elector organized a productive mining industry (Plate 17) that became one of the foundations of his country's wealth.

Fig. 36: Prospect of Dresden with the Royal Castle, Meissen plate

But Friedrich August, who loved his nickname Augustus the Strong, was not satisfied with just being one of the nine Prince-Electors, who had the right and the power to elect the Emperor of the German Empire. He aspired to be a king, and he also had ambitions to become Emperor.

His first step was to bribe the Polish Estates (Plate 18), who elected him King of Poland over a French prince who did not spend quite enough money to be elected. As King of Poland, Friedrich August called himself August II (Fig. 37) In order to get elected, he had promised to drive the Swedes out of the formerly Polish province of Livonia at the Baltic Sea. Sweden was the strongest military power around the Baltic Sea, much to the discomfort of the adjoining states: Russia under Peter the Great (Fig. 38), Denmark, and Poland/Saxony. These states formed a military coalition against Sweden, and in 1700 started a war, which later was called the Nordic War (1700-1721).

Wars are expensive, especially for the loosing side, and August II lost all of the important battles. The Swedes even occupied large parts of Saxony, and in 1706 August was forced to abdicate as King of Poland. His undiminished love of splendor, enormous war expenses and large foreign debts demanded more money than the country could provide.

In spite of his progressive attitude toward scientific and economic development, August was not free of remnants of medieval superstition. He and many of his contemporaries still believed in the philosopher's stone, which would solve all problems and answer all questions. And he was convinced that there was an "arcanum", the secret recipe which would turn base metals into silver and gold. Whoever possessed it could not only outdo the envied Louis XIV of France, he surely would become the mightiest ruler in the world.

Fig. 38: Medal from red stoneware with relief portrait of Tsar Peter the Great of Russia, *about 1715-1720*

So despite his preoccupation with the war, August immediately took notice when a royal courier brought him news from his chancellery in Dresden to the court in Warsaw. The district administrator of the Saxon city of Wittenberg in November of 1701 had reported an unusual incident to the Dresden chancellery. A Prussian lieutenant had presented himself to the administrator as authorized envoy of the Prussian King and requested the arrest of a fugitive from Prussian justice. To emphasize his demand, the lieutenant was accompanied by a detachment of Prussian soldiers, which - for the time being - had pitched their tents peacefully but conspicuously outside the city walls of Wittenberg.

Saxony and Prussia were on rather good terms, and the district administrator, Johann Jacob von Ryssell, did not want to take the chance of antagonizing Prussia. He ordered the arrest of the suspect, who turned out to be a nineteen year old man by the name of Johann Friedrich Böttger. But Ryssell was also cautious. He kept Böttger in Saxon custody after a first conversation with this "fellow from Berlin" had given him the impression that there was more to the case than the Prussian lieutenant wanted to reveal.

First of all, Böttger's citizenship was somewhat confusing, which was no surprise, because at that time more than 300 independent territories were crowded within the borders of the German Empire. Böttger's father had come from the archbishopric of Magdeburg originally. He left the city in 1680 to become mintmaster for the Thuringian Count Heinrich Ivon Reuss-Schleiz in the city of Schleiz. Johann Friedrich Böttger was born there in February 1682, but nobody knows exactly what day. The parish register only shows that the baby was baptized on February 5th.

About one hundred years later, someone wrote an addition into the register, which said that Böttger was born on February 4th. Böttger himself always claimed to be a Sunday-Child[1]. But the first Sunday in February of 1682 fell on the first of the month. The fourth of February was a Wednesday, and the day Böttger was baptized was a Thursday.

Since Böttger later was not even sure what year he was born, his claim of being a Sunday-Child should not be taken too seriously. Conventional wisdom in those days had it that being born on Sunday, under a lucky star, gave one the ability to discover secrets. Böttger later had a good enough reason to maintain his contention of possessing an important secret. Modern historiography has decided against Böttger, and chosen February 4th as his birthday (Fig. 39).

Fig. 37: August II, red stoneware, about 1710-1715

Fig. 39: Relief portrait of Böttger, *biscuit porcelain, 1982*

The mint in Schleiz, where his father worked, existed only a few years. The sovereign had had minted money that contained less gold or silver than it should have, and people would not take it for face-value. After the mint was closed, father Böttger moved his family back to Magdeburg in 1682, where he died the same year.

In the meantime, the city of Magdeburg had lost its independent statehood and had become part of Prussia. After a year of mourning, Böttger's mother married the Prussian town-major and fortification-engineer, Johann Friedrich Tiemann, who took great interest in the boy. He taught him not only mathematics and geometry, but also pyrotechnics. Young Böttger showed a special aptitude for chemistry, so his stepfather apprenticed him to the apothecary Friedrich Zorn in the Prussian capital of Berlin.

At first Böttger, who was fourteen years of age at that time, did quite well. He seemed to be diligent, curious and perceptive, but soon it became apparent that he was striving for a higher goal. He saw his future not in pills or ointments but rather in the search for the Philopher's Stone, the Red Tincture, the Arcanum, the Panacea, that would cure all ills and also would give eternal youth and everlasting life. Böttger experimented with goldmaking, and that got him into trouble with his master. He ran away twice, but each time reconsidered and begged forgiveness. Nevertheless he must have shown good conduct otherwise in Zorn's pharmacy, because his mother was able to persuade the apothecary to release him from apprenticeship early and make him a journeymen. A few weeks later, Böttger invited Zorn and his wife to witness an experiment in goldmaking.

Zorn considered this a good opportunity to prove to the obsessed young man once and for all that his hope of making gold form base metals was at best a pipe dream. He prepared the setting carefully and invited two relatives of clerical vocation to watch and to assist. Böttger was allowed to put an empty melting pot onto the hearth and to blow the fire until the pot was red-hot. Then he stood back. One of the clergymen dropped eighteen silver coins into the crucible and fanned the fire until the coins were molten. Böttger handed a pinch of his secret powder to the other minister, asked him to wrap it in paper, throw it into the molten silver and to cover the pot.

So it was done. After a short interval, the melting pot was taken from the fire, uncovered and its contents poured out. Instead of silver, gold came out of the pot. Gold of the highest quality, as was ascertained the next day. Böttger never revealed how he did it, but to those who watched he truly had made gold. Today there can be no doubt that he tricked his audience, but in those days, even the unbelieving Zorn was impressed.

The famous German philosopher and mathematician Gottfried Wilhelm Leibniz (Fig. 40) reported to the wife of the Prince Elector of Hanover Sophie on November 8th, 1701 that the Philosopher's Stone suddenly had appeared in Berlin, and that despite his doubts, he could not refute so many witnesses.[2]

Today it is possible to transmute metals, for instance to convert uranium into plutonium in a nuclear reactor. Nuclear scientists even have made a few specks of gold in a reactor at an expense that far outweighs the value of the gold. So it can be done, but not with a melting pot, a few coins, a hot fire and some strange powder.

There is no explanation of how Böttger got the gold he used for his tricks. He had no money of his own to buy the few ounces of gold he used for his performance. It was a perfect show of legerdemain, convincing and -as the apothecary Zorn had warned him before - very dangerous.

Despite Böttger's request to keep the transmutation a secret, it was the talk of the town a few days later. Zorn's pharmacy did a brisk business, because everyone wanted to see the young adept, who had found a way to make gold. Soon the rumors reached the Prussian Court, which was only three blocks away. King Friedrich I (Fig. 41) was a spendthrift. He, like August of Saxony, also had wanted to become a king, but this was not possible within the confines of the German Empire, where all the titles and ranks were neatly

Fig. 40: Relief portrait of Leibniz, *Böttger stoneware, made for the city of Leipzig in 1970.*

Fig. 41: King Friedrich I in Prussia, *relief portrait in red stoneware, after 1711*

and irrevocably tied up. Just as August had found his kingdom in Poland, Friedrich also went outside the borders of the Empire to his province of Prussia, later called East-Prussia, and made himself King in Prussia. This title legally was only valid inside the little province, but Friedrich quickly extended it to all his possessions within the Empire, and soon it became a generic term.

When Friedrich heard of Böttger's feat, he ordered Zorn to appear before him with the gold the young man had made. He listened to Zorn's story, kept the gold (later replacing it with a gold medal),and expressed his strong royal desire to see the now famous adept. The King was in dire need of some ready cash. He just had lavished six million Thalers on his coronation. The money he had dissipated were the state revenues for two years. With his treasury empty, Friedrich looked for ways to fill it up - the easier, the better.

Böttger panicked hearing the Kings command. He knew that the King believed in the possibility of transmutation, but he also was aware of the nasty royal habit first to find out - by means of inquisition and a little torture - whether a presumable gold-maker was a cheat or an adept. Böttger knew to which category he belonged, and he decided on the spur of a moment to disappear from Berlin.

Only 24 days after his great success, Böttger sneaked out of the city under cover of night and hid in the house of a merchant. Terrified, he learned that *Wanted* posters had been put up in Berlin, promising one thousand Thalers for his arrest: alive naturally, dead he was of no use for the King. After three frightening days, relatives of the merchant hid Böttger in a covered wagon and drove him across the border into Saxony, to the city of Wittenberg. When the Prussian King was told of Böttger's escape, he became furious. He immediately sent Lieutenant Menzel after Böttger. One day after Böttger had arrived in Wittenberg, the Prussian lieutenant showed up in the city, presented himself to the district administrator, and demanded the arrest and extradition of Böttger, without giving any reason except that Böttger was a Prussian subject.

The district administrator was a careful and deliberate man with a trace of timidity. He reported the mysterious affair to the Saxon Court in Dresden the same day and asked for instructions. While he was waiting for an answer, the Prussians meanwhile turned their heavy guns on him. They claimed that Böttger was a criminal, a murderer, who had poisoned two people. They also threatened reprisals and the

use of force if the request of their King was not honored immediately. That was something Augustus the Strong in Warsaw had to consider. His war against the Swedes had gone badly. He could do without a fight with his northern neighbour Prussia, he even expected some support from the King in Berlin.

On the other hand, a goldmaker would suit him just fine. The war had been expensive, two courts had to be maintained in style, and his coffers were almost empty. So Augustus had to make a wise decision. Böttger helped him to make it by appealing to him for protection, which put the King on technically sound legal ground, because he was able to tell the Prussians that he needed time to have the case investigated thoroughly. All further demands, requests and communications were to be directed - through proper channels -to King August personally. And while the Prussians would be kept busy by redirecting their extradition appeals, Böttger was to be brought to Dresden in utmost secrecy. His effects were to be well taken care of, especially the little bottles with secret liquids, and his papers were to be wrapped and sealed.

In the early morning of November 24th, 1701, at four o'clock, Böttger was led from his quarters near the Castle Church in Wittenberg (Fig. 42) to a waiting carriage. The carriage took a detour on its way to Dreden, because it was suspected that the main road was guarded by Prussian spies and soldiers. To keep the Prussians in the dark, the guards were left in front of Böttger's quarters, and his meals were brought in as usual for two more days. By that time, Böttger was safe. On November 28th, he arrived at the Royal Castle Moritzburg in Saxony, and from there he was brought to the so-called Gold-House, a part of the Royal Castle in Dresden that had been used as an alchemistic laboratory.

The prisoner knew what was expected of him, and he also knew that he could not deliver. Despite all his former tricks and his cheating, he was not a fraud at heart. Until his death he was convinced that gold could be made, given the right ingredients, the right methods, and sufficient money to delve deliberately into the secrets of nature. But that would have taken time, one of the many luxuries Böttger did not have.

The King's governor in Dresden, Prince Fürstenberg, gave the young man quarters in a wing of his palace in Dresden. Fürstenberg gave orders to keep him in strict custody, and allowed only two people to communicate with the prisoner.

Fig. 42: Castle Church in Wittenberg, biscuit porcelain in 1983. The portal of the church on which Martin Luther had affixed his 95 reformatory thesis stands out on this commenorative medal, biscuit porcelain

He still feared the Prussians might try to kidnap the gold-maker, or even worse, that Böttger could reveal the arcanum, the secret of goldmaking, to someone other than the King.

Böttger was not even permitted to open a window or to see a barber. One day he could not stand it any longer. He started screaming and yelling and went beserk. Governor Fürstenberg had him brought to castle Königstein (Fig. 43) for what would today be called a psychiatric observation. The results are not recorded, but shortly afterward Böttger was brought back to Dresden, and the conditions of his custody improved. He was moved to two comfortable rooms in the Royal Castle, with a view of a beautiful garden. Next to his quarters, a laboratory was installed, and he was allowed to hire some assistants: but he still remained a prisoner.

Fig. 43: Castle Königstein, the strongest 18th century fortress in Saxony, Meissen plate

Fig. 44: Saxon mining official by Kaendler and Reinicke, 1750

Despite his belief in the possibility of goldmaking, King August put a great deal of stock in the exact sciences. He ordered Gottfried Pabst von Ohain to supervise Böttger's experiments. Pabst von Ohain was a well educated scientist, who earlier had worked for Louis XIV of France. At the time of Böttger's arrival, he was one of the responsible managers of the royal silver mines in Freiberg, Saxony (Fig. 44). His special knowledge of metallurgy, melting and refining recommended him to August as the appropriate overseer for Böttger. Pabst von Ohain moved to Dresden for several months, but in March of 1702 returned to Freiberg. From there, he provided the goldmaker with all the necessary utensils and chemicals for his experiments. He would later play an important part in Böttger's life.

The young man, who was by then 21 years of age and full of zest for living, prepared an escape. On June 21st, 1703, he sneaked out of his comfortable prison. A young boy with whom he had communicated, had ordered horses for him and also had brought some of Böttger's personal belongings and clothes to the horse trader. Böttger rode all night, changing horses only once, trying to put as much distance between himself and his pursuers as possible. He could be sure that the King's men would try everything to get him back.

August's soldiers found him after five days, in an inn in the Austrian city of Enns. Böttger had identified himself as a baron to cover his tracks, but to no avail. The soldiers brought him back, first to Freiberg, and then on July 2nd to Dresden. Pabst von Ohain pleaded for the culprit, who by his escape had in effect forfeited his life. After Böttger had prom-ised in writing never to escape again, and to work on gold-making honestly and diligently from then on, the King had mercy on him. But his demands for gold grew more and more urgent. Whenever August's impatience grew dangerously, Böttger promised him tons of gold in a short time. He was so convincing that August would order his mintmasters to be prepared for the striking of a large amount of coins from gold to be delivered soon. That gold never came, and if August had not been in Poland most of the time conducting a war, Böttger's fate might have taken a turn for the worse.

Before his escape, Böttger in 1702 had met Ehrenfried Walther von Tschirnhaus (Fig. 45) at a dinner in the palace of Governor Fürstenberg. Tschirnhaus was impressed by the young man, by his knowledge and quick wit. He was a widely-travelled, well-educated scientist and philosopher, 31 years older than Böttger. Tschirnhaus was born in Kies-lingswalde in Upper Lusatia, presently Slawnikowice, Po-land. After studying medicine at the famous Dutch univer-sity in Leyden, he went on a five-year-journey through Europe. This "Gentleman's Tour" was considered to be the completion of a young nobleman's education in those days.

Back in Saxony in 1679, Tschirnhaus began experi-menting with glass. He constructed large burning mirrors to melt all kinds of metals and minerals in order to study their properties and reactions. Then he travelled to the Nether-lands and to Paris, where he became the first German member of the French Academy. In 1682, the birthyear of Böttger, Tschirnhaus and the philosopher Gottfried Wil-helm Leibniz founded the journal "Acta Eruditorum"

Fig. 45: *Relief portrait of* Ehrenfried Walther von Tschirnhaus

(Erudite Deeds). Tschirnhaus published a medical book, and then again began traveling. He met leading scientists and philosophers, corresponded all over Europe, and in 1696 he accepted a commission by Friedrich August I, then Prince-Elector of Saxony, to study all mines in the country. The idea was to find valuable stones or precious stones, and to investigate the possibilities of establishing manufactories in Saxony which would produce exportable goods from domestic raw materials.

During these investigations, and based on his experiments with glass, Tschirnhaus turned his interest to porcelain. At that time China and Japan were the only sources for porcelain, and their products were in such great demand in Europe and so expensive that the Oriental porcelain drained quite a considerable amount of money from Europe. So it was more than understandable that ingenious minds in Europe tried to lift the secret of porcelain making. The first reports of porcelain experiments in Europe are dated 1575. But neither these endeavours in Italy nor other attempts in the following centuries rendered true porcelain.

Tschirnhaus in 1698 first concerned himself with porcelain. He visited the famous potter city of Delft in Holland to learn how faience was made, and also studied the production of frit-porcelain in St. Cloud, France. Frit-porcelain is a pseudo-porcelain, closer to glass than to porcelain. Instead of clay, a special kind of artificially made glasslike material is used, called frit. Based on these studies, Tschirnhaus produced some white pearls with his burning mirrors after he had returned to Saxony. These pearls looked like porcelain, but actually were milk-glass. His affinity to glass technology, and the strong impressions he had received in St. Cloud lead him the wrong way. Porcelain is quite different from glass, and by following the methods of glass production Tschirnhaus went astray. Nevertheless, he made one very important discovery. He saw that clay would not melt under heat, it would only get soft. But the addition of even a small pinch of calcined bone made clay run like wax. The principle that certain minerals by themselves are not meltable, but that mixtures of these minerals with other minerals are not only meltable but also fusible, laid one of the foundations for the later invention of European porcelain.

This eminent scientist Tschirnhaus, acquainted with most of the intellectual giants of his time, took a liking to the twenty year old escaped apothecary's journeyman who pretended to be a goldmaker. And he was so impressed by Böttger at their first encounter that he remarked to Prince Fürstenberg that the young man was going to be a master in the sciences.

Tschirnhaus was the only person that could visit Böttger at any time and alone. Everyone else had to ask for permission from the Privy Secretary Michael Nehmitz. Nehmitz and Pabst von Ohain were charged by the King with the responsibility for Böttger and the supervision of his alchemistic experiments.

Augustus the Strong has been much maligned in German historiography. His baroque habits, his zest for life, and his many amorous affairs were in contrast to the Prusso-centered historical view of the following two centuries. He could not match the Prussian virtues of puritan life style, thriftiness and discipline, on the contrary, he was pictured as a despicable example of the degeneration of certain German rulers. But August actually was a much more enlightened ruler than his contemporaries. He had a keen interest in sciences and encouraged his leading scientists and technologists to meet and exchange ideas and experiences, not just for the sake of science itself, but to promote the establishment of new manufactories and to further economy, agriculture, and trade.

Tschirnhaus and Pabst von Ohain belonged to one of the groups that met occasionally, and Böttger sometimes participated in these discussions. It was a rather loose organization judging from all available reports, not a research group working sytematically on a scientific project.[3] But nevertheless, the free discussions and argumentations by knowledgeable men without doubt broadened their horizon and their understanding.

In September of 1705 Böttger was brought to the Albrechtsburg in Meissen (Fig. 46) to continue his work intensively. Five experienced mine and melting workers were sent from Freiberg to assist him. They were David Köhler, Samuel Stölzel, Paul Wildenstein, Johann Georg Schubert, Andreas Hoppe, and Balthasar Görbig, mason for the fireplaces in the laboratory. One year later, Böttger and three of his collaborators were brought to the fortress Königstein, where August kept some prisoners. He also had brought most of his valuables and state documents to the castle, because the Swedes had invaded Saxony and were marching toward Dresden. Böttger, who was considered valuable, was kept behind the impregnable walls of castle Königstein as an unidentified "Gentleman with three servants", which were David Köhler, Johann Georg Schubert and Paul Wildenstein.

Fig. 46: *View of Albrechtsburg and Elbe river, Meissen plate*

Böttger was bored at the castle. He could neither experiment nor research, at first he was not even allowed pen and ink. On the other hand, he had won a respite from the demands of the King for gold. He spent one year in inactivity, once he hesitantly participated in an escape scheme by some of the King's political prisoners but ultimately backed out of the attempt.

In September of 1707, after a peace treaty had been signed and the Swedish troops withdrew from Saxony, Böttger was brought to Dresden into a new laboratory in the eastern part of the city fortification, "Jungfern-Bastei" (Bastion of the virgin). August had been forced to renounce his kingship in Poland, and he had come back to Dresden. Shortly after Böttger had been moved to his new laboratory, August visited him and told him in no uncertain terms that he expected from him very soon large amounts of gold. He parted with the words: "Do right with me, Böttger, or else...". For Böttger, there was little doubt what August meant. The annals of alchemy are full of stories about the disgraceful end of goldmakers who had disappointed their patrons.

After the loss of the Polish crown August had more time to observe his goldmaker. He stayed in Saxony, concerning himself with the problems of his country. One of the problems was the lack of money. Knowing that his gold-making experiments could not save him, Böttger concentrated on another object the king was fond of: porcelain. Four months of experimenting in his new laboratory rendered the first pieces of real porcelain. A lab protocol of January 15, 1708 (Fig. 47) shows how organized and systematic he set up his tests.[4] The protocol, written in a kind of scientific dog-latin with a few interspersed German words, notes that Böttger fired seven mineral mixtures:

    N 1   clay only
    N 2   clay and alabaster in the ratio of 4:1
    N 3   clay and alabaster in the ratio of 5:1
    N 4   clay and alabaster in the ratio of 6:1
    N 5   clay and alabaster in the ratio of 7:1
    N 6   clay and alabaster in the ratio of 8:1
    N 7   clay and alabaster in the ratio of 9:1

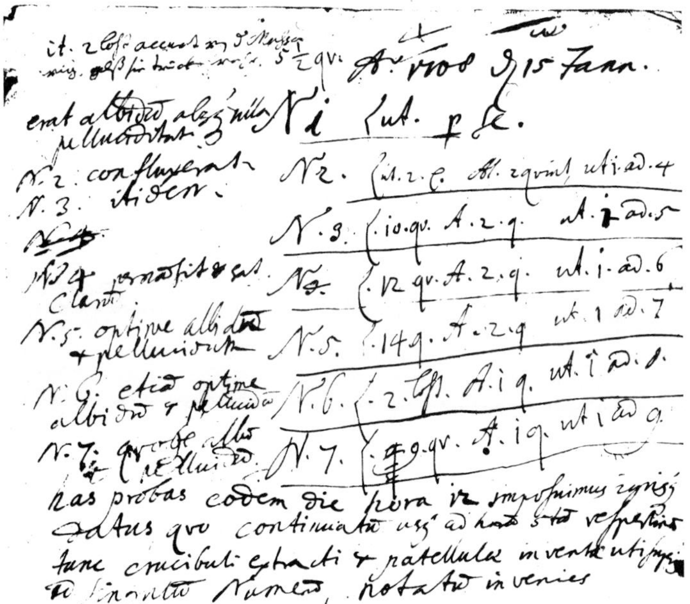

Fig. 48: Skyline of Freiberg, center of the Saxon mining industry, Meissen plate

Alabaster, a fine grained gypsum, was intended to bring the unmeltable clay to melting. The protocol also noted the results of a five-hour firing in the kiln.

N 1 was whitish but absolutely not translucent. N 2 and N 3 were collapsed. N 4 stayed in shape and was rather light in color, N 5 to N 7 were nicely white and translucent.[5]

It took Böttger a few more years until he and his collaborators had developed a composition usable for production of porcelain and a durable glaze. Before they could offer white porcelain for sale, they first perfected the red stoneware, but there is little doubt that the foundation for the invention of European hard paste porcelain was laid in that experiment on January 15, 1708.

And now a few words about an old controversy can no longer be avoided. At the turn of this century, a sometimes altercated dispute arose over the question of who actually had invented European hard paste porcelain. For some historians it seemed clear that only the well-educated, refined, and scientifically superior Tschirnhaus could have done it and not the unstable, sloppy apothecary's journeyman, Böttger the charlatan, who pretended to be a goldmaker. This discussion was influenced by the prevalent belief that great inventions and deeds could only be achieved by especially gifted individuals of the higher classes.

Progress in every field is not possible without singularly outstanding personalities, but they, too, start from a foundation others have laid, and they need the support and collaboration of others. What distinguishes them from others is that bit of additional curiosity, endurance, power of deduction, or courage. Böttger had these gifts, and taking off from the groundwork laid by Tschirnhaus, Pabst von Ohain, and his five assistants from Freiberg (Fig. 48) he found the secret of porcelain making.

Tschirnhaus had contributed valuable knowledge about the reactions of minerals under intense heat. He certainly encouraged, protected and guided Böttger, but his own experiments were on the wrong track. Coming from the production of glass, he thought that porcelain could be made by melting minerals, as is done with glass. Böttger, unencumbered by preconceived ideas, tried the ceramic route of sintering minerals, and he succeeded. When he produced his first porcelain, Tschirnhaus was still alive, he died in October of 1708. No records have been found showing that Tschirnhaus claimed priority for the invention. He was not without vanity and self-consciousness, and if he had in any

Fig. 47: First known lab protocol of January 15th, 1708 with Böttger's notes about experiments in porcelain making

way participated in producing the invention he would have spoken up and requested his part of the fame, but he did not. Later generations have tried to construe some sinister conspiracies by which Böttger supposedly had obtained Tschirnhaus's notes containing the secret of porcelain making. But if Tschirnhaus had found the secret why did he never produce porcelain? An invention can only be considered successful if a repeatable process is developed that produces the same results all the time. Tschirnhaus never produced anything that even faintly resembled porcelain, and therefore his notes - if Böttger really got hold of them - were of no great help for the invention of porcelain.

The whole discussion is only meaningful if the goal is to create a shining hero. An apparent hero is like the glistening tip of an iceberg, held high by a broad but not visible supporting base. Pabst von Ohain and Böttger's five assistants belong to this base. Some of them, like Köhler and Stölzel, later contributed important inventions of their own to further the development of porcelain making.

But Böttger made the breakthrough. In 1705/1706 on the Albrechtsburg, he concerned himself with ceramics, not really for the purpose of porcelain-making, but for the development of durable crucibles for his goldmaking experiments. These had to be imported from Hesse, and the large demand for the melting vessels certainly suggested the idea to produce domestic crucibles. It is doubtful whether Böttger seriously tried his hand on porcelain before he was brought to Dresden in 1707.[6] But when he started, it took him less than four months to combine the results of earlier experiments made by others, and to find the secret that had escaped them. For this, he rightly can be called the inventor of European hard paste porcelain.

After Böttger's first success, further development was rapid. In March of 1709, he presented a memorandum to the King about a number of inventions he had made, among them red stoneware and "the good white porcelain with the best glaze and all painting belonging to it".[7] In this memorandum, he put the porcelain invention into the same category as goldmaking and he asked for his freedom, since he considered his task fulfilled. August tersely responded that Böttger could expect his freedom only if he - starting December 1st, 1709 - would deliver at least 50,000 Ducats of gold a month until the promised 60 million Ducats were produced. At the rate of 50,000 Ducats a month, it would have taken Böttger 100 years to pay up.

Böttger hedged again. In his answer, he declared himself unable to deliver more than 10 million Ducats, and even to make that amount, he needed more time and more freedom. But August pushed him hard, and on Christmas of 1709 Böttger finally admitted in a long and larmoyant poem his complete inability to make gold, at the same time offering his life as a sacrifice for the many years of unfulfilled promises. August again was in Poland fighting the Swedes (Fig. 49). After the Russians had beaten the Swedes soundly in July of 1709, August had broken the peace treaty, reclaimed the Polish throne, and gone to war one more time. The recovery of his kingship and the prospect of making money with Böttger's inventions may have made him lenient.

Although Böttger confessed to his failure, he and the King still adhered to the belief that goldmaking was possible. August did not relax his demand for gold, and occasionally reminded Böttger to continue his experiments. In March of 1713, Böttger performed a transmutation in the presence of August and three other witnesses. One of them left a protocol[8] describing the complicated process by which Böttger changed copper into silver and lead into gold. Both pieces have been preserved and they are now in the Dresden Porcelain Collection (Plate 19). Despite the King's prodding Böttger fidgeted and procrastinated, always promising gold but never delivering. In his last contract with the King in December 1717, Böttger promised to tell the King the secret of goldmaking not later than January 1, 1719. August could not take him at his word, because at that date the alchemist already was in the throes of death.

But in 1709, when Böttger told the King in his memorandum about his useful inventions, August was interested. He

Fig. 49: Statue of August II, *Böttger porcelain, after 1723*

appointed a commission to investigate the proposals, but its members could not see the importance and viability of Böttger's ideas. Böttger got scared. He had compared the porcelain invention with gold-making for a good reason, because he feared for his life. Reports of a spectacular execution had reached Dresden. The Prussian King, from whom Böttger had escaped in 1701, had employed another goldmaker by the impressive name of Domenico Gaetano de Ruggiero from Naples. After Gaetano had led Friedrich I up the garden path for four years, the King had lost his patience and ordered him to be hanged. Dressed in a robe of Dutch gold, the unfortunate goldmaker lost his life on a gallow adorned with tinsel.

This news did not comfort Böttger, and three months after his first memorandum, he urgently repeated his proposals to the King. Despite the reluctance of his investigative committee, August saw the possibility of encouraging manufacturing and trade in his country. On January 23rd, 1710 he issued a royal order (Fig. 50) establishing a number of new manufactories, among them a porcelain manufactory.[9]

His order, published in German, French, Dutch, and Latin, reads like a prospectus for a limited stock company. He offered six percent interest for everybody who would buy shares for two years, and in addition, a reasonable recompense. Shareholders willing to take their repayment in porce-

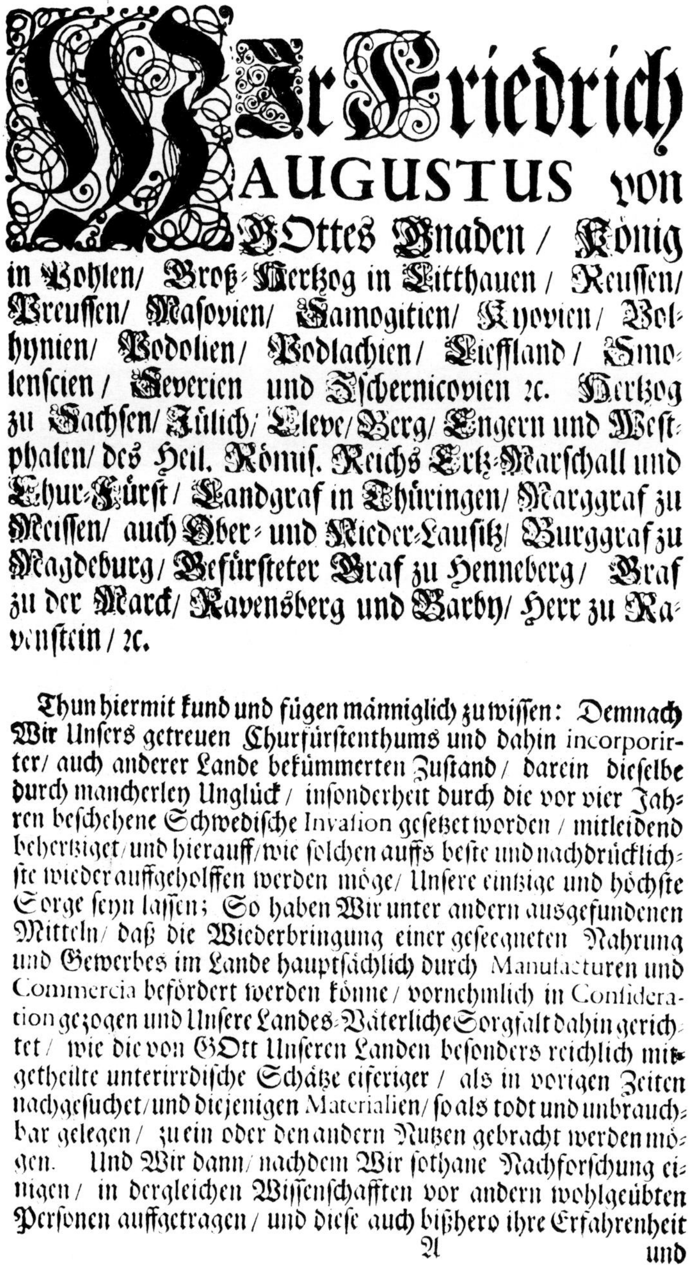

WIr Friedrich AUGUSTUS von GOttes Gnaden / König in Pohlen/ Groß-Hertzog in Litthauen / Reussen/ Preussen/ Masovien/ Samogitien/ Kyovien/ Vol-hynien/ Podolien/ Podlachien/ Liefland / Smo-lenscien / Severien und Tschernicovien 2c. Hertzog zu Sachsen/ Jülich/ Cleve/ Berg/ Engern und West-phalen/ des Heil. Römis. Reichs Ertz-Marschall und Chur-Fürst / Landgraf in Thüringen/ Marggraf zu Meissen/ auch Ober- und Nieder-Lausitz/ Burggraf zu Magdeburg / Gefürsteter Graf zu Henneberg / Graf zu der Marck/ Ravensberg und Barby/ Herr zu Ra-venstein / 2c.

Thun hiermit kund und fügen männiglich zu wissen: Demnach Wir Unsers getreuen Churfürstenthums und dahin incorporir-ter/ auch anderer Lande bekümmerten Zustand / darein dieselbe durch mancherley Unglück / insonderheit durch die vor vier Jah-ren beschehene Schwedische Invasion gesetzet worden / mitleidend beherziget/ und hierauff/ wie solchen auffs beste und nachdrücklich-ste wieder auffgeholffen werden möge/ Unsere eintzige und höchste Sorge seyn lassen; So haben Wir unter andern ausgefundenen Mitteln/ daß die Wiederbringung einer geseegneten Nahrung und Gewerbes im Lande hauptsächlich durch Manufacturen und Commercia befördert werden könne / vornehmlich in Considera-tion gezogen und Unsere Landes-Väterliche Sorgfalt dahin gerich-tet / wie die von GOtt Unseren Landen besonders reichlich mit-getheilte unterirrdische Schätze eiferiger / als in vorigen Zeiten nachgesuchet/ und diejenigen Materialien/ so als todt und unbrauch-bar gelegen / zu ein oder den andern Nutzen gebracht werden mö-gen. Und Wir dann/ nachdem Wir sothane Nachforschung ei-nigen / in dergleichen Wissenschafften vor andern wohlgeübten Personen auffgetragen / und diese auch bißhero ihre Erfahrenheit
A
und

Fig. 50: First page of announcement by August II about the establishment of manufactories, among them the porcelain manufactory

lain wares after two years were promised a discount of 25 percent on the regular price plus an advance credit of 3 to 12 percent in addition to the promised six percent interest. Nobody signed up for shares, so the King was forced to finance the new enterprises by himself. He did so reluctantly and irregularly. The porcelain manufactory always lacked sufficient funds, and the management system ordered by the King had clashes among its members built in.

Councillor of the Chamber Michael Nehmitz became director, Councillor of Commerce Mathis was responsible for the bookkeeping, and Böttger, still in custody in Dresden in 1710, became administrator of the manufactory, which was moved to the Albrechtsburg in Meissen in June of 1710 (Fig. 51)

The manufactory needed subsidies all the time, but even when the King ordered the payment of a certain amount, his treasury stalled, because the finances of the King were usually in bad shape. Böttger often had to borrow money.He never could keep the manufactory's funds separate from his own which later led to some accusations against him.

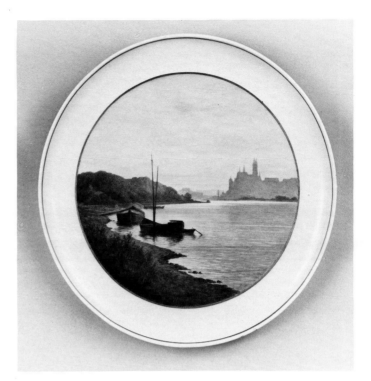

Fig. 51: View of Elbe river with Albrechtsburg in background, Meissen plate

The manufactory's administration was not quite business-like. Almost everyone involved with the manufactory tried to line his own pockets, including the directorate the King had appointed. Most of the underhanded dealings, the promissory notes and other shenanigans later were blamed on Böttger, who, although he certainly was a bad financial manager, was not a conscious defrauder.

In 1714 King August finally gave Böttger his freedom, under the condition that he would not leave Saxony, and that he would keep the arcanum a well guarded secret. One year later, he even gave the manufactory to Böttger's free disposition until the end of his days. If Böttger had wanted to get rich quickly, he could have used this opportunity. Many accusations of frivolous living have been heaped upon him, and indeed Böttger lived it up as good as he could in the comfortable custody the King kept him in. None of these accusations should neglect the fact that he was imprisoned from the nineteenth to the thirty-second year of his life. He drank and smoked excessively, as hard as he worked, and he was a glutton who entertained friends and sycophants generously.

For someone who is leading an unencumbered life without great trials and tribulations, it is possible to judge Böttger from a puritan and moralistic point of view. Böttger certainly would not measure up to normal community-accepted standards. But what was normal about his life? One part of it, his relations to women, is only fleetingly mentioned, even by his harshest critics. His housekeeper, Christiand Elisabeth Klünger, called "Maid Lieschen", seems to have had considerable influence over him, and expected him to marry her, which he steadfastly refused. Otherwise only general condemnations are known, like "excesses in drinking and love" or "he kept several mistresses like a nobleman".[10]

When these judgements were delivered about 150 years ago and repeated early this century public moral standards were so strict that love-life was taboo even if it could have contributed to a more derogatory description of his character. Today, the question is whether an investigation into Böttger's sex-life would aid in understanding his personality, whether it would have any redeeming value. Doubts seem justified, and so Böttger should be judged with the words of Shakespeare: "He was a man, take him for all in all."[11]

Intrigues, schemes and plots were almost a way of life at the court of August II and around it. Böttger's inventions promised easy income to everyone who found a way of getting his share of the money that was floating around uncontrolled. When Böttger died after a long illness on March 13th, 1719, his personal debts amounted to 8,564 Thalers, and the liabilities of the manufactory were figured at 22,563 Thalers, for which he was considered personally responsible. There can be no doubt that some of the manufactory's officials frequently dipped into the till. Böttger often complained that of 30,000 Thalers the King had allotted, only 9,000 Thalers found their way to him.

The bulk of the money was spent by the manufactory director Nehmitz, supposedly in the name of Böttger, but as Böttger claimed, without his knowledge. Even if this accusation was not quite substantiated, there is ample evidence that Nehmitz looked after his own interest from the beginning. Johann Melchior Steinbrück, the honest but in his loyalty to Böttger often strained inspector and chronicler[12] of the manufactory, recorded a number of fraudulent dealings. Nehmitz, for instance, took some red stoneware valued at 2,000 Thalers (Figs. 52 and 53) to the Leipzig Fair on Easter of 1710, where he sold most of it but did not bring back a penny for Böttger and the continuation of his work. The bookkeeper, Mathis, sold the best pieces in his quarters in Leipzig instead of offering them for public sale.[13]

It is a small wonder that other leeches tried to attach themselves to the manufactory, hoping to divert some of the cashflow into their own pockets. The arcanum was supposed to be kept a closely guarded secret, but Böttger himself occasionally dropped a hint or two from which smart entrepeneurs could gather the general idea. One of them was Johann Gottfried Meerheim, who first worked on the invention of the blue paint for underglaze porcelain decoration. He wanted to become bookkeeper, but fell out with Böttger. Later he exploited Böttger's desolate physical and mental condition to play up to him again. After Böttger's death, Meerheim claimed to know the secret of porcelain-making, and in order to keep him quiet, the manufactory employed him at a salary of 300 Thalers a year.[14] He just drew the money without doing anything useful except trying to find out the real arcanum, which he actually did not possess. Later, in 1725, the manufactory commission found out that Meerheim and his son David Conrad were secretly decorating Meissen porcelain outside the manufactory and selling it as porcelain with genuine Meissen painting.[15]

Fig. 53: Bottom of vessel in Fig. 52

Fig. 52: Small leaf-shaped bowl with flowering branches extending as handle, red stoneware, about 1708 to 1710

Another charlatan, who first claimed to have learned the secret of porcelain making from Böttger and Tschirnhaus, but later insisted that he had found it by himself, was Johann Georg Mehlhorn. To buy his discretion, the manufactory commission ordered his employment at the manufactory. Böttger first refused to do so, because he considered Mehlhorn a dangerous spy, but Mehlhorn found a way to overcome Böttger's resistance, and he was employed as vice-inspector in the laboratory.[16]

Meerheim and Mehlhorn for some years lived rather comfortably on account of their claims of possessing the arcanum. In 1732 Meerheim, who was a braggart, and his son were persuaded to write down the secret of porcelain. Their recipe contained all the necessary ingredients but also some superfluous ones. Doubting the ability of the Meerheims to really make porcelain, the chief painter Höroldt and two others recommended to the manufactory commission against a pension for them, arguing that a number of other people claiming knowledge of the arcanum would show up with similar demands.[17]

Höroldt had a low opinion of Mehlhorn and his son too. He proposed their removal to a "safe place" and the confiscation of their notes, because otherwise he feared that they would discover the secret.[18] A few years later Mehlhorn and Meerheim left Meissen, both unsuccessfully trying to establish porcelain manufactories outside Saxony.

As soon as the news of the invention of porcelain had travelled around Europe, Meissen became fertile ground for what is now called industrial espionage. The desire for porcelain was undiminished, and led to some strange deals. Despite the fact that he now was the proprietor of the only porcelain manufactory in Europe, August II still was after Oriental porcelain. In 1715 he began bargaining with the Prussian King Friedrich Wilhelm II, who in contrast to his father Friedrich I was thrifty and disinterested in the porcelain collection he had inherited. August II offered him 600 dragoons (Fig. 54), fully-equipped, including horses, for the 151 pieces of Oriental porcelain the Prussian King owned.

Fig. 54: Saxon Dragoon *by Kaendler, about 1750*

Fig. 55: Dragoon Vases, *Chinese export porcelain from the K'ang Hsi period with blue underglaze decoration. These vases were among the 151 pieces of East Asian porcelain from the Prussian King Friedrich Wilhelm I for which August II traded in 600 Saxon dragoons*

After some negotiations, Friedrich Wilhelm accepted in 1717. So the soldiers rode north to serve under a new flag, and the porcelain travelled to Dresden. Some of it is still exhibited in the Dresden Porcelain Collection, especialy the tall Dragoon Vases (Fig. 55).

Deals like that show the value and desirability of porcelain in those days, and since Meissen was the place where the secret was known, scoundrels and gentlemen hung around the pubs and inns of the city hoping to catch a piece of information or to bribe an employee of the manufactory. The first traitor was Samuel Kempe. He had worked for Tschirnhaus and later for Böttger. For theft he was punished with two years of incarceration but Böttger had him released earlier. Working again in Böttger's laboratory Kempe disappeared in 1713, taking along a chunk of the paste for red stoneware. In Plaue, Prussia, he helped Privy Councillor von Görne set up a manufactory for stoneware (Plate 20) which did not survive too long, because red stoneware slowly but surely was replaced by white porcelain.

Paul Wildenstein, one of the miners who had joined Böttger in 1705, reported in 1717 that he had been approached by some French speaking gentlemen who had tried to entice him to work for a "highly placed gentleman, who was interested in the arcanum"[19]. A bit more dangerous was the case of Conrad Christoph Hunger, who claimed to have worked with Böttger in 1717. The Austrian envoy to the Saxon Court, Count Vrimont, talked him into coming to Vienna to establish a porcelain manufactory. Hunger, however, could not find the necessary white burning clay in the vicinity of the Austrian capital.

In 1719 Samuel Stölzel, another of Böttger's early collaborators, was tempted to go to Vienna by the promise of a considerable amount of money. A business partner of Count Vrimont, Claudius Innocencius du Paquier, a merchant in war goods, wanted to get his porcelain manufactory near Vienna going. Hunger had worked there for two years without success, and du Paquier expected help from Stölzel. But it was not only the promise of money that brought Stölzel to treason. A note by inspector Steinbrück explains "the principal reason probably being that he has been held responsible in an impregnation matter in Freyburg...and that has prevented him from marrying in Meissen"[20].

In Austria Stölzel had similar problems to Hunger's in procuring white-burning clay. He recommended buying it in Saxony, from the same mine-owner who sold his clay to the Meissen manufactory, Veit Hans Schnorr in Schneeberg (near Aue). Since the manufactory did not always pay on time, Schnorr saw nothing wrong in selling his clay to customers outside Saxony if they paid cash. That was not expressly forbidden, nevertheless the Saxon customs officials were supposed to prevent the export of kaolin. Some wagons they were able to stop, but others found their way to Austria.

Hunger did not do well in du Paquiers manufactory, and in 1720 he moved on to Venice, Italy, trying to produce porcelain there. He claimed success after he got white clay from Schnorr in Saxony, and according to his memory, his Venetian patrons had brought in about fifteen hundredweights of kaolin from Schnorr's mine. Hunger gave this account in 1727, when he returned to Meissen and tried to get employment at the manufactory[21]. Some of his tales certainly were phrased to make him look good, and he probably also wanted to show his righteousness by denouncing other culprits.

Hunger testified that Schnorr had written to Venice that he expected the export of kaolin to be prohibited, but he still could deliver four hundred to five hundred hundredweights if they were ordered and paid for promptly. Since Hunger left Venice after his failure to produce usable porcelain in the spring of 1725, this offer by Schnorr must have been made before that time. Hunger's information urged the manufactory commission to some action. First it paid up all debts to Schnorr, gave him an advance payment, and strictly ordered him to sell kaolin to no one but the manufactory (Fig. 56)[22]. That still was not effective, so in 1730 the King issued a General Order prohibiting once and for all the export of white clay under the threat of severe penalties. In 1731 he had

to remind his authorities to seriously take measures at the borders against clay-smuggling[23]. Four months later, a customs official in Dresden accused Schnorr of clandestinely exporting clay again and an investigative team from the manufactory recommended that Schnorr's mine be locked with a strong door and that the door be guarded at all times[24].

Nothing evidently could stop the contraband, neither new General Orders in 1732, 1749, and 1764, nor an increase of the reward for informers from ten to one hundred Thalers[25]. Next to the arcanum, the white clay was the second most important part of porcelain making. Samuel Stölzel knew that only too well, when after some preliminary contacts with friends in Saxony, he in 1720 decided to return to Meissen. Du Paquier had not kept his financial promises, and Stölzel decided to part company with him. Before he sneaked out of the Vienna manufactory, he ruined the prepared porcelain paste, rendering it completely unusable. He also talked the young and gifted painter Johann Gregorius Höroldt into leaving du Paquier and accompanying him to Meissen. Stölzel was received back in good grace, and the present he had brought with him very soon led the Meissen manufactory to its first artistic peak.

Christoph Conrad Hunger - to leave no loose ends-for two years worked as a gold painter in Meissen, but he could not get along well with Stölzel and Höroldt. He left again in 1729 and tried his luck in Roerstrand, Sweden, in Copenhagen, Denmark and in St. Petersburg, Russia. He never was able to make porcelain, but left a number of impressive gilt decorations on porcelain (Plate 21).

Fig. 56: Proprietor's sign of August II on kaolin kegs

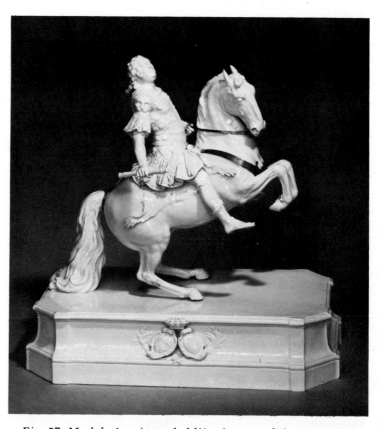

Fig. 57: Model of an intended life-size porcelain monument of August III that was never completed, Kaendler 1745

Plate 1: One of the pulls of the original Clemens-August-Hunt-Goblet by Kaendler and Ehder, 1741, now at the Westphalian State Museum of Art and Cultural History in Münster, FRG

Plate 2: New pull of the re-designed Clemens-August-Goblet, about 1975

Plate 3: Hunt Service, *form* Grosser Ausschnitt (Large Cutout) *with decoration* Hunting Scenes

Plate 5: Table adornment for the Hunt Service

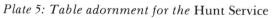

Plate 4: Candleholder of the Hunt Service, *about 1974*

Plate 6: Mocha set of the Hunt Service, *decorated with hunter's yarn stories*

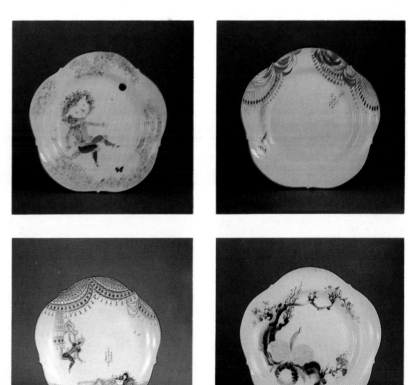

Plates 7 to 10
Plates form Large Cutout *with decorations*
Plate 7: Blütenreigen *(Flower Dance)*
Plate 8: The 1000 and one Nights
Plate 9: Gold Curtain
Plate 10: Blue Orchid

Plate 11: Plate made before 1924 and decorated after 1945 with substitute paints, mark see Fig. 6

Plate 12: Amazone with Amor *by Paul Scheurich*

Plate 13: Smoking Set by Zepner, 1966/1967

Plate 14: Tea Jar by Zepner, decoration Münchhausen's Tales *by Werner, dog on cover by Strang, 1966/1968*

Plate 15: Oberon, *king of the fairies, after* A Midsummer-nights Dream *by Peter Strang, 1969, garnished by Heinz Werner*

Plate 16: Titania, *wife of Oberon, by Peter Strang, 1969, garnished by Heinz Werner*

Plate 17: Mining Shaft *by Kaendler, designed 1752, later pull*

Plate 18: Polish Lady and Gentleman, *also called The Polish Handkiss, model by Kaendler 1743, later pull*

Plate 19: Gold and silver reguli supposedly made by transmutation by Böttger in 1713

Plate 20: *Black glazed coffee pot with gold painting, red stoneware from Plaue*

Plate 21: *Trembleuse of Chinese porcelain about 1700 with sprigged flowers, gilded and painted in enamel colors by Christoph Conrad Hunger. Ring on saucer to prevent sliding of the cup mounted in Paris about 1715*

Plate 22: Tureen from the Swan Service by Kaendler, Eberlein and Ehder, 1737-1741, later pull

Plate 23: August III, *model by Meyer 1752, later pull*

Plate 24: Monkey Band *by Reinicke 1747-1766*

Plate 25: Amphora Vase in the Wedgwood style, after 1792

Plate 26: Covered Box in the Wedgwood style, after 1792

Plate 27: Red stoneware in three colors, candleholder on the left is "iron porcelain"

Plate 28: Tankard with lid, marbled stoneware, decoration incised and gilt, about 1718, mounted pewter lid

Plate 29: Vase with sprigged acanthus leaves, polished, 1712-c. 1720, red stoneware, mounted in gilt bronce in Paris about 1745

Plate 31: Red stoneware cup with greenish yellow glaze, decoration cut through the glaze into the stoneware, 1710-1714

Plate 30: Red stoneware bowl with white test glaze, 1711-1714

43

Plate 32: Crinoline Group *by Kaendler, modelled in 1744, later pull*

Plate 33: Tailor Astride a Goat, *larger version, modelled by Kaendler in 1737, later pull*

Plate 34: Tailor Astride a Goat, *small version, modelled by Kaendler in 1740, later pull*

Plate 35: Tailor's Wife with Infant Riding a Goat, *modelled by Eberlein in 1740, later pull*

Plate 36: The Sleighride, *modelled by Kaendler, 1741, later pull*

Plate 37: Fox at the Harpsichord, *modelled by Kaendler in 1743, later pull*

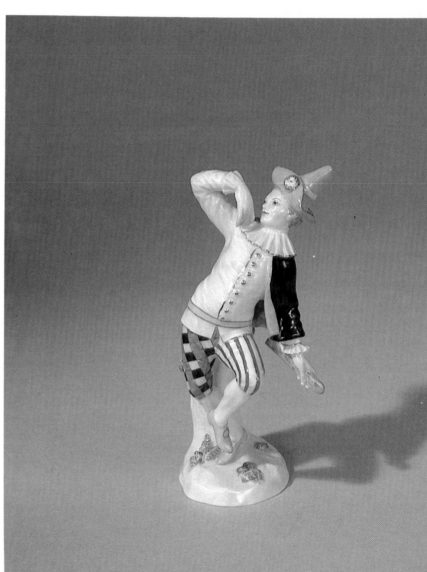

Plate 38: Two characters from the Italian Comedy by Kaendler, Left Harlequin twisting a pug dog's tail, right Gnaga with baby in swaddling clothes, 1772

Plate 40: Harlequin by Reinicke, 1743, later pull

Plate 39: Pantalone by Eberlein, 1744, later pull

Plate 41: Gardening Children *by Kaendler, 1740, later pulls*

Plate 42: Boy Teaching Dog *by Ehder, 1743, later pull*

Plate 43: Comedian Children *by Kaendler, 1765, later pulls*

Plate 44: Shepherdess and Shepherd *by Kaendler, 1750, later pulls*

Plate 45: Paris Peddlers *by Kaendler, female 1769, male 1741, later pulls*

Plate 46: Paris Peddlers *by Kaendler, 1756-1763, later pulls*

Plate 48: Map Vendor *by Reinicke, 1744, figurine probably made for the Duke of Mecklenburg because the map shows his Duchy*

Plate 49: Potter at the Wheel *by Kaendler and Reinicke, 1750, later pull*

Plate 47: Butcher *by Kaendler and Reinicke, 1750,* Button Maker *artist not ascertained c. 1747,* Cooper *by Kaendler, 1750, later pulls*

Plate 50: **Peasant's Wife with Basket** *and* **Peasant with Pitcher,** *modeller not known, 1752, later pulls*

Plate 51: Apple Harvest *by Kaendler and Meyer, 1753, later pull*

Plate 52: Japanese Man with Drum, Japanese Woman with Cymbals *by Meyer, year not known but before 1761, later pulls*

Plate 53: Two Malabars *by Meyer, 1751, later pulls*

Plate 54: Persian Nobleman Riding an Elephant with a Moor, *probably by Kaendler and Reinicke, 1747-1750*

Plate 55: Vase for mantelpiece, The Air, *by Kaendler, c. 1730, later pull*

Plate 56: Muse Thalia by Kaendler, 1748, later pull

Plate 57: The Seasons, *from left:* Spring, Summer, Autumn, Winter *by Kaendler, 1756 - 1763, later pulls*

Plate 58: Apollo and Daphne *by Kaendler, possibly 1762/ 1763, later pull*

Plate 59: Shepherd *by Punct, 1756 - 1763, later pull*

Plate 60: Boy as Shepherd, Girl as Shepherdess *by Acier, 1777, later pulls*

Plate 61: Motto Children *by Acier after drawings by Schoenau, 1775, later pulls*

Plate 63: The Good Father *by Schönheit, 1785, later pull about 1850*

Plate 62: The Good Mother *by Acier, 1784, later pull about 1850*

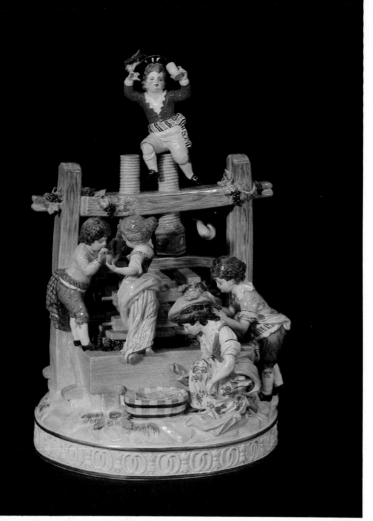

Plate 64: Children as Vine-Growers on Wine-Press *by Schönheit after Schönau, 1786, later pull*

Plate 65: Discovered Lover *by Kaendler, 1771, later pull*

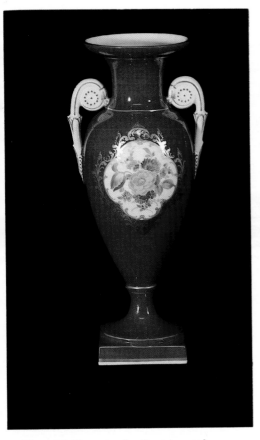

Plate 66: Vase in the Empire style

Plate 68: Silenus on a Donkey *in the version by Leuteritz, 1849 - 1853*

Plate 67: Silenus on a Donkey *in the version by Matthäi, after 1779*

Plate 69: Centerpiece in the "Second Rococo" style by Leuteritz, c. 1850, the basket was taken from an 18th century model, the figurines newly designed

Plate 71: Remodelled vase in the Empire style, the snake handles were introduced first in 1850 under Leuteritz

Plate 70: Crater Vase by Leuteritz, 1865

Plate 72: Jewel casket with flush mounted porcelain panels decorated in paste-upon-paste technique by Sturm. Figurines and group Juno on top by Theodor Paul Helmig, 1892/1893

Plate 73: Cinderella *by Hirt, 1881*

Plate 75: Slinking Fox *by Walther, after 1903*

Plate 74: North America *by Hoesel, 1906*

Plate 76: Girl in a Storm *by Ph. Lange, c. 1911*

Plate 77: Family Concert *by J. von Kramer, after 1903*

Plate 78: Tuba Player *from the* New Monkey Band *by Pilz, 1908 - 1912*

Plate 79: Concertina Player *from the* New Monkey Band *by Pilz, 1908 - 1912*

Plate 80: Dancing Couple *by Ehder, 1742*

Plate 81: Dancing Couple *by Punct, 1756 - 1763*

Plate 82: Dancing Couple *by Kaendler, 1770*

Plate 83: Dancing Couple *by Acier, 1770*

Plate 84: Dancing Couple *by König, 1912*

Plate 85: Amazone with Cupid *by Scheurich, 1933*

Plate 86: Peter Schlemihl by Münch-Khe, 1926

Plate 87: Decorated porcelain spoons from different periods

Plate 88: Tureen with lion masks, cover with pine cone shaped knob, model of the 1720s, later pull

Plate 89: Plate and covered bowl, Schoenau Prince-Electoral pattern

Plate 90: Oval covered Tureen on Plate with sprigged flowers, leaves and branches, c. 1750

Plate 91: Plate with plastic cherries and blossoms, c. 1745

Plate 92: Cup in Meissen called "Lemonshaped with pulled up handle." This form was first developed in Berlin about 1800 and called Campaner form. *The cornflower decoration was developed in the 1770s in Sèvres, France, for Queen Marie Antoinette. This cup 1800 - 1818*

Plate 93: Part coffee set, about 1850

Plate 94: Part coffee set B-form, designed by Leuteritz 1853 - 1855

Plate 95: Vineleaf plate, c. 1840, gilding worn off

Plate 96: Coffee pot in the Capo di Monte style, after 1865

Plate 97: Breakfast set designed by Leuteritz, c. 1890

Plate 98: Part coffee set X-form, designed 1943

Plate 99: Red stoneware cup with test gilding, 1715-1717

Plate 100: Covered footed bowl with Gold Chinamen, part of a set, about 1720-1725

71

Plate 102: Chinese scene in cartouche of beaker in Plate 101

Plate 101: Tall covered beaker with Chinoiseries about 1723-1725

Plate 103: Folio from the Schulz-Kodex with Höroldt's sketch of the Chinese scene in Plate 102

Plate 105: Detail from coffee pot in Plate 104

Plate 104: Coffee pot from a set with Höroldt Chinoiseries, silver and gilt mounts by Johannes Engelbrecht in Augsburg, about 1723-1725

Plate 106: Plate with Chinoiseries in reserves on border, about 1728

Plate 107: Red Ming Dragon

Plate 109: Black Dragon

Plate 108: Blue Dragon

Plate 110: Purple Indian Painting with gold dots

Plate 111: Coral-Red Indian Painting with gold dots

Plate 114: Polychrome Indian Flower Painting No. 5

Plate 112: Indian Rock, Flower and Butterfly *Pattern*

Plate 115: Polychrome Indian Flower Painting in two parts

Plate 113: Indian Rock, Flower and Bird Painting

Plate 116: Tischchen Pattern, gold shaded

Plate 117: Green Indian Painting No. 1 with gold dots

Plate 120: Chinese Flower Painting No. 6

Plate 118: Light Sheaf Pattern

Plate 121: Indian Branch Painting

Plate 119: Chinese Straw Pattern No. 3 with copper paints

Plate 122: Green Indian Painting No. 23

Plate 123: Very Light Indian Painting with Bird

Plate 126: Blue Indian Painting Old Manner

Plate 124: Rich Old Indian Purple Painting

Plate 127: Rich Sheaf Pattern

Plate 125: Indian Flower Painting after Rumberg

Plate 128: Chinese Butterfly

Plate 129: Vase with landscape after Dutch painting

Plate 130: Saucer with Harbour Scene in purple camaieu,
about 1730

Plate 131: Oval saucer for tureen with Battle Scene after
Rugendas, about 1740

Plate 132: Tea jar from a table set with Hunting Scenes,
about 1740

Plate 133: Vases with yellow ground color and Indian Flowers in reserves, AR-marks, 1730-1735

Plate 134: Part coffee set with yellow ground color and Chinese Scenes in reserves, recent production

Plate 135: Cup, saucer and plate with Green Watteau Painting

Plate 136: Plate with pastoral scene, about 1760

Plate 137: Coffee pot and cover with shadowed flowers (ombrierte Blumen)

Plate 138: **Full Flower Painting with Insects**

Plate 139: Flower Bouquet

Plate 140: Rose Painting

Plate 143: Painting No. 2 in Middle

Plate 141: Oblique Flower Bouquet with Royal Blue ring

Plate 144: Painting No. 2 Oblique

Plate 142: Spring Flower Painting

Plate 145: Painting No. 3 in Middle

Plate 146: Painting No. 3 Oblique

Plate 149: Old Polychrome Flower Painting with Copper Paints

Plate 147: Painting No. 4 in Middle

Plate 150: Yellow Rose

Plate 148: Painting No. 4 Oblique

Plate 151: Copper-Green Flower Painting

Plate 152: Tulip with Flowering Branch and Copper-Green Leaves

Plate 153: Painting No. 2 after Grillenburg with gold grass

Plate 154: Flowering Branch on Border, with Purple Grass

Plate 155: Naturalistic Flower Painting with Butterfly

Plate 156: Rose and Forget-Me-Not, Purple

Plate 157: Yellow Rose and Forget-Me-Not

Plate 158: Naturalistic Fruit Painting

Plate 159: Old Flower and Fruit Painting

Plate 160: Old Fruit and Flower Painting with Bouquets, Purple-Green with Insects

Plate 161: Light Bird Painting with Insects

Plate 162: Light Bird Painting on one Side

Plate 163: Exotic Bird Painting

Plate 164: Old Bird Painting on Branch

Plate 165: Game Animal Painting after Ridinger

Plate 166: Strewn Flowers No. 2b

Plate 167: Strewn Roses

Plate 168: Strewn Forget-Me-Nots

Plate 169: Strewn Roses and Forget-Me-Nots

Plate 170: Small bowl with angel in clouds

Plate 171: Watteau scene on plate with Royal Blue colored border, late 18th century

Plate 172: Plate with flower painting in sepia colors, about 1780

90

Plate 173: Copy of oil painting on plate, early 19th century

Plate 174: Cup with amorous scene, form Lemonshaped with Swan Handle, *about 1800 to 1813*

Plate 175: Portrait Cups, about 1800 - 1810

Plate 176: Biedermeier painting, about 1830 - 1840

Plate 177: Breakfast set with motifs after the animal fables by Aesop and La Fontaine, about 1850

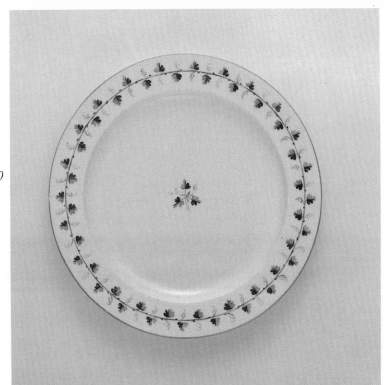

Plate 178: Early Vineleaf Pattern, *green overglaze, 1800*

Plate 179: Part coffee set with pattern Full Green Vine Wreath

Plate 180: Plastic relief contours highlighted by gold-bronze

Plate 183: Lower fields royal blue underglaze, upper fields simple gold-bronze

Plate 181: Simple Gold-Bronze

Plate 184: Simple gold-bronze and Strewn Flowers

Plate 182: Lower fields royal blue underglaze, upper fields contours highlighted with gold-bronze

Plate 185: Lower fields royal blue underglaze, simple gold-bronze, Strewn Flowers

Plate 186: Charger with copy of East Asian motif, about 1850

Plate 187: Showplate with gilt edge and flower painting, royal blue colored border, designed about 1850/1860, this plate made about 1935-1940

Plate 188: Vase with molten glaze by Grust, about 1900

Plate 189: Two vases with flowers made with different molten glazes, about 1900

Plate 190: Covered vase with Squirrel in Tree *pattern in blue paint underglaze, about 1910*

Plate 191: Vase painted by Braunsdorf

Plate 192: Showplate painted by Voigt

Plate 193: Commemorative plate for the 200th anniversary of the manufactory 1910

Plate 196: Plate by Richter

Plate 194: Plate by Hentschel

Plate 197: Plate by Barth

Plate 195: Plate by Richter

Plate 198: Plate by Baring

Plate 199: *Wall decoration,* Man rises into Outer Space *by Werner, 1976*

Plate 200: *Copy of a Watteau painting on a porcelain plaque, 19th century*

Plate 201: *Copy of a painting on a porcelain plaque, 19th century*

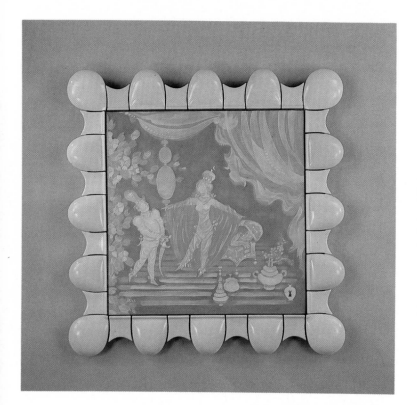

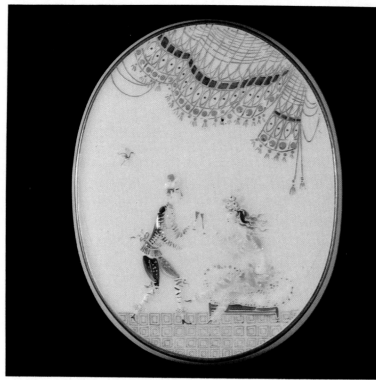

Plates 202 to 205: Four picture plaques from the present production

Plate 206: Chips for card games in a box with cover, about 1750

Plate 207 and 208: Covered boxes

Plate 209: Scent bottles, about 1740

Plate 210: Sewing kit with plastic relief decoration and scenes after Watteau in purple camaieu painting about 1750. The Meissen provenience of the kit has not been ascertained without any doubt but is probable

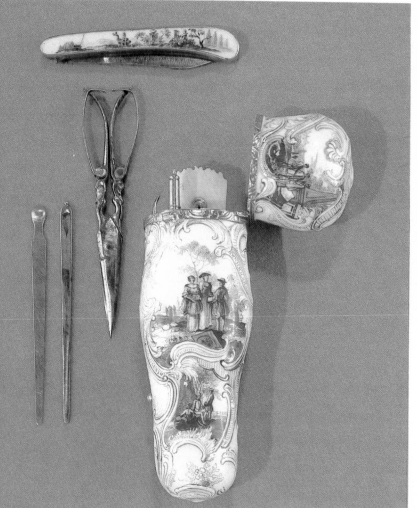

Plates 211 and 212: Eight pipe heads with different polychrome decorations

Plate 213: Meissen dolls' heads, 19th century

Plates 214 and 215: Tiled stoves, late 19th century

Plate 216: Eye-bath, about 1750

103

Plate 217: Tea pot with Gold Chinamen, Meissen porcelain, decoration Meissen or Ausburg

Plates 218 to 220: Coffee, chocolate and tea pot with ancient scenes, Meissen porcelain decorated by outside painter Johann Aufenwerth in Augsburg, about 1725-1728

Plate 221: Tea pot with mythological scene, Meissen porcelain decorated by outside painter Johann Aufenwerth in Augsburg

Plate 222: Part coffee and tea set, Meissen porcelain decorated by F.J. Ferner or his workshop 1745-1765

Plate 223: Oval Meissen tureen with outside painting by
Franz Ferdinand Mayer about 1750. Cover not originally
belonging to tureen with outside painting by unidentified
painter about 1750

Plates 224 and 225: Details of painting on tureen in Plate 223

Plate 226: Bowl with unidentified outside painting, about 1745

Plate 227: Plate from the Swan Service with flower painting by unidentified outside painter, about 1740

Plates 228 and 229: Plates with scenes in the Watteau style by unidentified outside painter, second half of 19th century

Plate 230: Detail of scene in Plate 229

Plate 233: Meissen plate with outside painting, third quarter 19th century

Plate 231: Cup and saucer with outside painting, late 19th century

Plate 234: Detail of painting in Plate 233 showing areas where paint chipped off

Plate 232: Detail of saucer in Plate 231

Plate 235: Cup and saucer made in the first half of the 19th century and decorated later by outside painter

Plate 236: Detail of painting in Plate 235

Plate 238: Detail of painting in Plate 237

Plate 237: Plate made between 1774 and 1817 and decorated in the second half of the 19th century by outside painter with a limited range of colors.

Plate 239: Children's busts modelled by Kaendler, two of the most imitated models of Meissen

Plate 240: Drinking Couple *of unknown origin with a faked*
Meissen mark, see Figs. 377 and 378

Plate 241: Reclining Man with a Bowl, *Meissen*

Plate 242: Imitation of the Reclining Man with a Bowl *in*
Plate 241 by the company of Voigt in Sitzendorf

Plate 244: Contrabass player *from the* Monkey-Band *made by the Oldest Volkstedt Porcelain Factory in Volkstedt*

Plate 243: Contrabas player *from the* Monkey-Band, *Meissen*

Plate 245: Contrabass player *from the* Monkey-Band *made by the Porcelain factory in Scheibe-Alsbach*

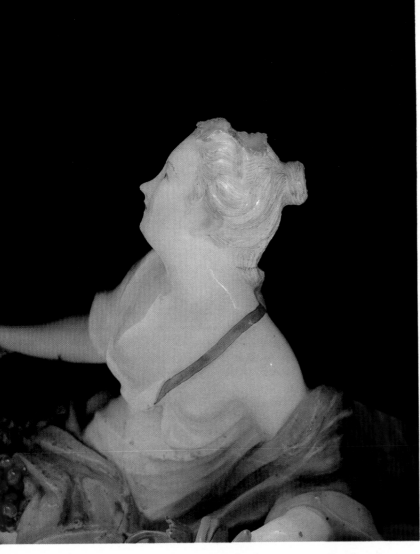

Plate 248: Reproduction of 18th century cup and saucer with Indian Flower Painting for the Metropolitan Museum of Art in New York, N.Y.

Plate 246: Detail from the group Silenus on a Donkey in Plate 67 showing the manner hair was painted in the 18th century

Plate 249: Reproduction of 18th century cup and saucer with Quail Pattern for the Metropolitan Museum of Art in New York, N.Y.

Plate 247: Detail from the group Silenus on a Donkey in Plate 67 showing how sparsely flesh parts were colored in the 18th century

When the manufactory started in 1710, it had twenty employees, administrative personnel included. At the time of Böttger's death the personnel roll named twenty-two employees:[26]

Officials

Doctor Nehmitz	monthly 30 Thalers
Inspector Steinbrück	25 Thalers
Clerk Klünger	8 Thalers
Court Silver Worker Irminger	20 Thalers
(he was stricken from the list on Jan. 1st, 1719)	
Johann George Mehlhorn	**20 Thalers**

Paste Preparers

David Köhler	12 Thalers
Joh. George Schubarth	12 Thalers
Samuel Stölzel	10 Thalers
(he deserted on January 5th of this year)	
Gottfried Gierich	10 Thalers

Kiln-Workers

Balthasar Gerbig	12 Thalers
Johann George Bormann	10 Thalers
Johann Andreas Hoppe	8 Thalers
Andreas Heinrich	6 Thalers
(he died last April)	

Thrower's

Peter Geithner	12 Thalers
Gottfried Lohse, is not paid by the regulations but separately	12 Thalers
Johann Christoph Krumbholz	10 Thalers
Joh. Daniel Rohrschuch	10 Thalers
Caspar Meissner	8 Thalers
Johann Donner	10 Thalers

Moulders

Paul Wildenstein	8 Thalers
Johann Kittel	8 Thalers
Michael Morgenstern	6 Thalers
George Fritzsche	5 Thalers
Johann Fritzsche, is paid separately with	5 Thalers
George Kirsten	4 Thalers
	....
	262 Thalers

From this has to be deducted this year for Irminger 20 Thalers for deserter Stölzel 10 Thalers	
	30 Thalers
and remains	232 Thalers
Furthermore are deducted the deceased Heinrich's	6 Thalers

Fig. 58: Lady and Cavalier at the Harpsichord, *model by Kaendler 1741, later pull*

After Böttger's death, the King did not appoint a new administrator, but instead, a commission of four members. They turned the financial tide and slowly the manufactory was able to produce a profit. Until 1719 no books were kept. From 1720 until 1737, the manufactory earned 50,526 Thalers and delivered porcelain to the disposition of the King and his appointees with a value of 117,364 Thalers[27]. By 1737, the number of employees had increased to about three hundred.

In 1730, King August II appointed his cabinet minister, Count Hoym, director of the manufactory. Hoym had vast authority which he used unabashedly to his own personal advantage. He entered into some secret business dealings with the French merchant Rodolphe Lemaire, who had the manufactory make a large number of porcelain pieces after Oriental originals[28]. Acting against a number of Royal Orders, Hoym and Lemaire finally became too careless. Complaints reached the King, and in 1731 August ordered Count Hoym to withdraw to his estates and remain there[29]. An investigation revealed that the Count had ordered the crossed swords mark to be left off porcelain for Lemaire, so he could sell the porcelain as Oriental wares. Sometimes the mark was painted over the glaze in a way that permitted its easy removal. Hoym also had the King's orders stopped or delayed to give preference to Lemaire's.

The Count lowered the prices for wares he or Lemaire bought, and they also tried to find out the arcanum. Against all rules, Hoym had permitted the Frenchman to freely move about the manufactory, where Lemaire gave orders and meddled into the manufacturing process.

Lemaire was taken into custody, and more than 2,700 pieces of porcelain were confiscated from his quarters, most of them undecorated. In Count Hoym's house, almost 1,600 pieces were found[30]. They all were brought to the "Holländische Palais" (Dutch Palace) in Dresden, the place that later was used for the royal porcelain collection. The confiscated pieces then probably received the blue crossed swords mark over the glaze. Many of them evidently remained in the royal porcelain collection; others were spread all over the world[31].

After the investigation was closed, Lemaire was ordered to leave Saxony within five days. Count Hoym, who had answered the accusations in a highbrow manner, spent the rest of his days in custody at Castle Königstein, where he committed suicide in 1736.

August II died in 1733. During the twenty-three years of the manufactory's existence under his reign, he had received porcelain with a total value of 1,674,503 Thalers at a preferential price. Of this amount, he paid only about one third. The rest was considered payment in kind by the manufactory.

The King's son and successor, Prince-Elector Friedrich August II, in October of 1733 became King of Poland as August III. (Fig. 57) He did not share his father's craze for porcelain, but the new manufactory administrator he appointed was very fond of it. It was his confidant, adviser and later Prime Minister Count Brühl, who could freely indulge in his inclinations since the King allowed him to procure all porcelain he wanted from the manufactory free of charge, an order August III reconfirmed in 1737[32].

The Count took full advantage of this privilege and some of the best designs of those years were made on his orders like the *Schwanen-Service* (Swan Service, Plate 22). Historiography has not been kind to Count Brühl. He is described as vain, as a show-off who desired to impress people as much as the King did. August III had not much interest in politics, he left the affairs of state to Brühl. He collected paintings, which may still be admired at the Dresden Art Collections, hunted (Plate 23), and enjoyed himself at lavishly arranged festivities. His Prime Minister encouraged him, because as long as the King sought diversion in games and plays, Brühl could conduct the affairs of state as he pleased. Contemporary observers described Brühl as a well-educated connoisseur of arts, amiable and completely unscrupulous.

Nevertheless, the manufactory under his administration saw its most productive and artistically most important period. The light, carefree attitude of the Rococo is found in many of the Meissen products made during the thirty years of Brühl's rule (Fig. 58). But the extravagant life-style of the

Plate 250: Chinese plate with blue underglaze painting from the K'ang Hsi period, this decoration was probably the model for the Meissen Onion Pattern

732

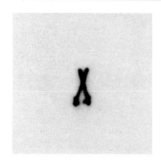

Plate 251: Meissen Onion Pattern on Plate, early 19th century and mark

Plate 252: Meissen Onion Pattern on Plate, 1924 - 1934

Plate 253: "Rich Onion Pattern", blue underglaze decoration highlighted with red and gold over the glaze

Plate 255: Green Onion Pattern

Plate 254: New Onion Pattern designed by Sturm late 19th century

Plate 256: Red Onion Pattern

Fig. 59 Friedrich II of Prussia *by Acier 1778, horse modelled by Schönheit*

Unfortunately for Saxony and the manufactory, Brühl's political abilities did not match the magnitude of his art appreciation. In Prussia, Friedrich II (Fig. 59), later called Friedrich the Great, prepared for an armed conflict with Austria under Empress Maria Theresia. He wanted to lead Prussia to a position of importance in Europe and he decided that the best way to do it was to weaken Austria.

Brühl's sympathy was with Austria: The catholic, historically legitimated center of the German Empire that played an important role in European affairs, rather than with the cold, intellectual, puritan upstart in Berlin, who was so averse to all the pleasures around which life centered in Dresden. Nevertheless, during the first Silesian War (1740-1742), Brühl cast Saxony's lot with the Prussian King, hoping for territorial gains. Prussia annexed Silesia, but Saxony came out emptyhanded. Then Brühl made contacts with Austria and signed a treaty by which Prussia felt threatened. The Count's action proved to be the downfall of Saxony and eliminated the country from the ranks of important and influential powers in Germany.

Friedrich II of Prussia had nothing in common with Count Brühl, except his penchant for porcelain. Despite his preoccupation with battles, victories, and defeats, he kept his eye on the Meissen manufactory. During the second Silesian War (1744-1745), the armies of Prussia and Austria/Saxony prepared for a decisive battle near Kesselsdorf, about 25km (15 m) to the southeast of Meissen. Nobody knew how it would turn out, but the day before the battle Friedrich ordered the removal of all porcelain in stock from the manufactory to Berlin. A scrupulously specific list enumerated everything that finally made its way to Prussia in fifty-two boxes[35]. In addition, some of the Prussian generals received gifts for which they correctly signed receipts.

Again, Prussia won the war, and a third time it clashed with Austria in the Seven-Years'-War (1756-1763). Saxony had again chosen the Austrian side (Fig. 60). Friedrich II was so enraged about what he considered Saxon and especially

Dresden Court also provided many opportunities to mock the foibles of prominent people. The famous monkey-band (Plate 24) is considered a parody of an orchestra Count Brühl had founded for his own glory.

The manufactory flourished as the sales figures show[33].

1730	26,930 Thalers
1740	38,319 Thalers
1742	82,330 Thalers
1746	135,162 Thalers
1752	225,560 Thalers

From the beginning of Brühl's administration in 1733 until 1752, a summary of twenty years produced these figures[34]:

Cash receipts of the cashier's offices in Dresden, Warsaw and Leipzig	1,776,164 Thalers
Deliveries to the King	1,016,844 Thalers
Total	2,793,008 Thalers
Expenses	1,358,917 Thalers
Profit	1,435,091 Thalers

The profit went into the royal treasury. The figures also show that the King still was the manufactory's main customer, receiving thirty six percent of the manufactory production, in fact much more, though, since the King was charged lower prices than the general public. Count Brühl was not a bad customer either. An inventory of the pastry shop in his castle Pförten in 1753 listed 2,676 groups and figurines, 868 pieces for table adornment, and 623 pieces of tableware. In March of 1754, a temple was delivered to the castle consisting of 264 pieces, 74 of them figurines, and until 1756 the tableware was increased by 786 pieces.

Fig. 60: Two Saxon officers by Kaendler, 1750

Brühl's perfidy that he had the Count's palace in Pförten sacked. In a short time, Prussian troops occupied most of Saxony, and Friedrich immediately had confiscated the stock of the three manufactory shops in Dresden, Leipzig and Meissen, which was carried in the books with a value of 300,000 Thalers but was actually worth much more. The porcelain was sold to Privy Councillor Schimmelmann, a Prussian dealer in war supplies, for 120,000 Thalers. He sold it to the Saxon Councillor of Commerce, Helbig, for a quick profit of 40,000 Thalers. Helbig took over the administration of the manufactory and kept it going despite severe problems.

At the beginning of the war, the chief painter, Höroldt, had been sent to Frankfurt on Main to keep him out of reach of the Prussian King. The other arcanists had been evacuated also, because it was known that Friedrich II was interested in them coming to Berlin. A porcelain manufactory had been founded there in 1751 that did not get off the ground and needed some professionals.

Helbig had taken over the administration of the manufactory without the Saxon King's consent, but there was nobody available to make decisions in this war situation. He leased the manufactory from the Prussians first for 24,000 Thalers rent annually and later for 60,000 Thalers, mostly paying with borrowed money. According to Saxon statistics, the Prussians received about 270,000 Thalers in cash, plus porcelain valued at 286,000 Thalers from the manufactory in the years between 1744-1745 and 1756-1763.

Friedrich II not only gave precise orders for porcelain to be made for him, he also took a personal interest in the manufactory. When he had a few days rest in Meissen in 1762, he visited the manufactory everyday, watching and advising the modellers and painters. He wanted the modelmaster J.J. Kaendler to go back to Berlin with him, but Kaendler refused. Some other Meissen workers took Friedrich up on his offers and moved to the manufactory in Berlin. Among them was Friedrich Elias Meyer, who was to become the most famous modeller of the Royal Prussian Porcelain Manufactory.

Three months before the end of the Seven-Years'-War, Friedrich II gave his last order for porcelain to the Meissen manufactory. He had sketched the details of the plastic relief he wanted on the set and also the decoration, and handed the sketches personally to Kaendler. According to his wishes, the set was to be called *Vestunen Service* (Fig. 61). It showed the first signs of a change in style the manufactory would undergo very soon.

August III and Count Brühl both died in 1763. Dresden had lost its role as one of the centers of culture and art in Germany. The Polish throne was gone for good, Saxony was impoverished, and the manufactory could not longer be a contributor to a playful court life because the festivities had come to a grinding halt. A new manufactory commission in 1764 was charged with the reorganization of the manufactory, and with finding new ways of artistic expression after the Rococo style had outlived itself. They were supposed to engage new artists with fresh ideas, and to see to an improvement of the economical and financial conditions.

The court reduced its demands on the manufactory. Between 1764 and 1810, it only received porcelain valued at 241,821 Thalers, les than the Prussians had taken in eight years. The profits rose during the first years after the war but then dropped. In the meantime, a large number of porcelain manufactories had sprung up in Germany and other European countries, and their competition was felt keenly in Meissen. In 1771, the manufactory had to report a deficit[36]. The administration had tried to cut costs by employing wives and daughters of manufactory workers among other things. They were employed for "ordinary blue painting, flower making, handle making and gilt polishing" because they were "cheaper than men" receiving only two thirds of the mens' wages. But the administration also looked at the moral side and proposed for the working women rooms separated from those of the men[37].

The wages generally had been lowered already during the war. In 1764 the system of monthly wages was abandoned, and the painters were paid by the piece. That took away the additional income they had earned by overtime work. Newly employed workers were hired at half or two thirds of the salaries of the older employees. In 1776, all wages were reduced drastically. Foreign competition and declining sales had brought the manufactory to a marginal existence. It had lost the touch and the feeling for the new taste and had been cut off from the development of porcelain designs during the war.

In 1764, the manufactory tried to find out what happened in Europe while Saxony had been involved in a destructive war. Two employees, Hummitzsch and Elsässer, were sent abroad and their reports must have been rather depressing. In Erfurt, Thuringia, they had found a dealer willing to sell Meissen porcelain even in countries where it was considered contraband, but only on a commission basis, he did not want to invest his own money. In Frankfurt on Main, dealers had Meissen porcelain in stock, but they did not display it, they kept it in closed boxes. About the products of other manufactories they noted in their journal[38]:

Höchst porcelain, very good but lacking good paints, good modeller for figurines, prices almost as high as those of Meissen. For love and money they could discover almost all secrets at the Höchst manufactory.

Frankenthal porcelain, nice pieces, good modelling by former Meissen workers, passable flower painting. Bros. Lücke, in 1757 escaped from Meissen, made very good articles. Manufactory in better shape than Höchst.

Ludwigsburg porcelain, not as white as Meissen, good modelling, but pieces are very fragile and decorated with bad paints.

Mannheim, they met with one of the Lücke brothers, he is not happy in Frankenthal, wants to go back to Meissen if a pardon and a yearly salary of 300 Thalers until the end of his days is promised.

Fig. 61: Plate from the Vestunen Service *for Friedrich II of Prussia*

Plate 257: Small cup in a quatrefoil shape with imitated Meissen mark (Fig. 960)

Plate 259: Red Dragon on charger, porcelain maker unidentified, decoration by porcelain painting shop of Gerhard Wehsener in Dresden 1981 mark in Fig. 975

Plate 258: Vase with Red Dragon, porcelain probably made by Galluba & Hofmann in Ilmenau, decoration by Arthur Voigtmann's painting shop in Dresden, mark Fig. 969

Plate 260: Red Dragon on ashtray, porcelain maker unidentified, decorated in Dresden by unidentified outside painter, mark in Fig. 976

Plate 261: Red Dragon on small plate made by VEB Porcelain Work "Weimar Porcelain" in Blankenhain, GDR, decorated by Arthur Rohleder in Meissen 1981, mark in Fig. 977

Plate 262: Red Dragon on plate with blue ground color on border, porcelain made by VEB Porcelain Work Reichenbach in Reichenbach, GDR, decorated by Production Co-Operative Meissen Porcelain Painting in Meissen about 1980, mark on plate

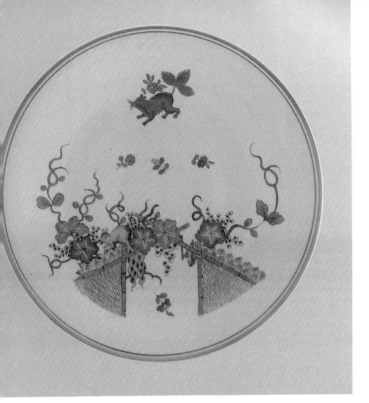

Plate 263: Plate decorated by Co-Operative Porcelain Painting Meissen, pattern called differently Flying Squirrel or Flying Dog or Flying Fox

Plate 265: Cup with two handles and faked AR-Mark (Fig. 723) probably decorated in the shop of Wolfsohn in Dresden, late 19th century

Plate 264: Plate decorated by Co-Operative Porcelain Painting Meissen, Sheaf Pattern and mark

Plate 266: Detail of painting on cup in Plate 265

Fig. 62: Duck-shaped tureen by Chr. G. Lücke, 1781

Fig. 63: Bust of Count Marcolini by Andreas Weger, 1809

Both Lückes, Johann Friedrich and Christian Gottlob, went back to Meissen the same year, where they were graciously received. The former in 1794 became overseer of the moulders (Fig. 62), he died in 1797. His brother had died as a pensioner one year earlier.

Besides the two emissarys, the manufactory also ordered two of its painters to seek employment in the French manufactory of Sèvres, and to report regularly about their experiences and the new developments in porcelain making and painting. In spite of everything, the manufactory remained in dire straits. In a bill of particulars of 1770, a number of problems were listed: The arcanists Schertel and Schatter were deadbeats, Schertel had falsified kiln reports. The arcanum was known only to a few people, which impaired technical progress. It was not a secret any longer, since it could be read in several books. The former arcanists did not like the new white clay from Seilitz, they preferred the clay from Schneeberg because they always got a tip for testifying that it was pure enough for use, even if it was not. Two employees had defrauded the widows support funds and escaped to Berlin. In 1763, when the manufactory had been taken over again by Saxon authorities, one third of the moulders and repairers had been incompetent for their jobs. Of the 76 workers employed by Meissen, four were tailors, one was a barber, one a pouch maker, three were shoemakers, one a carpenter, and two were soldiers. Also employed were one cooper, one clerk, one stockroom worker, one papermaker, one printer, one maker of trimmings, and one ropemaker. They all had found employment by "intrigues and illegal favouritism"[39]. The porcelain manufactory in Vienna was named as the most dangerous competitor, "because it finally has begun utilizing its natural advantages" in the Turkish trade. Austria and Turkey had a common border, and no customs duty was applicable for the transit of Vienna porcelain wares into an area that used to be one of Meissen's important markets. In addition, the Vienna manufactory sold its porcelain one third more cheaply than Meissen.

Count Camillo Marcolini (Fig. 63), who in 1774 became director of the Meissen manufactory, one year later reported to the King that his hopes of leading the manufactory to prosperity again had been dashed[40]. Other countries in the meantime had put import bans on Meissen porcelain to protect their own manufactories. Meissen wares were badmouthed, rumors were spread about the decreasing quality of Meissen porcelain, and the results of the propaganda were noticeable. Of 385 boxes of porcelain sent abroad in 1772, more than half were still unsold in 1775. Instead of the expected 128,770 Thalers in revenues, the manufactory had received only 63,355 Thalers. And despite all cost-cutting measures, expenses were climbing steadily.

Another reason for the decline of the manufactory was - according to Marcolini's report - the increasing competition of French and English stoneware. Wedgwood's cream- and Jasper-ware became especially popular with the middle classes, which could not afford porcelain but wanted to rise above earthenware. Saxony, so he complained, was flooded with English stoneware despite a 26 percent duty on it. In 1783, Marcolini demanded in even stronger terms that measures be taken against the blue and white Wedgwood ware, because the demand for blue and white Meissen porcelain had almost completely disappeared[41]. The dealers of Meissen porcelain threatened to stop selling Meissen if the import of the "incredible number of English stoneware" was not stopped. The customs duty for English stoneware was raised to 36 1/5 percent but it brought no revenues because the British government also had imposed duty on the import of Meissen porcelain. Saxon exporters were reimbursed for the duty payments in England out of revenues from the import duty for English stoneware. After three years, the books showed that the net revenues of the Saxon customs office amounted to less than 1100 Thalers.

Marcolini tried to answer the English competition in two ways. Wedgwood-like wares were produced in Meissen (Fig. 64, Plates 26 and 26), and he recommended a complete import ban for English stoneware. The King's economic council advised against an import or even a transit ban, pointing out the danger of retaliatory measures by other countries. Prince-elector Friedrich August III told Marcolini that there was no other way to protect the manufactory from harm "than to produce especially the current wares at cheap prices", and he earnestly advised the Count to immediately direct his attention to a reduction of prices and costs[42].

The problems with the English stoneware were solved during the Napoleonic wars, when the British fought France (1796-1815), and Napoleon (Fig. 65) in 1806 ordered a blockade of the European continent against all trade with England. But the relief this measure brought was far outweighed by the war itself, that in a short time engulfed all of Europe and closed traditional markets for Meissen porcelain.

By the end of the 18th century, the manufactory had lost most of its share in the Western European market. It concentrated more on Russia and the Middle East, mainly in the areas under Turkish rule that extended far into the Balkan, including Greece, Bulgaria, and most of the present states of Rumania and Yugoslavia. The manufactory also gave in to the tastes of its customers in these markets. Porcelain produced for Russia, for instance, did not match former Meissen standards in the quality of the paste or in the decoration. These were as close to mass produced wares as the manufactory could get at that time, and they could not be sold anywhere else but in Russia and Turkey. In order to fill the Russian orders, the manufactory neglected to accomodate its regular customers, who in 1804 complained to the Prince-Elector that they had to wait for years before they got their wares[43].

The Turkish trade, second in importance for the manufactory, declined at the end of the 18th century. Turkey and Russia were entangled in several wars, and concentrated their interest on other things than porcelain imports. In 1806, when the first war between Russia and France began, the Russian trade almost disappeared. Saxony was an enemy state for Russia, because it had taken sides with Napoleon, who as a reward had elevated the Saxon Prince-Elector to King Friedrich August I (Fig. 66).

Fig. 65: Small statue of Napoleon I, *about 1845*

Fig. 64: Pitcher in the Wedgwood style, about 1814-1818

Fig. 66: Saxon Prince-Elector Friedrich August III *who was elevated to King by Napoleon I, relief portrait in biscuit porcelain*

Plate 269: Detail of painting on one of the cups in Plates 267 and 268

Plates 267 and 268: Three cups made by the factory of Donath in Tiefenfurth probably decorated in Dresden late 19th century, mark in Fig. 833

Plate 270: Covered box with flower painting in the Meissen style made by the factory of C.G. Schierholz in Plaue, late 19th century, mark in Fig. 877

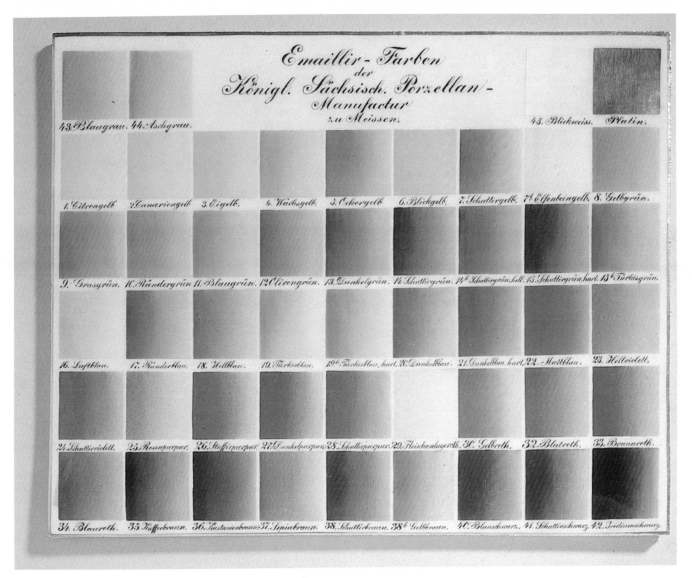

Plate 271: *Rectangular tile with 45 samples of Meissen over-glaze paints, before 1884*

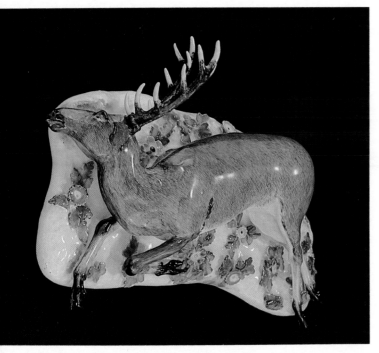

Plate 272: Felled Stag *by Kaendler, 1747*

Plate 273: Pointing Dogs, *18th century, later pull*

In 1805, manufactory sales still amounted to 155,964 Thalers. But by 1813, the beginning of the end for Napoleon, they declined to less than one sixth of that amount, to 24,378 Thalers. The manufactory had been reduced to a disorganized, deranged, badly administered, and demoralized institution with workers who had become accustomed to lazyness as the later-to-be manufactory inspector Heinrich Gottlob Kühn described the situation[44].

One serious problem was the lowering of the quality standards. Expecting a revival of the Russian trade, the manufactory produced immense quantities of a low grade paste that clogged the cellars of the Albrechtsburg, tying up all liquid assets of the manufactory. Furthermore, the White-Clay-Mine in Aue had delivered contaminated kaolin since 1812, and the arcanists had neglected to reject it. The whole paste supply for 1814 was thus spoiled, and the porcelain came out of the kilns yellowish or gray. "At first nobody could find out the reason for this sorry change, which destroyed the only advantage upon which the fame of the manufactory still rested: The quality of the paste. Thus the reputation of the manufactory took a hard blow, especially since neither designs nor painting were able any more to recommend Meissen porcelain"[45].

The secretiveness surrounding the arcanum, a long standing and well-nourished tradition in Meissen, brought the manufactory close to obsolescence. All over the world, the technology of porcelain-making had become known, but in Meissen the arcanists still guarded their secrets jealously. Kühn wrote that the most respected arcanists at Meissen was the one who best assumed an air of total mystery. This mystery-mongering prevented technical and technological progress. Equipment and working methods had become obsolete, and the manufactory had fallen far behind other manufactories in the ceramic field. Artistic development also had not kept pace with changing tastes, and whatever was offered as new by Meissen looked as if it was from a bygone period.

The manufactory had to be reformed, root and branch. After Marcolini's death in 1814, a new manufactory commission instituted a drastic price reduction to get rid of the large number of shelf-warmers, and it introduced considerable rebates for dealers. Auctions of substandard wares were held in the countryside, and at the end of 1814, sales had quadrupled compared to 1813, and revenues had risen to 106,713 Thalers.

Manufactory management was reorganized. A local administration was established in Meissen. It consisted of an economic manager, and a technical manager, called inspector. The director of the manufactory still resided in Dresden, but the local administration had more authority than its predecessors. Heinrich Gottlob Kühn, 26 years of age, became inspector, and because of his energy and efforts, the manufactory was able to turn away from the brink of ruin. One of his first successes was the abolition of the mystery of the arcanum, making it easier in Meissen for more people to research and experiment in ceramics. It was not easy for Kühn to get his innovations accepted by the manufactory personnel, a good many of whom still clung to outdated values and habits.

Some of the innovations were abandoned after a short while. Attempts to produce cheaper ware from lower grade pastes and the production of stoneware were soon stopped. The new administration made a surprise discovery. Despite the dire forecasts, the buying public still expected a high quality product if it bore the name Meissen. And so the experiments with pastes of different quality which started in 1817 were given up in 1824 (Fig. 67).

The new administration found well-qualified engineers and technologists - they still were called arcanists - and improvements of the technical equipment together with labor-saving devices very quickly increased the output of the manufactory. The new head of the painting department, Georg Friedrich Kersting, shook the decorators from their routine and apathy, and for the first time customers were able to order different decorations than the usual ones, if they paid a higher price for it. The manufactory also was willing

Fig. 67: Urn-shaped Vase with two mascaron handles made from paste II

to change old models within technical possibilities if a customer wanted them slightly different. Still, for years to come the manufactory could not break even financially.

A new boost for the manufactory was the sudden demand for old rococo figurines, groups, and decorative pieces, especially from customers in England. They soon were called "English Articles" (Fig. 68) and for the traders coming from England special model books in the English language were prepared. Old and almost forgotten models were brought to light again and the production of "English Articles" played an increasing role in the balance sheets of the manufactory. In 1830, about thirty-five percent of the total sales of the manufactory were realized by articles in the English taste, as they were known by then.

That year the manufactory was put on a new legal foundation. Until then, it had been property of the ruler. After Saxony had become a constitutional monarchy, the court budget was separated from the national budget, and the Saxon Estates (Landtag) had control of the national budget. The manufactory still needed subsidies, and during the discussions about its future, proposals were made to convert it into a privately-owned business enterprise. The creation of the German Customs Union in 1833, which lowered customs duties and tariffs between the German states, quickly turned the tide for the manufactory. Originally the Saxon government had asked for 9,000 Thalers in subsidies for 1834, but it withdrew its application during the budget discussions in the Landtag. It was already forseeable that the sale of Meissen porcelain had benefitted greatly from the German Customs Union, and, indeed, for the first time in thirty years, the manufactory could make a profit. It was a small one, only about 1,500 Thalers, but nevertheless, it was a profit. From then on, the manufactory was able to regularly show profits until World War I and contribute to the national budget. Only 1848 was an exception, and it brought new excitement

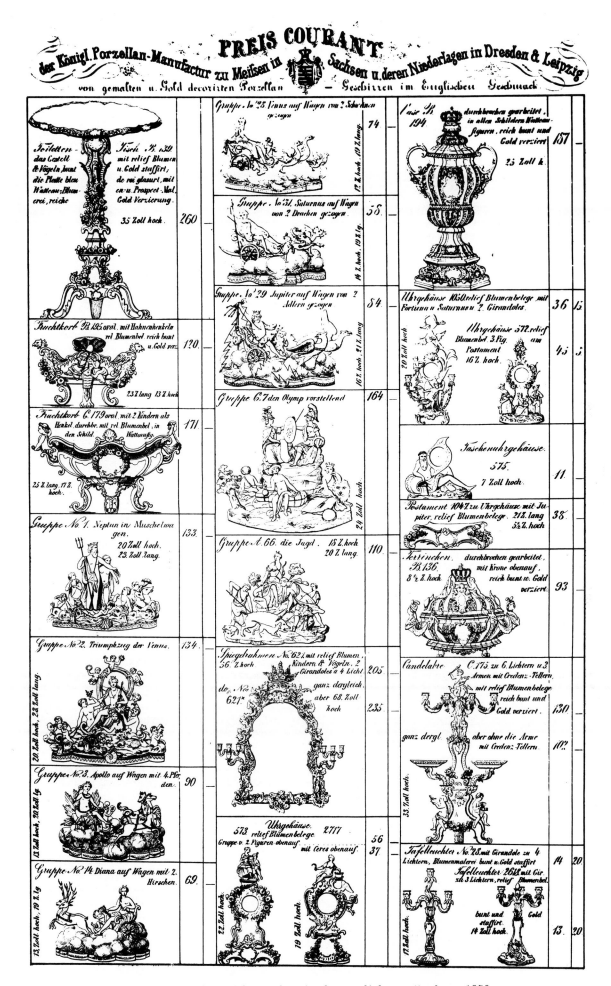

Fig. 68: Price list with articles "in the English taste", about 1850

Plate 274: Paste preparation

Plate 275: Repairing (bossieren) of a figurine

Plate 276: Placing a figurine in a saggar, a capsule protecting against direct fire

Plate 277: Porcelain kiln

Plate 280: Painting of plates with Onion Pattern

Plate 278: Preparation of paint

Plate 281: Transport of finished figurines to the stockroom

Plate 279: Painting of a Crater Vase

Plate 282: Registration of porcelain ready for sale

Fig. 69: Prospect of Meissen with Albrechtsburg in background, Meissen plate

Fig. 70: Prospect of the new manufactory buildings in the Triebisch valley in Meissen

to Meissen. The democratically-minded middle class, supported by the working class, tried to wrestle some of the political power from the ruling military and noble classes. In some German states revolutionary movements arose. The manufactory administration described these historic events from its point of view as "the unexpected sudden crowding together of savage gangs eager for booty" threatening order, property and life[46]. In order to protect the manufactory, the workers were supposed to arm themselves, and a list was circulated on which the manufactory employees had to note what kind of arms they owned. The manufactory workers evidently were a peaceful bunch. Of the 159 workers who were not members of the Communal Guard four owned shotguns, four had rifles, and forty reported pikes. But luckily, this ferocious army was never called upon for battle, since the revolution bypassed the manufactory. The uprising had left the workers with more self-confidence, though, because from then on they slowly but surely organized, and attended to their interests against the manufactory administration and its superior authority, the Saxon Treasury.

Shortly after the revolution the manufactory faced a new trial. The Saxon Heritage Foundation wanted to save the Albrechtsburg from further ruin and demanded its protection as a historical monument (Fig. 69). If the manufactory left the Albrechtsburg it would need new buildings, and the costs for them were estimated at 300,000 Thalers. At the rate of profit payments to the national budget in those years, the manufactory would have needed more than forty years to repay this investment plus interest. The value of the overall capital investment of the manufactory was figured at 400,000 Thalers, and for many members of the Landtag the proposed expense did not seem reasonable. Ideas were put forward to completely close the manufactory, to convert it into a limited stock company or to sell it outright. A Belgian finance group was interested in buying the manufactory, and negotiations were conducted intensely.

Finally, the government put an end to this by declaring that the manufactory not only contributed to the glory of the country but also was of value in the economic and financial field. This statement was reminiscent of the remark made by August II one hundred fifty years ago, that the manufactory had to serve the glory of the King and also the commerce. The money was appropriated, and in 1865 the manufactory moved into its new buildings in the valley of the little river Triebisch in Meissen, where it is today (Fig. 70). The new

Fig. 71: Saxon grenadiers in the Franco-German War of 1870/1871

Fig. 72: Part coffee set with Purple Indish *decoration*

Fig. 73: Showroom with Meissen porcelain, photography of 1899, on the right the monumental vase by R. Hentschel made for the Century Exhibition in Paris, France, in 1900

manufactory was equipped with modern machinery, the kiln capacity was doubled and the paste preparation was fully mechanized.

In 1866, Saxony was involved in another war between Prussia and Austria, and again chose the losing Austrian side. The military actions lasted only six weeks, but Prussian peace demands threatened the very existence of Saxony. Prussia annexed four sovereign German territories and also wanted to incorporate the state of Saxony. Only Austrian resistance against this plan saved Saxony. The other territories disappeared within the newly drawn Prussian borders. The manufactory was touched by the war too, but it already had stabilized, and the only effect was a drop in profits from 26,000 Thalers in 1865 to 4,629 Thalers in 1866. Starting in 1867, the manufactory contributed increasing amounts to the Saxon national budget. During the next ten years, for instance, it transferred 760,000 Thalers to the Treasury, paying back more than the new buildings had cost. The economic condition of the manufactory improved, demand for Meissen porcelain grew, and the number of workers increased from 325 in 1865 to 655 in 1880. At the same time salaries and wages were raised at an average of sixty percent.

Another war changed Saxony's history. She participated in the war of the German states against France 1870-1871 (Fig. 71) that resulted in the foundation of the German Empire under Prussian dominance. Saxony joined the Empire, forfeiting its own souvereignty. But the King remained on the throne and most domestic affairs still were in the domain of the Saxon state. Foreign affairs became a mater for the Imperial government, and the political power rested with the Prussian king, who had become hereditary German Emperor.

The manufactory benefitted from this change. One of the reasons for its growing prosperity was the rise of the middle class. It had become increasingly wealthy and economically influential but life-styles, standards of social behaviour and elegance still were set by the nobility. Without real political power, the burghers at least wanted to imitate the noble life of the ruling class, and they could afford to do so. Owning Meissen porcelain showed culture and refinement, not only by the figurines in display cases but also with a Meissen tea or coffee set for the afternoon (Fig. 72).

Also, the manufactory participated in a number of important exhibitions and fairs abroad. It showed its products in London, England in 1862, in Paris, France in 1867, in Amsterdam, Netherlands in 1877, in Melbourne, Australia in 1881, in Antwerp, Belgium in 1885, at the World Exhibition in Chicago, Illinois in 1893, and at the Century Exhibition in Paris, France in 1900. For Paris, the manufactory made a monumental vase, 2,35 m (92 1/2 in.) high, designed by R. Hentschel and painted with underglaze colors (Fig. 73).

Fig. 74: Exhibition of Meissen porcelain of the outgoing 19th century

Export sales were quite substantial. In 1909 they amounted to more than thirty percent of wholesale. The bulk of Meissen porcelain still remained in Germany. The Americas took second place, despite the fact that the U.S. had levied a sixty percent import duty on porcelain. England was the third largest buyer, France was on fourth, and Austria, in fifth place.

The celebration of the 200th anniversary of the manufactory in 1910 was occasion for joy and satisfaction. The director of the manufactory, Privy Councillor Gesell, could state: "The Royal Porcelain Factory already in the first century of its existence began to run a victorious course through the whole world and even today its artistic productions are in great demand. They are highly valued by modern civilization at the Rhine as at the Newa, at the Seine as at the Mississippi, at the Thames as at the La Plata."(Fig. 74)

Until the beginnning of World War I in 1914, the manufactory generally was in comfortable circumstances. For the years 1900-1913, the Saxon Treasury had estimated payments by the manufactory of 2.4 million Marks. It actually received from the manufactory's profits 2.8 million Marks[47]. The war stopped all exports except those to Austria, and the drain on the country's wealth left little money to spend on Meissen porcelain. Only by large subsidies from the Treasury could the manufactory be kept alive. After Germany had lost the war in 1918, its society, economy and finances were ruined. The future of the manufactory looked bleak.

In this situation Max Adolf Pfeiffer, who had been director since 1913, took over the manufactory as general manager. Pfeiffer followed a principle a famous American many years later phrased in these words: "Others ask why? I ask why not?" Instead of getting lost in the many problems of those years, he looked forward and initiated new projects. He expanded the manufactory, had new buildings erected, modernized the technical equipment, and started a new program for trainees. A lasting memorial to Pfeiffer is the "Schauhalle", an exhibition hall and museum of Meissen porcelain in the manufactory, which is open to the public (Fig. 75). It was built on his recommendation and inaugurated on January 1st, 1916, in the second year of World War I.

After Hitler had come to power in Germany in 1933, Pfeiffer was dismissed and the National Socialists tried to introduce their ideology in the manufactory. Four managers in twelve years, only one of them knowledgeable about porcelain, unsuccessfully worked on converting the manufactory into an obedient producer of Nazi-art. Their efforts failed, because they could not fight the force of more than two hundred years of history. Nor could they overcome the allegiance of the workers and artists to the high standards of Meissen. Very few pieces with propaganda value were made, such as medals commemorating military victories or honoring Nazi-leaders, paintings and decorations with Nazi-emblems, and in the area of figurines, only busts of Hitler

and the German president von Hindenburg were made[48].

During World War II, the manufactory had to produce white unpainted tableware, simple and unpretentious, and technical porcelain. The production of artistic porcelain decreased to forty percent of the pre-war volume. Because of allied air raids, the valuable, irreplacable collection of antique Meissen porcelain from the *"Schauhalle"* and the storerooms were brought to the vaults of the Albrechtsburg. Many of them disappeared in the turmoil at the end of World War II, which left the manufactory with a very uncertain future. But again, the manufactory would prove its viability and its right to call Meissen porcelain unique.

Fig. 75: Interior of the Schauhalle *at the manufactory in Meissen*

Chapter Three

Red Stoneware

Johann Friedrich Böttger's first ceramic invention ripe for production was the "Red Porcelain", or as it is called today, the red stoneware. In this field, it is not easy to claim that Böttger invented stoneware first. The Chinese produced red stoneware in large quantities, the Dutch copied these Chinese articles in red stoneware before Böttger's birth, and in England red stoneware was made earlier than in Dresden.

The basic manufacturing process was known and so were the necessary ingredients, but there is one important difference between earlier stoneware and Böttger's stoneware. Dutch, Chinese, and English stoneware is not as hard and dense as that one produced by Böttger. The Dutch stoneware still had many properties of earthenware. It is more porous, feels a little sticky to a wet finger, and its paste is rather coarse. With this paste only simple reliefs were possible, no intricate details (Fig. 76). English stoneware was much denser and firmer, but not of the same quality as Böttger's stoneware (Fig. 77).

He and his collaborators first concerned themselves with ceramic experiments in 1706 at the Albrechtsburg while trying to produce heat resistant crucibles for goldmaking. They probably tried out all available clays, regardless of the color. One of Böttger's workers, Paul Wildenstein, wrote thirty years later that Böttger and Tschirnhaus in 1706 had experimented with "red porcelain".[1] This testimony should be taken with caution. Tschirnhaus had tried to create something like artificial marble and tiles, but it is doubtful that Böttger took more than a fleeting interest in these attempts. But from Tschirnhaus' basic research in colored clays, he first developed red stoneware. Its superior quality over all the other stoneware can probably be explained by the fact that because of his goldmaking experiments, Böttger was accustomed to working with higher temperatures than the Chinese, the Dutch and the English potters. These higher temperatures increased the sintering process and made his stoneware harder and denser.

When Böttger in March of 1709 reported his invention of "red and white porcelain" to the King, he actually was only able to deliver the red stoneware. Eight months later, Böttger made detailed proposals for the artistic improvement of the stoneware by using sprigged flowers, by polishing, glazing, cutting, or adorning with semi-precious stones[2]. This, he stated, would not be possible with Chinese stoneware, because the Chinese paste was coarse and grainy. Besides copies of Chinese designs (Fig. 78) Böttger recommended that tableware, decorative pieces and figurines be made from the new material in the shape and style of silverware. As chief

Fig. 77: Cup with stamped relief decoration. English stoneware made by the Bros. Elers in Staffordshire about 1690. John Philip and David Elers had been silversmiths in Cologne, Germany. In the late 17th century they moved to England where they took up pottery

Fig. 78: Tea pot with relief decoration, not certain if of Chinese or Meissen origin, impressed Chinese looking mark

Fig. 76: Tea pot of Dutch stoneware with relief decoration after a Chinese model, made in Delft about 1680, red stoneware with impressed mark of Ary de Milde, Fig. 542

designer, he recommended the court silversmith Johann Jacob Irminger, who by royal order in 1710 started working for the manufactory, and in 1712 (Fig. 79), by another royal order he became head of the design department[3]. In the ten paragraphs of this directive, Irminger was ordered to invent new designs for complete sets and table decorations, to instruct the workers to inform the arcanists about every negative change in the condition of the paste, and most importantly, to produce wares not only "for foreign buyers and noble people of rank but also for the middle man." The middle man in this context were the groups between nobility on one side, and artisans, workers and peasants on the other. They included merchants, bankers, high-ranking civil servants and professionals, all those groups that later would be called middle class. In August's days, they had not reached the importance they would begin to acquire one hundred years laters. It is therefore remarkable that August II, in those absolutistic times, immediately saw to the widest possible distribution of the products of the manufactory, satisfying the demand of those who could afford them, and widening the base for the economic stability of the manufactory.

In the early 18th century, the theoretical foundations for the physical and chemical process in ceramics were unknown. It took almost another century and a half before scientists began research in the ceramic field. Even today, a number of questions remains unanswered[4]. Böttger and his co-workers were systematic empirics with a keen awareness of the different results of their experiments. At first, the stoneware vessels did not always come out of the kilns as Böttger expected they would (Fig. 80 and 81). He and his collaborators discovered that a reducing or an oxidizing flame (a shortage or surplus of oxygen) in the kilns changed the surface of the pieces. Actually, they did not know these technical expressions, which were coined much later. But Steinbrück in his chronicle of the first years of the manufactory[5] speaks of a very hot fire in which the surface of the vessels became grey instead of red, and a hot fire was a flame with an oxygen surplus. Not considering these pieces failures, Böttger called them "Eisenporzellan" (Iron Porcelain, Plate 27). Some of them were polished or ground, taking away the grey skin or leaving some of it as shadows or highlights for the decoration.

Polishing was the first method used to improve the finish of red stoneware pieces (Fig. 82), and quite a number were mounted with pewter, silver or bronze, some much later (Plate 29). Relief decorations were the next step (Fig. 83), cutting and grinding produced a large variety of shapes and finishes (Fig. 84), and very soon gilding became common to highlight elaborate decorations (Plate 28). Marbelized stoneware was made, probably by mixing a paste of different color with the red paste while throwing a piece on the potter's wheel or interchanging different pastes in a mould[6].

Fig. 79: Coffee pot and cover made of black glazed red stoneware, decorated with laquer paint and gold, design by J.J. Irminger 1710-1715

Fig. 80: Bowl from red stoneware, gotten out of shape while fired in the kiln

Fig. 81: Vase, about 1710, one of the early pieces showing bubbles and imperfections on its surface

Fig. 83: Coffee pot with relief and cut decoration, red stoneware, about 1710-1712

Fig. 82: Double handled cup and saucer, polished red stoneware, about 1715

Fig. 84: Tankard with cut and ground decoration, red stoneware with mounted silver lid, gilt inside, c. 1712-1713

In the first known inventories of the manufactory's store in Dresden and the manufactory itself, made in May and August of 1711, a "simpler paste" and a "heavy paste" are mentioned as variations. Since they were characterized as special pastes, then there must have been a standard paste, so Böttger evidently used at least three different pastes for the red stoneware. Depending on the ingredients and on the conditions of firing, they appear in dark or light red, brown, black or bluish[7].

A fourth paste was used for the yellow stoneware Böttger produced, but these pieces are by far outnumbered by the wares made from red stoneware.

The inventories of 1711 also show that within only sixteen months after the founding of the manufactory, a surprisingly large number of models and finishing techniques had been developed[8]. Almost 13,000 pieces of red stoneware were in stock at the manufactory in August of 1711, not including 5,900 tiles, which showed the productivity of the new enterprise that in 1710 had employed nine potters, two goldsmiths, two silversmiths, three enamelers, three painters and 29 glasscutters and grinders. Not all of them worked in Meissen, most of the vessels for instance were brought to the glasscutters and grinders in Bohemia to be finished there.

The manufactory inventory also lists 143 different moulds. Two of the mould descriptions show that at least some of the so-called *gemuschelte* (facetted) decoration (Fig. 85) already was applied in the moulds and not cut in later[9]. Two facetted tea-pots moulds are mentioned in the inventory, which also lists facetted tankards in unfired condition. Since stoneware can only be cut or ground after firing, the facets on these tankards must have been made by a mould.

Black-glazed pieces were made from the regular paste but fired at lower temperatures. After a first firing they were covered with a black glaze and fired again. (Fig. 86) Böttger also mentioned white and dark red glazes[10]. Some very early pieces with white or yellowish glazes have been preserved (Plates 30 and 31). It seems, though, that the white glaze did not meet Böttger's expectations, the inventories of 1711 make no mention of white glazed stoneware.

Lacquered ware is mainly black-glazed stoneware with colored and gilt decoration. It was called "cold painting" also because the decorations were applied on the glazed piece and not subjected again to a fire.

The first Oriental motifs were painted at this time (Fig. 87) the so-called *Chinoiseries*, for which Höroldt later became famous. In 1710, the manufactory employed two laquer painters, Johann Christoph Schiffler and Valentin Gotholf Wolff[11]. One year later, the court laquerer, Martin Schnell, began working for Meissen, most of the cold-laquered pieces are attributed to him. The personnel roll of 1712 lists under "Artists": Schnell, the goldworker Johann Carl Bähr, the painter Joh. Christoph Schäffler, and the filigree-worker Stefky. Each was salaried at 12 Thalers a month except Schnell who received 100 Thalers[12]. This high salary probably included a lump sum reimbursement for the gold he had to buy for gilding.

There are at least two groups of laquered wares, one in which the painting is still in good condition, the other one in which much of the decoration is worn off. The painting style in the better preserved group is - as a rule - more professional and artistically superior. This has led to the assumption that these pieces were painted by Schnell, while the other pieces were decorated by the other painters. This guess is as good as any, but proof cannot be offered, except for a few pieces that match the known decoration style of Schnell which can be seen on some wooden vases in the Dresden Art Collection.

The inventories of 1711 also show the use of red stoneware for plastic art. They enumerate:

Form 29   large female
Form 36   small picture of dwarf
Form 38   child's head (Fig. 88)
Form 42   Apollo's head (Fig. 89)
Form 43   Emperor's head
Forms 71 -81   Emperor's head
Form 67   large base for crucifix

Fig. 85: Tea pot with moulded facets, polished red stoneware, 1710-1711

Fig. 86: Two octagonal vases, red stoneware with black glaze, decoration cut through the glaze to the body, 1711-1714

Fig. 87: Tea pot and cover, red-brown stoneware with blackish-brown glaze, decorated with pale-red and brown laquer paints and gold, form designed by J.J. Irminger 1710-1714

Form 69   small base for crucifix
Form 143   crucifix
Form 70   picture of child bearing shell on head
Form 82   head of the fourth Prince-Elector, George
Form 83   picture of Judith (Fig. 90)
Form 84   head of St. Peter
Form 85   Emperor's head in relief
Form 86 - 96   Emperor's head in relief
Form 104   twelve small medallions with heads on
           them
Form 128   small round medallion, Mary of England
Form 129   small round medallion, Charles V

Fig. 89: Head of Apollo, *red stoneware, 1709-1711*

Fig. 88: Child's Head, *polished red stoneware, 1709-1711*

Fig. 90: Judith with head of Holofernes, *red stoneware, 1709-1711*

135

Not mentioned in the inventories are decorations with acanthus leaves or sprigged flowers and branches. They evidently were not made in the first 18 months, so pieces with this kind of decoration must be dated after August of 1711 (Fig. 91).

In 1713 Böttger was able to offer white porcelain for sale, and it quickly pushed the red stoneware off the market. Steinbrück in his chronicle of the manufactory noted that with increasing demand for the white porcelain in 1714 the sale of stoneware slackened. Cutting, facetting, laquering, enamelling, and adorning with stones were also abandoned and only polishing was continued[13]. The personnel role of 1719 no longer includes cutters and grinders, indicating the complete cessation of their work before June of 1719. That would allow the thesis that - except for those pieces facetted by the moulds - all pieces with cut, ground and enamelled decorations or those embellished with stones were produced before that time. Black glazed pieces were not mentioned, but since they were painted too, it seems reasonable to include them in the group of those wares not produced after June of 1719 anymore.

Production of red stoneware was decreased, and stopped completely about 1728. Price lists of the 1730s still carried red stoneware articles but they were unsold pieces that had been produced in earlier years. Stoneware was forgotten so fast that its formula was not even noted in the recipe book of 1741[14]. Also, the paste had been used up, so the ingredients as well as the manufacturing process fell into oblivion.

In 1907, the composition of Böttger's red stoneware was analyzed for the first time. The manufactory chemist William Funk experimented with red stoneware in order to find a new, usable paste, and about 1919 he had developed a red stoneware similar in appearance to Böttger's, but which was not the same. Funk's paste contained felspar, Böttger's did not. To get the right color, Funk had used a dye. Martin Mields, who later became technical director of the manufactory, improved the paste further. The manufactory called it Böttger stoneware, and used it mainly for figurines, medals, and coins, for which it is especially suited because it is not glazed, and much finer details can be worked out.

Max Adolf Pfeiffer, who was then general manager of the manufactory, was able to win the cooperation of some of the best known sculptors in Germany, who either agreed to have their designs made in stoneware and porcelain, or created new models. Gerhard Marcks worked for the manufactory (Fig. 92) as did Ernst Barlach (Fig. 93). Sculptors employed by the manufactory like Paul Börner (Fig. 94), Max Esser (Figs. 95 and 96), Erich Hösel (Fig. 97) and Erich Oehme (Fig. 98) contributed sculptural art to the manufactory. Animals always had been a main motif for Meissen figurines, and in 1922 the manufactory bought about twenty models from the estate of August Gaul (Fig. 99), who had been famous for his bronze animals.

Fig. 92: Grave Angel by Marcks, Böttger stoneware, 1920

Fig. 91: Bowl and cover with sprigged laurel leaves and blossoms, red stoneware polished inside the bowl and outside, 1711-1719

Fig. 93: Sleeping Peasants by Barlach, Böttger stoneware, 1923

Fig. 96 Mask of an Ape *by Esser, Böttger stoneware, 1923*

Fig. 94: Woman's Head *by Börner, Böttger stoneware, 1921*

Fig. 97: Pair of Lions *by Hösel, Böttger stoneware, 1939*

Fig. 95: Owl *by Esser, Böttger stoneware, 1921*

Fig. 98: Stud Maestoso *by Oehme, Böttger stoneware, 1951*

Fig. 99: Bear Cub *by Gaul, Böttger stoneware, 1922*

Willi Münch-Khe worked as a freelancer (Fig. 100) as did Alexander Struck (Fig. 101). Not all of the later animal sculptures are convincing especially not those made after 1950 (Fig. 102). They appear true to life and naturalistic, but they lack the expression and intensity of earlier pieces.

Böttger stoneware was and still is used for the considerable number of medals produced by the manufactory for outside orders. They shall be dealt with in Chapter 7. Only one special kind of medal shall be mentioned here.

One of the early medals made from red stoneware shows the head of Johann Friedrich Böttger (Fig. 103), on the reverse the crossed swords are incised. There is some disagreement about the genesis of this medal. The crossed swords sign indicates that the medal was made after 1723, because before that time the swords were not used as a manufactory mark. That means that the medal was made at least four years after Böttger's death.

If this portrait is based on an original picture of Böttger, then the original drawing must have been made in Böttger's last years, when his face was marked by exhaustion and sickness. Böttger was only 37 years of age when he died, but the man in the portrait looks much older[15].

The medal bears the inscription "LE BARON DE BOETTGER", and that has given some reason for doubts. Böttger was born a commoner and never was ennobled. But on his flight from Dresden in 1703 he had passed himself off as a Baron. Later, he explained to the King that he only had done so to get better treatment from the innkeepers. Nevertheless, the title stuck. Some of his collaborators called him Baron, and Steinbrück in his report to the King[16] refers to him by his real name on the first eighteen pages, but later calls him von Böttger or "the Baron". Steinbrück addressed his "Historic calendar" to the "High Noble born Baron Johann Friedrich von Böttger"[17]. None of the appropriate archives have found any entry proving Böttger's raise to the peerage[18], so it probably was a habit to refer to Böttger as "Baron", a title he evidently tolerated with a touch of vanity.

Another objection is based on the claim that the shape of the letters used in the inscription was not customarily used in the 1720s but rather, much later, at the end of the 18th century. The assumption therefore is offered that the medal might have been made to commemorate the 100th anniversary of the manufactory in 1810.

Against this theory speaks the fact that the production of red stoneware paste was abandoned about 1728, and the recipe was forgotten a dozen years later. To support this theory the claim was raised that some batches of red stoneware might have been preserved in the cellular vaults of the Albrechtsburg, and that this paste may have been used for the Böttger medal. But this is only an assumption without any proof, and a doubtful one at that[19].

So the question remains open, although more circumstantial evidence points to the 1720s as the time of creation of the medal. Only one thing is sure; all Böttger medals made later were based on this first one and the engraving it was modelled after. There are a number of them, issued on several anniversaries of his birth or death, on medals commemorating a visit to the manufactory, or on souvenir medals depicting the City of Meissen (Figs. 104 and 105).

Fig. 100: Roe Deer Fawn *by Münch-Khe, Böttger stoneware,*
1938

Fig. 101: Red Squirrel *by Struck, Böttger stoneware, 1939*

Fig. 102: Poodle *by Richter, Böttger stoneware, 1955*

Fig. 103: J.F. Böttger, relief portrait in red stoneware,
on reverse crossed swords incised, probably 1723-1725

Fig. 104: Medal with relief head of Böttger, Böttger
stoneware, 1972

Fig. 105: Commemorative medal with relief portrait
of Böttger, Böttger stoneware, 1982

Chapter Four
Sculptural Art

In his memorandum to the King of March 28th, 1709, Böttger had promised the "good white porcelain along with the very finest glaze". That was rash, because it took him another four years before he could offer white porcelain for sale. In January of 1712, he admitted in a letter to August II that he had underestimated the problems. Four weeks later he blamed his failure on the kilns, which were suitable for stoneware but not for porcelain[1]. It was not so much the porcelain paste that caused the delay, it was the difficulty of finding a glaze with thermic properties which matched those of the paste.

Experiments with all available clays in July of 1708 had led to the conclusion that the "white earth", kaolin from Schneeberg in the vicinity of the city of Aue, was well-suited for porcelain. Böttger tested and used other white burning clays for his porcelain, but in May of 1711 he finally realized the superior quality of the kaolin that was broken in the "White Andreas" mine belonging to Veit Hans Schnorr. In a memorandum to the King's administration he requested the Aue kaolin to be reserved solely for the manufactory.

A year earlier the King had received the first four pieces of white porcelain[2]. The delivery note does not say whether they were glazed or not. Some of them might have been, because three weeks later at the Easter Fair in Leipzig twelve glazed and five unglazed pieces of white porcelain were exhibited for show, not for sale[3]. Dr. Wilhelm Heinrich Nehmitz, brother of the manufactory manager Michael Nehmitz, in November of 1710 reported that while some of the white-glazed pieces had turned out well, others had turned out badly[4].

Dr. Nehmitz was one of the manufactory's first "arcanists", one of the very few people who knew the ingredients and methods of porcelain-making. The secret of the arcanum was so jealouly protected that even the size and the construction of the kilns was classified information. The workers were forbidden to make notes, and the arcanists hid their knowledge of specialized areas from each other.

In April of 1711, a new kiln for the white porcelain was fired the first time. It did not deliver the expected results, so Böttger proposed larger kilns. Eight months later, he complained about delays, because at the Albrechtsburg there was no suitable place to build the new kilns. He already had produced "two hundred to three hundred pieces" of white porcelain and he also claimed to have mastered the glaze problem. Böttger would need another year before he was able to make glazed porcelain with consistent results. He offered white porcelain for sale for the first time at the Easter Fair in Leipzig in 1713. Since he still had to work with small kilns, these pieces were small (Fig. 106). He probably had made cups, small bowls, pipe-heads and items in the shape of leaves similar to those red stoneware articles he had shown in 1710.

The paste Böttger had developed was usable but not altogether satisfactory. He knew about the superior qualities of the kaolin from Aue, but for his first pieces he used kaolin from the city of Colditz. He continued experimenting, turned again to the kaolin from Aue, and in 1717 finally found a mineral combination that produced a reliable paste. It was a mixture of Aue kaolin, Colditz kaolin, and alabaster, a fine grained calcium carbonate. This paste resulted in a calcareous porcelain, today called Böttger-porcelain. It was the only kind of porcelain produced until 1721, after that year step by-step alabaster was replaced by felspar.

Böttger-porcelain has a slightly yellowish color, partly from the mineral mixture but also from the firing method. Böttger's kilns burned with a surplus of oxygen, which gave the porcelain the yellowish tint.

Fig. 106: Small bowl with dragon, lion, roe deer and crane in low relief, Böttger porcelain about 1715

Fig. 107: Two bottles from the same mould, one red stoneware about 1711-1719, the other Böttger porcelain, 1713-1719

Fig. 108: Two tea jars with relief decoration of flowering trees and birds, the left from Böttger porcelain with gilding, about 1713-1720, the right from red stoneware, 1710-1715

Fig. 109: Vase with cover, lambrequin and flower relief decoration, painted with laquer colors, design by J.J. Irminger after 1711, this pull about 1720

Some of the first porcelain vessels were made in the same shapes and forms as red stoneware pieces (Figs. 107 and 108). The manufactory first used moulds developed for stoneware because they were the only ones available. But not all stoneware moulds were suited for porcelain. The softening effect of the glaze did not let the contours appear as sharp and clear as those on stoneware. The first glazes were rather thick, and soon it was realized that the different properties of porcelain also required a different treatment. It could not be cut, ground or polished like stoneware, and new forms and shapes were necessary.

August II had charged Johann Jakob Irminger with designing new vessels, and also with instructing and training the moulders and throwers at the manufactory. But it is impossible to identify all of Irminger's designs with certainty (Fig. 109). In many cases, he probably only sketched details, which the manufactory workers took up and realized, and in some cases he merely gave general advice.

From 1713 until 1719, the porcelain forms in Meissen were developed under the general influence of Irminger. But he evidently lost interest in working for the manufactory, and he showed up in Meissen less and less frequently. Böttger either did not encourage him to design more models or the already introduced models seemed sufficient and were repeated[5]. Irminger withdrew from the manufactory around 1720, when relief decorations were replaced by painting under the influence of Höroldt.

Sharp-edged decorations like laurel leaves or acanthus leaves, known from red stoneware, appear less frequently on Böttger-porcelain, because the thick glaze diminished the effect of this kind of plastic decoration. This applied also to all red stoneware finishes that required cutting or grinding. Under Irminger's influence relief or sprigged flowers and branches and fruits became prevalent, especially roses, vine-leaves (Fig. 110) and forget-me-nots. Oriental shapes were

In 1721, a group of dwarves was created (Fig. 111 and 112) after etchings by Jaques Callot made in his book *Varie Figure Gobbi*, which later were repeated by other artists in even more grotesque variations. They look a little simple and not very artistically executed, but that is not the fault of the unknown modeller, the original etchings depicted the dwarves this way. Besides these dwarves, no other figurines seem to have been made in the 1720s until the year 1728. The manufactory employed only one modeller for sculptural art, Georg Fritzsche, who probably made some of the dwarves after Callot. He also might have modelled some of the earlier pagodas, but no records have been found to verify attributions[7].

Until 1727, the manufactory was without a sculptor. That year Johann Gottlieb Kirchner was engaged. He was twenty-one years of age, and had been trained as a sculptor in wood and stone. His brother was court sculptor in Dresden, where he owned his own shop. The new modeller only reluctantly went to Meissen, he still preferred wood and stone to porcelain. Kirchner was unhappy in Meissen, and after one year he asked for his dismissal, citing health reasons. While he went to Weimar to work as sculptor, the manufactory tried its luck with Johann Christoph Ludwig Lück, who became modelmaster, but was dismissed after only ten months as "unsuited" for his job. In 1730, Kirchner was called back to Meissen, this time by a royal order, because August II wanted impressive tall statues and elaborately designed decorative porcelain from his manufactory. Kirchner became modelmaster in 1731, but he never lost his aversion to porcelain.

Fig. 110: Vase with relief decoration of vine leaves, bunches of grapes and two women's masks, Böttger porcelain, 1713-1720

copied with preference to "Blanc de Chine" (white Chinese) wares, which actually were slightly creme-colored. These usually unpainted pieces were exported from China to Europe in the early 18th century. The prunus-relief, later a popular Meissen decoration, was frequently used for *"Blanc de Chine"* vessels. In Chinese flower symbolism the prunus or white plum blossom stands for the coming of spring.

Only a few figurines in Böttger-porcelain are known to the art world. The Chinese goddess Kuan Yin, which had been copied in red stoneware, was repeated in porcelain, as was the child's head (Fig. 88). August II appeared in porcelain (Fig. 49) but mainly copies of Chinese figurines were made. Many so-called pagodas (Fig. 35), a small statue of Confucius, and a Chinese woman with a fish in a basket are known from this time.

The manufactory also attempted to make figurines of Christian saints and other biblical characters. The inventory of the King's porcelain collection of 1721 spoke of "Two pieces, statues of St. John" and "One Dolorosa, heavily cracked in the fire"[6]. These statues probably were intended as parts of a crucification group which was never completed. The inventory of 1721 also mentions dogs, frogs and lizards, proving that these animals were made between 1713 and 1721 mainly during Böttger's administration, or at least were designed during that time.

Fig. 111: Figure of a dwarf after Callot, Böttger porcelain with thick glaze, artist not ascertained about 1720-1725

Despite his lack of enthusiasm, Kirchner made the first important statues and figurines in Meissen. Among them were an elephant (1731), a rhinoceros (1731), a lion (1732, Fig. 113), a bear (1732, Fig. 114), a leopard (1732), a lynx (1732, Fig. 115), several birds, probably the monkey with a snuff box (1733, Fig. 116), and a Foo dog (1733, Fig. 117). Most of Kirchner's animals are rather large, some up to 34 inches high. Here it can be perceived that he originally was accustomed to thinking in sculptor's dimensions. This applies to many of his creations, be it a grotesque vase (71 cm, 28 3/8 in. high), a statue of St. John Nepomuc (52 cm, 21 in.), or a tall statue of an evangelist originally made for the chapel of the Japanese Palace in Dresden (100 cm, 40 in.). Kirchner also designed plastic decorations for table sets and clock-cases. He was never quite satisfied and often disagreed with the moulders and repairers at the manufactory, with whom he did not get along well.

Fig. 112: Monsieur Piperouk and Marquis de Sauterelle confessing his love, *dwarf figurines after Callot, Böttger porcelain partly gilt,* Monsieur Piperouk *also garnished with Schwarzlot (black enamel) which was mainly used for line decorations, artist not ascertained, about 1720-1725*

Fig. 113: Lion modelled by Kirchner in 1731, later pull

144

Fig. 114: Bear *by Kirchner, 1732, later pull*

Fig. 116: Monkey with Snuff Box, *modeller not ascertained but probably Kirchner, 1732/1733, later pull*

Fig. 115: Lynx modelled by Kirchner 1732/1733, later pull with slightly larger tongue than original

Fig. 117: Foo Dog probably modelled by Kirchner about 1732/1733, later pull

He also had problems with a new modeller, the twenty-five year old court sculptor, Johann Joachim Kaendler, who had been appointed his collaborator and assistant in June of 1731. Kirchner probably realized that Kaendler had a special feeling for the possibilities and the limits of porcelain modelling. Kaendler also was able to improve the working atmosphere, and to increase the willingness of the workers to follow his inspirations.

First Kaendler assisted Kirchner in completing a series of large animals for the Japanese Palace. Working on this task, he soon gained a touch for the inherent properties of porcelain (Figs. 118 and 119). Porcelain was not conducive to large or monumental plastic art, its special flair coud be developed only in smaller pieces.

At first, the manufactory commission still preferred Kirchner over Kaendler for his "inventions and other ways"[8]. King August had told Kirchner and Kaendler to cooperate but their relationship evidently was strained. The tension arose not only because Kirchner was unstable, worked irregularly, and was often absent without explanation while Kaendler was a diligent and systematic worker, but also because Kirchner slowly realized Kaendler's superiority.

Both of them had the title "modelmaster," with Kirchner in the senior position. But Kaendler's salary was higher, which led Kirchner to demand a raise and other benefits. The manufactory commission felt unable to fulfill Kirchner's wishes so he resigned from his job. On April 28th, 1733, the commission noted in its diary that Kirchner had been dismissed in February of that year "because of permanent in disposition"[9].

Kirchner's resignation was easily accepted because the commission in the meantime had come to the conclusion that Kaendler was capable of replacing Kirchner fully. He had shown his ability by designing a number of animal figurines enumerated in his work report for the time between June of 1731 and December of 1732:

> A large eagle on a pedestal with a wingspread of more than 1.75 m (70 in.).
> An osprey, 90 cm tall (36 in.).
> A sea gull on a pedestal with sea shells.
> Another osprey tearing a carp to pieces.
> A large owl.
> A hawk on a pedestal, partly finished.
> A water fowl on a pedestal with rushes.

In addition, Kaendler had made a tall statue of St. Peter, and he had been working on an ure-ox fighting with a wild boar, and a statue of August II on horseback.

This was more than Kirchner had been able to do. When Kaendler could work freely after Kirchner's resignation, his creativity had no bounds. In 1734 he made 34 four-legged animals and twenty-seven birds ordered specifically by the court, and he added five quadrupeds and twenty-three birds of his own.

In the years to come, Kaendler produced a number of rather large figurines and statues, among them the *Padua Rooster* (Fig. 120) and the *Virgin Mary with Child* (Fig. 121). He repeated this motif a few years later (Fig. 122), as religious themes were appreciated by the catholic and baroque ruler and his entourage. Among those pieces was a group of evangelists' statues (Fig. 123), which were repeated and changed several times, and are still in production today. Added later was also a number of *Saints*.

With the reign of Louis XV of France (1715 - 1774), the coquettish, seemingly carefree and pleasure-loving Rococo style spread all over middle-Europe. It also influenced plastic art in Meissen, and together with the baroque beginnings this period is considered the manufactory's best, since porcelain matched the Rococo style perfectly. Kaendler continued to create groups and figurines after biblical or mythological themes (Fig. 124), but his figurines turned more and more to contemporary life, to habits, foibles and also to social shortcomings of his time (Fig. 125). His honesty in depicting them contributes to the undiminished appreciation of Kaendler's small creations even today.

They were not all his own ideas. Kaendler also used engravings, etchings or drawings by contemporary or older artists, and transformed them into porcelain. Many of them

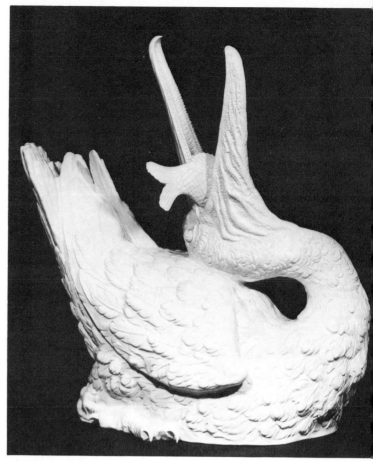

Fig. 118: Pelican devouring a fish, model by Kaendler in 1732, later pull

Fig. 119: Goat, model by Kaendler in 1732, later pull

Fig. 120: Padua Rooster, *model by Kaendler about 1733-1735 and renewed by him in 1750*

Fig 122: Virgin Mary with Infant Jesus, *model by Kaendler 1738, later pull*

Fig. 121: Virgin Mary with Child Jesus, *model by Kaendler c. 1733-1735, later pull*

Fig. 123: Evangelist Mark, *model by Kaendler 1740/ 1741, later pull*

Fig. 124: Bath of Apollo, *model by Kaendler 1748, the group consists of thirteen single pieces*

Fig. 125: Gipsy Sorceress, *model by Kaendler 1748-1763, later pull*

are still in the manufactory archive, at the Dresden Porcelain Collection, or in the collection of the Green Vaults in Dresden. Not at all afraid of competition, Kaendler employed a number of congenial modellers in his department, cooperating with them, having his designs finished by them and giving them enough room for their own creations.

The first modeller to join him was Johann Friedrich Eberlein (1696-1749), who worked at the manufactory from 1735 until his death. In 1739 Johann Gottlieb Ehder (1717-1750) followed. Four years later Peter Reinicke (1715-1768) came to Meissen and created many of the series of small figurines, and in 1748 Friedrich Elias Meyer (1723-1785) completed the quintet of Rococo modellers in Meissen. Meyer left in 1761 to become modelmaster at the Royal Prussian Porcelain Manufactory in Berlin. Together with Kaendler (Fig. 126), who in 1740 had become head of the plastic art department and in 1749 received the title of Court Commissioner, these modellers are responsible for the large variety of models and forms and the depiction of Rococo life and tastes in the miniature shapes of their porcelain creations.

Kaendler had begun in 1736 with the Handkiss-Group (Fig. 127), two single figurines which belonged together. They are stable even without pedestals, and the feet of the lady are modelled properly under the crinoline. Courting pairs, still showing baroque influences, are now called "Crinoline Groups", and they have been made in varying situations. (Plate 32)

At this occasion a few sobering words seem necessary. Quite a number of porcelain collectors and even some custodians of collections and museums tend to consider their valuable treasures as unique, one of a kind, the only original pull, and the standard sample. Valuable they are, unique they are not, except for a very few. The manufactory always pulled a considerable number of figurines and groups from the same moulds, it produced in small series. Of the 34 four-legged animals and twenty-seven birds Kaendler created in 1734 on orders of the court, sixteen of each were to be delivered that year. But since the human hand does not copy itself, they all differ slightly, even if the difference is not easily recognizable.

Fig. 126: Johann Joachim Kaendler, black silhouette painting on a Meissen plaque

So it is not possible to declare one piece an original, and another slightly different one a later pull because of its variations. The modellers and repairers did not follow slavishly the shape of the piece pulled first. Since they very early used some kind of a modular-design principle and also changed the models to accomodate special orders or even because they wanted some variety themselves, there can be several different shapes of the same group (Figs. 128 to 130). The difference lies not only in the painting. This group also appears with a little covered cylindrical bowl on the epergne the Moor is holding (in Basel, Switzerland, Pauls-Eisenbeiss Foundation), without the Moor (Museum in Dijon, France), with a jester and a goat instead of the Moor (Metropolitan Museum of Art in New York, N.Y.) with a bagpipe instead of the Moor (Christie's, London, October 17, 1977) or with a birdcage on the table. The groups were all made about the same time, and if a claim as to originality should be raised, then only for those groups that exactly fit Kaendler's description of 1737: "One new small group begun, as a noble lady is sitting on a chair holding a coffee cup in her right hand, but the left is kissed by a male person in finery, behind the woman a Moor is standing with a salver, who serves". All other groups of this kind not matching Kaendler's description would have to be characterized as later pulls, if the meaning of "original" is narrowed to a point. But all of the groups mentioned are originals, in spite of their variations. A few months after he had made his first model, Kaendler reworked the back of the chair to let it appear as canework, and even later he adddded the pug-dog in the lady's lap.

Fig. 127: Handkiss Group *by Kaendler, 1736*

Fig. 128: Handkiss Group *modelled by Kaendler c. 1737-1740, right hand of Moor broken off*

Fig. 130: Lady with Moor *modelled by Kaendler c. 1737-1740, variation of group in Fig. 128, Gentleman is replaced by a table with a coffee set*

These samples show that figurines or groups were not considered untouchable once they were designed. They underwent changes, and were altered if a new idea of arranging the parts seemed more convincing. Therefore it is not possible to apply the same criteria to Meissen porcelain as can be applied to a painting. The Mona Lisa is unique, this Handkiss-Group exists in at least eighteen original pulls[10]. Its components, like the Moor or the pug-dog, also can be found as figurines by themselves, or as parts of other groups. Meissen porcelain was not produced to create a singular work of art for a singular person. It was something to be used and enjoyed by many people. Price or rarity limited the number of these people, but nevertheless no one should say today that his piece of antique Meissen porcelain is the only original one in the world. And nobody should base scientific or other judgements solely on those pieces which are available to him.

Crinoline groups not only showed amorous scenes, they also depicted court life and the diversions of noble people. Kaendler also poked fun at some of the peculiarities of the upper class. In 1737 he modelled the *Tailor astride a Goat* (Plate 33). The story behind it is supposed to be this: Count Brühl's tailor had asked the Prime Minister for an invitation to a dinner at the Royal Palace. Brühl promised him that he would be at the table one day, which was absolutely unthinkable. Then the Count ordered Kaendler to model a tailor on a goat. Brühl put this piece on the dinner table thereby fulfilling his promise.

Many old stories cannot be verified with certainty, the same applies here. Kaendler noted in his work report of May 1737 that he modelled the group "on demand", but he did not say who had demanded it. In European folklore, the tailor and goat were reputed to be unusual relations, and medieval songs and tales said some very nasty things about the love of tailors for she-goats[11].

Kaendler made five original pulls of this group, but none of them seems to have survived. All pieces which are now privately owned or in museums are pulls made in the 19th or in the 20th centuries. In 1740 Kaendler made a new smaller version of the group (Plate 34), 24.8 cm (9 3/4 in.) tall instead of 44 cm (17 1/2 in.). About the same time, Eberlein made a matching group of a *Tailor's Wife on a Goat*, nursing her

Fig. 129: Handkiss Group *as in Fig. 128, right hand, right arm, and neck of Lady broken off and repaired, replaced arm and hand of Lady might account for the large bowl she is holding. Close scrutiny will reveal slight differences to Fig. 128 in many details. The Gentleman does not touch the Lady's hand with his lips, he holds his tricornered hat a bit differently, index and middle finger of his right hand under the Lady's arm are spread wider, the hilt of his sword is closer to his body, there are different flowers on the base, etc.*

Fig. 131: Fröhlich and Schmiedel with Mousetrap by Kaendler, 1741, copy from an old glass plate negative

Fig. 132: The Dentist, *modelled by Kaendler in 1741, later pull*

baby (Plate 35). The tailor and his goat must have been a motif appreciated all over Europe. It was copied twice by the porcelain manufactory in Ludwigsburg, Germany, once in Höchst, Germany, several times in Derby, England, and even in stoneware by a manufactory in Staffordshire, England.

Favorite targets for ridicule were the professional jesters at the court of August II. One of them was the Court Juggler Joseph Fröhlich, whose temperament matched his name. He was merry with a ready wit. His counterpart "Baron" Schmiedel was rather sulky and melancholic. Both were highly intelligent, otherwise they would not have survived as court jesters. They could say the most outrageous things and get away with saying them provided they said them wittily. Kaendler has modelled them in various situations, each by himself and also together as groups. Some of the pieces were made on orders, others Kaendler made of his own volition, such as the *Sleighride* (Plate 36). At first one sees only a lady in a one-horse open sleigh, an owl and a monkey and a man with a pointed hat embracing the lady from behind. This hat was the trademark of Fröhlich, and closer scrutiny reveals that the lady bears the features of Schmiedel. Schmiedel was terrified by mice, and this fear always was good for a laugh when someone scared him with one (Fig. 131).

The dentist in the group with that name is supposed to be a likeness of Fröhlich too (Fig. 132). The same group without the patient and the man standing to the left while the boy harlequin is to the right is called *The Quack,* and shows Fröhlich as a snakeoil salesman at a masquerade in the court of the Royal Castle in Dresden. The boy is supposed to be his assistant, Christoph Kirsch.

Another satirical group is the *Fox at the Harpsichord,* modelled in 1743 (Plate 37). At first it was thought to be a mockery of the Viennese Court Conductor Johann Joseph Fux (Fux is pronounced like Fuchs in German, which means fox). The lady is supposed to be the opera singer Faustina Hasse-Bordoni known for her explosive temper, which she once demonstrated publicly by starting a free-for-all on the opera stage. All samples are without sheet music on the harpsichord except for a piece at the Metropolitan Museum of Art in New York, N.Y. that shows the notes of an opera.

Opera and comedy were preferred amusements of August III and his court. Understandably the fixed characters of the

Fig. 133: Shepherd group under a tree by Kaendler c. 1750

Italian comedy - already modelled earlier in red stoneware -were repeated in porcelain (Plates 38 to 40) by Kaendler, Eberlein and Reinicke. They made three series of comedians. The first one, by Reinicke, was made in 1743 and 1744, the second series about 1764, and the third one between 1771 and 1775. Outside these series other characters of the Italian Comedy were created as singles or pairs at other times.

Children were also a favorite subject. They were dressed as adults, as was usual in those days, and shown in adult poses, like the series of *Gardening Children* (Plate 41), a boy teaching a dog by Ehder (Plate 42), the series of *Amorettes* or the *Child Comedians* (Plate 43).

Jean Jaques Rousseau's call "Back to Nature" not only was modelled in Meissen porcelain (Plate 44), it was heard by the ruling class. Its members were so influenced by it that they decided to dress up like ordinary people and to move their favorite games and diversions into open air. The large number of shepherds and shepherdesses with their fancy dresses and their playful attitude is less a depiction of real life than a rendition of dressed-up noble people (Fig. 133). But this has never impaired the great popularity of the Meissen shepherds and shepherdesses.

In between, the manufactory had to attend to less amusing business if the court ordered certain representative objects. After the Austrian princess Maria Theresia became Empress of the Holy German Empire in 1740, the manufactory had to produce a series of busts of her ancestors (Fig. 134). Kaendler and Reinicke shared in the work on this order. But it seems that this series was never delivered in its entirety to the Austrian court, because several of the busts were found in private possession soon afterwards.

Kaendler and his collaborators sought their motifs in real life too. They modelled a large number of artisans, peasants and trading people. The *Paris Cryers* or *Paris Peddlers* were made after etchings of the French Count de Caylus, which themselves were based on drawings by Edmé Bouchardon (Plate 45). There are two series of *Paris Peddlers*. In the first one, several were made by Reinicke and one is ascribed to Kaendler (Plate 46). These figurines were rather large, so after 1753 Kaendler and Reinicke modelled a new series, whose figurines were smaller and more graceful.

Between 1740 and 1760 Kaendler and Reinicke also made a large number of artisans, craftsmen and various other tradespeople. (Plates 47 to 49 and Fig. 135). The miners (Plate 17) also are from this time period. Peasants and rural life were other subjects Kaendler concerned himself with (Plates 50 and 51). The first peasant figurines were made in the 1740s, but until now it has not been possible to find out exactly who modelled which peasant figurine when. It seems, though, that a number of the peasant figurines were created after Kaendler's time, probably even early in the 19th century.

Far away countries and the strange people and animals there caught the interest of the Europeans. Augustus the Strong even financed an expedition into Africa, and the treasure cabinets of rich people contained many trophies from foreign countries. So it was only natural that the Meissen manufactory produced figurines and groups showing unusual people and their habits.

Chinese had been a favorite object of plastic art from the beginning (Fig. 136). They now were joined by the Japanese, another inscrutable people arousing curiosity (Plate 52 and Fig. 137). India inspired Meyer to create his male and female Malabars in two sizes (Plate 53). The name "Malabar" was taken from the Malabar Coast of India extending along the Arabian Sea. The supposed riches of Persia influenced the group *Persian Nobleman on an Elephant with a Moor* (Plate 54), in another version called *Sultan on an Elephant*. It was probably created by Kaendler and Reinicke in the middle of the 18th century. The Moor - already encountered earlier - was a favorite figure in many groups, especially since every European ruler with self-respect felt his importance being enhanced by the number of black Africans in his employ.

Kaendler never lost his penchant for mythological and allegorical themes. Every so often he returned to them. In the 1730s he modelled vases to be put on a mantelpiece represent-

Fig. 134: Bust of the Austrian Emperor Albert by Kaendler and Reinicke c. 1744

Fig. 135: Fisherman, artist not ascertained, c. 1745, Fishwife by Kaendler c. 1746, later pull

152

Fig 136: Group of Chinese, probably by Meyer c. 1755

Fig. 137: Japanese Woman with Two Children *by Kaendler, year unknown, later pull*

ing the four elements Earth, Water, Fire and Air (Plate 55). The muses intrigued him as well, in 1748 he modelled a series depicting those friendly daughters of Zeus and Mnemosyne, who preside over the nine arts and sciences (Plate 56).

During the Seven-Year's-War, from 1756 to 1763, Kaendler modelled a series of *Seasons* (Plate 57), another allegorical theme on which Meyer already had tried his hand in 1746 and 1747. Kaendler later created a third series of *Seasons*, representing them by amorettes, and a fourth series was made by Johann Carl Schönheit in 1782, this time with children.

At the time of the Seven-Year's War, the European power struggle that extended to North America as well, tastes and styles slowly but noticeably began to change. Wars are never conducive to lighthearted art, and the influence of the sober and frugal Prussian life style, so averse to flippancy and fun, did not pass by the Meissen manufactory. While Höroldt was sent abroad Kaendler stayed at the Albrechtsburg, continued working there, and produced many of his designs for the Prussian King. Most of the files of these years were lost, so it is not possible to exactly determine what was made in Meissen during the war.

At the end of the fighting, only Kaendler and Reinicke were left from the old team that had been joined in 1761 by Carl Christoph Punct. Eberlein had died in 1749, Ehder in 1750, and Meyer had left for Berlin in 1761. Kaendler himself had refused an offer from the Prussian King Friedrich II, but that did not save him from facing accusations of having treacherously collaborated with the Prussian enemy. He could refute them, but his standing with the new administration never reached its former amiability.

Despite large orders from Friedrich II, who very often gave precise instructions down to the last detail, Kaendler still was able to follow his own intuition. One of the last pieces of his art, unencumbered by ideas of others, is the group *Apollo and Daphne* (Plate 58), made before the Saxon government took over the manufactory again after the war had ended. After that, plastic art in Meissen brought forward no new ideas of its own. Old series, figurines and groups were re-modelled and re-worked, not always to their disadvantage. Punct made some new shepherds (Plate 59) and shepherd-esses, several allegorical figurines, elements and representations of commerce, agriculture and the five senses.

Reinicke crowned his work for the manufactory with a new version of the *Monkey-Band* Kaendler had originally had made around 1750. Reinicke's band shows his mastery of small details especially evident in the faces of players and singers (Plate 23).

Reinicke died in 1768, and Punct had succumbed to tuberculosis in 1765. Kaendler was the only survivor of the Rococo period of the manufactory, which had outlived itself. In impoverished, ransacked, and war-beaten Saxony there was no mood for fun and games. New ideals, philosophies, and standards were sought for life under the changed circumstances so completely different from the gay, elegant, lighthearted time of the Rococo.

Kaendler worked for the manufactory for 44 years until his death in 1775. He was the creator of a porcelain style that had influenced porcelain art all over Europe. His feeling for the properties and possibilities of porcelain, his involvement in contemporary life, and his highly developed sensitivity for all facets of life in his time is expressed in his models. As naturally as the Baroque style slid over into Rococo, Kaendler changed his style smoothly without a hitch. The thousands of figurines, groups, statues and decorative pieces he and his co-modellers created are still considered the pinnacle of porcelain art, because they represent ambience, mood, pleasures, conflicts, and also philosophy of contemporary life in the most perfect way. But they are not just images. By analytically and critically pointing out the follies and inadequacies of a way of life they became historic witnesses. This is certainly one of the reasons for their lasting popularity.

After the Seven-Year's-War, Kaendler appeared outmoded, antiquated, and out of touch with reality. From France, the new style of Louis XVI had travelled to Saxony. Its Neo-

Classical inclination was something Kaendler had his difficulties with, especially because it was the first time when porcelain - in contrast to the previous period - was supposed to be plain and simple.

The rediscovery in Germany of Greek and Roman antiquity was strongly influenced by the German art historian Johann Joachim Winckelmann and his book "Reflections about Copying the Greek Works of Art in Painting and Sculpting", published in 1755. In his opinion, plastic art in Meissen had only produced "ridiculous dolls", and his characterization of the antique Greek art as having been dominated by "Noble simplicity, serene magnificence" soon became the catch-phrase for the new art style.

The Meissen manufactory, having been isolated by the war for seven years, had missed the new trends and tastes. It was sitting on its large stock of Rococo pieces, now considered silly and laughable. In 1764, the manufactory sent the painter Hummitzsch and the modeller Elsässer abroad to explore the new tastes especially in France. One of their tasks was to find a new modeller for Meissen who was well-versed in the new style. They found a "skilled young man, not yet 20 years of age, who had studied for 10 years at the Royal Academy of Sculpture" in Paris by the name of Delaistre[12]. Delaistre was not quite satisfied with the salary that had been offered to him, but he had agreed to go to Meissen. A week later, influenced by his father, he went back on his word.

With the help of Mme. Huet, the Paris representative of the Meissen manufactory, Hummitzsch and Elsässer found another young man. This second choice was Michel Victor Acier, 28 years old, who took the offer but demanded a salary that was fifty percent higher than the manufactory had intended to pay, plus free quarters in Meissen and some other benefits.

In Meissen, Acier became modelmaster along with Kaendler. He was preferred by the court, and although Kaendler officially still was head of the plastic art department, Acier was not subordinate to him. Orders went over Kaendler's head directly to Acier, and their relations soon deteriorated. Kaendler became embittered, rude, and ill-humored. Acier, with his cool, composed, stand-offish attitude was not touched too much by this, but the workers suffered under Kaendler's rough treatment.

Johann Carl Schönheit, an assistant of Kaendler, became a modeller under Acier. His place was taken by Christian Gottfried Jüchtzer. Both soon developed into model designers in their own right.

Acier combined Neo-Classical ideas with a touch of sentimentality and homeliness in his figurines and groups. There was nothing of the spontaneity and liveliness Kaendler excelled in. Everything had to be dignified, measured, and soulful according to the taste of his time. His *Girl with a Broken Mirror* (Fig. 138) invites contemplation of what Kaendler might have made out of this misfortune and the bad omen connected with it. Acier's shepherds and shepherdesses (Plate 60) are quite different from those of Kaendler and his school (Plate 44).

Acier created a new series, the *Devisenkinder* (Motto Children), after the different mottos on the pedestals (Plate 61). They show Cupid, the Roman god of love, busily inflaming hearts, putting them to the test and finally joining them. Schönheit quickly followed Acier's style, and they collaborated perfectly. Acier's *The Good Mother* (Plate 62) and Schönheit's *The Good Father* (Plate 63) are some examples of their work. Very often Acier sketched and started the new models while Schönheit finished them. His own creations followed the intentions of his master very closely (Plate 64).

Acier's figurines and groups appear rather stiff and composed compared to those of Kaendler. That should not be taken as a quality judgement. In his style, Acier mirrored the mood of his time the same way Kaendler did for the periods of the Baroque and the Rococo. If Acier's creations might not have the same appeal today that Kaendler's do, the reason is probably a subconscious preference for happiness and warmth over the cold realities of modern life.

Despite Acier's competition, Kaendler by no means was at his wit's end. His adaption to the new taste was slow and he never succumbed completely to it, but as Neo-Classicism became more elaborate and luxurient, Kaendler was able to get accustomed to it. His powers of imagination and creativity never left him, as shown by the group *Discovered Lover* (Plate 65), and *Mercury* (Fig. 577), a group he made one year before his death in 1775.

Hummitzsch and Elsässer in 1764 had sent news back from Paris about a new kind of porcelain. On July 7th of that year Hummitzsch wrote: "I forgot to report that all French porcelain figurines are without glaze and therefore are called biscuits"[13]. In Meissen experiments with biscuit porcelain that had been developed in Vincennes, France in 1751 were begun immediately. Its unglazed surface was reminiscent of alabaster or marble, the material Greek and Roman statues were made of[14]. Biscuit porcelain offered itself for classical themes and when the manufactory had mastered the technological process about 1780, it produced a considerable number of biscuit pieces.

Johann Gottlieb Matthäi, an apprentice at the manufactory between 1773 and 1776 who had been employed as a modeller since 1779, created one of the first biscuit pieces, the statue of a Gladiator (Fig. 139). Jüchtzer, who after Acier's resignation in 1781 had unofficially become head of the plastic art department, also made a large number of biscuit pieces in the Neo-Classical style. One of the more famous is the group of the *Three Graces* (Fig. 140).

The influence of the blue and white Wedgwood ware led the manufactory to produce figurines and groups similar to Wedgwood's Jasper ware. In contrast to the decorative pieces of Jasper ware (Plates 25 and 26 and Fig. 64), these articles never really caught on.

Fig. 138: Girl with Broken Mirror *by Acier c. 1776*

154

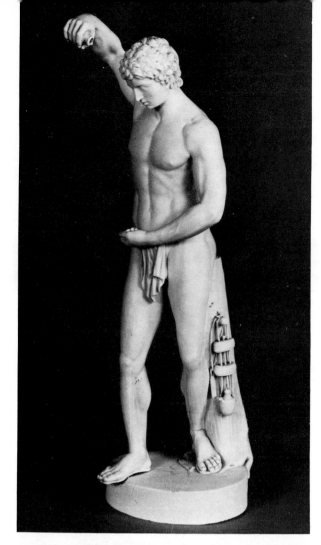

Fig. 139: **Gladiator** *by Matthäi c. 1781*

Fig. 140: **The Three Graces** *by Jüchtzer, 1784, later pull about 1820*

The extension of Neo-Classicism, the French Empire style, manifested itself in Meissen mainly in vessels (Plate 66) which, with later variations, have survived until today.

After Acier's resignation, the manufactory lacked a strong personality guiding artistic development and setting a style. In addition the ensuing Napoleonic Wars left no chance for artistic creativity. Under the directorship of Count Marcolini, design work for new models was slowed down in the 19th century, and from 1808 to 1812 stopped altogether. The manufactory tried everything it thought it could sell, but it suffered from the fact that after Neo-Classicism and Empire, no new style or even partially accepted standards or criteria of art had evolved.

Competition became stronger too, especially from neighbouring Thuringia, where a number of porcelain manufactories made cheaper porcelain, often copying Meissen. The market was flooded with porcelain and appealing, but less expensive stoneware. Sales of Meissen products went down, in 1807 the manufactory could not sell its products at all, and in 1810 it had to close down for a time because it produced only unsalable goods for its own warehouse.

Plastic art in Meissen declined and painting became more important. Busts of famous people from antiquity to contemporary rulers were modelled, which were very true to paintings and drawings but very boring. The Biedermeier style escaped the manufactory almost entirely in plastic art. Only the rediscovery of the old Rococo figurines and groups in the late 1820s, especially by English collectors, gave the manufactory a chance of survival. Special orders for changes in the originals were gladly accepted as long as the pieces could be sold. After Ernst August Leuteritz became modeller in 1843 and head of the plastic art department in 1849, he "modernized" many of the old models. This period today generously is called Second Rococo.

The group *Silenus on a Donkey*, originally created by Meyer in 1760, is one example of the changes pieces were subjected to. In Meyer's version, the group consisted of the drunken Silenus on a donkey, his foster son Bacchus, the patron god of grape-growing and wine in Greek mythology, supporting him and a tipsy looking putto in front of the donkey holding on to a tendril of vine. A price list of 1765 describes the group which matches the piece in Fig. 141 as being composed of four figurines. The irregularly shaped base sprigged with flowers was common before the Rococo bases with rocaille decoration were preferred.

Meyer's creation did not sell too well, its proportions were not in accord with the taste of the time and the usual Meissen shapes. Some years later the group was altered to make it more popular. A work report of February 1777 notes that Schönheit and Acier modelled a new version with four figures, one more than in Meyer's design. A drawing by Johann Gottlieb Matthäi, who already has been mentioned, shows the changes (Fig. 142), his sketch is still in the manufactory archive.[15] In his drawing the center of the group with donkey, Silenus and Bacchus is preserved, but the putto is moved to the rear of the donkey, facing away from the viewer. In the putto's place the new version shows a barebreasted girl called Flora. She was not a new design but taken from the top of a clockcase made about 1760 or a little earlier (Fig. 143). The base was altered too. Instead of the "terrace", as the irregularly shaped base was called, a Rococo base was used. That changed the size of the group. While the original was 19 cm (7 1/2 in.) high and 18 cm (7 3/32 in.) wide, the new model in the version shown by Matthäi was 21.6 cm (8 1/2 in.) high and 22.9 cm (9 in.) wide (Plate 67).

The new group sold much better and was ordered frequently. But in the middle of the 19th century the girl must have been considered too suggestive. After 1849 under Leuteritz she was turned away from the viewer now showing her back (Fig. 144 and 145). Bacchus became a smiling and handsome young man and the donkey was covered with paint (Plate 68). That was in accord with the artistic conception in the second half of the 19th century, when all areas that had been left white in the 18th century were generally painted, especially the flesh parts.

Fig. 141: Silenus on a Donkey *by Meyer, c. 1760, picture from an auction catalogue of 1934*

Fig. 143: *Top of clockcase model no. B 102 with figurine* Flora *used for the new version of the group* Silenus on a Donkey

Fig. 142: *Drawing by Matthäi for the re-designed version of* Silenus on a Donkey, *after 1779*

Fig. 144: Silenus on a Donkey *in the version created under Leuteritz between 1849 and 1853*

Fig. 145: Sketch of the group Silenus on a Donkey *from a price list of c. 1853-1854. Despite two major changes the group retained the model no. 2724, which the original had received c. 1760*

Fig. 146: Candlesticks by Leuteritz, 1863-1865, the figurines were taken from 18th century models, the candlesticks newly designed

The new version of the Silenus group was not necessarily an improvement. Still it was produced and sold in considerable numbers, even after the manufactory got a complaint in 1908. Count du Chastel pointed out that the change was not to the advantage of the piece[16]. The girl, so he said, made the composition disharmonic, she made the group too heavy on the left side and since she was showing her back, the piece had completely lost its front or viewing side. The manufactory noted this complaint and left the group as it was at that time. But the hint was not lost. Today the group again is made in the original shape designed by Meyer.

Leuteritz changed quite a number of 18th century models according to what he considered contemporary taste. He modified groups, took single parts from others, and combined them with components he had designed himself and which did not harmonize with the old models (Plate 69 and Fig. 146). This was not the modular-design principle of earlier years, it was closer to cannibalizing the 18th century models. The Meissen manufactory embraced this Second Rococo for lack of sound stylistic sense.

Next to this Neo-Rococo other revivals were tried. The Gothic style was discovered, classical influences were recognizable and Louis Seize again. Regency, Empire and Renaissance contributed to a kind of eclecticism that could be observed all over Europe and found one of its expressions in the Victorian style. Nobody saw anything wrong in jumbling together different styles, it was the taste of the time.

Leuteritz himself created some pieces in the Neo-Gothic manner (Fig. 147). He also designed large crater vases in the Greek style (Plate 70) which were decorated after original paintings.

The Empire style, with its cool, lifeless elegance, was modernized by more plastic attributes. Fancifully arched snake handles were developed in 1850 (Plate 71). From Sèvres the "paste upon paste" (pâte-sur-pâte) technique was adopted, and after many tries successfully introduced in Meissen in 1878. The delicate transparent reliefs were achieved by apply-

Fig. 147: Goblet in the Neo-Gothic style by Leuteritz, 1849

Fig. 148: Vase with paste-upon-paste decoration in reserves, blue colored ground, c. 1890

ing with a brush several layers of viscous porcelain paste on an already fired piece, varying the thickness of the application (Figs. 148 and 149). This technique also was combined with other kinds of plastic decorations (Plate 72).

Most figurines of the second half of the 19th century do not distinguish themselves by originality, many of them produce the effect of miniaturized statues. The manufactory did not employ modellers with ideas of their own. Rather it bought the rights to reproduce statues, monuments or busts that had originally been sculpted in stone or metal, or it had models made by outside sculptors (Fig. 150 and Plate 73).

Leuteritz' successor, Emmerich Andresen, who took over the plastic art department in 1886, was even more fond of reproducing monumental works of art in small porcelain copies. He visited art exhibitions hoping to find something that could be modelled in porcelain. Andresen continued the pompous Victorian style despite the change in art appreciation that announced itself. Meissen plastic art was criticized as old-fashioned, but the manufactory looked at its balance sheets and saw that this kind of art still sold well.

But Art Nouveau (Jugendstil) slowly but surely reached Meissen - late, but not too late. At the Dresden Art Exhibition in 1897 Walter Schott showed his *Girl Playing Bowls.* Andresen did not like the statue at all, and he had to be pushed to buy the reproduction rights in 1898. Since then, the porcelain version (Fig. 151) which comes in two sizes, is one of the steadily selling figurines still produced today.

At the Century Exhibition in Paris in 1900, the manufactory mainly showed "improved" 18th century models. They simply were re-worked without a feeling for the period that had inspired them, but with pedantic attention to details. They appear stiff and without expression, still they were successful at that time (Fig. 152). But these pieces were the last stand of the Victorian period. New ideas were in the offing. When Erich Hösel became head of the plastic department in 1903, the manufactory finally liberated itself from the style confusion of the 19th century. Hösel encouraged artists and modellers to study nature and to travel abroad for new impressions. He had voyaged to the Middle East and to America, and the group North America (Plate 74) was one of the results.

Fig. 149: Plate with Psyche *in paste-upon-paste technique, c. 1890-1895*

Fig. 150: Dying Warrior *by Roeder, 1884*

Fig. 152: Singer and Songstress *in the "Second-Rococo" style by Ruedrich after 1870*

Fig. 151: Girl playing Bowls *by Schott, 1898*

Fig. 153: Elephant *by Walther, after 1903*

159

Fig. 154: Girl with Rabbits *by Bochmann, after 1903*

Fig. 155: Four Children on Bench *by K. Hentschel, 1906*

Hösel was able to attract a considerable number of artists who were able and eager to try their hands on motifs of nature, and to express modern feelings in porcelain. Animal figurines were taken up again, and in this area Paul Walther, modeller of the manufactory, excelled especially (Fig. 153 and Plate 75). The modellers employed by the manufactory as well as outside artists could create new models, unrestricted by narrow art conceptions, as free and natural as impressions came to them. Max Bochmann's *Girl with Rabbits* (Fig. 154), Philipp Lange's *Girl in a Storm* (Plate 76), Konrad Hentschel's *Four Children on a Bench* (Fig. 155), Theodor Eichler's *Lady in Evening Gown with Wrap* (Fig. 156) and Alfred König *Ladies with Hats* (Fig. 157) are but a few

Old styles were taken up again, not to be copied, but to be executed with a modern understanding of the 18th century. The Munich sculptor Joseph von Kramer modelled the group *Family Concert* (Plate 77), which was at the time considered one of the best interpretations of Rococo life with modern means and a sensitive artistic understanding.

Otto Pilz renewed the monkey-band by Kaendler and Reinicke in a modern version (Plates 78 and 79). At first the manufactory could not identify with Pilz's designs at all. Pilz' often grotesque and whimsical ideas were accepted only after Hösel stood up for him.

About 1910, plastic art became more sprightly and animated, leaving Art Nouveau behind. The *Dancing Couple* by Alfred König (Fig. 158) took up a theme that had been a favorite of the manufactory at all times. The differences in style and expression can be seen on Plates 80 to 84, showing dancing couples from several periods of the manufactory.

Hösel also did something very important for the manufactory, its historic continuity, and its reputation. He restored the 18th century models which had been treated so badly during Leuteritz' reign to their original shapes. Using old moulds and the work reports by Kaendler and his co-workers, Hösel continued his toilsome task even after he had retired in 1929, until his death in 1951. If new pulls of 18th century figurines, groups, and decorative porcelain again appear like or at least very close to the originals, it is mainly due to Hösel's tireless efforts.

Max Adolf Pfeiffer, influenced plastic art considerably. Before he came to Meissen, Pfeiffer had been head of the Schwarzburger Werkstätten für Porzellankunst (Schwarzburg Workshops for Porcelain Art). There, he had given many young and talented sculptors a chance. When he asked them to work for Meissen, they came and created some of the most important works of plastic porcelain art in this century.

Fig. 156: Lady in Evening Gown with Wrap *by Eichler, 1910*

158: Dancing Couple *by König, 1912*

Fig. 157: Ladies with Hats *by König, 1911*

One of them was Paul Scheurich, who as a free lancer made more than one hundred models for the manufactory. On the occasion of his 100th birthday in 1983, Scheurich was celebrated as the most gifted and important porcelain designer since Kaendler. He was born in New York as the second child of German immigrants who went back to Germany nine months after his birth. His brothers in 1916 returned to the United States. August the older one became a violoncellist with American Philharmonic Orchestras, and Viktor his younger brother was cameraman and director of photography with Columbia Pictures in the 1920s and 1930s. But Paul Scheurich stayed in Germany.

He studied plastic art, and in 1909 designed his first work in porcelain for the Schwarzburg Workshops, then under the management of Max Adolf Pfeiffer. Scheurich got offers from manufactories in Berlin and Nymphenburg, Germany, but Pfeiffer, who in the meantime had become commercial manager in Meissen, succeeded in signing him up for the Meissen manufactory exclusively. The close relationship and collaboration between Pfeiffer and Scheurich was fruitful, and Scheurich used the artistic freedom he found in Meissen to create figurines and groups still considered unsurpassed (Plate 85). In 1913, he modelled five characters from the Russian ballet *Carnival* that had impressed him very much when it was performed by the Petersburg Russian Theater in Berlin in 1910 (Plate 12 and Fig. 159). These figurines were still generously garnished but very soon Scheurich became very careful with paint, often using it only for highlighting, and some of his groups he left completely white (Figs. 160 and 161).

In 1933 the manufactory received a hard blow when its artistic freedom was curtailed. It no longer was allowed to decide which designs should be accepted and produced. The Saxon State Treasury had appointed itself the sole judge over the artistic development of the manufactory. To the moral

Fig. 159: Dancer and Danseuse *from the Russian Ballet* Mardi Gras *by Scheurich, 1913*

Fig. 160: Drunkard *by Scheurich, modelled in 1922, this pull 1952*

standards of bureaucrats, some of Scheurich's creation appeared too piquant. His *Lady Falling off a Horse* (Fig 162) was rejected by the Saxon Treasury for "reasons o decency"[17]. Scheurich, who already had received most of the payment for the group, was requested to deliver a substitute It too was rejected, not because the Treasury did not like it but because it had changed its mind.

The Industrial Fair in Paris of 1937 was approaching and for lack of convincing exhibits Scheurich's models were selected to represent Meissen in Paris, among them the *Lady Falling off a Horse.* It was awarded the "Grand Prize" in Paris, as were five of Scheurich's other creations. Even the rejected substitute *Lady with a Hind* (Fig. 161), of which a few pulls had been made, received the highest award at the Paris Fair. But *Lady Falling off a Horse* was not mentioned in the manufactory catalog of 1938 any more. "Decency" had won again.

In 1934, after Pfeiffer had been dismissed by the new national socialist leadership in Meissen, Scheurich terminated his contract with the manufactory. After his success in Paris the manufactory bought a few more pieces from him, but Scheurich's close connection with Meissen could not be revived. He died in 1945.

Scheurich was the most important artist Pfeiffer won for the manufactory. Others like Ernst Barlach (Fig. 93), Gerhard Marcks (Fig. 92), Willy Münch-Khe (Fig. 100 and Plate 86), Erich Oehme (Fig. 98) and August Gaul (Fig. 99) already have been mentioned. One other productive sculptor, Max Esser, created new and interesting animals in porcelain while working for the manufactory from 1920 to 1926 (Figs. 95, 96 and 163).

Another outside artist was Ludwig Nick, from whom the manufactory purchased some models between 1927 and 1932 (Fig. 164). But the most influential of these artists was Emil Paul Börner, who was a painter as well as a modeller, and from 1930 until 1937 was head of the artistic departments of the manufactory. He designed only a few works of plastic art (Fig. 165 and 166) but his artistry is impressed on the many coins, medals and plaques he created. For the Nikolai Church in Meissen, he made a monumental memorial for the Meissen citizens killed in action in World War I (Fig. 167). He also made a carillon of thirty-seven porcelain bells, chiming from the steeple of the Frauen Church in Meissen since 1929.

About plastic art during the years of national socialist reign in Germany, there is nothing of importance to report. What happened after that has been described in Chapter 1.

Fig. 161: Lady with Hind *by Scheurich, designed 1931, first pull 1935*

Fig. 162: Lady Falling off a Horse *by Scheurich, first pull in 1937*

Fig. 164: St. Christopher *by Nick*

Fig. 165: Bell with singing Angels *by Börner, 1930*

Fig. 163: Elephant as candleholder *by Esser, 1924*

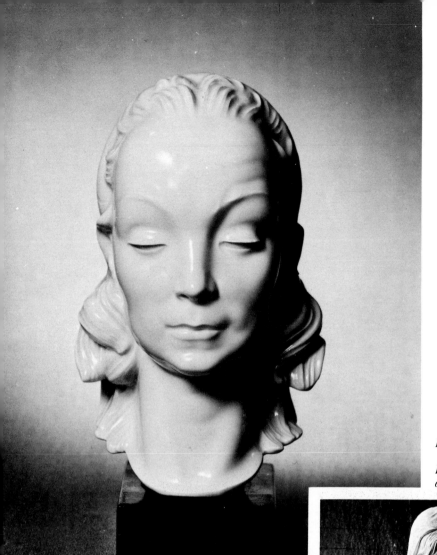

Fig. 166: Woman's Head *by Börner, 1930*

Fig. 167: *Part of a Memorial for Meissen citizens killed in action in World War One by Börner*

Chapter Five
Tableware

Among the things he promised to make from porcelain, Böttger in 1709 mentioned complete dinner sets as precious as those made of silver. He never lived to see his promise fulfilled, it took more than twenty years until the first sets of dinnerware were made. The inventories of 1711 show that the manufactory produced tea and coffee pots, cups, sugar pots, creamers, butter dishes, salt cellars and bowls but they were not designed to match. They were modelled as single pieces, as were the tankards, mugs, and bottles mentioned in the inventory. Among the almost 13,000 pieces listed, there were only thirty-five plates of one design. Meals were still eaten from silver or pewter plates for many years to come. Even the inventory of the Royal Porcelain Collection in the Dutch Palace of 1721 does not register a single dinner or dessert plate[2].

Spoons (Plate 87) and fork and knife handles were made from the beginning (Figs. 168 to 170). The blades and the metal parts of the forks were attached by cutlers outside the manufactory. These objects remained in the production program of the manufactory at all times, and they are still made today.

Since painting had not been mastered yet most of the first porcelain vessels received plastic decorations. That changed when Höroldt after 1720 quickly developed the art of porcelain painting.

Early in the 1720s, the first matching breakfast sets were made, and at the end of the decade, the first dinner sets. But their porcelain pieces still were plain, and they only became sets by the matching decoration. For handles and knobs small animals, lions heads or stone-pine cones were applied (Plate 88). Plastic decorations on tableware were not introduced until Kaendler became modelmaster in Meissen in 1731. His first complete set with a uniting plastic decoration was probably a dinner set for Count Friesen made in 1731. Friesen had married an illegitimate daughter of Augustus the Strong, and became cabinet minister of the King. No verified piece of the Friesen set has been found.

Fig. 168: *Two-pronged fork and knife, handles polished red stoneware, c. 1710-1715*

Fig. 169: *Knife with pistol-shaped handle of polished red stoneware, blade silver c. 1710-1715*

Fig. 170: *Fork and knife from a set of twelve pairs, decorated porcelain c. 1750-1760, mounting ring gilt silver, metal parts mounted in Paris, France, late 19th century by E. Taburet-Boin*

In 1732, Kaendler made a dinner set for the Swedish King, Adolf Frederik I, which is now in the collection of the Royal Castle in Stockholm, Sweden (Fig. 171). In this set, which is elaborately painted, relief decorations of small blossoms connected by tendrils are found only on the borders of the plates.

In 1732, August II ordered a tea-set, and one year later a Coronation Set was made for his successor August III. The plates were still without plastic decoration, but the edges of larger bowls were cut into arches (Fig. 172).

Count Sulkowski, also a cabinet minister of the King, in 1735 ordered a dinner set that started the long series of Kaendler's plastic designs for tableware (Fig. 173). Sulkowski was deposed in 1738, and Count Brühl replaced him. He also ordered dinner sets in 1733 and 1736 which are only known from the work reports in the Meissen archive.

These first sets were made on special orders, and they were not supposed to be repeated exactly. But elements of their plastic decorations and the arched cuts of their edges were incorporated in new designs, or the old designs were modernized. From the *Sulkowski* pattern, the *Old Ozier* pattern emanated about 1736, also in the style of wickerwork (French: *ozier*, Fig. 174). This pattern was further developed into *New Ozier* (Fig. 175) between 1741 and 1745.

One of the most elaborate dinner sets ever made was ordered by Count Brühl in 1737. It was called *Schwanen Service* (Swan service), and supposedly consisted of more than two thousand pieces. The whole surface of the plates was modelled in low relief, showing various animals and water plants which hinted at the meaning of the name Brühl, i.e. bog or fen (Fig. 176). Kaendler and Eberlein worked together on this set, which shows a pure, naturalistic style. Brühl kept it at his Castle Pförten for *Schau-Essen* "show dinner's" and for display of his wealth (Plate 22). Most of the original set was kept by his family until the end of World War II, when the pieces were scattered all over the world. But the manufactory continues to make pulls from the old moulds for other customers, and most of them are not only garnished but also decorated.

Fig. 171: Parts from the dinner set for the Swedish King Adolf Frederik I by Kaendler, c. 1730, stylized flowers in low relief and painted coat-of-arms

Fig. 172: Plate from the Coronation Set for August III

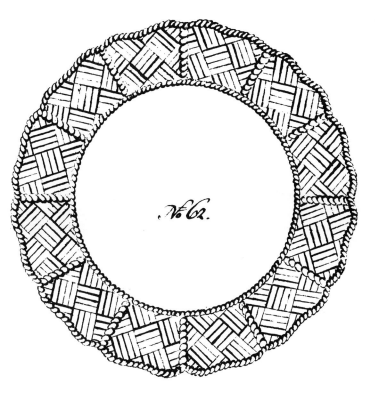

Fig. 173: Drawing of a plate from the Sulkowski Pattern

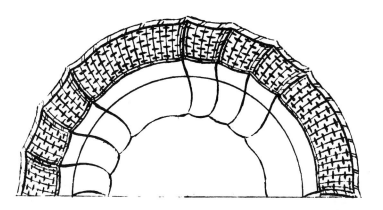

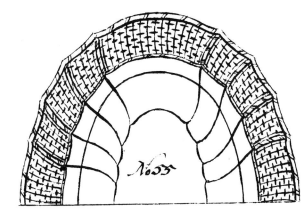

Fig. 175: Drawing of New Ozier Pattern

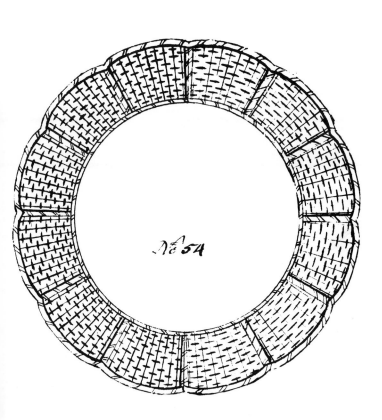

Fig. 174: Drawing of Old Ozier Pattern

Fig. 176: Plate of the Swan Service

The Swan pattern belongs to those designs that have survived until today, and still are among the patterns in the regular production program of the manufactory. The others are the earlier mentioned *Sulkowski, Old Ozier,* and *New Ozier* patterns. They were joined by the *New Brandenstein* pattern (Fig. 177), that was developed from the *Old Brandenstein* pattern (Fig. 178), the *New Marseille* pattern (Fig. 179), and *the New Dulong* pattern (Fig. 180), a modernization of the *Old Dulong* pattern (Fig. 181). They all were created between 1741 and 1745.

But the most successful pattern was designed in 1745 by Kaendler. He called it *Neuer Ausschnitt* (New Cutout) and it is plain except for the wavy edge cut (Fig. 182). At first it probably was only a partial set consisting of the basic pieces for a simple and unpretentious dinner set for middle class customers. During the 19th century it was extended to become the set with the largest number of different parts. It is appealing even by itself but it also offers a plain surface for painting of all kinds, an idea that was taken up again by Ludwig Zepner with his design *Large Cutout* in 1973 (Plates 6 to 10).

During the 18th century a large number of plastic patterns was developed. A list of 1790 and another one of 1830 show drawings of them[3]. The years mentioned in the description denote the period of design. Except for those patterns pointed out especially only dessert plates with these patterns were available.

Fig. 179: New Marseille *Pattern*

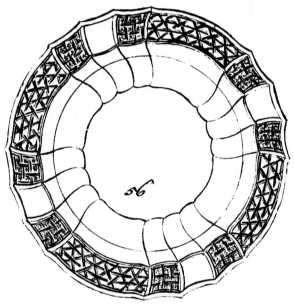

Fig. 177: New Brandenstein *Pattern*

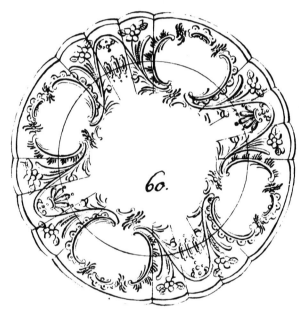

Fig. 180: New Dulong *Pattern*

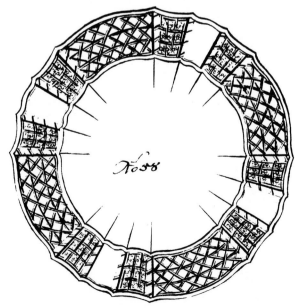

Fig. 178: Old Brandenstein *Pattern*

Fig. 181: Old Dulong *Pattern*

168

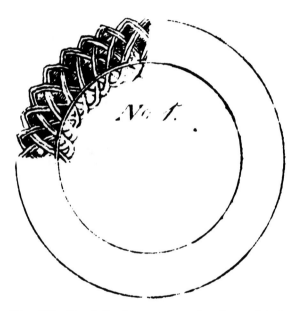

Fig. 182: Plate of New Cutout Pattern

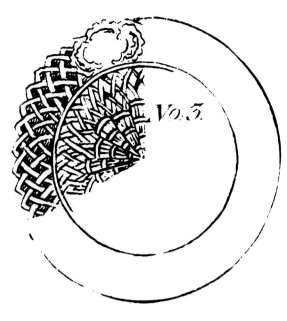

Fig. 185: No. 3 Basketweave on border, ledge and well with three cartouches, border pierced. 1764-1773

Fig. 183: No. 1 Basketweave on border and ledge, pierced. 1774-1814

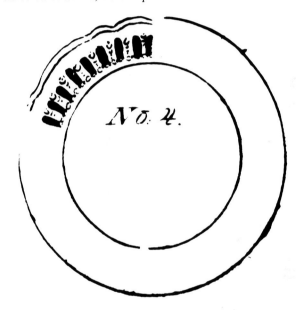

Fig. 186: No. 4 With pierced border, formerly called No. 2x. 1774-1814

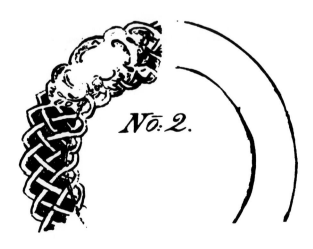

Fig. 184: No. 2 Basketweave on border and ledge with three cartouches. 1764-1773

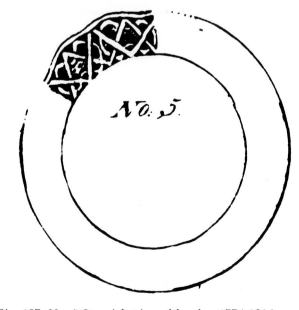

Fig. 187: No. 5 Spanish pierced border. 1774-1814

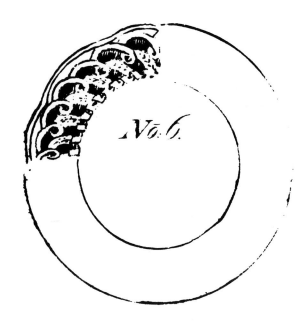

Fig. 188: No. 6 With pierced border. 1774-1814

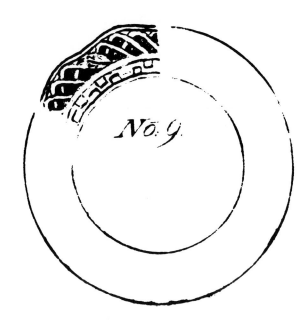

Fig. 191: No. 9 Border pierced. 1764-1773

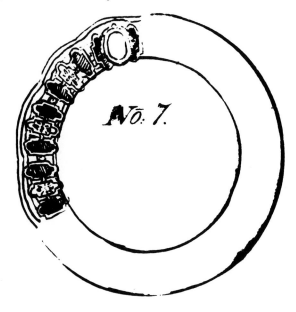

Fig. 189: No. 7 Border simply pierced, Schoenau pattern. 1774-1814

Fig. 192: No. 10 Schubert pattern, border pierced or not pierced. 1774-1814

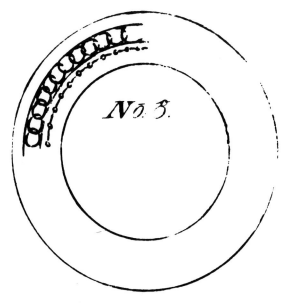

Fig. 190: No. 8 Chain pattern on border, pierced or not pierced. 1774-1814

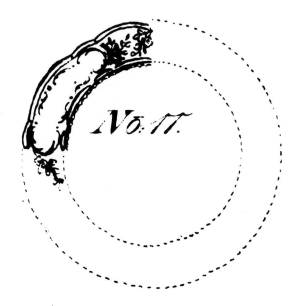

Fig. 193: No. 11 Border with four scrolled cartouches, part set. 1746-1756

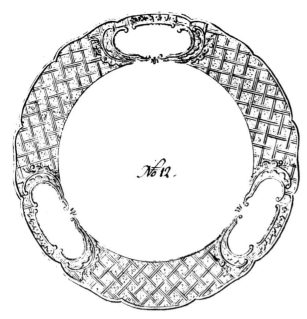

Fig. 194: No. 12 Lindish *pattern on border with three cartouches, available as dinner set. 1746-1756.*
No drawing: No. 13 Dinner Plate, larger version of No. 28

Fig. 197: No. 17 Gotzkowsky *pattern, flower relief continuing from border into well, with four cartouches on border, not pierced, (compare No. 52), available as dinner set. 1741*

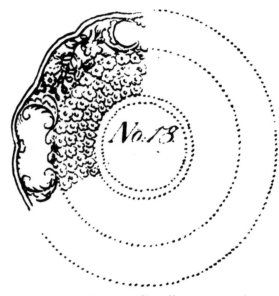

Fig. 195: No. 14 Lindish *pattern on border, ledge and well, with four cartouches on border protruding into ledge (in some lists misprinted as No. 41 and corrected by hand). 1746-1756*

Fig. 198: No. 18 Saucer, relief all over except in center of well, with four cartouches on border, not pierced

Fig. 196: No. 15 *Border relief with three cartouches, not pierced. 1746-1756*
No drawing: No. 16 Turkish plain entwined

Fig. 199: No. 19 With border relief, not pierced. 1764-1773

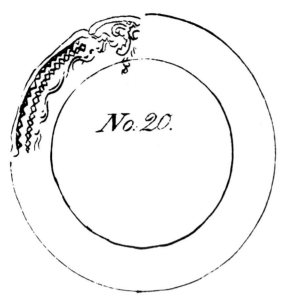

Fig. 200: No. 20 Ornamental relief (in German: Zierratenkante) on border, not pierced. Available as dinner plate and
as soup plate. 1746-1756

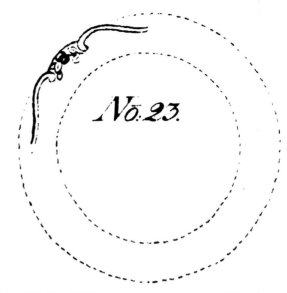

Fig. 203: No. 23 Four wings on border and fruits on edge, not
pierced. 1746-1756

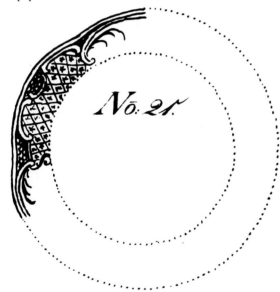

Fig. 201: No. 21 Ornamental relief (Zierratenkante), not
pierced, part set. 1746-1756

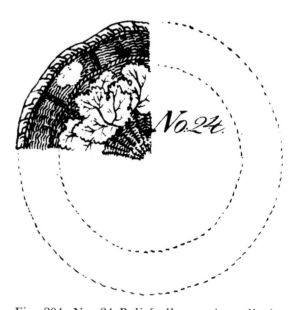

Fig. 204: No. 24 Relief all over, in well vine-leaves, not
pierced. 1746-1756

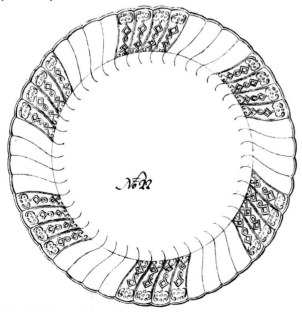

Fig. 202: No. 22 Turkish wound with ornaments, not pierced
(set was completed in 1910). 1746-1756

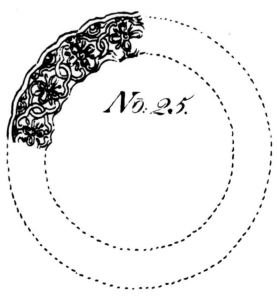

Fig. 205: No. 25 Ornamental relief (Zierratenkante) on
border, not pierced. 1764-1773

Fig. 206: No. 26 Flowers on border, wreath of flowers on edge, not pierced. 1746-1756

Fig. 209: No. 29 Relief border with four scrolled cartouches, not pierced. 1746-1756

Fig. 207: No. 27 Gothic pierced. 1774-1814

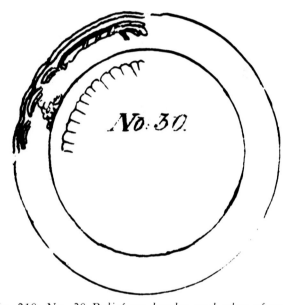

Fig. 210: No. 30 Relief on border and edge of well, not pierced. 1746-1756

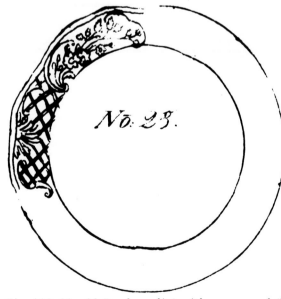

Fig. 208: No. 28 Border relief with weave and flowers, not pierced,, available as dinner plate and as soup plate, see also Nos. 13 and 68. 1746-1756

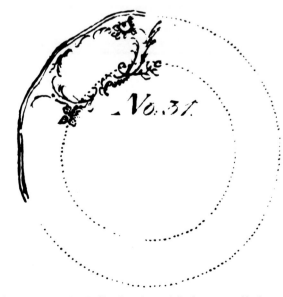

Fig. 211: No. 31 Relief border with three scrolled cartouches. 1746-1756

Fig. 212: No. 32 Prussian design or Prussian Musical Design with musical instruments, available as dinner plate and as soup plate. 1761

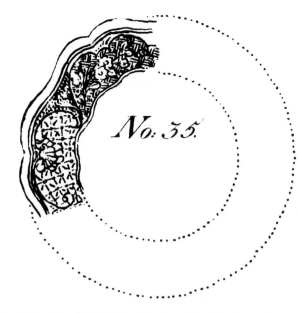

Fig. 215: No. 35 Brühl's Medley (Brühlsches Allerlei), part set. 1742

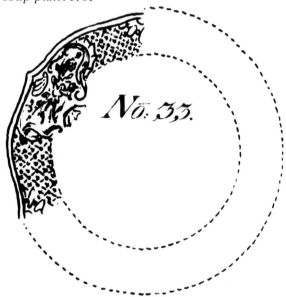

Fig. 213: No. 33 Relief on border with three filled cartouches, not pierced. 1746-1756

Fig. 216: No. 36 Relief border with braided edge, part set. 1757-1763

Fig. 214: No. 34 Ornamental border relief, not pierced. 1746-1756

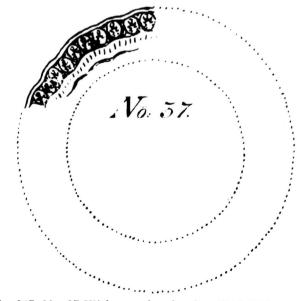

Fig. 217: No. 37 With acanthus border. 1764-1773

Fig. 218: No. 38 With rosette border, pierced or not pierced. 1774-1814

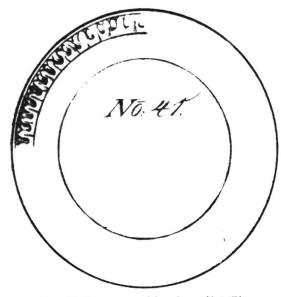

Fig. 221: No. 41 Ornamental border relief (Zierratenkante), not pierced. 1774-1814

Fig. 219: No. 39 Relief border, not pierced. 1757-1763

Fig. 222: No. 42 Relief border with tendrils of vine and bunches of grapes. 1764-1773

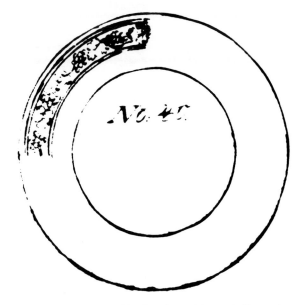

Fig. 220: No. 40 Relief border with tendrils of vine and pears. 1774-1814

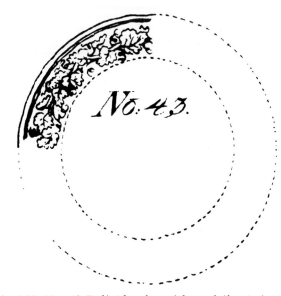

Fig. 223: No. 43 Relief border with tendrils of vine without bunches of grapes. 1764-1773

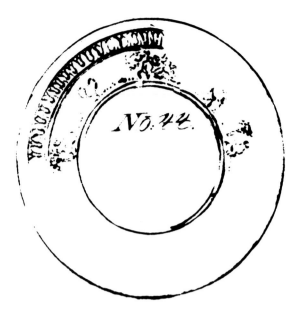

Fig. 224: No. 44 Relief border with figures. 1774-1814

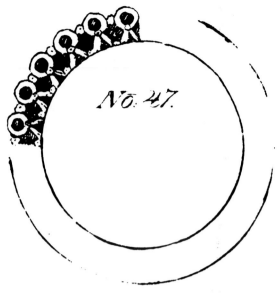

Fig. 227: No. 47 Rounded bows on border, pierced or not pierced. 1764-1773

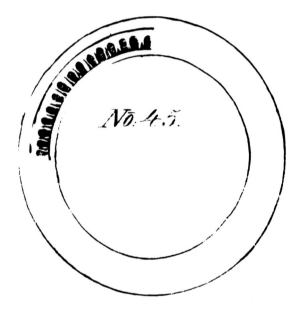

Fig. 225: No. 45 Manteuffel Pattern, pierced or not pierced. 1774-1814

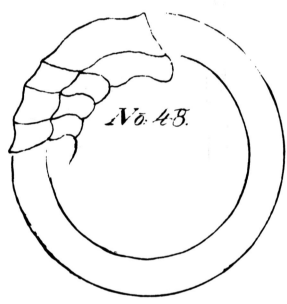

Fig. 228: No. 48 With 20 wavy lines from edge to periphery of well (the list of 1790 says: "overlayed with forget-me-nots", but the illustration does not show any flowers). 1746-1756

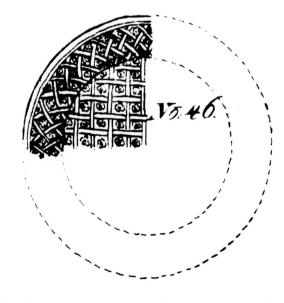

Fig. 226: No. 46 Weave and forget-me-nots all over, not pierced. 1746-1756

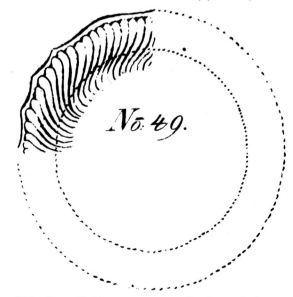

Fig. 229: No. 49 Narrow wavy ribs from below edge to periphery of well. 1746-1756

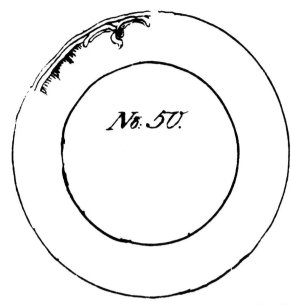

Fig. 230: No. 50 With narrow relief below edge. 1746-1756

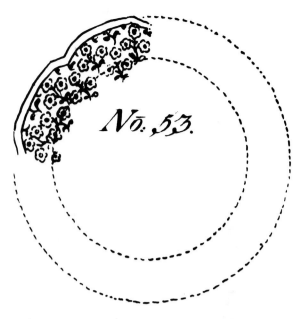

Fig. 233: No. 53 With strewn forget-me-nots on border and ledge. 1746-1756

 No. 54 Old Ozier, *see Fig. 174*
 No. 55 New Ozier, *see Fig. 175*
 No. 56 New Brandenstein, *see Fig. 177*

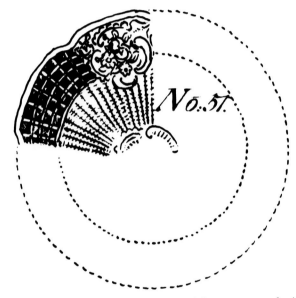

Fig. 231: No. 51 Relief all over with one cartouche in center of well and three cartouches on border. 1746-1756

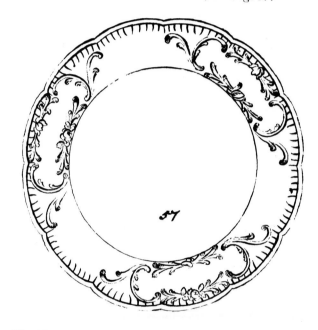

Fig. 234: No. 57 New Spanish *pattern, complete set. 1746-1756*

 No. 58 Old Brandenstein, *see Fig. 178*
 No. 59 Old Dulong, *see Fig. 181*
 No. 60 New Dulong, *see Fig. 180*
 No. 61 New Marseille, *see Fig. 179*
 No. 62 Sulkowsky *pattern, see Fig. 173*

Fig. 232: No. 52 Variation of Gotzkowsky Pattern (No. 17) with four plain spaces on border instead of cartouches. 1744

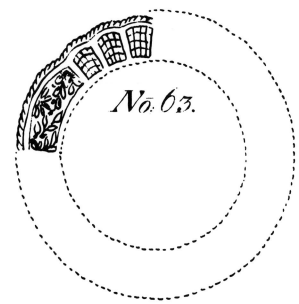

Fig. 235: No. 63 Relief border, not pierced (in some price lists misprinted as No. 36), in 1830 also available pierced. 1746-1756

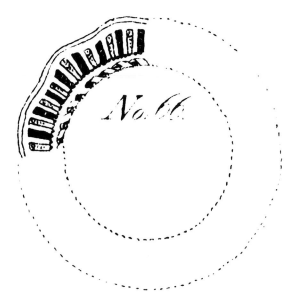

Fig. 238: No. 66 Schoenau pattern, with wound ribbon on ledge, not pierced, in 1830 also available pierced. 1764-1773

Fig. 236: No. 64 Relief on border, ledge and periphery of well with three small cartouches on border, not pierced. 1774-1814

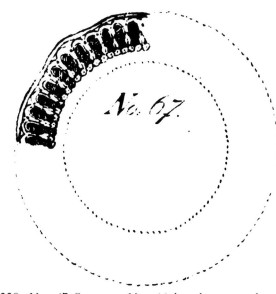

Fig. 239: No. 67 Same as No. 66 but larger and without ribbon. 1764-1773

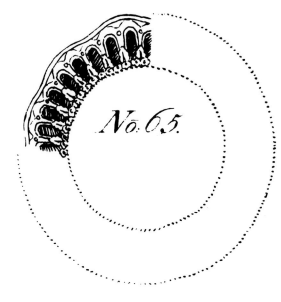

Fig. 237: No. 65 Relief border with forget-me-nots, not pierced, in 1830 also available pierced. 1764-1773

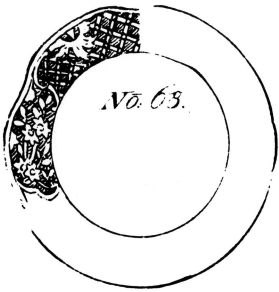

Figs. 240 and 241: No. 68 King's Pattern, similar to No. 28, in two versions, the second one with additional flower branches around well. 1757-1763

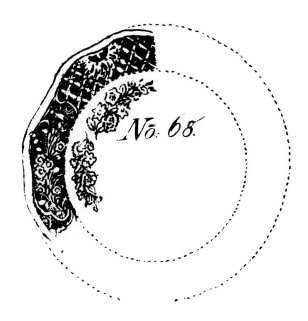

Fig. 244: No. 71 Border and ledge with relief flowers, flower bouquet in center of well. 1746-1756

Fig. 242: No. 69 Schoenau Prince-Electoral *Pattern, with wound ribbon, pierced, part set. 1774-1814, (Plate 89)*

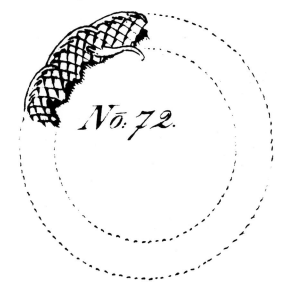

Fig. 245: No. 72 With scaled border. 1757-1763

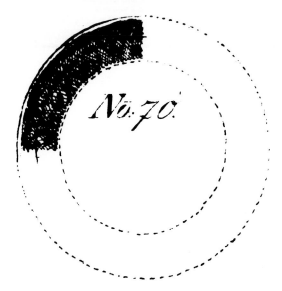

Fig. 243: No. 70 With fine lacework border. 1774-1814

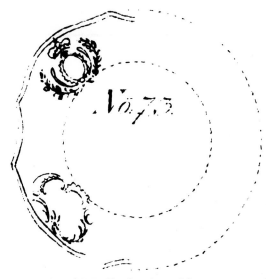

Fig. 246: No. 73 Relief border with two cartouches and two escutcheons. 1746-1756

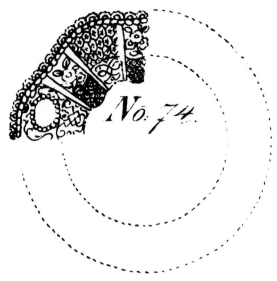

Fig. 247: No. 74 With elaborate relief on border continuing over ledge into periphery of well. 1746-1756

Fig. 250: No. 77 Relief border with four cartouches and wound ribbon on edge. 1734-1737

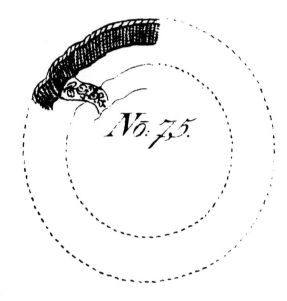

Fig. 248: No. 75 Narrow relief border similar to New Ozier with six flowering branches protruding into well. 1746-1756

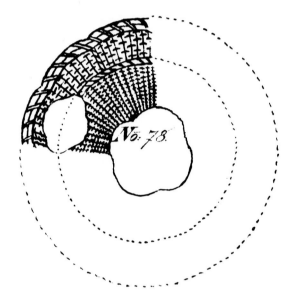

Fig. 251: No. 78 Relief border continuing into well, four plain cartouches on border, one larger cartouche in center of well, wound ribbon on edge. 1746-1756

Fig. 249: No. 76 Border with three plain and three scrolled shells. 1746-1756

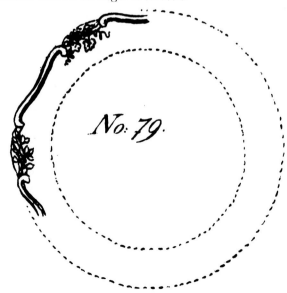

Fig. 252: No. 79 Narrow border relief with six arches on edge separated by flowers. 1746-1756

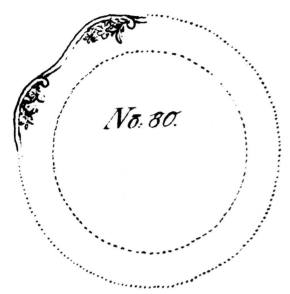

Fig. 253: No. 80 Narrow border relief with eight arches below edge and four sprays of flowers. 1746-1756

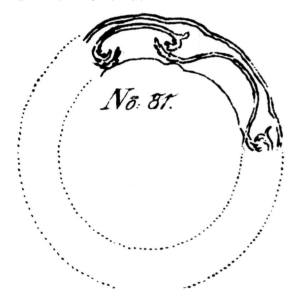

Fig. 254: No. 81 English Pattern, border relief with four long and four shorter arches, part set. 1746-1756

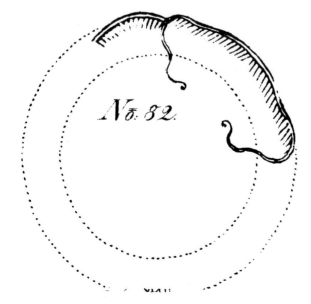

Fig. 255: No. 82 Border relief with four scrolled arches protruding into well, similar to No. 94. 1746-1756

The list of 1830 ends with No. 82. The list of about 1790 continues but does not show any more illustrations beyond No. 84.

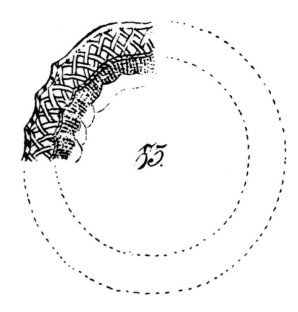

Fig. 256: No. 83 Dessert plate, pierced.

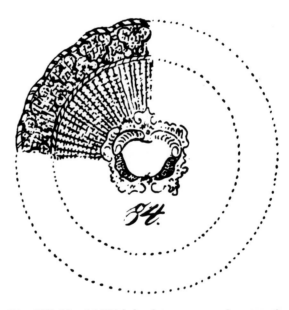

Fig. 257: No. 84 With basket weave and cartouche in well.

Beginning with No. 85 the patterns in the list of 1790 are only described, some of them even without a number. These descriptions are repeated here and - where possible - the patterns are identified or illustrated. All of them were designed before 1790.

No. 85 Prince-Electoral or King's pattern (probably similar to Nos. 28 and 68)
No. 86 Dessert plate, pierced (probably matching a Turkish cup)
No. 87 Dessert plate, pierced
No. 88 Ditto
No. 89 Ditto
No. 90 Ditto
No. Ditto without cartouches in well, after Steinauer

Table dishes with relief
No. 91 Part set with rose garlands and scaled well
No. 92 With rose garlands and ribbed well
No. 93 Swan Pattern (see Fig. 176)

No. 94 not described
No. 95 not described
No. 96 Part set with leaf ornaments
No. 97 Part set, not described
No. 98 Part set, similar to Prussian Musical Design No. 32
No. 99 Part set with three cartouches and blossoms of forget-me-nots
No. 100 Part set with blossoms of forget me-nots
No. 101 Part set with ornamental shells
No. 102 Part set, not described
No. 103 Part set with strewn relief flowers
No. 104 Part set with tulip pattern
No. 105 Part set with ribbed or flame pattern
No. 106 Part set with rose pattern
No. 107 With ribbed squares
No. 108 Ribbed all over
No. 109 Lobed and plain
No. 110 Lobed different kinds
No. 111 Scaled pattern
No. 112 Turkish plain wound (handwritten remark added later says: "is No. 16")
No. 113 Wound pattern
No. 114 not described
no No. Wafer shaped cutout
no No. *Old Cutout*
no No. *New Cutout* (see Fig. 182)
no No. Coffee set in the shape of fruits
No. 115 Dessert plate, small perforations
No. 116 Dessert plate with piercing on edge
No. 117 Ditto with six arches

The list also contains some illustrations which are not explained in the text as the *Ordinary Ribbed Pattern* (Fig. 258) and the *Ribbed Pattern with French Cut Edge* (Fig. 259) or a plate in the shape of a leaf (Fig. 260). Besides the patterns named in the lists some others were designed, for instance the *Schneeball Service* (Snowball Set) of about 1738 - 1740 (Figs. 261 and 262), the *Festoon Set* already mentioned (Fig. 62) or the pierced *Rosette Pattern* (Fig. 263). Other patterns have been found that do not match the descriptions exactly (Fig. 264). They might have been variations of a pattern or a combination of two patterns. Plastic decoration during Kaendler's time knew only few bounds. Vessels were generously covered with applied flowers (Plate 90) and sometimes plates were already filled with porcelain fruits and plants (Plate 91).

This style was abandoned in the last third of the 18th century in favor of Classic and Empire shapes and forms. Very few of them emanated from Meissen. The manufactory borrowed ideas from France, England and even Prussia (Plate 92 and Fig. 265). Handwritten price lists with hand-drawn sketches[4] show the forms Meissen developed during the Marcolini period from 1774 to 1814 (Fig. 266 and 267). Only the Old Form had come down from earlier times, the other shapes had been newly developed and these designs were the only ones the manufactory had in its regular production program.

Beginning about 1830, some of the old 18th century forms were taken up again when interest in the style of the Rococo increased. Some of the part sets of the Kaendler time were completed, especially the form *New Cutout*, for which 550 different parts were developed.

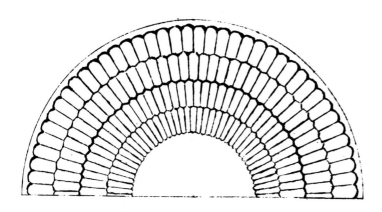

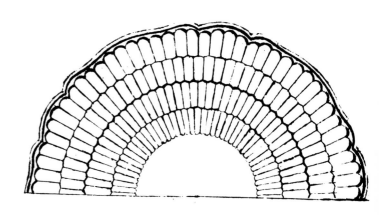

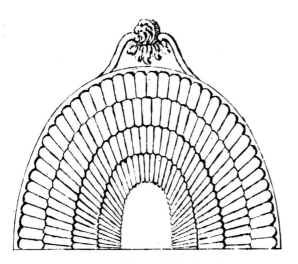

Fig. 258: Ordinary ribbed pattern

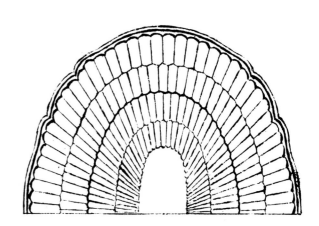

Fig. 259: Ribbed pattern with French cut edge

Fig. 260: Leaf-shaped plate

Fig. 262: Vase with Snowball pattern and birds

Fig. 261: Saucer from Snowball Set

Fig. 263: Pierced Rosette Pattern

Fig. 264: Plate with a variation of plastic relief pattern no. 14 with only three cartouches on border and a fourth one on well

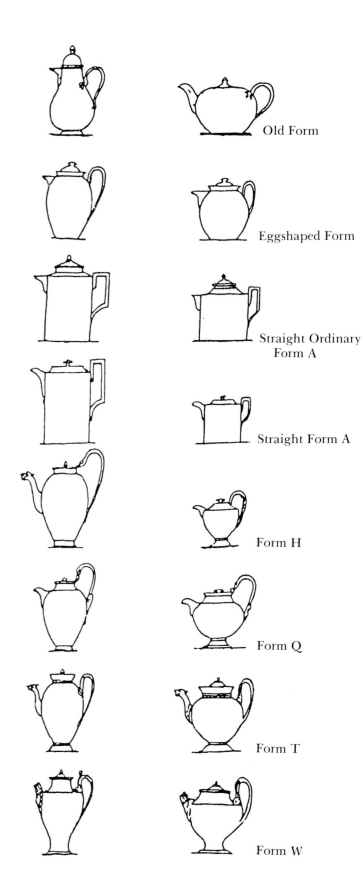

Old Form

Eggshaped Form

Straight Ordinary Form A

Straight Form A

Form H

Form Q

Form T

Form W

Fig. 265: Coffee pot and creamer influenced by the Wedgwood style with Classicistic elements on handles and on the spout of the coffee pot, after 1780

Fig. 266: Drawings of Meissen forms of coffee and tea pots offered between 1774 and 1814

Old Form, plain handle

Old Form, antique handle

Conical with plain handle

Conical with antique handle

Straight with antique handle, No. 1

Straight with antique handle, No. 2

Lemonshaped Form with plain handle

Lemonshaped Form with pulled up handle

Lemonshaped Form with Swan handle

Bulgy with pulled up handle

Bulgy with Swan handle

Form O, No. 98

Form P, No. 5

Form P, NO. 43

Form Q, NO. 74

Fig. 267: Drawings of forms for coffee and tea cups offered between 1774 and 1814

When the manufactory struggled onto its feet after the Napoleonic Wars, its modellers and designers could not come up with new ideas of their own as technologists, technicians, and even managers did. Marcolini's order not to design new forms had squashed the incentive of the Meissen modellers. In 1831 they began to copy cut glass patterns (Fig. 268). This so-called T-series was a deviation from the usually pretty sound stylistic sense of the manufactory (Fig. 269). Most of the cut glass copies were abandoned at the end of the 19th century. The manufactory itself was never happy with them, and in order to forget them as quickly as possible, the form numbers of the cut glass pieces in the T-series were assigned to new designs. (See chapter on Marks and Markings, Model Numbers).

With a few variations, the Empire shapes could be adapted to the Biedermeier period. The stripe decoration usually connected with Biedermeier already had been used in the late 18th century, and it suited the Biedermeier taste (Plate 93). In Meissen Biedermeier style was expressed with modernized old forms taken from different periods of the manufactory (Plate 94 and Figs. 270 and 271).

In the middle of the 19th century Historism and Eclecticism influenced the design of tableware the same way it affected plastic art (Figs. 272 to 284). Plates and vessels were overloaded with relief decorations, some purely ornamental, others in Neo-Gothic, Neo-Renaissance or Neo-Classical styles. Naturalistic relief decorations became popular. Vine-leaves and grapes, for which the manufactory had always had a penchant (Plate 95) were preferred. Covered with the new cheaper gilding, these articles found buyers, and some of them became so popular that they are still produced today. Others were very shortlived. In 1851 more than 260 articles were taken off the production program, some of them only a few years old (Figs. 279 and 280).

For a relatively short period after 1865, the manufactory also turned to the wrongly-named *Capo-di-Monte* style, that had become very popular. The manufactory in Capo di Monte had only existed from 1743 until 1759, and used a stylized lily as its mark (Fig. 285). The letter N with a crown above (Fig. 286) was the mark of a manufactory in Naples, Italy, that operated from 1771 first in Portici and from 1773 until 1821 in Naples. Its moulds and models were acquired by the manufactory of Ginori in Doccia near Florence, Italy. This manufactory quickly developed into a factory and produced the bulk of the so-called Capo-di-Monte pieces. They were so much in demand that Meissen, too, made porcelain of this kind (Plate 96), but it did not, as many other factories did, mark it with the crowned letter N, it applied the crossed swords mark. Competition in this field was so great that Meissen let these products disappear after a few years.

When at the end of the 19th century this styleless style began to outlive itself, the manufactory slowly moved away from it and took up old elements for new forms, maintaining the representative character of tableware that was sought by the buyers. (Plate 97) The manufactory only reluctantly approached the Art Nouveau style, which turned away from the overstuffed Victorian style. Art Nouveau was a movement that made a break with the past. The manufactory did not feel able to join too easily, because its strength lay in the preservation and the permanent development of the old.

In 1897, Konrad Hentschel designed the *Crocus Breakfast Set* (Fig. 287) which found reasonably good acceptance.

Konrad Hentschel and his brother Rudolf had received their first training at the manufactory, but had completed their artistic education outside. They were able to understand the reasons for the rise of Art Nouveau. Modellers and painters having grown up artistically in the manufactory could not detach themselves from the principle of historic continuity, and therefore never found a sound relation to the new style.

The manufactory had to look somewhere else for Art Nouveau designers. It commissioned Henry van de Velde, expecting a new design for a dinner set that would match the new furniture and furnishings of Art Nouveau. The set delivered by van de Velde in 1903-1904 won the applause of the new art scene, but it was unsalable (Fig. 288).

Preisverzeichniss von Dessertgefässen etc.

in der Kön. Porzellan-Manufactur in Meissen und in deren Niederlagen in Dresden und Leipzig, mit Vergoldung.

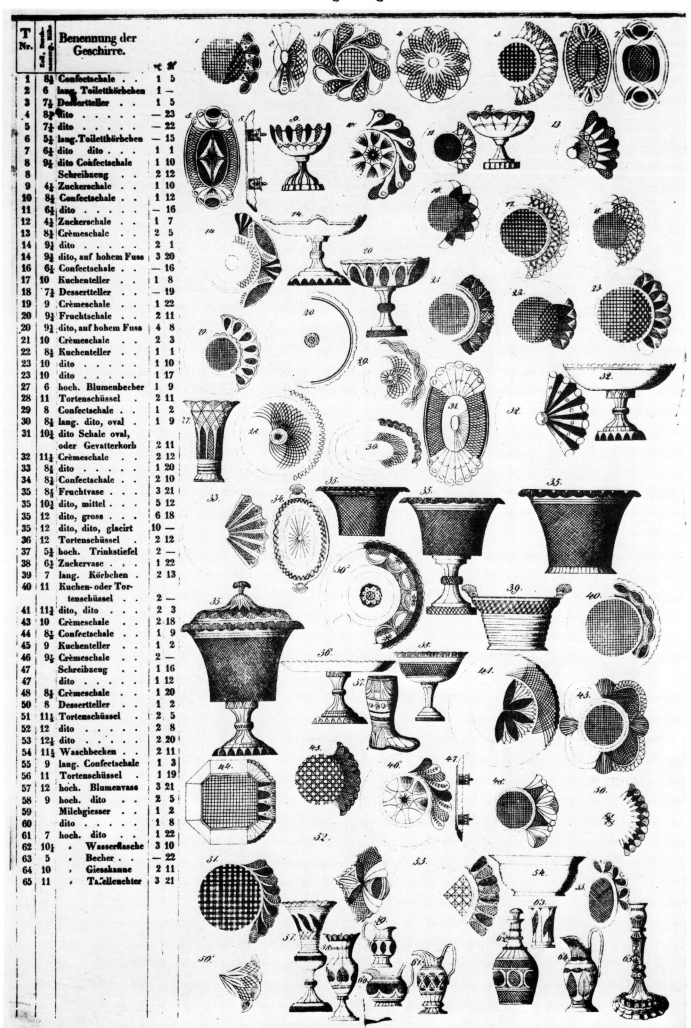

T Nr.	Zoll, Durchmesser o. Höhe	Benennung der Geschirre.	₰	ℳ
1	8½	Confectschale . .	1	5
2	6	lang. Toilettkörbchen	1	—
3	7½	Dessertteller . .	1	5
4	8½	dito	—	23
5	7½	dito	—	22
6	5½	lang. Toilettkörbchen	—	15
7	6¼	dito dito . . .	1	1
8	9¼	dito Confectschale	1	10
8		Schreibzeug . .	2	12
9	4½	Zuckerschale . .	1	10
10	8½	Confectschale . .	1	12
11	6½	dito	—	16
12	4½	Zuckerschale . .	1	7
13	8½	Crèmeschale . .	2	5
14	9¼	dito	2	1
14	9¼	dito, auf hohem Fuss	3	20
16	6¼	Confectschale . .	—	16
17	10	Kuchenteller . .	1	8
18	7½	Dessertteller . .	—	19
19	9	Crèmeschale . .	1	22
20	9¼	Fruchtschale . .	2	11
20	9¾	dito, auf hohem Fuss	4	8
21	10	Crèmeschale . .	2	3
22	8½	Kuchenteller . .	1	1
23	10	dito	1	10
23	10	dito	1	17
27	6	hoch. Blumenbecher	1	9
28	11	Tortenschüssel .	2	11
29	8	Confectschale . .	1	2
30	8½	lang. dito, oval .	1	9
31	10¾	dito Schale oval, oder Gevatterkorb	2	11
32	11¼	Crèmeschale . .	2	12
33	8½	dito	1	20
34	8½	Confectschale . .	2	10
35	8⅝	Fruchtvase . . .	3	21
35	10¾	dito, mittel . . .	5	12
35	12	dito, gross . . .	6	18
35	12	dito, dito, glacirt	10	—
36	12	Tortenschüssel .	2	12
37	5¾	hoch. Trinkstiefel	2	—
38	6¾	Zuckervase . . .	1	22
39	7	lang. Körbchen .	2	13
40	11	Kuchen- oder Tortenschüssel . .	2	—
41	11¾	dito, dito . . .	2	3
43	10	Crèmeschale . .	2	18
44	8½	Confectschale . .	1	9
45	9	Kuchenteller . .	1	2
46	9½	Crèmeschale . .	2	—
47		Schreibzeug . .	1	16
47		dito	1	12
48	8½	Crèmeschale . .	1	20
50	8	Dessertteller . .	1	2
51	11½	Tortenschüssel .	2	5
52	12	dito	2	8
53	12½	dito	2	20
54	11¼	Waschbecken . .	2	11
55	9	lang. Confectschale	1	3
56	11	Tortenschüssel .	1	19
57	12	hoch. Blumenvase	3	21
58	9	hoch. dito . .	2	5
59		Milchgiesser . .	1	2
60		dito	1	8
61	7	hoch. dito . .	1	22
62	10¼	„ Wasserflasche	3	10
63	5	„ Becher . .	—	22
64	10	„ Giesskanne	2	11
65	11	„ Tafelleuchter	3	21

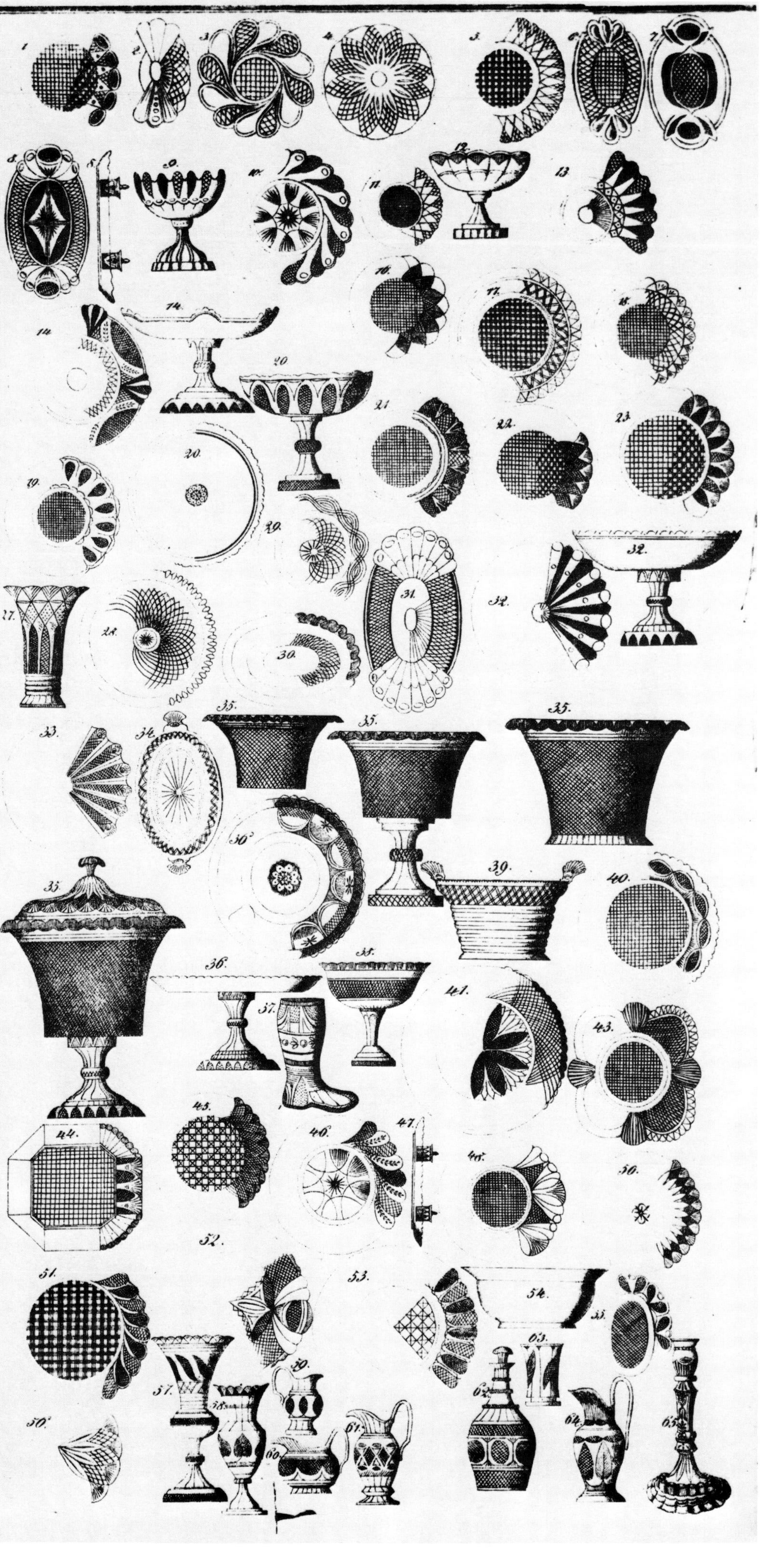

66	5	hoch. Becher .	1	—
68	6	„ Pokal .	1	15
69	9	Dessertteller .	1	9
70	9½	dito	1	17
73	14½	Tortenschüssel	3	12
74	15	dito	4	—
75	8¾	dito	1	—
76	8¾	Fruchtschale .	2	10
77	11½	dito	2	15
79	11¾	Schale, oval .	2	16
80	6¾	Crèmeschale .	—	21
81	10	lang. dito . .	1	16
83	12	lang. dito . .	3	16
84	6¼	Compotschale .	—	17
85		Salzfass . . .	—	8
86	9	Crèmeschale .	2	4
87	7½	Zuckerschale .	1	13
88		Flacon . . .	3	3
89	5	hoch. Becher	1	2
90	5	„ Zuckervase	1	10
91	14½	Tortenschüssel	3	21
92	12½	dito	2	13
93	13	Credenzplateau	3	12
95		Rumflasche . .	1	17
96	14½	Waschbecken .	4	10
97	11¼	Giesskanne . .	3	19
98	3¼	Zuckervase . .	1	4
99		Flacon . . .	1	20
101		Theebüchse .	2	7
103		Flacon . . .	1	17
105		Eisbecher . .	—	11
106	8¼	hoch. Blumenvase	1	18
107	8	Dessertteller .	1	—
108	9	lang. Confectschale	1	15
109	8¾	dito . .	1	4
110		Senfbecher . .	1	13
111		Butterbüchse .	2	16
111	7½	Dessertteller .	1	11
112		Zuckerdose .	3	2
112		Dessertteller .	—	19
113		Tasse . . .	1	11
113	6¾	Compotière . .	—	15
114		Handleuchter .	1	6
115		Salzfass . . .	—	15
116	9	Dessertteller .	1	8
117	11½	lang. Confectschale	2	8
118		Kindertasse . .	—	13
119	8	hoch. Zuckervase	2	14
120		Dessertteller .	1	11
121	9	Dessertschale .	—	23
122		Fidebusbecher .	—	15
123		Cigarrenbecher	—	21
124		Handleuchter .	—	23
125	11	lng.Zwiebackschale	1	19
126		Zuckerschale .	1	20
127		Salz- u. Pfeffergefäss	—	22
128	11	Fruchtschale .	3	—
129		Bouillontasse .	2	3
130		Toilettschälchen	1	—
131	11	Fruchtschale .	3	6
131		Saladière . .		
132	6½	hoch. Blumenvase	1	22
133		Blumenbecher .	1	9
134		Tasse . . .		
135		Salzfass . . .	—	20
136		dito, auf Delphin		
137	6	hoch. Spielleuchter	1	6
138		Tafelleuchter .		
139		Füllhorn, gross		
140		Flacon . . .		
141	11½	lng.Zwiebackschale		
142		Confectschale .		
143	7	lang. Zuckerschale		
U.12	15½	hoch. griech. Korb		
U.11	13	hoch. dito . .		
U.83	7	Füllhorn . . .		
U.84	4¾	dito		
	18½	Etagère, gross .		
	15	h. Etagère nach U. 15		
	11½	h. Etagère mit Stern		
	13	Schale auf Fuss U. 15¹		
	11	dito . . . . U. 15²		
	8¾	dito . . . . U. 15³		
	15	Schale auf Fuss mit Stern etc. 1 .		
	11	dito 2 . . .		
	9	dito 3 . . .		

Fig. 268: Two pages of a price list of c. 1845 showing articles with cut glass patterns

Fig. 269: Plate with cut glass pattern, about 1840, decorated in blue and gold, most of the lustre gilding is worn off

Fig. 270: Part coffee set form T, in the 1830s re-named Bie-dermeier Form

Fig. 271: Biedermeier Form with Braided Edge

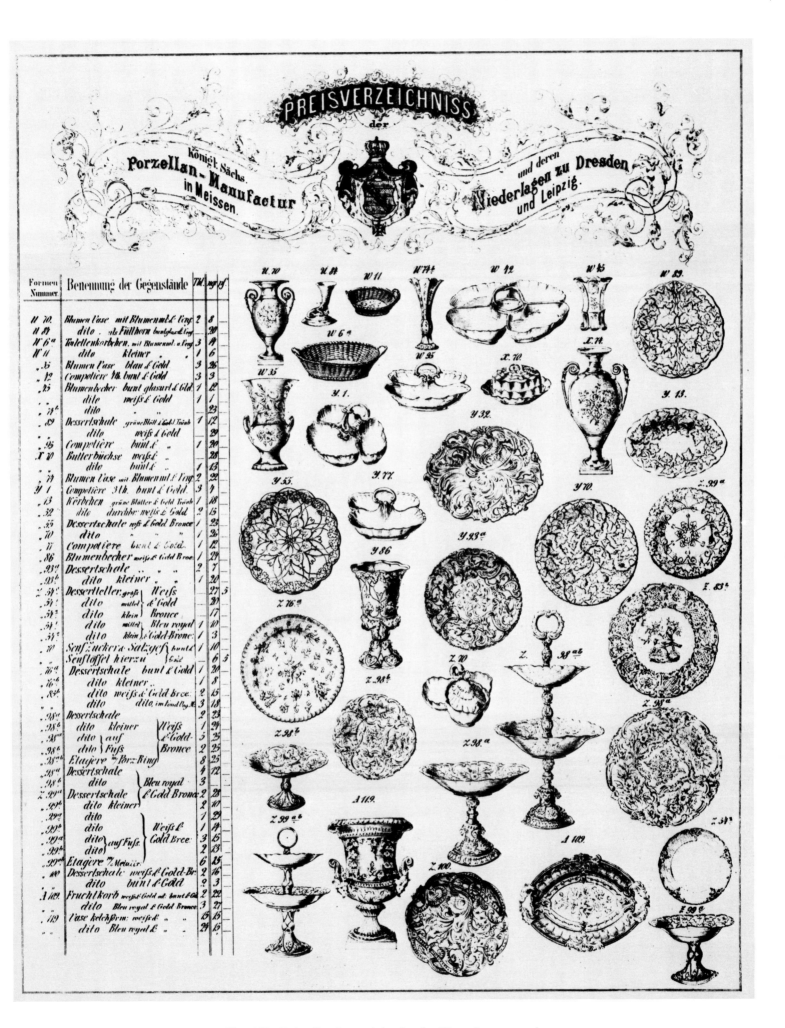

Fig. 272: Price list for articles in the Victorian taste, about 1850

189

Fig. 273: Saucer from Biedermeier Set with Braided Edge, relief decoration on edge highlighted in green or blue paint overglaze, after 1834

Fig. 276: Saucer form no. V. 24a, first made in 1839, som contours highlighted with blue or green rims

Fig. 274: Saucer from Biedermeier Set with Braided Edge, relief decoration on edge and ornaments on saucer painted with lustre gold

Fig. 277: Saucer with plastic rose decoration, edge orname gray and blue, form W 33, first made in 1841

Fig. 275: Saucer form no. V 24a, first made in 1839, lustre gilding worn off

Fig. 278: Cup with plastic rose decoration once gilt, form 33, first made in 1841

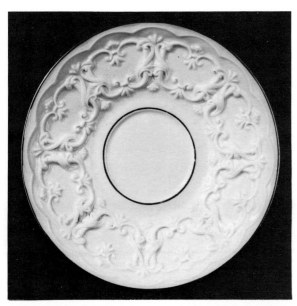

Fig. 279: Saucer with relief decoration, form W 100, first made in 1843, taken off the production program in 1851

Fig. 282: Saucer with relief decoration, in cartouches polychrome flowers, oval reserves raised and painted turquoise, form X 78, first made in 1847

Fig. 280: Saucer with relief decoration and vine-leaves painted in green overglaze, form X 43, first made in 1844, taken off the production program in 1851

Fig. 283: Saucer with relief decoration and gilding, made between 1840 and 1855

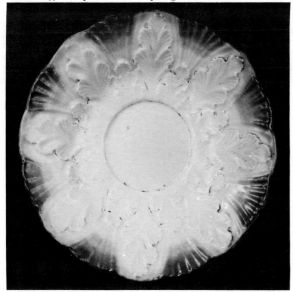

Fig. 281: Saucer with oakleaf relief decoration highlighted with blue, form Y 33a, first made in 1847

Fig. 284: Saucer with relief decoration in the Neo-Gothic style, about 1855

191

Fig. 286: Marks of the porcelain manufactory in Naples, Italy, 1771-1821

Fig. 287: Plate from the Crocus Set by K. Hentschel

Fig. 288: Tureen and Plate from the van de Velde Set

A set by Richard Riemerschmid (Fig. 289) also was received well by the art critics, but the buying public stayed away from it after its appearance on the market in 1905. The manufactory had hoped to find in Riemerschmid's design a substitute for the *Onion Pattern*, which it considered worn out and copied by too many other factories. Elements of the designs by van de Velde and Riemerschmid later were used in other forms, but the attempt of the manufactory to employ two of the most famous artists of Art Nouveau turned out to be a commercial failure.

One of the reasons was that these artists did not quite master the material, which was new to them. For reasons of stability van de Velde's design required much thicker porcelain than was usually used. This problem could have been solved if the designs had sold. Later, the manufactory required outside designers to first get acquainted with the properties of porcelain by studying the manufacturing process and spending a certain time in the manufactory.

But the main obstacle was the philosophy of Art Nouveau. It wanted to produce artistic designs by industrial methods. The Meissen manufactory was not the right place to realize this philosophy, because it could not mass produce. In addition, buyers of Meissen porcelain did not identify the Art Nouveau articles with Meissen. Especially Reimerschmid's design was considered too simple and rustic, and the old *Onion Pattern* beat it hands down. Sales figures showed that modern designs were responsible for only ten percent of the returns. The old Meissen forms were still preferred, and the manufactory, as a commercial institution, had to limit its experiments.

The encounter with Art Nouveau was brief, but it influenced many of the designs to follow. Paul Börner, who joined the manufactory in 1911, designed tableware that won acclaim for its functional, simple elegance. Not all of Börner's ideas for tableware succeeded in Meissen, but many of them were picked up by other factories. Of the three table sets Börner designed, only one was produced by the manufactory (Fig. 290).

At all times, the manufactory experimented with new forms (Plate 98), not exeedingly eagerly, sometimes even reluctantly. But the reluctance did not stem from a refusal to follow changing tastes. The manufactory officials were cautious, they felt that not everything promoted as "new" and "modern" had a chance of survival. Whenever the manufactory adopted modernistic styles, these products shared the fate of those styles, they disappeared after a short bloom. This was especially true for some designs of the 20th century, when the pace of life became faster and tastes changed ever so quickly. The creations of that time would never be suspected to have come from Meissen (Fig. 291) but they were necessary, because every new generation in Meissen has to find out for itself that the lifeline of the manufactory is the preservation of the old, from which it can safely venture to new creativity.

In 1983, the manufactory began a remarkable undertaking. It presented the newly designed Japan form at the Fall Fair in Leipzig (Figs. 292 and 293). All shapes of this table set were designed to suit the Japanese table and eating habits that require quite different vessels. The manufactory was awarded a gold medal for this new set at the Leipzig Fair. It is kind of a poetic justice that Meissen now offers its reverence to the Orient, from which it has received so many ideas and incentives.

Fig. 289: Plate from Riemerschmid Set

Fig. 290: Part set Börner Form, designed 1929/1930

Fig. 291: Place setting from coffee and tea set designed 1924-1934 with green ground color

Figs. 292 and 293: Parts from the set Japan Form, *designed 1982/1983*

Chapter Six

Painting and Decorations

The list of immediately available decorations at the manufactory presently includes more than 730 different kinds of painting. These are only a part of the decorations developed in the manufactory since 1710 and they have proven to be the ones demanded most often. But any decoration or painting ever applied in Meissen still can be ordered today. It might take a little longer, but the manufactory will do it.

It is impossible, and that is just not a figure of speech, to describe all painting and decorations Meissen has ever applied on porcelain. The manufactory, for instance, often took orders for special kinds of decorations, including portraits of the orderer's family. Certain decorations were only made once and never repeated again. Privately owned pieces with these decorations rarely are shown in public. Even today, decorations occasionally come into view which were hitherto completely unknown.

This chapter can only deal with decorations typical of Meissen, and not with unique painting. Even then the wealth of examples seems overwhelming, because the painters at the manufactory seem to have had limitless new ideas for adorning and beautifying white porcelain.

The beginning was toilsome. The development of paints for porcelain decorations proved to be even more difficult than porcelain-making itself. Böttger did not live to see the kind of porcelain painting he had promised the King, and the elaborate plastic decorations on the red stoneware and the porcelain pieces made during his time certainly were substitutes for the polychrome and blue painting the manufactory was not yet able to offer. In 1713, Böttger ordered some of the white ware to be decorated with sprigged blossoms and twigs, but he did not mention any color painting. He himself was experimenting with paints from time to time. In July and August of 1717 he worked on several paints, and also on a method of gilding that seemed promising (Plate 99) but then he made no further experiments.[1] Böttger evidently had lost interest in his paint research, because in October of that year he stated that the white porcelain actually needed no painting. But if someone wanted it decorated, it should be done "the Japanese Way". This was cold painting with laquers on the glazed pieces. They could not be fired again, and the laquer was only sitting on the glaze. Many of these decorations wore off after a short time because they chipped, peeled off and cracked. Only a few pieces with preserved cold painting have survived (Fig. 109), but there are some more around with traces of laquer pointing to previous decorations. This laquer painting curiously also can be found on large, almost life-size animals made between 1728 and 1735 at a time when enamel painting already had been perfected. These animals were made of an inferior paste that cracked in the sharp fire, leaving crevices and large fissures. The flaws were filled with mortar, sawdust mixed with glue, papermaché or plaster of Paris, and after these materials had hardened the animals were covered with laquer paint to hide all faults and cracks[2]. But this makeshift patching was required by the unusual size - up to 28 inches - of the animals demanded by August II. That was a task the manufactory was not able to master yet.

In the 1710s, cold painting was the only way to get colors on porcelain. In 1717 the manufactory inspector, Steinbrück, reported that laquer paints were still used in addition to gold, silver, and the first enamel paints. Underglaze paints still had not been developed.[3]

At first, only plastic relief decorations were highlighted by painting. The manufactory did not employ painters until 1720. Before that year, the pieces were sent to the goldsmith Johann George Funcke in Dresden to be decorated. A file of 1719 says that Funcke had already painted porcelain for six years, which means that he must have started working for the manufactory the same year Böttger was able to offer his first white porcelain for sale.[4]

Funcke, encouraged by Böttger, successfully experimented with enamel colors, developing green, blue, yellow, black, light and dark purple between 1713 and 1718. Böttger himself contributed a green and a dark red enamel paint. The first gold and enamel decorations show rather thick layers of paint, protruding over the glaze with stark colors. They appear a bit heavy and lifeless and these decorations are garnishings rather than painting (Fig. 294). But soon free painting developed independently of the plastic reliefs. Before 1717, the ornamental Laub - und Bandelwerk (Leaf and Strapwork) appeared in colors and also in gold (Fig. 295). The first *camaieu* landscapes were painted at this time too. For them only one color was used and the effect was achieved by applying several tones of the same color in varying thickness (Fig. 296). These first *camaieu* decorations today look pinkish-violet partly changed to gray. Originally they probably were painted with an iron red paint which might have faded over the years.

For gold ornaments, at first gold leaf was used that was not very durable. In 1717 Böttger had come up with a usable process for the application of gold and silver decorations. It was a fulminating gold solution that under certain conditions exploded. On porcelain, this gold color showed a pinkish lustre similar to mother-of-pearl.

In Dresden two gilders, Johann George Funcke and Johann Jacob Gäbel, were under contract with the manufactory for ornamental decorations and gilding. Still, for a long time all so-called *radierte Goldchinesen* (etched Gold Chinamen) were ascribed to *Hausmaler* (outside painters) in Augsburg.[5] For these decorations, first the contours were finely painted on the glaze, then the areas within the contours were completely filled with gold. After firing in the

Fig. 294: Chocolate cup with plastic relief decoration highlighted by gilding, about 1718/1719

Fig. 295: Cup and saucer with strap-and-leaf work, 1713-1720

Fig. 296: Cup with European landscape in pinkish violet color, about 1719

Fig. 297: Portrait of Johann Gegorius Höroldt on a Meissen plaque

muffle kiln, the next step was a meticulous engraving of all details with an agate stylus before the gold decoration was polished.

Today doubts about definite statements that etched Gold Chinamen were only made in Augsburg seem justified. A manufactory bill of delivery of February 1720 mentions six saucers and cups "completely gilt on the inside, on the outside with suchlike figures", suchlike meaning gilt.[6] Another bill of delivery of 1725 speaks of saucers and cups for the King of Sardinia "finely enamelled on the outside with Gold Japanese Figures". The difference between Chinese and Japanese was not taken seriously in Meissen at that time, to the writer of this bill they all looked alike. Other documents show that Gold Chinamen were painted in Meissen even in 1738, when they were precisely described as "etched" figures. Several pieces at the State's Museum in Schwerin, GDR, at the Dresden Porcelain Collection and some privately owned pieces bear the letters "JF" written in ink on the bottom. It stands to reason that all the pieces sent to Funcke in Dresden for gilding and decoration were identified with his initials. Since these pieces are decorated with etched Gold Chinamen they seem to be proof that this kind of painting was done for the manufactory too and not only by outside painters in Augsburg (Plate 100).

Polychrome painting with enamel colors still had to wait for perfection for a few more years, until the deserter Samuel Stölzel brought Johann Gregorius Höroldt to Meissen from Austria (Fig. 297). This young man, who was twenty-three years of age, had worked in Vienna as wallpaper painter. He preferred Chinese motifs in his painting of them. He had also decorated porcelain at the manufactory of du Paquier. Despite Stölzel's promise to deliver a "well trained painter", Höroldt's knowledge about porcelain paints was rather limited. He brought to Meissen only a red enamel paint for overglaze decoration, but even this paint looked much better than those the manufactory had used before.[7]

At first Höroldt worked in a flat he had rented in Meissen. The paints were prepared for him at the manufactory by David Köhler and Samuel Stölzel. Höroldt did not work on new paints until 1923. One year earlier, his painting shop had been moved to the Albrechtsburg. His turning point from painter to paint technologist can be ascertained quite precisely, it was on April 30th, 1723, early in the morning. That day, after a short illness, the arcanist David Köhler died and the only one at his deathbed was Höroldt. He never could refute the suspicion of having copied parts of Köhler's paint recipe book between the time the arcanist had died and the time he notified the manufactory administration. After Böttger's demise, Köhler had been the most experienced and ingenious technologist at the manufactory, solving a number of problems on which Böttger had given up on. Of the eighty-two pages of Köhler's recipe book nine were missing. It was never found out who had removed them.

But after 1723, Höroldt quickly developed new paints, utilizing one important piece of information Köhler had kept a secret. The ingredients in a paint are important, but the flux added to the paints is also significant. Only the right flux fixes the fusion point of a paint to a temperature at which the glaze softens slightly and paint and glaze can be fused.

Between 1723 and 1731, Höroldt came up with sixteen new enamel paints which are still the basic paints for porcelain decoration today. With his new paints, he was also able to design new painting motifs. Chinese scenes were much in demand, and Höroldt sketched a large number of them. Most of the sketches are still preserved in the *Schulz-Codex* at the Museum of Arts and Crafts *(Museum des Kunsthandwerks)* in Leipzig, GDR.[8] These gray wash-drawings were drafted between 1720 and 1740 and also include European scenes, ornaments, flowers and plants.

Pinpricks on some of the sketches show that they actually were used in the Meissen painting shop. Carbon dust was powdered on the porcelain pieces through the little holes made by the pins, outlining the details of the motif. For many decorations, the sketches can be found in the *Schulz-Codex* (Plates 101 to 103). Execution of the sketches was mainly left to the painters Höroldt employed (Plates 104 and 105). His own hand can only be proven with certainty on about sixteen pieces he signed personally. The so-called Chinoiseries were so popular that they appeared even in small sizes on elaborately decorated porcelain (Plate 106 and Fig. 298).

Among the painters who specialized in *Chinoiseries* were Johann Ehrenfried Stadler, Johann Gottlieb Erbsmehl, Christian Friedrich Herold, Johann Christoph Horn, Johann Gottlob Hermann, Johann Tobias Locke and Adam Friedrich von Löwenfinck. Some of their work can be identified by signatures or monograms.

Höroldt's relationship to the manufactory was peculiar. He was not put in a hierarchical position as head of the painting department with a number of painters employed by the manufactory. He was instead a subcontractor. Even after he had moved his shop to the Albrechtsburg, he was paid by the pieces he delivered. With increasing demand for painted porcelain, Höroldt employed more and more painters, for whom he set the wages himself. He also paid them without the manufactory knowing his wage scale. By 1724, Höroldt had employed twelve painters, and he treated them badly, according to their complaints. His personal traits are not valued highly, he had a streak of meanness, was jealous of gifted painters working for him, and showed a rather uncontrolled ambition.

But Höroldt also created the unique Meissen painting style. He taught his apprentices and journeymen to exactly follow his kind of painting to the last little detail. That is still the rule in Meissen today. Höroldt's business practices led to an investigation in 1730. It showed that Höroldt only paid about half of the amount he charged the manufactory for the painted pieces delivered as wages to his painters, sometimes even less. He pocketed between 3,000 and 4,000 Thalers a year, while his best paid painter had to live on 324 Thalers per year.

There was nothing illegal about this, but it was considered immoral. The King ordered a change of the whole system. All painters were now employed directly by the manufactory. Höroldt received an annual salary of 1,000 Thalers. That was a hard blow for him, considering his earlier income. Even his appointment as head of the painting department and the title Court Commissioner could not console him. Neither did his appointment to First Arcanist, which gave him complete control over all technical departments of the manufactory.

Höroldt almost completely stopped painting after this decision was made in 1731. His best painters subsequently received a fixed salary of 156 Thalers per year. Before that time, they had earned by overtime work another 150 to 170 Thalers. Höroldt punished them for complaining by taking away the overtime work. The painters in turn petitioned the King to again permit overtime work, which he did to a certain degree.

Although Höroldt reduced his work for the manufactory to managerial functions after 1731, he still added new ideas for painting motifs to the many he had developed before.

Because the court wanted Oriental styles in large numbers, the earlier decorations were influenced by East Asian motifs (Fig. 299). The Japanese Kakiemon style[9] had considerable influence on Meissen painting. One of the first motifs to be copied was the *Rich Old Yellow Lion* (Fig. 300). Until today the Dragon Pattern in many color variations is very popular (Plates 107 to 109). Before 1918 the red dragon highlighted with gold, called the *Court Dragon* was reserved for the Saxon Court.

Also influenced by Kakiemon porcelain was the *Quail Pattern*, which was copied almost exactly (Fig. 301). In Meissen painting after Japanese and Chinese motifs today still is called Indian Painting *(Indischmalerei)*, because early in the 18th century everything in Asia was considered as belonging to India. In its list of immediately available decorations, the manufactory at present carries more than 250 kinds of Indian Painting, varieties of the same pattern included. The most popular ones are shown on Plates 110 to 128.

Already during Böttger's time European motifs had been

Fig. 298: Plate with Chinoiseries *in four elongated reserves on the border and flower and ornament decoration, c. 1740*

Fig. 299: Plate with painting in the Kakiemon style, c. 1725

Fig. 300: Plate with Rich Yellow Lion *Pattern about 1728-1730, polychrome painting in the Kakiemon style*

197

Fig. 301: Cup and saucer with pea-green ground and Quail Pattern, on the bottom the sign of the turners Schieffer (Fig. 666d), about 1730

Fig. 302: Tea pot with cover, landscape painting in silver, about 1725

Fig. 303: Coffee and tea set with polychrome Harbour Scenes in quatrefoil gold framed cartouches, about 1740

198

painted on porcelain. Höroldt took up ideas of Dutch, Flemish and French painters and transferred them onto porcelain (Plate 129 and Fig. 302). Harbour scenes are known in many variations (Plate 130 and Fig. 303), and battles scenes were painted by five painters who specialized in this genre (Plate 131). Hunting scenes were popular as always (Plate 132) and most of these patterns originated with Höroldt, although some designs might have been influenced by his top painters. The *Fable Animals* (Fabeltiere, Fig. 304) seem to show the irrepressible phantasy of Adam Friedrich von Löwenfinck. His *Chinoiseries* also show a recognizable difference from the sketches of Höroldt. The two men did not get along well, and because of the intolerable conditions in the painting shop and his personal debts, Löwenfinck in October of 1736 fled from Meissen. His later work at several manufactories, especially in Höchst and Hagenau, shows his versatility as painter and the extent of his talent, lost to Meissen.

On special orders, the manufactory painted all desired coats-of-arms on porcelain. The first verified piece of Meissen porcelain with a coat-of-arms was made in 1714[10]. It was simple, but with the improvement of paints the possibilities were increased for the depiction of the often intricate coats-of-arms.

About 1725 Höroldt also was able to fulfill King August's desire for porcelain with colored backgrounds. Except for reserves left white, the whole piece was covered with one color. The reserves then received polychrome painting (Plates 133 and 134 and Fig. 305). The first paint suitable for colored grounds *(Fondmalerei)* was yellow. Later different shades of green, a yellowish green, apple-, pea- and sea-green were added as were powder- and lavender blue, purple, tomato-red and mouse-gray. Gold and dead leaf brown also were used for colored grounds.

Pastoral scenes were taken up late in the 1730s, and the French painter Watteau was copied heavily on Meissen porcelain. The Green Watteau Pattern was considered the most desirable (Plate 135). The first set with this decoration was made for the daughter of August II as a gift for her marriage to the King of Sardinia. Later pastoral scenes with simple instead of noble people, sometimes rather earthy, joined this genre (Plate 136).

Flowers were a favorite decoration on East Asian porcelain, and they appeared very early in Meissen too, at first only as relief decoration on red stoneware and early porcelain. But in the 1720s Höroldt developed his Indian Flowers mainly as decoration for larger vessels (Fig. 306).

Early in the 1730s, European Flowers or Dry Flowers joined the flower patterns. They evidently were copied from woodcut illustrations in botanical books, because they appear a bit lifeless and stiff. Some of them also were painted with a shadow, they are called *Ombrierte Blumen* (Shadowed Flowers, Plate 137). In many flower patterns insects also can be found.

About 1745, flower painting became livelier. The manufactory began to use mainly German Flowers *(Deutsche Blumen)* without shadows which were painted after nature, the whole palette of Meissen colors was utilized. The range of flower decorations was extended continually (Plates 138 to 157). The so-called Strewn Flowers *(Streublümchen*, Plates 166 to 169) were developed for two purposes after 1730. A considerable number of porcelain pieces came out of the kilns in perfect shape but with little black spots from iron oxide, with little pocks that could be ground off but left a dull spot in the glaze, or with little pinprick holes in the glaze. In many cases, these imperfections could be covered by painting with Strewn Flowers. The kilns also delivered many pieces of substandard quality not worthy of being decorated with expensive decorations. Outside painters eagerly sought white porcelain of lower quality grades, and in order to prevent the sale of white ware a Modest Painting *(Schlichte Malerei)* for porcelain of lower quality came into being.[11] Later, it was called Reject Painting *(Ausschussmalerei)* and even applied on porcelain of the lowest grade that was supposed only to be sold to manufactory employees. Not only flowers were used for this kind of painting, also simplified Indian Painting patterns were applied.

Fig. 304: Plate with polychrome Fable Animal, *about 1735-1736*

Fig. 305: Pitcher with mounted lid, purple ground color with Quail *Pattern in reserves. On bottom impressed former's sign of Johann Elias Grund (Fig. 666c), about 1735-1740*

Fruit, bird and animal painting joined the Meissen repertoire in the first half of the 18th century (Plates 158 to 165). They followed the course of flower painting, and like them, gradually replaced most of the polychrome oriental motifs.

Augustus the Strong in 1710 had demanded from his newly established manufactory porcelain with blue underglaze decorations in the manner of the Chinese Ming period. He felt justified in this demand since Böttger in his first memorial to the King already had promised six colors for porcelain painting, among them the desired blue for underglaze decorations. He was confident because the basic technique had been known for a long time. Delft tiles and fayence and Hamburg stoneware were decorated with blue ornamentation, as were Rhenish beermugs and wine decanters made from stoneware. The main ingredient of the blue paint was cobalt in various compounds, a metal that was readily available in Saxony.

Böttger experimented with cobalt and since the theory of chemical reactions was still unknown, it was trial and mostly error. There were two problems he was not able to overcome. Cobalt compounds react as flux on porcelain, they tend to flow and muddle contours of decorations and also cause the glaze to run off. Furthermore, Meissen porcelain is fired at much higher temperatures than Chinese porcelain or fayence, and the blue Meissen paint of the early years was easily discolored at high temperatures.

Despite his promise to the King and his many experiments, Böttger never was able to develop a usable and reliable paint for underglaze decoration. August had promised a reward of 1,000 Thalers to anyone who would develop a blue underglaze paint. Besides Böttger, other workers of the manufactory tried to invent the blue paint. The former cabinetmaker Johann Georg Mehlhorn, a jack-of-all-trades who was given to boasting, told newspapers that he knew how to make blue paint and that he could prove it if he were just given the necessary facilities. Böttger took him up on his bragging and provided him with the demanded kiln and the required ingredients. Mehlhorn could not come up with a satisfactory blue paint, but he improved the porcelain paste somewhat and reduced the flowing of the existing blue paint.

More successful was the arcanist David Köhler, an early collaborator of Böttger's. In 1717, he mixed the first usable blue paint that stayed blue even at high temperatures. In 1720, August II was presented with samples from Mehlhorn's and Köhler's work, and each of them hinted that he considered himself the rightful recipient of the reward. August preferred Köhler's blue over Mehlhorn's, but he pretended to have difficulties in remembering his promise. Nevertheless, he held out the prospect of a "just remuneration" if Mehlhorn and Köhler would continue to work on the improvement of the blue paint. Both men finally were awarded a bonus, though they never saw the 1,000 Thalers.

Köhler was the only one who really knew the secret of the blue paint. In 1720 he tested twenty different cobalt ores with unsatisfactory results. But one year later he made an important discovery. On a new paste which contained felspar and less alabaster, the blue paint stayed much better. So he developed new glazes containing felspar and he also added kaolin to the paint. These changes were the stabilizing factors for the blue underglaze paint.[12]

In all probability, Höroldt stole Köhler's recipe for the blue paint after Köhler had died. But not being too familiar with porcelain technology, he evidently did not understand immediately all the intricacies of the recipe. One thing seemed to have escaped him completely. Köhler had not used just cobalt oxides, he had combined them with kaolin and thus protected them against the aggressiveness of the melting glaze that often ruined the blue paint. In the years after Köhler's death, the work reports often speak of dissatisfying results.[13] With the help of Samuel Stölzel it took Höroldt until 1733 before he could stabilize the blue paint by developing a new glaze that agreed with the paint.[14] From then on the art of blue painting under the glaze was mastered even if occasionally a backlash occured.

Underglaze blue was necessary for copies of Chinese motifs and especially of the Japanese Imari porcelain. Imari was the shipping port for a large number of porcelain makers around the city of Arita on the Japanese island of Kyushu. In present usage, "Imari" is defined as porcelain with blue underglaze decoration highlighted with iron-red and gold painting over the glaze. The Imari technique was used in Meissen as soon as the blue paint was usable (Fig. 307). Other East Asian motifs were copied too (Fig. 308), often in combination with a brown colored ground on the outside of the vessels (Fig. 309).

Fig. 306: Vase (Schlossvase) with Indian Flowers, about 1730

Fig. 307: Plate with Imari decoration, about 1730-1735

Fig. 308: Flat bowl with blue underglaze painting of Chinese seascape, c. 1720-February 1722, mark in Fig. 583

Fig. 309: Saucer and pitcher with brown ground color outside and blue underglaze decoration inside, from different periods, saucer made in the 1720s, mark in Fig. 584, pitcher made 1774-1775, mark in Fig. 596

The most famous pattern painted blue under the glaze is the *Onion Pattern* to which for reasons that shall become understandable a whole chapter in this book is dedicated. The *Strawflower* or *Immortelle Pattern*, mentioned in the chapter about *Onion Pattern*, is another popular decoration. Flowers of various kinds also appear in blue under or over the glaze (Figs. 310 and 311). Painted in the same color was a set first offered on the price list of 1765 as "Children a la Raphael". In the meantime it has been discovered that they are not copies of children sketched or painted by the Italian Renaissance painter Raphael, but that most of them were inspired by the etchings of the French painter Jaques Stella.[15] For most of the playing naked children, the originals by Stella have been found, a few cannot be traced (Fig. 312).

The constant demand for Meissen to produce novelties was felt in the painting department too. The department was not in a good condition. Höroldt neglected his duties, and his jealousy prevented good painters from giving their best. For example Höroldt would order painters of battle scenes to paint flowers, only because he had an indistinct feeling that the painter might become too uppity.

His relationship with Kaendler deteriorated. Very often Kaendler had to wait a long time for Höroldt's approval of a new design or model, and Höroldt felt that Kaendler's plastic decorations on tableware left not enough space for painting. There was a lot of bickering and backbiting going on between them. In 1734, the situation finally came to a first clash. Kaendler and the manufactory inspector, Reinhardt, an enemy of Höroldt's, lodged an official complaint against the First Arcanist. Kaendler complained about the poor quality of the porcelain paste, for which Höroldt was responsible, and about Höroldt's procrastination. A commission appointed by the King found no grounds for the complaint and Kaendler lost. He came out of the affair with a reprimand, but Reinhardt was arrested as ringleader of a conspiracy and dismissed from his job at the manufactory.

Kaendler did not give up. About 1739 he wrote down a bill of particulars against Höroldt[16], noting that the output of the seventy workers employed by the painting department was bad. White porcelain was ruined by carelessness, and in Kaendler's opinion Höroldt did not even teach his apprentices to draw a proper line, nor would he touch a brush himself.

Höroldt answered in kind, accusing Kaendler of incompetence and renitence. The complaints against Höroldt were well-founded and supported by a number of manufactory employees, but nothing happened to him because he got protection from high officials, among them the Prime Minister, Count Brühl.

The matter was solved by the approaching Seven-Years'-War. The King ordered Höroldt to go to Frankfurt-on-Main, out of the reach of the Prussian King, who would have liked to get hold of the man who knew all the secrets of porcelain-making and painting in Meissen. While he was in exile, Höroldt drew his full salary, which was paid by the King. After the war he returned to Meissen, but retired two years later in 1765.

Despite his unfortunate personal traits, Höroldt introduced a porcelain painting style that became pacesetting for all manufactories in Europe and even today is as alive as it was 250 years ago. That applies also to the large variety of paints he developed. His really productive time lasted only about ten years, but in this short span, he laid the groundwork for the art of porcelain painting that has lasted up to this day.

The Seven-Years'-War brought nothing new to painting in Meissen. As with plastic art, painting too had lost the touch for the changed tastes. An Art School founded by the Saxon regent Xavier was supposed to renew the Meissen style. Its head, the Court Painter Christian Wilhelm Ernst Dietrich, became supreme judge for all art matters concerning the manufactory. He ordered the painters to be trained on Greek and Roman samples and on Italian and Dutch paintings. The result were neatly painted copies with every brushstroke on its proper place, stiff and without expression. The manufactory commission released Dietrich in 1770 from his

Fig. 310: German flowers in blue underglaze painting, 1850-1924

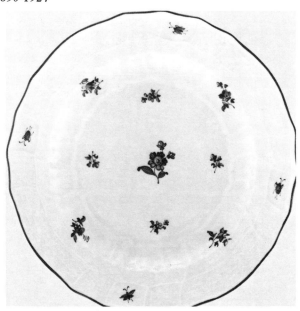

Fig. 311: Plate with plastic relief and modest painting blue over the glaze 1850-1924

Fig. 312: Plate with child playing badminton, painting blue underglaze, crossed swords with dot between the hilts, about 1765-1770

appointment, but the style he had introduced remained. It is characterized by elaborate border decorations with hoops, wreaths, ribbons, flowering branches, garlands and festoons. He also introduced peacock's feathers and angels (Plate 170).

In the last quarter of the eighteenth century, literature influenced painting in Meissen also. Miniature painting depicting scenes from books and plays became popular (Fig. 313). After 1780 Royal Blue colored grounds appeared often (Plate 171). This paint had been developed in France and was copied in Meissen. Also fowl of all kinds were inspired by samples from the French manufactory in Sèvres. Meissen painting became sentimental too and flowers in black and sepia colors fitted this style (Plate 172).

In 1783 Johann Eleazar Schenau, co-director of the Dresden Academy of Arts, became supervisor of the Meissen painting department. In his younger years, he had painted a number of very appealing family scenes. By the time he joined the manufactory, he already had turned to a rather pompous depiction of religious, mythological, and historical subjects which then also were chosen as motifs for Meissen painting. Done in a heavyhanded way, this style haunted the manufactory for decades to come (Plate 173). Occasional breakouts from this staid boredom are quite rare, but they show that there was still life in some Meissen painters (Plate 174).

The 19th century began with more of the same. Portrait cups (Plate 175) and city prospects, gold and silver ornaments on blue colored grounds, edge-to-edge fruit and leaf painting show the lack of artistic ideas. The most important order of these years was a dessert set for the Duke of Wellington, the victor over Napoleon I at Waterloo. The Emperor in Vienna and the Kings of France, Prussia and Saxony had their manufactories make parts of a complete set of several hundred pieces for the Duke. To Meissen fell the desert set consisting of more than 130 pieces. The set can still be seen at Apsley House in London, England, where it is shown as *Saxon Service*.

The *Wellington Set* was made under Georg Friedrich Kersting who had been appointed head of the painting department in 1818.[17] He tried to get some fresh air into the musty paint shop and to replace the immovable painting style with livelier and sprightlier decorations. But the plastic art department had discovered cut glass patterns and produced them with a fervor. These patterns left not much room for imaginative painting and Kersting's efforts only brought few fruits (Plates 176 and 177). Nevertheless, he developed some new paint colors for the manufactory, some with a little help by industrial espionage in Sèvres, and he found a new gilding method that saved a considerable amount of gold.

Economic problems after the Napoleonic Wars induced the manufactory to think about more efficient and less costly decoration methods. A simple instrument for drawing gold lines on plates already had been in use. It was working basically like a fountain pen with a guide running along the edge to keep the instrument at proper distance from the edge. It was also possible to vary the width of the line from a hairline to wider stripes.

Pattern printing also was tried. On a prepared copper plate an etching of the intended decoration was engraved. Then the engraved lines were filled with paint, excess paint was carefully removed. By pressing tissue paper on the plate the paint was transferred to the paper. While the paint was still wet, the paper was rolled on the porcelain piece with a felt covered roll leaving the decoration on the porcelain. In 1814, experiments with blue transfer printing under the glaze were conducted without satisfying results. Later methods were developed mainly with sepia, black, blue and red colors. But transfer printing in Meissen did not get its way against hand painting. It only survived for a very limited number of motifs, today called *Aquatinta* decorations (Figs. 314 and 315) for which now steel plates instead of copper plates are used.

Besides the blue underglaze paint a green paint for underglaze decoration was something the manufactory always was searching for. It also tried to improve the overglaze green paint. Green was made from copper oxide that after about forty to fifty years develops a faint lustre that is very much

Fig. 313: Covered cup and saucer, ground color royal blue, polychrome painting of lovers, crossed swords mark with star, about 1774-1780

Fig. 314: Plate with landscape in Aquatinta technique

Fig. 315: Plate with Roses in Aquatinta technique

appreciated and also proof that the decoration is at least almost half a century old. Experiments with new green paints were conducted all the time without convincing results. Count Marcolini in an order in 1777 exclaimed: "We need paints that stick, stick perfectly" after newly tested green paints again did not show the required properties.[18]

Tests with chromium oxide in 1817 finally led to a new green paint for underglaze decoration that became famous in connection with the *Vineleaf Pattern (Weinlaubmuster)*. The vineleaf motif had been used before for overglaze decorations (Plate 178) but now it was extended to the *Full Green Vine Wreath (Voller grüner Weinkranz)* as it is called officially (Plate 179). Like the blue *Onion Pattern* the *Vineleaf Pattern* is one of the unbeatable sales runners of the manufactory.

Another green underglaze decoration, the *Pointed Arches (Spitzbogendekor)* with vineleaves in the arches did not become as popular (Fig. 316). In modern times an interesting method of combining underglaze and overglaze painting was developed first for the Hunting Scenes on the form *Large Cutout* (Plate 3). Part of the decoration is painted green under the glaze and the fine details are applied with overglaze paints. New Flower Painting in blue is done the same way. This technique results in a remarkable plasticity and depth of the decoration.

In the 18th and the early 19th centuries, the heads of the Meissen painting school came from outside the manufactory. They knew all about academic painting but nothing about porcelain. In 1825 Professor Hartmann, superintendent of the painting school submitted designs for twenty-nine new forms of tableware. He felt that the manufactory needed some outside inspiration. His designs looked interesting but unfortunately most of them were technically not practicable. His meddling was answered by the Saxon Treasury with the strict order for Harmann to stick to painting. Should he still intend to make new proposals, so the Treasury wrote, he should take into consideration the peculiarities of porcelain-making as well as the economic and financial implications.[19]

Desperate for financial recovery the manufactory even filled orders for decorations it considered abhorrent. In 1828 Professor Hartmann objected against the wish of a customer in Buenos Aires, Argentina, who wanted an oakleaf border decoration in blue color and the painters at the manufctory agreed with him. Still it was made not only for the Argenti-

nian customer, it was also offered at the manufactory owned sales stores in Dresden and Leipzig. The Treasury confessed its understanding for the reluctance of the manufactory to produce decorations for the "less developed taste" but reminded it that it was not only an art institute. If the customers persistently demanded old flower decorations, now considered in bad taste, the manufactory had to give it to them, because it also had to see to the "procurement of the necessary operating funds".[20]

About the same time as the green underglaze paint new gilding methods were invented. Höroldt already had

Fig. 316: Saucer with decoration Pointed Arches in underglaze green, gilt rim and gilt circle in well, about 1831-1834

improved on Böttger's gilding method, but the amount of gold needed was still considerable. In addition, the gilding required treatment after firing. The gold came out of the kiln with a dull grey-brown color. It had to be polished with an agate tipped instrument or a so-called Blutstein (hematite)[21] to give it the golden shine. Today stiff glass-fiber brushes or rotating wheels are used. On larger areas, the fine polishing scratches on the gold are visible at close scrutiny.

This gilding method required a large amount of gold, because the paint contained forty to sixty percent pure gold. About 1815 a light gilding was tried using only half the gold necessary until then. It still was polishing gold (Poliergold) but applied in a much thinner layer. That had some disadvantages because the polishing often damaged the thin gold skin, very intricate ornaments could not be painted with the light gold and it wore off much easier. It also could not be used around edges, only on reasonably plain areas.[22]

In 1818, Kersting improved on the light gilding by using a different adhesive medium. To fix the gold preparation - or any paint for that matter - to the glaze, oil of turpentine was used, especially Dicköl (Thick Oil), a sticky concentrate of oil of turpentine with a high resin content. Kersting found out that Spiköl (Spike Oil)[23] was much better suited for light gilding. But even his preparation was only usable if the gilding was fired by itself without polychrome painting. The necessary fixing temperatures for these two decorations were so different that one of them suffered if fired to the temperature required for the other. If fired with polychrome decorations Kersting's light gilding did not achieve enough shine when polished.

Kersting also participated in developing another gilding technique devised by the manufactory's technical manager Heinrich Gottlob Kühn in 1827. Occasionally it is called Triangelvergoldung (Triangle Gilding) because of a small red triangle in red color that was painted on pieces with this kind of gilding next to the crossed swords marks on the bottom (Figs. 317 and 318). It too was a polishing gold but with an even lower gold content, only about one fourth of the amount needed for the heavy gilding preparation, as the older method was called. Pieces with triangle gilding had to be fired at higher temperatures as usual and the triangle on the bottom probably indicated this fact. It is the alchemist's sign for fire, and alchemistic signs were used at the manufactory even in the 20th century.

But the triangle gilding did not fullfil the hopes of the manufactory either. A breakthrough was finally achieved by Kühn in 1830 with the invention of Glanzvergoldung (Luster Gilding). It brought several advantages not only because it needed even less gold but also because it came out of the kilns already shining and did not require polishing. Although it was more durable than the light or the triangle gilding it wore off in heavy use too. Kühn improved on the new method a few more times but he never was able to match the qualities of the old heavy gilding, which is still employed for more valuable articles. Lustre gold is also applied on certain articles, and for figurines and groups another gilding technique with powder gold is used.

For garnishing a so-called goldbronze was developed, which is lustreless after firing. Before a piece is covered with liquid glaze the parts to be gilded are protected by a kind of wax that repels the glaze. Then the unglazed parts are painted with a gold preparation. After firing the gold has a dull finish since it was applied on the porous parts of the porcelain piece and not on the glaze. This goldbronze looks rather heavy and distinguished (Plates 180 to 185).

About 1855/1860 the demand for gilt porcelain slackened. With Historism new decoration styles arose. East Asian motifs of a different kind were introduced (Plate 186) and the crater vases in the Renaissance style were decorated again with copies of paintings. A platinum paint applied on a tortoise shell colored ground was perfected (Fig. 319) and from the manufactory in Limoges, France, enamel painting on a blue ground was adopted (Plate 70 and Fig. 320).

And finally even ornamental hardware on furniture was done the honor to be depicted on Meissen porcelain together with graces and putti (Fig. 321). These decorations have not survived, they were too closely related to the taste of their time that itself lived from borrowed ideas and feelings of earlier historic periods. Historism seems like the attempt of the rising middle class to make up in a summary procedure for all of those times past when it had been without influence and political power. It could give the burghers their own roots in history and make it easier for them to identify with the present. It was a purposive style that vanished when the purpose disappeared after World War I that turned Europe upside down. Today only a few designs of the second half of the 19th century are still salable. Many of the elaborately painted and gilt show plates were created in the period of Historism (Plate 187).

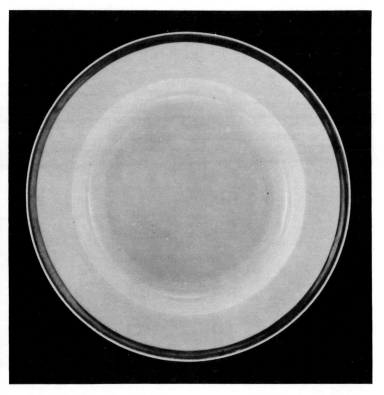

Fig. 317: Soup plate with gilt band around border in Triangle Gilding, about 1830

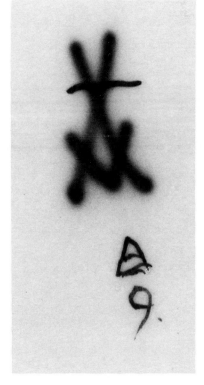

Fig. 318: Mark on bottom of soup plate in Fig. 317, triangle, figure 9 and line across swords in red paint overglaze

Fig. 319: Crater Vase *by Leuteritz with platinum painting on tortoise-shell colored ground. After the painting* The Procession of Bacchus *by Haehnel*

Fig. 321: *Showplate with allegorical rendition of Autumn with three graces and putti playing musical instruments. Relief ornaments in the style of furniture hardware, after 1880*

Fig. 320: Crater Vase *by Leuteritz with painting a lá Limoges after* The Procession of Alexander *by Thorwaldsen*

But as it was with plastic art, new ideas announced themselves already. Experiments with colored crystallized and molten glazes brought new incentives to porcelain decoration but were not received too well by the public (Plate 188). When Ludwig Sturm became head of the painting department in 1880 old patterns were modernized, paste-upon-paste painting was extended and high temperature paints (Scharffeuerfarben) were developed (Plates 189 and 190). They were underglaze paints and besides the already known blue and green colors for underglaze decorations new colors extended the palette. First ox-blood red in 1888 and then until 1893 light and dark dove-gray, sky-blue and dark-blue as well as shades of green, blue-green, grey-brown, soft-red, and yellow appeared. These soft but bright colors required new motifs and the painters working for the manufactory came up with them.

Julius Eduard Braunsdorf, raised in the tradition of the manufactory he had joined in 1858 as an apprentice, was the first one to explore new possibilities. His naturalistic flower painting soon changed to an impressionistic and decorative style (Plate 191). Another flower painter was Otto Eduard Voigt, who participated considerably in the development of the high temperature paints (Plate 192 and Fig. 322).

Theodor Grust (Plates 188 and 193) supported energetically Art Nouveau in Meissen and that furthered the work of the brothers Konrad and Rudolf Hentschel. Konrad died in 1907 but Rudolf continued designing new decorations for the manufactory (Plate 194). Paul Richter (Plates 195 and 196) contributed new decorations for tableware as did Arthur Barth (Plate 197) who later concentrated more on landscapes. Influential too was William Baring (Plate 198) and he later excelled especially with stylized figure and animal painting with underglaze paints. Paul Börner, already mentioned before, in the 1920s and 1930s set new standards with his imaginative and decorative painting style (Fig. 323).

After World War II at first plastic art prevailed and painting took second place. Only after 1970 Heinz Werner, Rudi Stolle and Volkmar Bretschneider brought painting to new importance. The newly designed decorations (Plates 6 to 10) are not without risk for the manufactory because most of

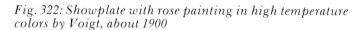
Fig. 322: Showplate with rose painting in high temperature colors by Voigt, about 1900

Fig. 323: Vase with flower painting by Paul Börner, about 1930

them are only suited for the new shape of the form *Large Cutout*. One of the strengths of the manufactory was always its continuity. Any new painting style was applicable to all forms and shapes of porcelain and vice versa. This will not be possible with the decorations for the form *Large Cutout*, most of them are only designed for this particular shape and they do not fit on the traditional shapes. It has to be seen how the manufactory can reconcile the new decorations with its vitally necessary tradition.

An important but rarely described part of decorations are the gold ornaments, lines and bands. At Höroldt's time they were an indispensable component of the whole decoration, and from then on gold ornaments on edges and borders as well as framing ornaments for painting always belonged to many Meissen decorations. Today the large number of gold ornaments has been reduced to a little over seventy and those that have proven to be the most popular are shown here (Figs. 324 and 325).

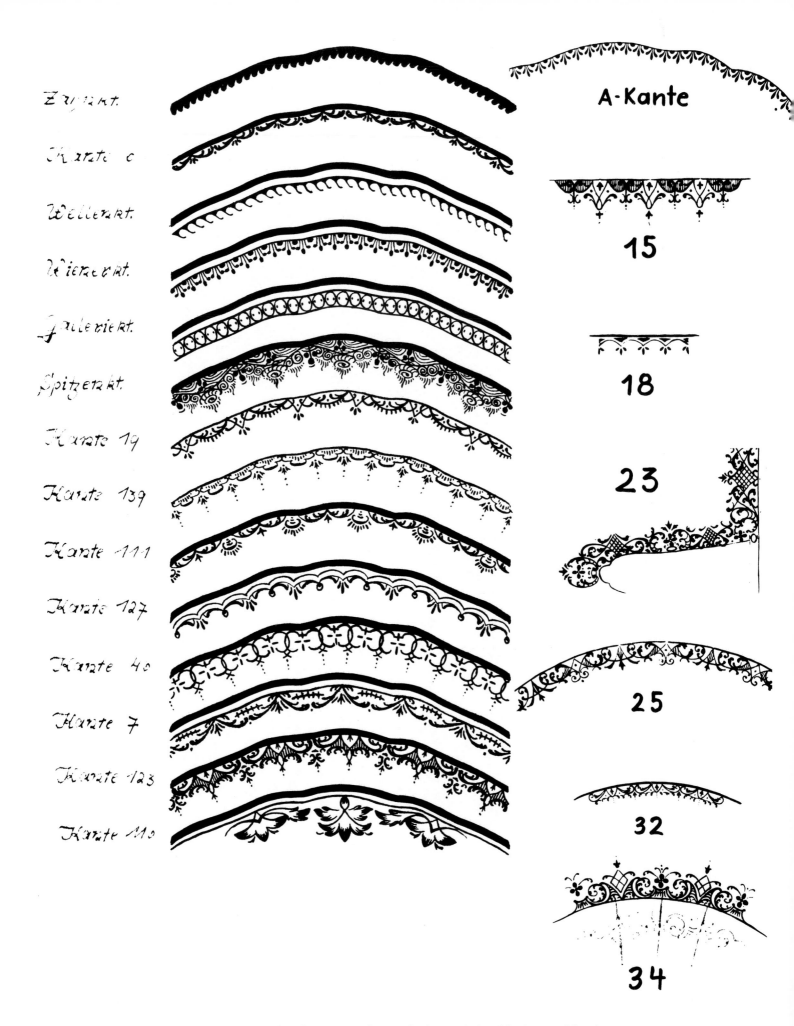

A-Kante

15

18

23

25

32

34

Fig. 324: Presently mostly demanded gold edges and border decorations

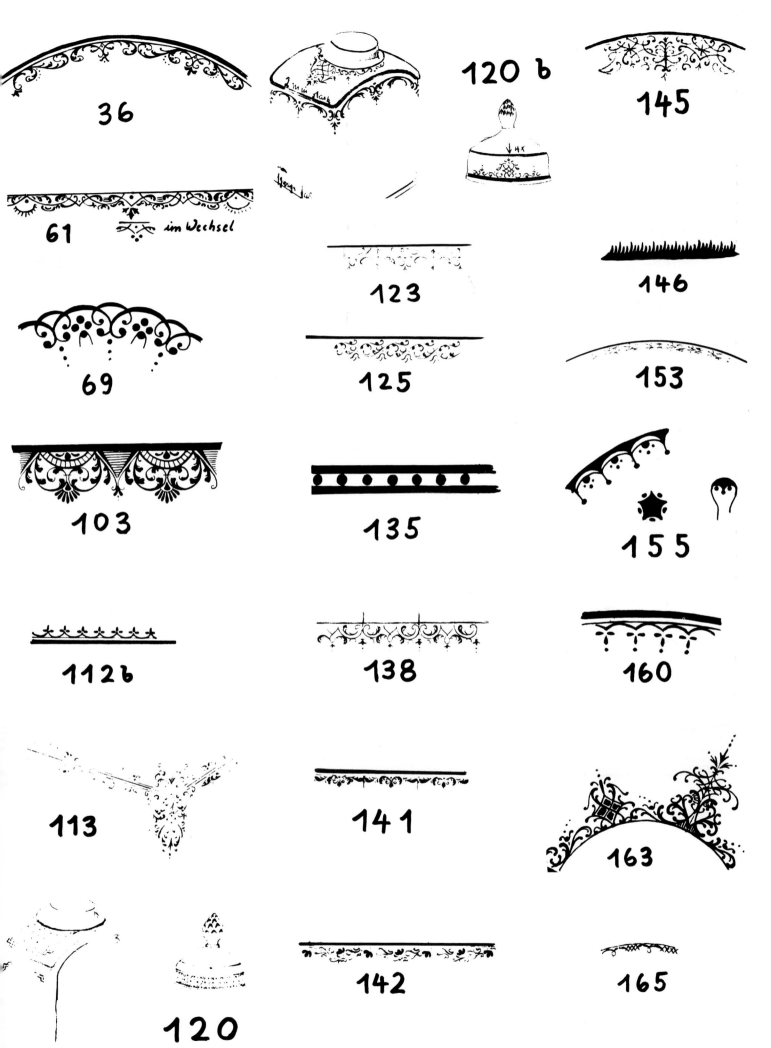

36

61   im Wechsel

69

103

112b

113

120

120 b

123

125

135

138

141

142

145

146

153

155

160

163

165

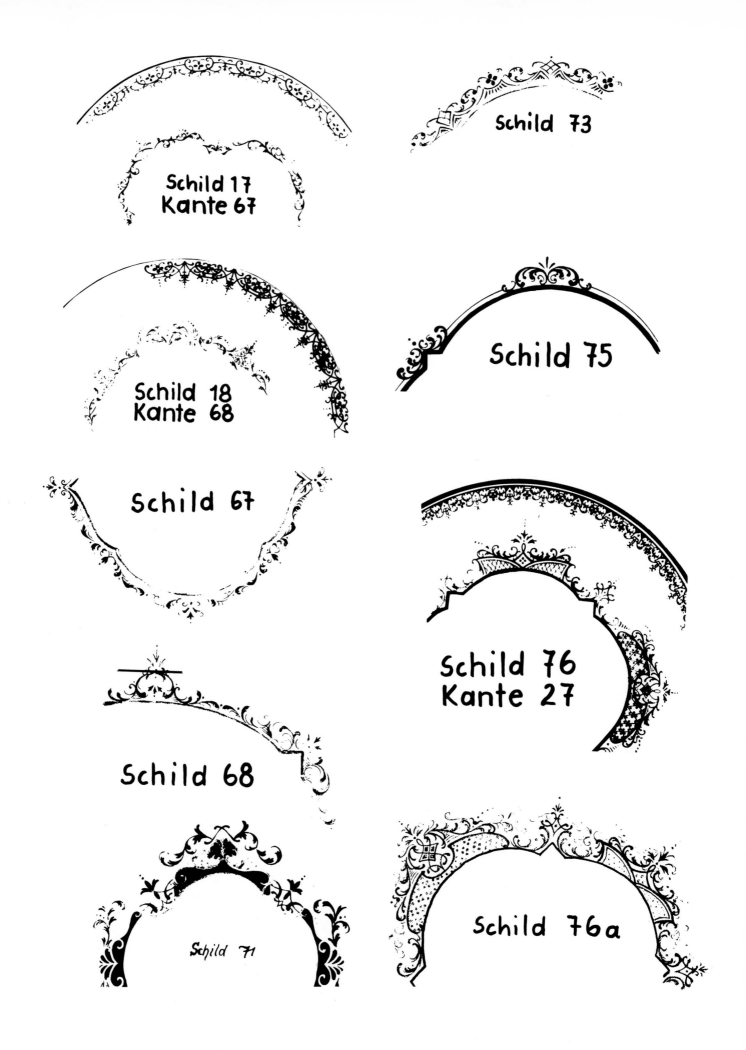

Schild 73

Schild 17
Kante 67

Schild 18
Kante 68

Schild 75

Schild 67

Schild 68

Schild 76
Kante 27

Schild 71

Schild 76a

Fig. 325: Mostly demanded gold frames and cartouches

Chapter Seven

Medals and Coins, Lithopanes, Tiles, Knick-Knack and Technical Porcelain

Among the first pieces made by the newly established manufactory were commemorative medals. At that time every ruler had himself, his ancestors, his royal friends or those he admired immortalized in gold or silver, and the new red stoneware seemed noble enough to be used for medals too. From already existing silver medals often plaster moulds were taken and used for the stoneware medals. The plasticity of the red stoneware allowed the impression of surprisingly fine details, and the flat areas were ground smooth on the early medals to enhance the relief portraits.

Not very many medals from the first years have been preserved, probably only a few were actually made. Known are medals showing - naturally - Augustus the Strong himself, his father Johann Georg IV, Peter the Great of Russia (Fig. 38), who supported August in the war with the Swedes, one Friedrich II, probably of Gotha, Friedrich I in Prussia (Fig. 41) and the contemporary Pope Clemens XI. King August had a good reason to honor the Pope and to show that he was a faithful Catholic. About 190 years before, his predecessor Prince-Elector Friedrich the Wise had hidden the church reformer Martin Luther (Fig. 326) after Luther had been banished and outlawed by Pope and Emperor. Friedrich also supported actively the spreading of protestant beliefs, and his brother and sucessor Johann, for all practical purposes, had established the Lutheran Church in Saxony.

Augustus, successor to the Prince-Electorate of Saxony in 1694, wanted to become a king and if possible, even Emperor of the German Empire. He saw his only chance for a kingdom in Poland. There the monarchy was not hereditary, but a king was elected for life. In 1697 three top candidates had emerged from a number of aspirants, two German Princes and a French one. Augustus was among them, and he was well-prepared. He spent large amounts of money to convince the Polish *Sejm* (Diet) that he was the right man, he got the Emperor of the German Empire on his side, and finally even gained the support of the Pope, who had a decisive voice in predominantly Catholic Poland.

Augustus paid a price for the Pope's assistance by converting to Catholicism. This conversion was not much more than a gesture. Augustus could not lead Saxony back to Catholicism, and he had not the slightest intention of doing it. But outwardly he had to show his sincerity and faith to the Pope. One way of doing it was to produce religious medals and plaques in Meissen, which would please the Catholic Church. Besides plaques with general religious motifs (Figs. 90, 121-123) he also had depicted exponents of the counter-reformation like Mary the Catholic of England, who tried to restore Catholicism in England after her father Henry VIII had broken with Rome.

Count Brühl, while he was director of the manufactory, collected these medals, and in 1753 he owned 21 of them, described in an inventory record as "15 different portraits, round and six half-length portraits of His Majesty", who at that time was Augustus III. Not very many medals from this period are preserved.

During the following years medals seem to have faded into the background. They were revived only after Josiah Wedgwood perfected his Jasper ware around 1775. His relief plaques became so popular that Meissen could not avoid joining the trend. The manufactory experimented with white relief on blue or green grounds. Larger pieces came out satisfactorily (Fig. 65, Plates 24 and 25), but smaller ones often appear blurred (Fig. 327). Altogether, Meissen never reached the liveliness and inventiveness of Wedgwood Jasper ware.

Much better were plaques and medals made from biscuit porcelain (Fig. 328). About 1820, the King of Saxony sug-

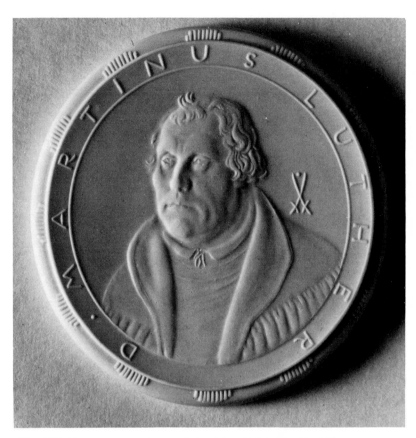

Fig. 326: Commemorative medal with relief portrait of Martin Luther, originally designed 1924 to 1934, re-minted on the occasion of Luther's 500th birthday in 1983

Fig. 327: Small plaque with white relief of angels on blue background in the Wedgwood style, early 19th century

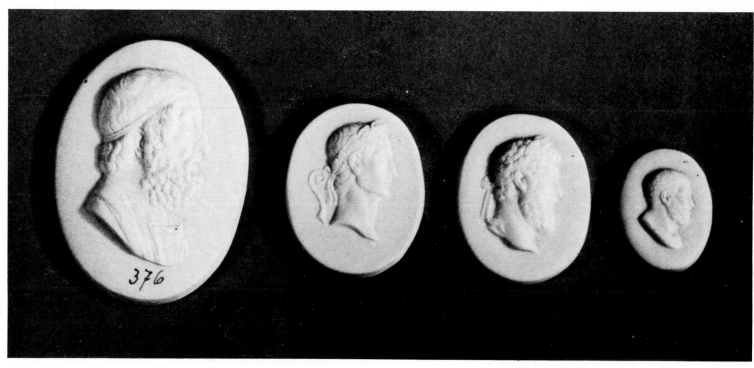

Fig. 328: Four small medals with relief portraits, biscuit porcelain, early 19th century

gested that the manufactory reproduce some silver medals in biscuit porcelain. He himself is depicted on a medal (Fig. 66), some of his relatives on others. Medals were cast to commemorate the introduction of a constitution in Saxony in 1830, the dedication of the Martin Luther Memorial in the city of Wittenberg, and to honor famous Germans like the poet Johann Wolfgang Goethe. His portrait on a biscuit medal was designed in 1824 by the medal maker A. Bovy especially for minting in porcelain. It was repeated in 1932 in red stoneware and in porcelain at the 100th anniversary of Goethe's death. In contrast to the 19th century medals, those of 1932 bear the crossed swords mark.

A list of articles in Low Relief (*Basrelief*) of 1851 describes 74 articles in production at that time.[1] The numbering system of this list ends with the number 147, which could indicate that 73 items had been dropped before 1851.

The systematic production of medals began only in the third century of the manufactory. Since 1910, almost 2,500 medals have been manufactured. Most of them were made from red stoneware, those made from porcelain were not glazed - only a few glazed samples exist - because the glaze blurs the details. Red stoneware also was preferred, since unglazed biscuit-porcelain easily became dirty.

Medals were produced in greater numbers with metal dies. Most of them were designed by Emil Paul Börner, who had joined the manufactory in 1910, and in 1930 became its artistic director. He was mainly responsible for the new emphasis on relief decorations and medals.

Organizations, schools, churches, (Fig. 329), merchants, and even private persons could order commemorative medals. The range of motifs goes from the 1000th anniversary of the City of Meissen to an honorary prize for rabbit breeders, and from New Years' Plaques to the State Convention of Saxonian Trichinosis Inspectors. Many of the medals and plaques were designed by Börner, others by Paul Scheurich, Richard Langer, Erich Oehme, Ludwick Nick, Max Esser and Erich Hösel.

Medals were also issued to collect donations for certain purposes, for charity, reconstruction of churches and museums, for memorials (Fig. 330), libraries and sportsgrounds. After Germany had lost the first World War and the Treaty of Versailles burdened her with harsh conditions, medals were minted to express political sentiments, to protest the French occupation of the industrial area along the Ruhr river or the separation of Upper Silesia from Germany in favor of Poland.

Fig. 329: Commemorative medal for the 800th anniversary of the Johannes Church in Plauen, Germany, 1922

Fig. 330: Donation medal for a memorial in the Leuchtenburg castle, Germany, for soldiers killed in action in World War One, 1922

Fig. 331: 10 Pfennig coin for the department store of Henry Seligmann in Hannover, Germany, 1921

Fig. 332: 5 Reichsmark coin, 1921, averse and reverse

At this time, the German people knew that it had to pay reparations to the victors of World War I, especially to France, that would bleed Germany white. Many Germans tried to protect at least a bit of their small fortunes which already had been depleted by the war. They collected and saved all available gold and silver coins. Even some denominations down to 20 Pfennig (about 5¢ at that time) were made from silver and most of these disappeared. Others containing copper or nickel had been used for the war effort. Suddenly an acute shortage of change developed and a solution had to be found. Cities printed paper money in small denominations or issued "Emergency Money" made from silk or linen, from wood, or even from gelatine. The Meissen manufactory from 1920 to 1922 also minted emergency money (*Notgeld*) from Böttger stoneware and porcelain for a number of cities and for stores (Fig. 331). The coins minted for stores were only valid as voucher, and could not be used in general circulation. The city coins could be circulated only within the confines of the cities that had issued them.

Strangely enough, the state of Guatemala in 1920 also ordered 2 Peso pieces in stoneware and porcelain from the manufactory.

For the German Reich and the State of Saxony the manufactory made a number of emergency coins. There is some disagreement among experts as to whether these coins really were in circulation as legal tender. Some feel that the coins were only specimens that were never issued as money, and had been minted for collectors only. Others insist that these coins actually were used as emergency money, and they cite as proof a 1922 law about the exchange of emergency money into regular currency, that also lists coins made from porcelain or stoneware.[2]

Both opinions are right - to a certain degree. There is no doubt that emergency money minted for cities, utilities or stores was in internal use within the issuers' jurisdictions. Each issuer was responsible for the redemption of his emergency money. Altogether, the Meissen manufactory in 1920 and 1921 produced emergency monies for 39 clients, among them the city of Meissen.[3]

Besides this locally valid money, the manufactory also minted emergency money for the German Empire. Its history is somewhat confused. Early in the 1920's, the manufactory proposed the production of porcelain and stoneware coins to the German Treasury. The Treasury declined the offer - as it had done already in 1917 - because it felt that these coins could easily be falsified and would not be very durable.[4] The Art Commissioner at the Department of the Interior, on the other hand, encouraged the manufactory to quickly introduce emergency coins because of their collectors' value and their promotional value for art.

The manufactory in 1920 produced a number of specimens of Imperial emergency money in denominations of 10 Pfennig, 20 Pfennig, 50 Pfennig, 1 Mark, 2 Marks, 3 Marks, and 5 Marks (Fig. 332). These coins never became legal tender, they were only test pieces.

In 1920 the manufactory also made emergency coins for the State of Saxony in denominations of 20 Pfennig, 50 Pfennig, 1 Mark, 5 Marks, 10 Marks and 20 Marks. They were test pieces too and not in circulation. Collectors' demands induced the manufactory in 1921 to mint three thousand sets of Saxon emergency money with the date 1920 until the Saxon Treasury intervened and ordered the manufactory to cease at once minting pieces with the year 1920. The manufactory also was advised not to produce the Imperial coins any more and the Treasury even threatened disciplinary proceedings if this order was not complied with by the manufactory management.[5]

The Imperial coins and the Saxon coins dated 1920 never were allowed as legal emergency money. With Saxon coins bearing the year 1921 it is different. Some coins of the Saxon series of 1921 were actually in circulation. The denominations of 20 Pfennig, 50 Pfennig, 1 Mark and 2 Marks were admitted as legal tender within Saxony from January 1st, 1921, until December 31st, 1921. The pieces valued at 5 Marks, 10 Marks, and 20 Marks were designated collectors' items and only sold with an additional charge of 50% of the face value or, if sold as a complete set of all seven coins, at a

Fig. 333: Set of Saxon emergency money in case, 1922

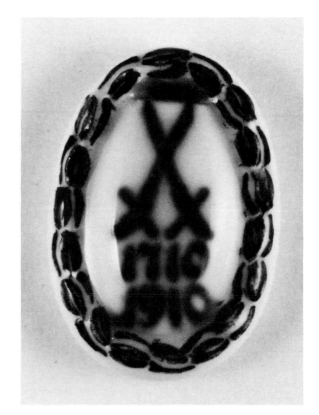

Fig. 334: Commemorative pendant for the 200th aniversary of the Meissen manufactory in 1910

Fig. 335: Token for one pot of coffee in the cafeteria of the manufactory, the combination of one coffee bean with two ears of barley indicates the ingredients of the coffee, after 1919

price of 50 Marks, 12.30 Marks more than the combined face value.[6] Some of the 5 Marks, 10 Marks and 20 Marks pieces were made with gilded edges, because their metal predecessors were gold coins.

The Treasury allowed the manufactory to produce 40,000 complete sets of the 1921 series, but at the end of 1921 Meissen had minted

52,099 5 Marks pieces
55,105 10 Marks pieces
49,481 20 Marks pieces

In April of 1922 the manufactory relinquished the dies to the Saxon Treasury after it had stopped regular production of Saxon emergency coins as of December 31st, 1921.[7] Probably to satisfy collectors it was allowed to mint 2,000 pieces each of the 20 Pfennig, 50 Pfennig, 1 Mark and 2 Marks pieces of the never valid 1920 series of Saxon emergency coins. These pieces were produced in 1922 but bore the year 1920.

The remaining sets were neatly packaged in little upholstered red boxes with the sign of the crossed swords and sold to collectors (Fig. 333). In 1923, when inflation in Germany had become rampant, the price of one set of Saxon emergency coins had risen from 50 Marks to 2,400 Marks. At this time one U.S. Dollar was worth 4,200,000,000,000 German Marks. The manufactory produced a few medals and tokens for its own use too (Fig. 334 and 335).

Commemorative medals were a regular part of the manufactory's production. After Adolf Hitler's ascension to power in 1933, medals were made for political purposes. Hitler himself appeared on several coins as did other Nazi leaders. Börner, the initiator and main designer of many of the Meissen medals, left the manufactory in disgust after four years of Nazi management. He returned to the manufactory after the end of World War II and again designed porcelain for Meissen and other factories until his death in 1970.

Shortly after World War II, the manufactory resumed production of commemorative and occasional medals and plaques. Some of them were issued in limited editions, others were made in large runs of up to 70,000. They depict persons and events in history, culture and politics, they honor people and organizations, and also promote political ideas and goals (Figs. 336 to 338). While in former years the diameter of the medals was between 4 and 5 cm (1 9/16 in. and 2 in.) later diameters between 6,5 cm and 8 cm (2 9/16 in. and 3 5/32 in.) began to be preferred, because they had more space for intricate artistic reproduction or design. Some of the medals were square or rectangular with slightly rounded corners or curved sides (Fig. 40). A few of the medals are decorated with gold or colors which were applied by hand.

Until 1982, the Meissen manufactory has produced more than two-thousand medals. Roughly 1,500 of them were created after 1946. It seems strange that in a time in which

Fig. 336: Medal after a coin minted in 1610 in the city of Rostock at the Baltic Sea

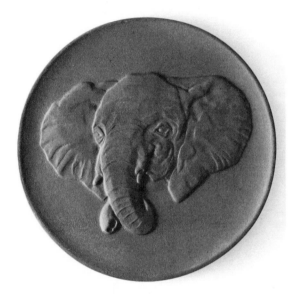

Fig. 337: Medal for the 20th anniversary of the Animal Park in Berlin, GDR, 1974

Fig 338: Medal for visitors of the Meissen manufactory

Fig. 339: Medal with the Great Seal of the City of Quedlinburg, about 1980

everything seems collectible, Meissen medals are neglected. There are even numismatic circles and dealers who never have heard of ceramic coins and medals, which were not only produced by Meissen but by other factories too. One reason could be that only a few books about this field are available, and they are not only hard to find, they are all written in German.

The most thorough listing until now can be found in the six volumes by Karl Scheuch (bibliography nos. 209-211). Because he could not find a publisher, Scheuch published offset copies of his typewritten manuscript himself. A new and very ambitious listing is in the works in the GDR. A team of numismaticists plans five volumes of a handbook in which they want to show all medals made by the manufactory between 1819 until 1932 and from 1946 until 1979 (bibliography no. 276). Medals issued during the Nazi rule in Germany from 1933 until 1945 will not be included. For these nearly 200 medals the books by Scheuch will still have to be consulted. The reason for these omissions are legal restrictions in the GDR prohibiting the reproduction of fascistic and militaristic symbols, and of motifs that are detrimental to the preservation of peace or contain other inflammatory connotations. The extension of these restrictions to reference books leaves scientifically unacceptable voids.

The Meissen manufactory itself is not eager to issue publications or even public announcements about its medal production. Most of the designs stemmed from artists outside the manufactory and did not always match the artistic taste in Meissen. But they are produced for customers as a kind of public service provided by the manufactory. Since it is impossible to get any organized information about new medals made in Meissen, collectors or people interested in starting a collection only accidentally learn about new issues. That is another obstacle which prevents Meissen medals from becoming objects of systematic collection.

Since medals and plaques offer themselves as souvenirs, many cities in the GDR have them made for visiting tourists. They mostly show points in the cities' histories, but also depict scenes of contemporary life. (Figs. 339 and 340). For the State's Museums in Berlin, GDR, the manufactory produces scaled down reproductions of some of their famous exhibits in Böttger stoneware and in biscuit porcelain (Figs. 341 to 343).

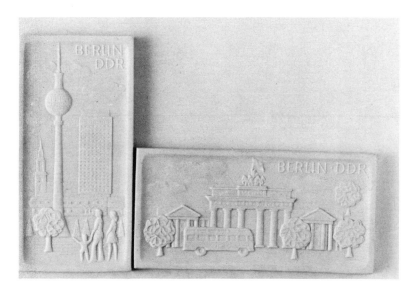

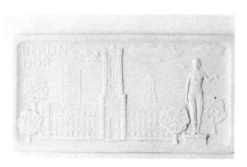

Fig. 340: Three plaques showing points of interest in Berlin, GDR, biscuit porcelain, about 1980

Fig 341: Scaled down reproduction of the lintel decoration of a door to an ancient temple in Sudan built in the third and second century B.C., now at the State's Museums in Berlin, GDR, about 1978

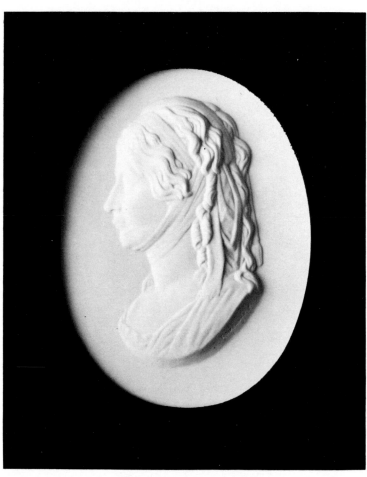

Figs. 342 and 343: Relief portraits of the Prussian Princesses Friederike and Luise in biscuit porelain with wooden frame, after a statue by J.G. Schadow finished in 1797, now at the State's Museums in Berlin, GDR

Lithopanes

During the rather sentimental period of the Biedermeier, which began in the 1820's and tapered off in the 1860's, wealthy burghers in Germany developed a taste for a more elaborate but cozy decoration of their homes. The newly offered transparent porcelain plaques called lithopanes suited their taste and the manufactory included these articles in its production program.

But Meissen did not invent them. They were first made by Paul de Bourgoing in 1827 in Paris, France. He modelled scenes on porcelain plaques, varying the thickness of the paste. These scenes could only be seen clearly if light was transmitted through the plaques, similar to modern photographic transparencies. The technical process is not very difficult. First, a wax plate has to be made with the intended picture carved in intaglio. The thinner parts allow transmitted light to pass through, and by varying the thickness, plastic effects can be achieved in soft tones (Fig. 344).

From the wax plate a gypsum mould is taken, which is filled with porcelain paste. The resulting cast is dried and then fired once. Lithopanes as a rule were not glazed.

A Saxon merchant, Carl Friedrich Höltzel, in August of 1828 brought fourteen French lithopanes back from Paris and recommended to King Anton that the Meissen manufactory could easily copy and sell them at reasonable prices.[8] He also pointed out that in France lithopanes were protected against copying by a *Brevet d' Invention*, something like an early patent, for ten years and therefore the prices were high. He had paid 37 1/2 Thalers for the fourteen pieces, the most expensive of them was priced at 7 1/3 Thalers.

In November of 1828, the King ordered the manufactory director, von Oppel, to give his opinion about the possibilities of production and the marketability of lithopanes. Von Oppel's reaction showed his indignation about outside meddling in manufactory affairs. The minutes of a meeting of the manufactory administration on December 1st, 1828, state: "...besides it was expressed by all that Mr. Hölzel has not offered the manufactory anything new."[9]

The manufactory had bought some French lithopanes at the Easter Fair in Leipzig that year and copied some of them in the manufactory and some outside. But the administration did not put much trust in them. Instead of acquiring new samples or developing some in the manufactory itself, the administration decided to wait for a possible demand by the public.

The King was not satisfied with this attitude. On the last day of 1828 he expressed his desire for an immediate lithopane production at the manufactory and he wanted them of a better quality than the French samples.[10] Lithopanes soon became an important sales article for the manufactory in commercially strained times, and they sold well despite the competition from Paris and the Royal Porcelain Manufactory in Berlin, Prussia. At the Leipzig Fair in the fall of 1829 buyers from Prussia bought about 400 Meissen lithopanes, which was remarkable because there was a high import duty on lithopanes in Prussia in order to protect the manufactory in Berlin.

Still, lithopanes made in Berlin very soon became dangerous for Meissen.[11] They were improved to a better quality, and appeared pure white, while the Meissen lithopanes in the 1840s were slightly brownish-yellowish. The paste in Meissen then was changed to render white lithopanes but the time for these articles slowly neared its end.

In 1836, at the Easter Fair in Leipzig 6.5% of the sales were accounted for lithopanes. In 1840 at the St. Michael's Fair it was 12% and two years later it had gone down to a little over 5%.[12] From then on interest in lithopanes slackened even more. The yearly financial report of the manufactory for 1847 still speaks of a rising demand, especially from North America[13] but that was only a passing event. In the following years it became evident that lithopanes had outlived themselves. Sales went down steadily and in 1851 thirty percent of the 255 different lithopanes in the price list were stricken. After 1860 lithopanes were taken off the list of currently available wares completely. But they still were made on special order and the manufactory files show that even in the 1920s orders for some of the lithopanes were filled.[14]

Fig. 344: Three Girls at the Water, *lithopane no. 200*

Fig. 345: Lithopane no. 151 Jesus as a Boy, *later called* Girl under a Tree

217

After World War II, the manufactory resumed regular production of some lithopanes. A price list of 1970[15] offers thirteen lithopanes (the list of lithopanes in the back of this book shows which ones were taken up again after World War II). Two of these lithopanes had been taken out of production in 1851 because they did not match the taste of the public any more. Another one (no. 151) formerly called "Christ as a Boy" now was listed as "Girl under a Tree" (Fig. 345).

Present day interest in lithopanes has encouraged the manufactory to contemplate production of more of these porcelain transparencies. The technical department at the moment is working on a further improvement of the paste for lithopanes, and it is the intention in Meissen to offer more of them in the near future.

It could not be ascertained whether the 19th century lithopanes were marked at all. It seems rather doubtful and there are not enough verified old lithopanes around any more for comparison. Some lithopanes are known, though, which bear the crossed swords in blue. One of them *Square in Front of the Royal Castle in Dresden* (no. 118) some time ago was shown in an art dealership in Braunschweig, Germany. It bears the blue crossed swords on the lower edge. But this no. 118 was not only made on order in April of 1924, it also was listed as currently available in the price list of 1970. So the question remains whether this lithopane was made in the 19th century, in 1924 or even as late as 1970. Until now there is no definite proof that lithopanes made in the 19th century were marked with the crossed swords in blue. But then, there is no proof that they were not.

Besides lithopanes, lithopanic lampshades and hanging lamps were made, most of them with motifs that already had been used for lithopanes (Fig. 346). A list of these items follows the list of lithopanes in the back of this book.

One lithopane, though, will not appear in any list. In the 19th century, one of the modellers at the manufactory, whose name is not known, made for himself and for his friends a lithopane with a frivolous scene showing a half-naked woman. This lithopane was made and distributed clandestinely. That was the peak of pornography in those days, so it is doubtful that many copies could have been produced, and officially this lithopane never was a product of the Meissen manufactory.

Fig. 346: Lithopanic lampshade

Marmorphan

At the time when lithopanes were on the decline, the manufactory thought it had found another promising novelty. In 1848 manufactory director Heinrich Gottlob Kühn reported to the Saxon Treasury that a new product had been invented with the capacity of increasing sales.[16] For seven years the manufactory had experimented with a porcelain that was supposed to look like marble. Kühn sent thirty-eight sample pieces made from this material to the Treasury, describing them as similar to the famous Italian marble from Carrara. The marble-porcelain was white and slightly transparent.

Kühn recommended the new material for "articles in an ancient style" and especially for "almost lifesize busts". He let it be known that the manufactory had given considerable thought to the question of naming the new product, and had come up with two proposals "Marmorphan" (simulated marble) and "Marmoroit" (similar to marble).

The Treasury did not think much of these Neo-Greek concoctions and decided to call the material simply "Marble Porcelain" for the time being. It proved not to be necessary to discuss the name again because marble porcelain had no future. It soon disappeared and no known and identified piece is left of the objects Kühn sent to the Treasury enumerated on an accompanying list. This list can be found in the back of this book. The marble porcelain episode was so short and produced so few pieces that today even experts confess to have never heard of this material and of pieces made of it. If pieces are still around, they probably are considered as a kind of biscuit porcelain.

Tiles, Wall Decorations and Pictures

In 1905, the manufactory embarked on a completely new and unusual undertaking. On the outside of one of the buildings belonging to the Royal Castle in Dresden, the artist August Walther in 1876 had painted a large sgrafitto-work, 100 m long and 10 m high (323 feet by 33 feet), showing all the Princes of the House of Wettin who had ruled what later became Saxony since the year 1123. They were depicted with horses and entourage two and a half times their actual size. Around the turn of the century, this huge painting was almost destroyed by climatic influences and by air pollution. The Meissen manufactory proposed a reconstruction of the painting faithful to the original but on ceramic tiles (Fig. 347).

From 1905 until 1907 the picture was painted on 25,000 tiles which join perfectly and close. The tiles were put up in 1907 and endured climatic and chemical aggressions. During the British and American air raids on Dresden in February of 1945 a number of tiles were broken by bomb splinters and flying debris. It took the manufactory some time to reinvent the special ceramic paste that had been used from 1905-1906 and the colors developed for the tiles. In 1979 finally the *Train of the House of Wettin* was completely restored (Fig. 348).

The manufactory also contributed ceramic wall decorations, interior and exterior, to architecture. Some restaurants and coffee houses in the GDR were adorned with large wall pictures made from Meissen porcelain.[17] One elaborate wall decoration (Plate 199) is in the United States, unassembled in private possession.

Copies of famous paintings on porcelain plaques were begun during Marcolini's time in the late 1770s. Not only portraits of famous people were painted on porcelain, among them George Washington, but paintings by Watteau (Plate 200), Angelica Kauffmann, Canaletto and other artists were copied in smaller size on porcelain plates and framed like pictures (Plate 201). Production of these copies, now considered unsuitable for porcelain, reached its peak in the second half of the 19th century. Today pictures on porcelain are still made, but their motifs are no longer taken from oil paintings. They are mainly developed by the Meissen artists especially for porcelain (Plates 202 to 205).

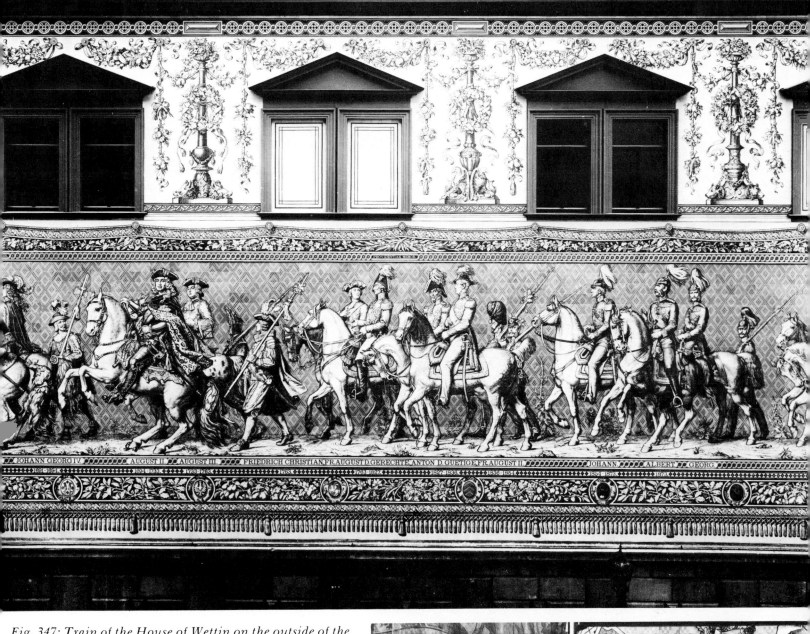

Fig. 347: Train of the House of Wettin on the outside of the Royal Castle in Dresden, part of the painting on tiles showing, among others, August II and August III

Fig. 348: Part of the Train of the House of Wettin during cleaning and repair work

There was no field in which the Meissen manufactory was not active. In the early years it even produced ceramic coffins. A story passed on over the centuries tells of an incident at a funeral. A lady of high birth, so the tale goes, had died, and her relatives wanted her to be interred in a Meissen coffin. But when the coffin was lowered into the grave it slipped out of the ropes and to the dismay of the mourners broke apart hitting the ground, releasing the lady's body. Immediately the rumour circulated that the Dresden coffin makers had bribed the professional pall bearers to let the coffin slip on purpose because they were afraid that this new competition might reduce the sale of their wooden coffins. Shortly afterwards, the manufactory gave up production of coffins. It is not known whether it did so because of this incident or for another reason.

Porcelain seemed to be more suited for life and its joys than for death, not only for the decoration of rooms but also for personal adornment. Drop-shaped painted lockets to be mounted in gold or silver as pendants had been made since the early 19th century (Fig. 349). Even smaller plates were intended to grace rings (Fig. 350) or brooches (Fig. 351). They still are in the regular manufactory production program.

For card games, the manufactoy offered little boxes with chips (Plate 206), and boxes for snuff or pills or other gentlemen's necessities are known from the early 18th century (Plates 207 and 208). They came with a loose lid but more often the lid was mounted with metal, preferably silver or gold. Ladies could choose between all kinds of scent bottles (Plate 209), a useful accessory since in the 18th and 19th centuries the prevalent lack of personal hygiene could only be overcome by strong perfumes. Pastille burners, (Fig. 352) which came in different shapes, had a similar function.

Little sewing kits for travel or quick mending, but also for special needles to lace stays, were favorites among the well-to-do ladies (Plate 210). For young mothers they often came in the form of babies in swaddling clothes which were made by many manufactories.[18] Some of these babies also were made as signets or as pipe-stoppers. For the smoking gentleman not averse to a little frivolity, pipe-stopers in the shape of ladies legs were available. They were called *Flea-Legs* (Fig. 353) because of a little flea usually painted on the leg above the stocking.

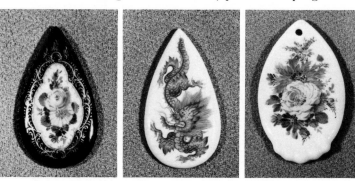

Fig. 349: *Three porcelain plates with overglaze decoration for pendants*

Fig. 350: *Porcelain plates for rings*

Fig. 351: *Porcelain plate for a brooche and a mounted brooche plate*

Fig. 352: *Pastille burner by Kaendler and Ehder c. 1743*

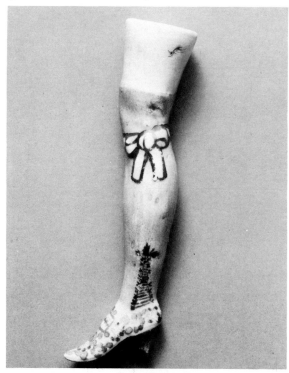

Fig. 353: Flea Leg *as pipe-stopper c. 1750-1760*

Pipe heads had been made from clay long before European hard-paste porcelain was invented. So it was only natural that the new material was used for these articles too (Fig. 354). Most of them were elaborately painted and decorated (Plates 211 and 212), to be used with pipes sometimes three feet or longer because in those pipes the smoke cooled off before it reached the sensitive taste buds.

Children were not neglected either. For them doll's heads were made to be put on bodies made of stuffed cloth and dressed up in fancy clothes (Plate 213). Strong competition from the cheaper and often more ingenious Thuringian doll head makers limited the production of these articles in Meissen.

In the 19th century the manufactory made fanciful mantelpieces for fireplaces. It also produced tiled stoves with handpainted tiles (Plates 214 and 215). For these tiles, a special paste was necessary that did not really fit into the regular Meissen production program. And because the Teichert factory in Meissen sold tiled stoves of excellent quality which could be bought much more cheaply, the manufactory made its stoves only in limited numbers.

Commemorative plates for all imaginable occasions were another branch of the manufactory program (Figs. 355 and 356). Among them were Christmas plates (Figs. 357 and 358). In 1909 the first Christmas plate was offered for sale, and they were issued regularly, sometimes even two different motifs the same year. After 1959 Christian motifs on these plates were replaced by general winter scenes or scenes from fairy tales, and instead of Christmas plates they were referred to as year plates.

Fig. 356: Commemorative plate for the 1000th anniversary of the city of Meissen

Fig. 354: Pipe heads early 19th century

Fig. 357: Christmas plate 1936

Fig. 355: Commemorative plate for the 200th anniversary of the Meissen manufactory

Fig. 358: Christmas plate 1940

And not to leave out anything, the manufactory also made articles for hygienic purposes (Plate 216) and for nursing care (Fig. 359). Known are also porcelain plates for house numbers[19] and a vast variety of technical porcelain, ranging from porcelain insulators for telegraph lines,[20] to thread guides for spinning and weaving machines, to muffle kilns for dental ceramics and laboratory porcelain. Especially these laboratory implements were produced in considerable numbers (Figs. 360 and 361). In the 18th century, they at first were made for use within the manufactory but soon they became regularly offered articles for sale. In 1955, the manufactory gave up production of technical porcelain altogether in order to concentrate on artistically important porcelain.

Fig. 359: Nursing cup

Figs. 360 and 361: Laboratory vessels

Chapter Eight
Outside Painting, Imitations and Copies of Meissen Porcelain

The beauty and value of Meissen porcelain made it an object of desire from the beginning. This desire was not always stilled legitimately. Porcelain was stolen, sold underhandedly, and painted outside the manufactory, injuring its reputation. In May of 1717, inspector Steinbrück and the arcanist Nehmitz, on Böttger's orders made a search in the manufactory for hidden porcelain. In the cellar where the ingredients for the paste were washed, they found two boxes filled with white porcelain. In a room above the kilns, three baskets of porcelain were hidden, and in a closet in the bookkeeper's office they detected about 130 pieces of porcelain, some of them broken but quite a number still usable.[1]

Thefts and smuggling of porcelain out of the manufactory were something that has never been stopped completely, even now. But while petty thievery of decorated pieces only meant a financial loss for the manufactory, the carrying away of the white porcelain touched a raw nerve as did later the official sale of white ware by the manufactory itself.

Painted and decorated porcelain is considerably more expensive than white articles and very soon some people saw a chance to pocket the difference by decorating white Meissen porcelain themselves. There are two expressions for those people: *Hausmaler* (outside or home painters) and *Pfuscher* (botchers). The latter name was chosen because these painters butted into the manufactory's trade. Porcelain literature in the meantime has made *Hausmaler* a respectable name, but in the eyes of the manufactory, they too were botchers and counterfeiters (Fig. 362).

Today the work of the early *Hausmaler* is considered as valuable as original Meissen painting of the same time, or even more so (Fig. 363). Especially the home painters in Augsburg are appreciated highly (Plate 217). The members of two families, the Aufenwerths and the Seuters, began very early to procure white Meissen porcelain and to decorate it.

Johann Aufenwerth, whose signature JAW can be found on some pieces,[2] evidently was the first one to decorate white ware from Meissen with Gold Chinamen, polychrome Chinoiseries, and mythological scenes (Plates 218 to 221). It was not his main profession, he was a goldworker in a addition to his other trades, and probably decorated porcelain only occasionally between 1713 and 1728. Aufenwerth evidently was not without wit. A tankard at the Museum of Arts and Crafts in Hamburg, Germany, shows the painting of a monkey on a table busily painting a coffee pot.

His daughter Elisabeth Anna who in 1722 married the goldsmith Jakob Wald, also painted Meissen porcelain. She signed with ornaments containing the intertwined letters EAW or AW.[3] Elisabeth Anna must have continued painting (Fig. 663) porcelain even a long time after her marriage, because two tankards signed with her full name bear the date 1748.

Another Aufenwerth daughter, Sabina, in 1731 married the merchant and coffeehouse owner Isaac Hosennestel. From her the signature SAW is known.[3] She evidently decorated porcelain only occasionally, although her sister produced a considerable number of painted pieces.

The two Seuter brothers made most of the Augsburg decorations. Abraham in 1726 was granted a privilege by the Augsburg city council for the decoration of porcelain with gold and silver. He and his brother Bartholomäus began with Gold Chinamen (Fig. 364), then painted polychrome *Chinoiseries* and later took up many other popular motifs.

The Augsburg painters had the same decorating ideas as Höroldt had in Meissen. Some of the Augsburg motifs were copied from Meissen, for others they used etchings. Hunting scenes were copied from the drawings of Johann Elias Ridinger, another Augsburg citizen with whom they were acquainted. Ridinger's motifs also were copied in Meissen, and later in other German manufactories.

Fig. 362: Teapot with cover, c. 1725-1735, decorated later by unidentified outside painter with polychrome Chinoiseries

Fig. 363: Tea pot with cover with etched Gold Chinamen, about 1720-1725, painter not ascertained

Fig. 364: Chocolate cup made about 1720, painted with Gold chinamen after 1725 probably by one of the Seuter brothers

Ignaz Bottengruber in Breslau, Silesia, was another important outside painter of the early period. He decorated Meissen porcelain probably between 1720 and 1730, later he used Vienna porcelain, which was more readily available. His motifs are rather cheerful Arcadian landscapes, bacchantic and mythological scenes (Fig. 365), and hunting and military events.

In Bayreuth three outside painters were working: Johann Christoph Jucht, Rudolf Christoph Drechsel, and the more important Johann Friedrich Metzsch. In 1731, Metzsch tried to get employment at the Meissen manufactory as gilder and painter, claiming that August II already had received gracefully pieces painted by him. He offered to decorate a tea set for the King as a sample of his abilities, and then have the ruler decide on his request for employment. Metzsch wanted to set up his shop in Dresden, not in Meissen. The manufactory did not like this idea because it feared "that he would employ journeymen and botchers", and by clandestinely decorating and selling Meissen porcelain take business away from the manufactory.[4]

Feeling that his chances were slim, Metzsch tried to entice some employees of the manufactory to escape and join him, but this "Bayreuth Conspiracy", as it is called in the files, was discovered, and some manufactory employees ended in jail. Metzsch then returned to Bayreuth, where he worked as home painter until 1751 (Fig. 366). That year he joined the manufactory in Fürstenberg, Germany, as painter. Some of his pieces are signed with the letters F.M. or with his full family name, Metzsch. Often the city name, written as Bayreith or Bayr., and a year were added. A typical part of Metzsch's decorations is a shell-shaped design, also called a bat wing, which he often used in his ornaments.

Very little is known about F.J. Ferner, who operated a painting shop in Thuringia or in Saxony. His decorations include cavaliers, ladies, horsemen and shepherd scenes in a limited number of colors, among which a pale iron-red was preferred. Some pieces have been found on which Ferner took Meissen porcelain with sparse blue underglaze painting and decorated it over with polychrome painting, adding his own decoration in the white areas (Plate 222).

This method of painting over simple Meissen underglaze decorations can be found quite often. It evidently became more and more difficult for the outside painters to get white porcelain from Meissen, and they had to make do with already decorated pieces. Their own painting they squeezed into the remaining white areas or they applied it on the inside of bowls, which were usually left white by the manufactory, except for border ornaments. Outside painters covered the blue underglaze decoration or highlighted it with gold (Fig. 367).

Franz Ferdinand Mayer in Pressnitz, Bohemia, worked as outside painter from about 1745 until 1778, but he preferred older Meissen porcelain from the 1720s. His decorations often are found on white porcelain pieces rejected by the quality control of the manufactory because of imperfections. Besides mythological motifs, hunting and shepherd scenes, he painted landscapes and situations of rural life (Plates 223 to 225).

An unusual kind of decoration was applied by August Otto Ernst von dem Busch in Hildesheim, Germany. By profession he was a canon, and his decoration work seems to have been a hobby in the years between 1745 and 1775. Von dem Busch incised line drawings into the glaze with a diamond and then filled the incisions with lamp black (Fig. 368). Most of the pieces decorated by him are signed with the name Busch and a date. The earliest known date is 1745, the latest year 1775.

Of a number of other outside painters their names are known but it is difficult to ascribe to them decorated pieces with certainty. On the other hand, painted Meissen porcelain is around for which an outside painter has not been ascertained (Plates 226 and 227). It seems rather difficult to shed more light on this field, but fortunately there are still

Fig. 366: Meissen plate decorated by outside painter Johann Friedrich Metzsch about 1735-1751

Fig. 365: Cup and saucer made about 1723-1725, decorated by Ignaz Bottengruber about 1730

scholars around who from time to time contribute new enlightenment.

The Meissen manufactory was not too happy about the botchers. Böttger in 1717 already complained about the increasing number of outside painters. Some were connected with the manufactory as Johann Gottfried Meerheim, who later got 300 Thalers hush-money per year because he claimed to know the arcanum. He dabbled as a painter at the manufactory, but his work was criticized as inconsistent. Outside the manufactory he worked in cahoots with his son David Conrad on decorating Meissen porcelain with rather crude painting.[5] They sold it in Dresden and in some spas in Bohemia and the manufactory figured its losses from the competition of these botchers at one thousand Thalers.

Johann Georg Mehlhorn was another "arcanist" who had been employed by the manufactory in order to buy his silence. He worked in the paint laboratory of the manufactory and secretly decorated porcelain on the side. Later in 1748 his son Johann Gottlieb Mehlhorn, a painter at the manufactory, was arrested for botching.

Many of the painters of the manufactory took home white porcelain, decorated it and sold it. One of the worst culprits was Höroldt himself. An investigation in 1732 revealed that he kept several boxes with porcelain in his home. His house-maid Katharina Nitzschner was called as witness in this investigation and she testified that she had seen three boxes filled with porcelain and observed a lively traffic with porcelain in and out of Höroldt's home. Höroldt defended himself by claiming that he had paid for the white porcelain but he circumvented the issue that the white ware increased in value considerably after he had painted it. His defense was the contention that he was not employed directly by the manufactory at that time and he assured the investigation committee that he had given up his private enterprise in 1731, the year he signed an employment contract with the manufactory.[6] Höroldt got off the hook, he was too valuable to the manufactory, but his house-maid was sentenced to three weeks in jail or three Thalers fine for "denunciation".

Knowing Höroldt's character and greed a little one cannot discard the impression that he continued his home painting after 1731, especially since his salary from the manufactory had been set at one third or less of his former income. Other manufactory painters did the same thing to better themselves. A few were caught and punished, others could avoid discovery. Those who identified the pieces painted by them are mentioned in the chapter "Marks and Markings".

It seems impossible to distinguish pieces with home painting by Meissen painters from those decorations made in the manufactory itself. Höroldt drilled his painters to a certain kind of painting technique and the manner of painting taught at the manufactory the painters repeated at home. It would even have been difficult for most of them to develop a new style.

But at all times some of the more imaginative Meissen painters decorated porcelain with motifs of their own. They could buy white porcelain of the lowest quality grade at reasonable prices and also pieces of better quality and paint them with anything they liked. One of the privileges of the Meissen workers is the kiln benefit. They are permitted to have a certain number of painted pieces fired in the muffle kilns of the manufactory. In former times there were almost no restrictions but today this benefit is limited.

Pieces with unusual decorations created this way can be encountered occasionally and they are puzzling even for experts because they cannot be classified in any known category. Apprentices too paint or garnish unsalable pieces for practice. Often very beautiful painting thus appears on porcelain of such a low quality grade that is not even sold to the manufactory employees. They are confusing since they are neither regular manufactory painting nor outside decoration, but they still were made by Meissen painters in the manufactory.

While it was difficult for the manufactory to prevent the illegal home painting of its own painters, it tried to limit the large number of crude outside decorations that were sold as genuine Meissen to unaware buyers. The introduction of the letters M.P.M., K.P.F. and K.P.M. painted in blue under the glaze on the bottom of certain pieces was an attempt to meet the problem (see chapter "Marks and Markings").

Another one was the idea of restricting the sale of white ware, but it never became more than an idea despite all efforts to realize it. Since the manufactory always produced more white ware than it could decorate, it had to get rid of the surplus of white pieces from time to time. Only the quality grades "Medium Good" and below were sold white, but the botchers did not care about that too much because their customers usually did not know the difference.

Fig. 367: Meissen plate with early Onion Pattern, *the blue underglaze decoration is covered over the glaze with an identical and finely engraved gold pattern probably made in Augsburg 1730-1740*

Fig. 368: Tureen and cover made after 1750, decoration by outside painter von dem Busch and signed by him with the year 1774

In 1729, the manager of the manufactory-owned store in Dresden, Samuel Chladni, complained that botchers sold their products cheaply compared with the Meissen prices and that the good Meissen pieces could not be sold. One month later, manufactory director Count Hoym forbode the sale of white porcelain altogether, but Chladni, who was sitting on a large stock of white articles, asked if it would be advisable to sell them anyway but note the name of the customers who bought white ware[7]. The King agreed with Chladni, but exempted reputable people from the duty to give their names. Chladni still could not get rid of the large number of white pieces, so in January of 1730 he proposed that the manufactory should produce only as much white ware as it was able to decorate[8].

The problem could not be solved, and the King had to be asked for a decision. It came on May 19th of 1731, and said that white porcelain should not be sold but that excess white ware at least should be decorated with a few sprays of flowers or similar painting[9]. Some years later, at a date which has not been determined yet, but is known to have been before 1764, a special marking was introduced for porcelain sold white, a short incised line in the glaze through the crossed swords mark (Fig. 369)

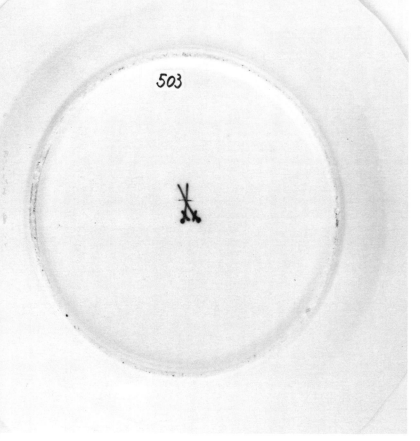

Fig. 369: Mark on plate in Plate 228, one incision through the crossed swords is a sign that the manufactory had sold the plate undecorated

That was not sufficient either. White ware was still smuggled out of the manufactory by workers. They also could buy *Brack*, the lowest quality grade for usable porcelain, and this inferior porcelain also found its way to outside painters.

In 1761 Councillor von Nimptsch, a member of the manufactory commission, reported that in his absence whole table sets of undecorated porcelain had been sold, even white figurines. They were "painted by certain people in Dresden and sold to unwitting people as manufactory products", von Nimptsch complained, He asked August III for a law forbidding outside decoration under threat of jail sentences[10]. He also told the King that the thrower Figolowsky had confessed to the theft of 200 Thalers worth of porcelain.

August III took up the recommendation. On August 27, 1761, in the midst of the Seven-Years'-War, he found time to

issue a General Order against botching, because he felt that outside painting not only "cheated the public but also weakened trust in the quality of the products of Our Porcelain Manufactory."[11] Botchers were threatened with jail, to no avail. On April 25, 1775, the order was repeated and extended. Not only botchers should go to jail - if caught -also traders selling Meissen porcelain with outside painting and even landlords who tolerated the work of botchers in houses they owned[12]. The order of 1775 explicitly mentions that botchers were working in Meissen and in Dreden, and that their demand for white porcelain had caused defraudations and peculations at the manufactory.

Even people of rank participated in this shady business. A former Russian colonel by the name of Gileski was expelled from the city of Meissen in 1779 because he secretly had bought white porcelain from Meissen workers to have it decorated by outside painters. The colonel was admonished not to continue these illegal deals, and he was able to leave Meissen unharmed because of his social position[13].

At the beginning of the 19th century when the manufactory was in dire straits financially, it sold everything it could find a buyer for. Price lists of that time offer white tea and coffee sets in all available shapes, as well as dinner sets with tureens and bowls. On one of the lists in the manufactory archive there is a handwritten remark: "For completely white pieces 11 1/2 percent discount, export 5.5 percent"[14].

That all changed in 1819, when the old regulations against the "white sale" were reinforced. White articles were no longer sold at a discount price, on the contrary, an additional charge of two thirds of the regular white price was levied on them. That measure was supposed to make outside painting less profitable[15].

New conditions for the sale of white or only partially decorated porcelain were set in 1846. Pieces in the English taste, mainly meaning pulls of 18th century models, could be bought white only with an additional charge of one third of the regular white price. For articles with gold decoration only, the surcharge was 50 percent, and for pieces with Modest Painting *(Schlichte Malerei)*, it was 33 1/3 percent. Porcelain with large areas of royal blue ground color but without polychrome painting could only be bought for double the regular price.

That was a hard blow for the outside painters whose margin of profit decreased considerably. Luckily, there were exceptions for people who were not under suspicion of using porcelain for shady deals, especially those connected with the court or in respectable positions. In those cases, the manufactory reviewed and decided every single request, and if a good customer or a dealer ordered white articles even if they were figurines and groups, the manufactory was generous. Some of these white wares found their way to outside decorators because even people in high positions are not always averse to a quick, profitable deal.

From the last third of the 19th century until 1914, outside painting again increased dangerously. The number of botchers grew as rapidly as the demand for decorated porcelain, but many of the outside painters sacrificed quality for quantity. Some of the outside painting was not too bad, it was probably made in the early stages of the new botching movement (Plates 228 to 230). Later, the outside painters became more and more careless, because only quick painting brought money, and quick painting means crude painting (Plates 231 and 232).

Flower painting was a favorite subject with the botchers, but they did not always have the right paint available. They were not able to match the Meissen colors, but they did try to get close. Some botchers even used laquer paints. Very often, this kind of decoration chipped and wore off easily, leaving ugly spots (Plates 233 and 234). Although, the right paint and proper painting determine a good decoration, the firing in the muffle kilns is as important, and many of the botchers in those years only had makeshift kilns without a proper temperature control. Often, the painting stayed dull because it had not been fired at a high enough temperature, and the paint had not been fused to the glaze.

It also was usual to marry pieces with different hues of the glaze, something the manufactory never would have done. Cheap gilding was supposed to distract the attention from the slight difference in color, but the cheaper it was, the more easily it wore off (Plates 235 and 236). The range of colors available to the botchers was rather narrow, and their polychrome painting stands no comparison with Meissen (Plates 237 and 238).

Everything was copied, the motifs of Indian Painting included (Figs. 370 and 371). All of this was done on Meissen Porcelain with the crossed swords mark. Not only white porcelain was used but also pieces with simple red or blue lines around border and ledge, which were painted over. Incisions through the crossed swords indicating porcelain of substandard quality carefully were removed by grinding off the glaze, and with it, the incisions. Since the incisions often only had cut the glaze but not gone through the blue swords, it was possible in most cases to grind them out. The price for this operation was a dull spot or a slightly indented small area in the glaze on top of the crossed swords (Fig. 372 and 373).

Sometimes fakers tried to hide these spots with flux or by using fillers. There is a long list of more or less secret recipies for filler material that can be used on porcelain. Some of them are quite strange concoctions. One recipe recommends a mixture of eggwhite and finely sieved lime, this combination was used frequently. Another one is as odorous as the purpose it was intended for. It says: Macerate Gruyere cheese in water for three days, add two or three naked snails and mix with an equal part of quicklime. But be it eggs or cheese, all fillers left an irregular spot in the glaze above the mark and that is a hint that somebody has tampered with it.

Some fakers worked in a large style like the *Sächsische Porzellanfabrik von Carl Thieme* (Saxonian Porcelain Factory by Carl Thieme) in Potschappel near Dresden, which will be encountered a few more times later in this book. In 1914, the Meissen manufactory conducted an investigation about the practices of the Thieme factory by questioning some of its own painters, who formerly had worked for Thieme[16]. They reported that in Potschappel, modest painting on Meissen porcelain was carefully removed with acids, especially aqua regia (nitrohydrochloric acid). Then the pieces were decoated with popular and price-raising painting as copies of Watteau and Hunting Scenes.

One of the most popular decorative patterns was the red dragon. The painter and trader J.G. Schneider in Bautzen, Saxony, bought pieces with the simple *Red Dragon* and highlighted the dragon with gold, transforming it into the

Fig. 370: *Meissen* Rock and Bird *Pattern on plate*

Fig. 372: *Mark on cup in Plate 231, incisions designating substandard quality of the piece are ground out leaving a dull spot, below the spot the crossed swords mark appears lighter in color*

Fig. 371: *Imitation of Meissen* Rock and Bird *Pattern by outside painter*

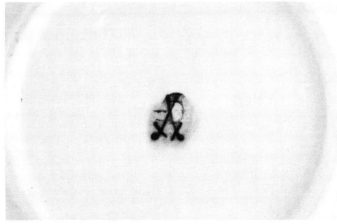

Fig. 373: *Mark on saucer in Plate 231 with ground out incisions, the two incisions going through the crossed swords could not be removed completely, to the left of the swords remnants of the incisions are still visible*

Court Dragon, that was only to be made for the Royal Court in Dresden and for nobody else. He also added the letters *KHC* on the bottom. That was a proprietor's mark of the 18th century, and Schneider sold his handiwork as antique Meissen porcelain.　The manufactory took some of the fakers to court. In the Schneider's case, it succeeded, he was sentenced to five months in jail for fraud. The Imperial Court followed the opinion of the manufactory that a Meissen mark also covered the decoration.[17] It reconfirmed its decision in 1921, but left a loophole open. Someone who decorates Meissen porcelain for his own use or as gift without the intention of bringing it into commercial traffic was allowed to do so. This provision was aimed at the many ladies and daughters of wealthy burghers and noblemen, who considered porcelain painting an amusing pastime. They did not intend to sell their artworks, it was only made for their enjoyment or that of their beloved.　Still these pieces appeared on the antiques market. In a debate in the Saxon Diet in 1908 the Saxon Secretary of the Treasury Dr. von Rüger had an explanation for it, when he said "all humans are mortal and from their estates such pieces come into commercial traffic." The secretary lamented the fact that privately decorated Meissen porcelain was finding its way from estate sales to antiques dealers and he did not see anything that could be done against it.[18] Since there was no intention of cheating deliberately, and not all antique dealers realized that decorations had been made by outside painters, the manufactory could not do much. It warned and occasionally treatened, but it has no leg to stand on when it comes to private decoration of Meissen porcelain, especially if the painter clearly indicates that the piece was not painted in Meissen. (Fig. 374).

In its zeal to stop botching, the manufactory occasionally overshot its goal. A porcelain dealer and painter in Dresden in 1981 sold a showplate with a Saxon landscape to a customer by the name of Kramer, who said he wanted it for his father's 70th birthday. Little did the dealer know that Mr. Kramer was an employee of the Meissen manufactory looking for Meissen pieces decorated outside the manufactory. Since the dealer was also a porcelain painter, his store seemed a fertile ground for a clandestine investigation. One week after the sale, the manufactory wrote a stern letter to the dealer accusing him of having decorated the plate and pointing out to him the illegality of his doings. And then it said that it was not going to take him to court because the painting was "not too bad". But the manufactory demanded

the sale price back, a written promise by the dealer never to do it again and the surrender of all Meissen pieces he had decorated for the removel of the crossed swords mark.

The dealer was surprised. He protested his innocence and told the manufactory to check its files for a copy of a bill of sale, because this plate with the decoration on it had been bought directly from the manufactory. In Meissen the people in charge mulled over this answer for a month and then peevishly admitted to having made a mistake. It was indeed a plate with "not too bad" original Meissen decoration. To obscure its humiliation, the manufactory now accused the Dresden dealer in strong terms of having tried to deceive poor Mr. Kramer by telling him that he was going to buy a plate decorated by the dealer and painter. But that was only a rearguard action, and after the dealer had talked the matter over at the manufactory the whole affair was considered closed.[19]

Copies of Meissen decorations on porcelain made by other manufactories are innumerable. Occasionally on those pieces, perfect Meissen painting can be encountered. Painters trained at the manufactory left for certain reasons and opened up their own shop or joined other painting shops. They took along the brushstroke they had learned in Meissen, and the kind of painting at which the manufactory excelled (Fig. 375).

The old and most sought after patterns belong to porcelain history and are free for all. Only decorations developed after 1919 are protected as are those for which a copyright has been obtained. Some porcelain factories today print old Meissen patterns on their products, such as the *Hutschenreuther AG* in Selb, Bavaria, satisfying the demand for porcelain with old Meissen patterns for those who cannot afford the more valuable originals. There is nothing illegal or immoral about it. The adoption of old Meissen patterns today is simply proof of their immortality.

Meissen plastic art was faked too, but this was not possible as homework. It had to be done in a porcelain manufactory or a factory. Copies of Meissen figurines and groups without a Meissen mark are not uncommon. Other manufactories tried to get their marks as close to the Meissen marks as possible, as shall be explained in the chapter "Imitations of Meissen Marks".

Among the most copied items are the children's busts modelled by Kaendler (Plate 23). They appear with some regularity at antique auctions, often signed with some kind of AR-mark (Fig. 376). At auctions in Washington, D.C. in

Fig. 374: Plate with outside decoration on a Meissen plate made before 1924, painting by outside painter after 1980 with his initials on the bottom

Fig. 375: Meissen flower painting on a plate decorated by a paintress trained in Meissen and later working in a porcelain painting shop in Leipzig, GDR, about 1981

Fig. 376: Faked AR-mark on imitations of Kaendler's Children's busts (Plate 239) sold at an auction in Washington, D.C.

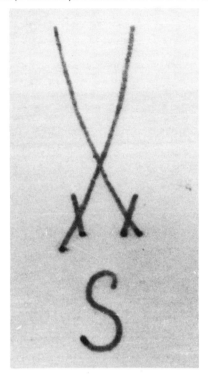

Fig. 377: Mark on group in Plate 240

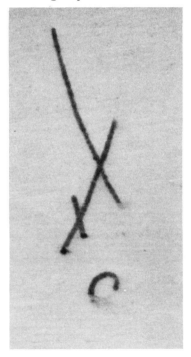

Fig. 378: Mark on group in Plate 240 after removing part of the colorless nail polish covering the bottom

Fig. 379: Mark on bottom of figurine in Plate 241, additional markings have been scratched off, scratches blackened for better identification

1975-1976 no less than three pairs of these children's busts were offered. At one of the auctions in February of 1976, one pair was described as "Pair Antique Augustus Rex Bust Portraits, Young Girls" and they were offered with an estimated price range of $350 to $450. The gavel fell at $350, and if they had been real Augustus Rex period pieces, the auctioneer should have been sued for incompetence, because most serious collectors or museums would have paid twenty or thirty times the amount realized if the busts had been what the auction catalogue promised.

Fakes of Meissen *Crinoline* groups abound, as do animal and especially bird imitations, in which the Samson manufactory in Paris, France, excelled. The already mentioned Thieme factory in Potschappel is suspected to have produced fakes of 18th century Meissen figurines and groups. Since it imitated the marks of Meissen too, there is no way of identifying the maker of these pieces, because other manufactures faked Meissen pieces with Meissen marks too.

Sometimes a faker proceeded quite crudely. The group in Plate 240, by no means showing any similarity to the Meissen style, was sold as Meissen at an auction. On the bottom was the crossed swords mark. But the faker must have crossed the signals. He applied the mark on the bottom and added the letter S. That was one of the marks used by Samson in Paris for his imitations of Meissen porcelain. Closer scrutiny of this curious piece revealed that the bottom, which originally had been unglazed, was covered with a thin film of unknown consistency. Careful treatment with all kinds of chemicals finally gave way to nail polish remover, identifying the cover as colorless nail polish. And at the same time, it became clear why the polish had been applied, because the remover took the mark away too. It probably had been drawn with a modern felt pen (Fig. 377 and 378).

But that was not all. On the back of the base a small golden anchor was hidden within the decoration. This sign was used by the porcelain manufactory in Chelsea, England, from about 1758 until 1769, and it too was a fake. But the faker of the Meissen mark either had overlooked the already faked Chelsea anchor, or he thought that Meissen was more valuable.

Not all fakes are made that stupidly, but since collecting fakes is not a usual hobby, and most people who own fakes either do not know or keep quiet about it, it is not easy to find samples for publication. Excellent copies were made by the factory of the Brothers Voigt and its successor Alfred Voigt in Sitzendorf, Thuringia. They very carefully copied every single detail (Plates 241 and 242). Their mark was an attempt to delude buyers into thinking that it showed the crossed swords of Meissen (Fig. 379). The Voigt factory imitated Meissen models from about 1887 until the early 20th century.

The Thuringian factories were famous for their Meissen copies, and they picked those models that sold best. Among

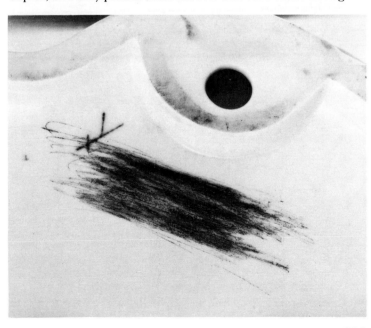

them was the Monkey Band (Plate 24), which was imitated by a number of small factories. Even today some of them are still producing the Monkey Band, but now with a mark that clearly identifies the pieces as not being made in Meissen (Plates 243 to 245).

There are a few hints for the indentification of fakes. Meissen porcelain always has a bluish white hue to it, most other porcelains look white or slightly creme-colored. Some fakes were copied by taking a plaster mould from an original Meissen piece and using it for the pull of the fake. These pulls are always smaller than the original. A porcelain piece shrinks about 16 percent in all directions in drying and firing, so figurines and groups made from moulds taken from originals are smaller than the originals. Good libraries and museums can help in finding out the size of the originals. Many books dealing with special areas in the porcelain field, catalogues, and museum files contain details about size, width, and depth of figurines and groups with which suspicious pieces can be compared.

But even the trained eye of a layman can detect a pull from such a mould. When the original piece is modelled, all details, sharp edges, creases and even noses have to be slightly exaggerated. Shrinking will diminish the exaggerations, and glazing will soften the contours to their intended appearance. A piece made from a mould taken from a glazed original will not show clearly small details. Sharp edges will be rounded and a copy of this kind appears rather faded in the intricate parts.

Another physical test is weight. Meissen porcelain is denser than that of other manufactories and factories, and therefore heavier. Fakers know that and at a time when it still paid to make spurious copies of Meissen plastic art they took more paste for their imitations to give them more weight. That is not without risks because the more solid a piece is, the greater is the danger of cracks and fissures. To avoid this, figurines and groups usually are hollow. But they need a little hole to let the air escape at the high temperatures in the kilns. If the vent holes could not be made in the bottom, they were cleverly hidden in Meissen pieces, and were almost imperceptible. Copyists and fakers were less careful, they often put the holes on clearly visible spots if it was more convenient.

Eighteenth century figurines with blue eyes are extremely rare, they usually got brown eyes. So if a figurine or group reputed to be of the 18th century provenience looks at the prospective buyer with blue eyes he should take another look.

Garnishing is another clue. In the 18th century fleshparts were only sparsely highlighted by painting (Plate 246), and hair was indicated with thin lines over the base color clearly separated from each other (Plate 247). In the 19th century, fleshparts were painted all over and the lines in the hair disappeared. A fake copied from a 19th century pull of an 18th century model, for instance, probably will be garnished and painted in the 19th century style and thus give itself away as not being an original.

A completely different matter are the "reproductions" or "recreations" of old Meissen models by other companies. The Nelson Rockefeller Collection in New York, N.Y. offers a number of those pieces. By limiting the edition of some of the figurines, the Rockefeller Collection asks prices for them that have no relation to the value. A 1980-1981 catalogue of the Nelson Rockefeller Collection offered a pair of "Meissen Cocatoos - Originally designed by Johann Kaendler and executed in Meissen in the 18th century...recreated in today's finest porcelain" in a limited edition of 200 pairs at $1,200 a pair. A "Meissen Bittern" in a limited edition of 150 could be had for $1,500 plus $7.00 shipping and handling charges.[20]

The five-piece place setting of the recreated Meissen Swan Service was $625, and for anyone who knows the originals this recreation only can create a shudder. The porcelain manufactory in Vista Allegre in Portugal, which made these recreations for the Rockefeller Collection is producing good porcelain, but its products are still not of Meissen quality. The porcelain paste is quite different from that of Meissen,

and the plastic decoration is rather a bit wish-washy compared with that of Meissen. And why should a serious connoisseur of Meissen porcelain buy a coffee pot from the "recreated" Swan Service for $775 if he can have the real thing for about one fourth less?

The legal implications are somewhat unclear. These "recreations" are not fakes, because on them it is clearly indicated that they were not made by the Meissen manufactory. There is no copyright protecting old Meissen forms and models. So the "recreations" can be made with legal impunity. With the moral question it is different, but this is not the place to discuss morals in business.

The Smithsonian Institution in Washington, D.C. is also in the reproduction business, but it restricts itself to copies of pieces in its own collection, and the prices are more reasonable. A reproduction of a 18th century vase with Indian Flower Painting in the Hans Syz Collection of the Smithsonian Institution in 1980 was available for $100. It was made by Lenox in the U.S.A., and at that price it cannot have been handmade and handpainted, as the original is. Doubts seem justified about the Smithsonian's advertising claim that this piece will be "amid a collector's most prized porcelains".

For people with limited means, the Metropolitan Museum of Art in New York, N.Y. offers smaller pieces, for instance cups and saucers after old Meissen models (Plates 248 and 249 and Fig. 380). They are clearly identified for someone who knows a little bit about porcelain as having been made by the Haviland factory in Limoges, France. Some of them are even identified as reproductions (Figs. 381 to 383).

Fig. 380: Reproduction of 18th century Meissen cup and saucer made for the Metropolitan Museum of Art in New York, N.Y.

Fig. 381: Mark on cup in Fig. 380

Fig. 382: Mark on cup in Plate 248

As long as the Meissen manufactory is able and willing to produce all these pieces from its own genuine moulds and in its time-honored way of handmaking, the justification for these reproductions or "recreations" seems to be lacking. The manufactory today can make more than 200,000 articles which it made in the past, the same way they were made when they were designed, among them are all of the pieces now being reproduced or "recreated". The manufactory's pieces would be genuine Meissen porcelain with its unique and inimitable paste, its careful handcraftsmanship, and its unmatched colors and handpainting.

But all attempts by others to make capital out of the fame of Meissen also suggests another thought. Since 1710 Meissen products have been considered worth of faking, imitating, reproducing, and recreating. That says something about the high esteem in which Meissen porcelain is held, about its value, and its desirability then, and evidently today.

Fig. 383: Mark on saucer in Plate 248

Fig. 384: Early Meissen Onion Pattern with all fruit stems pointing outward, about 1740

Fig. 385: Plate with Onion Pattern, Royal Porcelain Manufactory Berlin, shortly before 1800

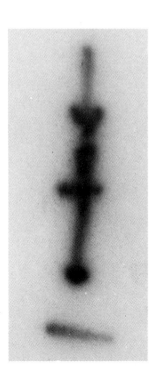

Fig. 386: Mark on plate in Fig. 385

Chapter Nine

Onion Pattern

The best known, most widely distributed and most copied porcelain decoration created in Meissen is without doubt the *Onion Pattern*. More than sixty European and Oriental factories used this very popular decoration, calling it a number of fancy names from *Ming Tree* over *Vienna Woods* to *Blue Nordic*. But *Onion Pattern* is *Onion Pattern* by any other name, even though it has nothing to do with onions at all.

White and blue porcelain from the Orient was very much in demand in Europe at the turn of the 18th century. After Dutch, English and French East India Companies had established a flourishing trade with China under the in 1644 newly installed Manchu (or Tsing) Dynasty, the Chinese quickly adapted to the European craze for white and blue porcelain. This kind of porcelain had already been produced in the earlier Ming Period, but in the 17th century the Chinese improved it, occasionally to an almost lifeless perfection. They sold it in great numbers to traders, and it became fashionable among rich Europeans, commanding high prices.

Augustus the Strong demanded from his new porcelain manufactory large plates, bowls, dinner services and vases with blue underglaze decoration. (Chapter 6 explaines how difficult it was to develop blue painting under the glaze). While the manufactory experimented with blue paint, the Chinese influence in form and decoration remained strong. The model for the *Onion Pattern* probably was a flat bowl from the Chinese K'ang Hsi Period (1662-1722), which is now at the Dresden Porcelain Collection (Plate 250). The earliest samples of the later Meissen *Onion Pattern* are dated about 1728. They show that the Meissen painters followed the original closely. But the Meissen versions nevertheless were alienated copies of a Chinese model that was not really understood by the painters, so they converted it into something they were more familiar with (Plates 251 and 252).

The *Onion Pattern* as it is known and used today basically was created in 1739 after Höroldt had perfected the blue paint. In the meantime, it underwent several changes, often to eliminate parts that were more difficult to paint, because the less qualified painters were employed with blue painting.

Occasionally this pattern is called the bulb pattern, and the flower in the center has been described as aster, peony or chrysanthemum. Since no book about Meissen seems to be able to avoid a discussion about the *Onion Pattern*, this one too shall try to put some order into the *Onion Pattern* terminology.

If anything is certain about this pattern, then it is the fact that the fruits or bulbs around the border were definitely not supposed to be onions originally. Scholars agree that the fruits on the copied Chinese originals resemble peaches and pomegranates alternating. Peaches were known in Saxony, so they came out close to their natural appearance. Pomegranates were known at least by name, because they are mentioned in the bible,[1] and they must have been introduced in Europe too, since they can be seen on a number of still lifes by Dutch and Flemish painters of the 17th century. The first versions of the *Onion Pattern* indeed show fruits resembling pomegranates (Fig. 384), but as the years progressed, the fruits were simplified and looked more and more like onions. Thus the name *Onion Pattern* came into being.

The large blossom, which keeps the balance to the bent bamboo cane in the well, often is called an aster. Typical asters have a center disk surrounded by one circle of flat enlongated petals (actually flowers). The blossom in the *Onion Pattern* is more bulbous with several rows of alternating petals. Its original was in all probability the tree or mountain peony, common in China, which is shrubby with

a permanent wooden stem and can grow up to 1.80 meters (6 feet). This would explain the long winding stem and the matching height of bamboo cane and flower.

The tree peony probably was unknown to the Meissen painters. On the other hand, they must have been familiar with chrysanthemums, which - when stylized - have a certain resemblance to peonies. So the flower evolved as a hybrid between tree peony and chrysanthemum. But since the chrysanthemum belongs to the aster family, the happy conclusion can be drawn that all the descriptions of the flower in the *Onion Pattern* could be considered right - more or less.

As mentioned before, the original pattern of 1739 underwent a few changes. At first, all the fruits on the border were pointing inward with the stem on the edge. After a few years this arrangement was changed. The fruits began to point inward and outward alternately. Also, the painting became a bit flat without the slight shadows of earlier years. More and more, the once lively decoration became a repeatable pattern. It is still painted by hand in Meissen, but the painters have not the least tolerance for individual interpretation as they do in other decorations, especially the new ones.

The *Onion Pattern*, as it should continue to be called, very soon became popular and was turned out in large numbers. The manufactory administrators liked it, because it was cheaper to produce than other decorated wares. It could be painted by lower paid "blue painters", even by journeymen and apprentices.[2] Also, it did not need a third firing, which was necessary to fix enamel decorations. The painting was applied after the first light firing on the still-porous piece, which then was covered with glaze liquid and subjected to sharp firing.

The comparably reasonable price for Onion Pattern ware contributed to its popularity, and yet another development made it the favorite of the middle classes. In 1745 Johann Joachim Kaendler designed his form *New Cutout (Neuer Ausschnitt)*, that lent itself perfectly to the *Onion Pattern* and like it has survived all style changes.

As always when there is a sale to be made, others jumped on the bandwagon. Manufactories in France, England, Switzerland, present day Belgium, Denmark, Japan, and naturally in Germany, copied the *Onion Pattern*. At the Smithsonian Institution in Washington, D.C., there are a few plates from the household of President John Quincy Adams.[3] He probably bought them while he lived in Berlin as ambassador to the Prussian Court from 1797 to 1800 (Fig. 385). Among the *Onion Pattern* plates of President Adams, there is one made by the Royal Prussian Manufactory in Berlin, at that time the capital of Prussia. It shows the scepter mark of the manufactory with a short blue line underneath (Fig. 386). This special mark with the short blue line not only indicates that the plate was decorated at the Berlin manufactory, but also that the plate was made late in the 18th century.

The manufactory in Berlin was one of Meissen's important competitors and adopted quite a number of Meissen decorating ideas, among them the *Onion Pattern*. It produced porcelain with this pattern from the 18th to the 20th century (Figs. 387 to 390).

Toward the end of the 18th century underglaze blue decorations seemed to have lost their attraction for the buyers of Meissen porcelain, and the manufactory decreased its prodution considerably. So it is possible that Adams could not find a complete set of Meissen *Onion Pattern* while he lived in Berlin, and had to add some pieces made by the Prussian manufactory.

Only later, "painting in blue which had been almost entirely given up, had to be in 1819 again taken up and

Fig 387: Plate with Onion Pattern, *Royal Porcelain Manufactory Berlin, 1837-1844*

Fig. 389: Plate with Onion Pattern, *Royal Porcelain Manufactory Berlin, second half 19th century*

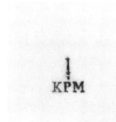

Fig. 388: Mark on plate in Fig. 387

Fig. 390: Mark on Plate in Fig. 389

young people were employed for it".[4] In the second half of the 19th century, when house furnishings became darker and heavier in their appearance, the *Onion Pattern* seemed to complement perfectly the new elaborate furniture style preferred by the wealthy middle class. After 1865, the production of *Onion Pattern* wares increased to new heights[5]. *Onion Pattern* became a craze. Table clothes and napkins, enamelled cooking pots and metal boxes, skirts, shawls, and blouses with *Onion Pattern* appeared in the 1880's, and today again they are produced in large quantities.

Most of the presently available *Onion Pattern* pieces in the antiques market were made in the period after 1865. This pattern was also available with certain decorative improvements. It was offered with a gilt edge, or the fruits and plants were heightened with gold and red contours (Plate 253). With these modifications, it became the *Rich Onion Pattern*.

Demand grew so rapidly that a number of European factories copied the *Onion Pattern* and reproduced it not only on porcelain but also on stoneware. The copy-mania reached such proportions that the Meissen manufactory thought of giving up this pattern altogether or changing it drastically. At the end of the 19th century, Ludwig Sturm, the head of the painting department in Meissen, designed a new *Onion Pattern*. He chose different fruits and flowers and arranged them symmetrically (Plate 254). But as is true with things people have become accustomed to, "new and improved" in this case was not a good sales pitch for the revised *Onion Pattern*. Production of Sturm's design soon was given up. The attempt to replace the *Onion Pattern* by the new Riemerschmid design a few years later also failed, as mentioned

before. *Onion Pattern* also was painted in green and red over the glaze, but these pieces were not produced in series (Plate 255 and 256).

Onion Pattern was not protected by a copyright, so everybody could use it. The Meissen Manufactory thought of a way to protect its *Onion Pattern* products and to make them quickly identifiable as Meissen porcelain. This need became especially urgent after Carl Teichert in Meissen in 1879 began producing porcelain with *Onion Pattern* and applied a mark that contained the name "Meissen".

The Meissen manufactory decided to make it easy for everybody by repeating the crossed swords mark in the *Onion Pattern* decoration itself. The swords were painted inside the lowest part of the bamboo cane (Fig. 391). When this was done for the first time has been a subject of considerable discussion, but the precise date is important because it provides a clue to the age of an *Onion Pattern* piece.

The manufactory does not seem to be sure of the date itself. In some of its publications, the year 1886 is mentioned, in others the year 1893.[6] Which was it? It is with certainty neither year. A publication launched by the manufactory in a trade journal in 1887 does not yet show the swords in the bamboo cane.[7] So it could not have been 1886. A perusal of the manufactory files finally turned up the right date. In 1890, the director of the manufactory wrote to the Saxon State Treasury that "for about two years now" the crossed swords had been paintd within the decoration. That would point to 1888 as the first year and also mean that all Meissen *Onion Pattern* ware without the swords in the bamboo cane was made before 1888.[8]

Fig. 391: Detail of Meissen Onion Pattern, *crossed swords in the lower part of the bamboo cane introduced in 1888*

Fig. 392: Cutting board, A. Heckmann, Annaburg, after 1874

Fig. 393: Mark on cutting board in Fig 392

This means of identification was more than necessary, as the following case shows. In 1894, a merchant from Berlin by the name of S. Kommen established an office in Meissen and started an exaggerated advertising campaign, offering "10,000 excellent genuine Meissen *Onion Pattern* sets" consisting of 45 pieces each for the price of $4.25 per set.[9] That was a steal even in those days and orders poured in. A few days later the customers received letters apologizing for a little mistake. The ads -so the letters said - should have pointed out that the sets were imitations of the genuine *Meissen Onion Pattern.* But since the esteemed customers had shown interest, the prepaid sets would be mailed anyway, the letters continued. Most of the customers kept them because it did not seem worthwhile to them to start arguments with the merchant, and in addition, who wanted to look like a fool for believing that a 45 piece Meissen set could be had for $4.25?

The dinner sets were made from simple, rather coarse earthenware, produced by the factory of A. Heckmann in Annaburg, Saxony (Figs. 392 and 393). Heckmann had not done anything wrong, the *Onion Pattern* was not copyrighted, but the District Attorney in Berlin finally brought in an indictment against the merchant Kommen and his clerk Gerson. He demanded jail sentences of six months for Kommen and two months for Gerson. The attorney for the two accused defended his clients with the argument that nobody in his right mind could expect to buy a genuine Meissen dinner set for a trifle. The promise "genuine Meissen *Onion Pattern*", so he added, only meant that the pattern was a genuine copy of the original. The court agreed with him and found the accused not guilty.

This generous interpretation helped all the other imitators of the *Onion Pattern*, and legalized even exact copies of the pattern of the Meissen manufactory. Two of these copies confuse many collectors. One is called *City of Meissen Onion Pattern (Stadt Meissen Zwiebelmuster)*, the other one *Karlsbad Onion Pattern (Karlsbader Zwiebelmuster)*. Both are actually the same, and they are identical with the original Meissen pattern as it was used after 1865.

In 1863, the potter Carl Teichert founded a factory for tiled stoves at the New Market in Meissen. Tiled stoves, often taller than a man, were very popular for centuries. Heated with soft coal or wood, the thick, heat-absorbing tiles kept a room warm by slowly radiating heat over many hours. But the tiles were not very satisfactory in those years, the glaze cracked easily, they discolored, and often they were not fireproof.

About 1860, Gottfried Heinrich Melzer, by profession a repairer at the Meissen Manufactory, had invented a new kind of tiles which later became famous as "Meissen Tiles". Melzer could not raise the money he needed for the establishment of his own tile factory, so he cooperated with Carl Teichert, whose factory greatly benefitted from Melzer's invention after Melzer died in 1867. Teichert did not survive him for long. He lost his life in the Franco-German War of 1870-1871. One year later the factory became a limited stock company (*Aktiengesellschaft*). At that time, 225 employees produced six thousand tiled stoves per year.

The Company now called *"Meissner Ofen - und Chamottewaaren Fabrik, vorm. C. Teichert"* (Meissen Stove and Fireclay Factory, formerly C. Teichert) not only became known for its tiled stoves, in 1879 it decided to go into porcelain production too. It copied some of the forms and decorations of the Meissen manufactory, but the bulk of the tableware it produced was decorated with the famous *Onion Pattern*, copied to the last detail and handpainted, as it was done at the Meissen Manufactory.

The first porcelain pieces had a slightly greyish tint, they, were speckled with little black spots, and very often they showed little cracks from the sharp fire (Fig. 394). On the bottom the name Meissen was impressed (Fig. 395). The factory quickly improved its porcelain paste and the method of firing, and soon came up with porcelain that at first glance could be taken for a product of its more renowned neighbour (Fig. 396). In 1882 the factory registered a trademark that contained the name "Meissen" which became a source of considerable confusion (Fig. 397).

In 1884, the factory advertised as its specialty "The well-known and popular Meissen *Onion Pattern* in all varia-

Fig. 394: Bowl with Onion Pattern, *C. Teichert, Meissen, about 1880*

Fig. 395: Mark on bowl in Fig 394

Fig. 396: Plate with Onion Pattern, *C. Teichert, Meissen, after 1882*

Fig. 397: Mark on plate in Fig. 396

tions"[10], and in 1885 it changed its name to *"Meissner Ofen-und Porzellanfabrik, vorm. C. Teichert"* (Meissen Stove and Porcelain Factory, formerly C. Teichert). At that time, porcelain production already had become an important part of the company's business.

Carl Teichert had a twin brother, Ernst, born a few minutes later and therefore called his "younger" brother.[11] Ernst also founded a factory in Meissen in 1869, called *Sächsische Ofen- und Chamottewaarenfabrik Meissen-Cölln"* (Saxonian Stove and Fireclay Factory Meissen-Cölln). When it became a limited stock company in 1872, Ernst Teichert left and founded his own *Porzellanfabrik Ernst Teichert* (Porcelain Factory Ernst Teichert) at the *Fabrikstrasse* in Meissen in 1884. He also produced porcelain with *Onion Pattern* (Fig. 398), and adopted a trademark that could be mistaken for the mark of the Meissen Manufactory (Fig. 399) especially if it was applied rather generously and viewed upside down (Fig. 400).

The Meissen Manufactory did not like this mark, and applied for its cancellation in the trademark register. In 1888, it came to an agreement in which the new proprietor of the factory, Christian Teichert, a son of Ernst Teichert, promised not to use this trademark any more. Ernst Teichert had died in 1886. The Royal Manufactory offered to grind out this mark from all porcelain still in stock at the Teichert factory, and the files show that Christian Teichert shipped not less than 38, 148 pieces to the Meissen Manufactory for the removal of the marks.

Then the Porcelain Factory Ernst Teichert registered a new mark in 1888 (Fig. 401) and another one with the added work "Meissen" in 1900 (Fig. 402). They were applied in several variations (Fig. 403). The factory produced porcelain with *Onion Pattern* from 1884 until 1923, when the Meissen Stove and Porcelain Factory, formerly C. Teichert bought all

Fig. 398: Plate with Onion Pattern *by Ernst Teichert, Meissen, 1884-1888*

Fig. 399: Mark on plate in Fig 398

Fig. 400: Variations of the Ernst Teichert mark in Fig. 399

Fig. 401: Mark of Ernst Teichert after 1888

MEISSEN

Fig. 402: Mark of Ernst Teichert after 1900

Fig. 403: Variations of the Ernst Teichert mark in Fig. 401

shares of the Ernst Teichert factory and discontinued porcelain production there.

The flourishing Meissen Stove and Porcelain Factory, formerly C. Teichert also took over in 1925 the Porcelain Factory of Stockhardt & Schmidt-Eckert in Meissen. It had been founded as a pottery and fireclay factory by J.F.W. Kollrepp in 1860, became a limited stock company in 1891, and was bought by Stockhardt & Schmidt-Eckert in 1919. But even then, it still was called *Kollrepp-Werk* (Kollrepp-Work) in Meissen. Beginning in 1926, porcelain production of the Teichert group was concentrated in the Kollrepp-Work. Sales were very good until the world depression in 1930 hit the Teichert group hard.

In 1928 Teichert's porcelain sales had peaked at more than one million marks. In the first half year of 1930, they had fallen to 106,000 marks[12]. In July of 1930 the last porcelain was fired, and then production was discontinued altogether. That was the end of the *City of Meissen Onion Pattern*.

For some unexplained reason the wrong assumption has survived that the Meissen Stove and Porcelain Factory, formerly C. Teichert and the Porcelain Factory Ernst Teichert had been granted a license by the Royal Porcelain Manufactory to reproduce the *Onion Pattern*[13]. One of the reasons for this assumption might be that the *Onion Pattern* of both Teichert factories were identical to that of the Meissen Manufactory. Another one certainly is the fact that the word "license" indeed played a certain role in the *Onion Pattern* business in 1930.

After the Teichert group had given up porcelain production, the Porcelain Factory L. Hutschenreuther in Selb, Bavaria, bought "the models for the *Meissen blue Onion Pattern* dinner-ware with all production rights usual in the trade",[14] and immediately started production (Fig. 404). The pieces were marked with the regular L. Hutschenreuther trademark (Figs. 405 to 408), but were advertised as *Meissen Blue Onion Pattern*.

Fig. 404: Plate with Onion Pattern, *Hutschenreuther AG, Selb, c. 1980*

Fig. 405: Mark on plate in Fig. 404, in use since 1969

Fig. 406: Mark of Porcelain Factory Lorenz Hutschenreuther, 1856-1920

Fig 407: Mark of L. Hutschenreuther, 1887

Fig. 408: Mark of L. Hutschenreuther, 1920-1969

The Meissen Manufactory intervened and demanded that the L. Hutschenreuther factory cease making porcelain with *Onion Pattern*. It based its request on an agreement of the German porcelain factories, which said that nobody was permitted to copy a pattern or a decoration of another producer unless he had copied it before October 1st, 1919.[15] Decorations "belonging to porcelain history" were free for all even if they had not been copied before 1919. The term "porcelain history" was not explained, but later it turned out that mainly Meissen decorations of the 18th century were meant.

The L. Hutschenreuther factory was able to prove that it had produced pieces with *Onion Pattern* in 1874-75, using the method of printing the pattern on porcelain. Though porcelain with *Onion Pattern* since then never had been part of the regular L. Hutschenreuther production, the factory was able to comply with the agreement of the German porcelain factories. From then on it also carefully avoided any mention of the fact that it had bought the rights to the *Onion Pattern*. The company only declared that it had bought forms and models from the Meissen Stove and Porcelain Factory.

But the L. Hutschenreuther factory made one concession. It promised not to sell its *Onion Pattern* as *Meissen Blue Onion Pattern*, but only as *Hutschenreuther Blue Onion Pattern*.[16] For many years, this porcelain was just one of the many patterns offered. But after nostalgia became part of life, the demand for *Onion Pattern* grew considerably, and for the Hutschenreuther factory, porcelain with the *Onion Pattern* became an important part of business after 1955.[17]

The *Hutschenreuther Onion Pattern* is printed, not painted by hand, because the cost of handpainting would be prohibitive for a factory that produces porcelain for everyday use. Nevertheless, Hutschenreuther's advertising still draws upon the long history of *Onion Pattern*, intimating that the pattern is a part of Hutschenreuther history: "*Hutschenreuther Blue Onion. A legend in porcelain. Traditional fine china retains eternal worth. The perfect example: Blue Onion* by Hutschenreuther. This cobalt blue decoration, originating in the middle of the 18th century, has lost nothing of its mystique over the years and merges artistically the fruit floral motives of ancient Asia".[18]

But the history of the *City of Meissen Onion Pattern* is still not complete. The Meissen Stove and Porcelain Factory, formerly C. Teichert in 1885 acquired the porcelain factory of Tschinkel in Eichwald, Bohemia, about 80 km (50 miles) from Karlsbad. Bohemia at that time was part of Austria, which had imposed high tariffs on the import of porcelain. By producing in Austria, the *Meissen Stove and Porcelain Factory* tried to avoid the customs duties. For its branch in Eichwald, the factory in 1886 registered the same trademark in Austria that it already had registered in Germany four years earlier (Fig. 397).

But business was not as good as had been expected. The Austrian ceramic industry was strong and influential and had no love for the German competitor. Nasty rumours were spread about the bad financial situation of the factory in Eichwald. Its German stockholders became nervous, and in 1899 the factory was sold to B. Bloch, who had operated a porcelain and stoneware factory in Eichwald since 1871.

One of the conditions of the sale must have been the continuing use of the "Meissen" trademark (Fig. 397) by B. Bloch, despite the fact that all legal connections between the two factories had been severed. The *Meissen Stove and Porcelain Factory* had the registration of this mark renewed in Germany and Austria in 1896. When the ten-year protection period expired in 1906, B. Bloch registered the same mark in his name in Austria and his company renewed it every ten years.

The *Meissen Stove and Porcelain Factory* tolerated Bloch's use of the mark and kept the same mark registered in Germany. The *Onion Pattern* of Eichwald was identical to that of the *Meissen Stove and Porcelain Factory*, which was a copy of the Royal Manufactory's pattern. (Fig. 409) It also was called *Karlsbad Onion Pattern*, but it basically was the same as *City of Meissen Onion Pattern*.

Fig. 409: Plate with Onion Pattern, *B. Bloch, Eichwald, Bohemia, after 1899*

For the period before 1900, it is not easy to distinguish whether porcelain with *Onion Pattern* and the same mark was made in the city of Meissen or in Eichwald. After 1900, the factory in Meissen added the word MEISSEN to its mark on the bottom. It was colorless impressed before the first firing and then glazed over. The Meissen factory also printed on porcelain for export the words "Made in Germany" in blue under the glaze. That addition makes it possible to state that porcelain with the mark in Fig. 397 and one or both of the additions just mentioned were made by the *Meissen Stove and Porcelain Factory, formerly C. Teichert* between 1900 and 1930.

In 1921, the factory of B. Bloch was converted into a limited liability company *Eichwald Porcelain and Stove Factory Bloch & Co.* At that time, Bohemia had become a part of Czechoslovakia, a new state that had been created in 1918 after World War I, when the Austrian Empire was dissolved. In 1924, the company registered six more marks (Fig.410) in order to prevent the use of any similar looking mark by other factories. In addition, it used several other marks (Figs. 411 to 416), some of them on porcelain with *Onion Pattern*.

In 1930, after the *Meissen Stove and Porcelain Factory* had discontinued porcelain production, the Eichwald factory still sold porcelain with *Onion Pattern* and the mark in Fig. 397 in Germany. Since the Eichwald factory had no connection with Meissen, the Meissen Porcelain Manufactory was able to obtain an injunction forbidding the Eichwald factory the use of this mark[19]. Bloch & Co. accepted this without objection, and promised not to use this mark in Germany any more. A little too late, the Meissen Manufactory realized that the renunciation of the mark only applied to porcelain sold in Germany. For porcelain exported into other countries, the Eichwald factory still used the old mark. On porcelain exported to Germany, the mark in Fig. 417 was applied.

In 1939, Germany had occupied the Czechoslovakian provinces of Bohemia and Moravia and annexed them. The Eichwald factory, partly Jewish property, had to be sold under duress in 1939 and became *Eichwalder Porzellan-, Ofen-und Wandplattenfabriken Dr. Widera & Co.* (Eichwald Porcelain, Stove and Walltile Factories Dr. Widera & Co.). Now it also came under German jurisdiction, and the Meissen Manufactory again sued to have the mark discontinued, this time successfully. In 1942, the Eichwald factory was ordered to cease using a mark with the name "Meissen

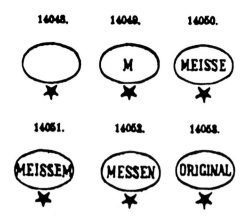

Fig. 410: Marks registered for B. Bloch in 1924

Fig. 411: Mark used by B. Bloch after 1900

Fig. 412: Mark used by B. Bloch after 1900-1920

Fig. 413: Mark used by B. Bloch and Bloch & Co. 1913-1940

Fig. 414: Mark used by B. Bloch 1915-1920

Fig. 415: Mark used by B. Bloch and Bloch and Co. 1918-1940

Fig. 416: Mark used by B. Bloch and Bloch & Co. 1918-1939

Fig. 417: Mark used by Dr. Widera & Co. 1940-1945

Fig. 418: Mark used by Dr. Widera & Co. 1940-1945

Fig. 419 Mark of Duchcovsky Porcelan since 1947

Fig. 420 Mark of Duchcovsky Porcelan since 1947

surrounded by an oval line with a star beneath".[20] After that, the mark in Fig. 417 was used, as was a new one registered in 1940 (Fig. 418).

After World War II the factory was expropriated by the Czechoslovakian Government and with two others combined to the nationally owned enterprise "Duchcovsky Porcelan".[21] Eichwald was renamed Dubi and the branch of Duchcovsky Porcelan located in Dubi continued to produce porcelain with *Onion Pattern*. It immediately reintroduced the old mark (Fig.397). The export organisation of the German Democratic Republic intervened in Czechoslovakia against this mark and the Czechoslovakian export organisation Keramika in Prague promised in 1951 to see that the Dubi branch of Duchcovsky Porcelan did not use the disputed mark any more. Instead the factory in Dubi introduced a new mark (Fig. 419). This mark was unusual, because the Czechoslovakian factory used the German words *"Original Zwiebelmuster"* (Original Onion Pattern).

There is little doubt that the factory speculated on the fame of the Meissen *Onion Pattern*. This mark (Fig 419) always appears with the new trademark of the company Duchcovsky Porcelan (Fig. 420), which resembles the old mark of B. Bloch (Fig. 415) except that the letter E for Eichwald was replaced by the letter D for Dubi.[22]

The now VEB State's Manufactory in Meissen again asked for an official intervention against the mark "Original Zwiebelmuster", and since the German Democratic Republic and Czechoslovakia were friendly states, the Czechoslovakian authorities promised to discontinue the use of this mark. But despite the fact that these negotiations were conducted on a high level, the Czechoslovakian export organisation Keramika ignored all agreements, and continues to sell porcelain with this mark until this day.

In addition to these factories, a large number of other porcelain and stoneware factories in Germany and abroad copied the *Onion Pattern*, so much that not only the Meissen Manufactory but also the *Meissen Stove and Porcelain Factory* felt forced to sue some factories for their misuse of the name Meissen. One of them was the factory of Oscar Schaller in Schwarzenbach in Bavaria, which added the words *"Meissen Zwiebelmuster"* (Meissen Onion Pattern) or *"Dekor Meissen"* (Decoration Meissen) to its regular mark (Figs. 421 and 422) that itself showed a removed kinship to the mark of the Manufactory.

The German Supreme Court in 1926 decided that the expression *"Meissen Zwiebelmuster"* (Meissen Onion Pattern) was in the public domain as a generic name, and its use should be permitted as long as it did not imply that porcelain marked or sold with this term was manufactured in Meissen[23].

At the same time the court decreed that the expression *"Dekor Meissen"* could not be used by factories outside Meissen. The factory of Oscar Schaller's successor then changed its mark and later also its *Onion Pattern* (Fig. 423).

This judgement was the basis on which the Meissen Porcelain Manufactory in 1930 demanded the renunciation of a mark used by the porcelain factory of Bros. Schoenau, Swaine & Co. in Hüttensteinach, Thuringia (Fig. 424 and 425). The factory quickly had adopted this mark after the *Meissen Stove and Porcelain Factory, formerly C. Teichert* had announced it would discontinue porcelain production. Bros. Schoenau, Swaine & Co. already earlier had run into problems with the Meissen Manufactory because of its use of another mark (Fig. 426). After the factory in Hüttensteinach realized the seriousness of the manufactory's intent to protect its rights, it used only its regular trademarks on porcelain with *Onion Pattern* after 1930 (Figs. 427 and 428).

Figs. 429 to 492 show *Onion Patterns* by other factories and their marks. Those porcelain pieces which resemble the original closest are depicted first. They are followed by those that deviate more from the Meissen Manufactory's pattern. Figs. 493 to 526 show *Onion Pattern* on earthen- and stoneware arranged after the same principle and Figs. 527 to 536 are marks observed on pieces with *Onion Pattern* for which photographs were not available.

Fig. 421: Plate with Onion Pattern *by Oscar Schaller in Schwarzenbach, 1892-1926*

Fig. 424: Plate with Onion Pattern, *Bros. Schoenau, Swaine & Co., Hüttensteinach, 1929-1930*

DEKOR Meissen

Fig. 422: Mark on plate in Fig. 421

BAVARIA

Fig. 423: Regular Mark of Oscar Schaller and Oscar Schaller Successor after 1892

Fig. 425: Mark on plate in Fig. 424

Fig. 426: Mark of Bros. Schoenau, 1887-1900

Fig. 427: Plate with Onion Pattern, *Bros. Schoenau, after 1900*

Fig. 431: Plate with Onion Pattern, *Greiner factory in Rauenstein, late 19th century*

Fig. 428: Mark on plate in Fig. 427

Fig. 432: Mark on plate in Fig. 431

Fig. 429: Tureen by Fr. Chr. Greiner in Rauenstein, late 19th century

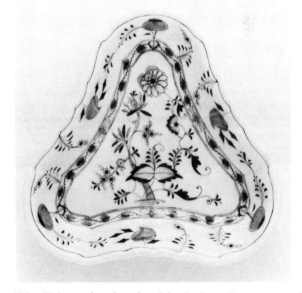

Fig. 433: Triangular bowl with Onion Pattern, *maker unidentified*

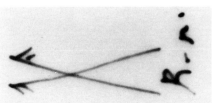

Fig. 430: Mark on tureen in Fig. 429

Fig. 434: Mark on bowl in Fig. 433

241

Fig. 435: Plate with Onion Pattern, *early 20th century, no mark, maker unidentified*

Fig. 438: Cup and saucer, porcelain factory Porsgrund in Norway, 20th century

Fig. 439: Mark on plate in Fig. 438

Fig. 436: Plate with Onion Pattern, *Hermann Ohme, Niedersalzbrunn, 1882-c. 1930*

Fig. 437: Mark on plate in Fig. 436

Fig. 440: Plate with Onion Pattern *made c. 1980 in Nova Role, Czechoslovakia*

Fig. 441: Mark on plate in Fig. 440

Fig. 442: Plate with **Onion Pattern**, *F.A. Reinicke, Eisenach, 19th century*

Fig. 446: Mustard pot with **Onion Pattern**, *made in Japan for Lipper International and Blue Danube Inc. New York, N.Y. after 1950*

Fig. 443: Mark on plate in Fig. 442

Fig. 447: Mark on pot in Fig. 446

Fig. 444: Charger with **Onion Pattern**, *Mimosa, Japan, c. 1978*

Fig. 445: Mark on charger in Fig. 444

Fig. 448: Solitaire with **Onion Pattern**, *made in Japan for Lipper International and Blue Danube Inc. New York, N.Y. after 1964*

Fig. 449: Mark on Solitaire in Fig. 448

Fig. 450: Quatrefoil bowl with Onion Pattern, *maker unidentified, late 19th, early 20th centuries*

Fig. 451: Mark on bowl in Fig. 450

Fig. 454: Small plate with Onion Pattern, *Japan, after 1920*

Fig. 455: Mark on plate in Fig. 454

Fig 452: Cache-pot with Onion Pattern, J. Kronester, Schwarzenbach, Bavaria, about 1980

Fig. 453: Mark on cache-pot in Fig. 452

Fig. 456: Cup and saucer with Onion Pattern, *made in Japan for Seymour Mann, New York, N.Y. c. 1964-1978*

Fig. 457: Mark on cup in Fig. 456

Fig. 458: *Twelvecornered plate with handle on top*, Onion Pattern, *maker unidentified, early 20th century*

Fig. 459: Mark on plate in Fig. 458

Fig. 460: *Tea jar with* Onion Pattern, *German, after 1970*

Fig. 461: Mark on tea jar in Fig. 460

Fig. 462: *Mustard pot with* Onion Pattern, *Gerold & Co. Tettau, Bavaria, after 1948*

Fig. 463: Mark on pot in Fig. 462

Fig. 464: *Cutting board with* Onion Pattern, *Gerold & Co. Tettau, Bavaria, c. 1980, impressed number 1379*

Fig. 465: *Small footed cup with* Onion Pattern, *Gerold & Co. Tettau, Bavaria, c. 1980*

Fig. 466: *Mark on cup in Fig. 465*

Fig. 467: *Moustache cup with* Onion Pattern, *maker unidentified, possibly Japan, c. 1975*

Fig. 468: *Mark on moustache cup in Fig. 467*

Fig. 469: *Plate with* Onion Pattern, *E. & A. Müller, Schönwald, Bavaria, 1904-c. 1930*

M. P. M.

Fig. 470: *Mark on plate in Fig. 469*

Fig. 471: *Bottle opener with* Onion Pattern, *handle by VEB Porcelain Combine Kahla, GDR, c. 1980, no mark*

Fig. 472: *Cup and saucer with* Onion Pattern *by Henneberg Porcelain, Ilmenau, GDR, after 1973*

Fig 473: Mark on saucer in Fig. 472

Fig. 476: Plate with Onion Pattern, F.A. Reinicke, Eisenberg, 1927-1960 and mark on plate

Fig 474: Cup and saucer with Onion Pattern, China, about 1980

Fig. 475: Mark on cup in Fig 474

Fig. 477: Plate with Onion Pattern, Henneberg Porcelain, Ilmenau, GDR, c. 1949-1973

Fig. 478: Mark on plate in Fig. 477

Fig. 481: Plate with Onion Pattern, VEB Porcelain Combine Kahla, GDR, c. 1980

Fig. 482: Mark on plate in Fig 481

Fig. 479: Plate with Onion Pattern, Seltmann in Weiden, Bavaria, after 1954

Fig. 483: Plate with Onion Pattern, VEB Porcelain Combine Kahla, GDR, after 1957

Fig. 480: Mark on plate in Fig 479

Fig. 484: Mark on plate in Fig. 483

Fig. 485: Plate with Onion Pattern, VEB Porcelain Combine Kahla, GDR, after 1957

Fig. 489: Plate with decoration inspired by Onion Pattern, Rosenthal, Selb, Bavaria, c. 1980

Fig. 486: Mark on plate in Fig. 485

Fig. 490: Mark on plate in Fig. 489

Fig. 487: Plate with Onion Pattern, Nikko, Japan, c. 1980

Fig. 491: Vase with Onion Pattern blue overglaze, Co-Operative Meissen Porcelain Painting, c. 1980

Fig. 488: Mark on plate in Fig. 487

Fig. 492: Mark on vase in Fig. 491

249

Fig. 493: Charger with Onion Pattern, Burslem, England, after 1910, earthenware

Fig. 494: Mark on charger in Fig. 493

Fig. 497: Plate with Onion Pattern, Villeroy & Boch, Dresden, after 1874, earthenware

Fig. 498: Mark on plate in Fig. 497

Fig. 495: Plate with Onion Pattern, Bates, Walker & Co. Burslem, England, 1875-1883, earthenware

Fig. 496: Mark on plate in Fig. 495

Fig. 499: Plate with Onion Pattern, Villeroy & Boch, Dresden, after 1874, earthenware

Fig. 500: Mark on plate in Fig. 499

250

Fig. 501: Plate with Onion Pattern, Brown-Westhead, Moore & Co. Hanley, England, 1862-1904, earthenware

Fig. 505: Plate with Onion Pattern, J. Uffrecht, Haldensleben, 1894-1924, earthenware

Fig. 502: Mark on plate in Fig. 501

Fig. 506: Mark on plate in Fig. 505

Fig. 503: Plate with Onion Pattern, Johnson Bros. Hanley, England, after 1885, earthenware

Fig. 507: Plate with Onion Pattern, maker unidentified, earthenware

Fig. 504: Mark on plate in Fig. 503

Fig. 508: Mark on plate in Fig. 507

251

Fig. 509: Plate with Onion Pattern, *maker unidentified, no mark, earthenware*

Fig. 511: Plate with Onion Pattern, *maker unidentified, no mark, earthenware*

Fig. 510: Plate with Onion Pattern, *maker unidentified, no mark, earthenware*

Fig. 512: Plate with Onion Pattern, *Keller & Guerin, Luneville, France, c. 1900, earthenware*

Fig. 513: Mark on plate in Fig. 512

Fig. 514: Plate with **Onion Pattern,** *maker unidentified, no mark, earthenware*

Fig. 517: Plate with **Onion Pattern,** *maker unidentified, no mark, earthenware*

Fig. 515: Plate with **Onion Pattern,** *maker unidentified, earthenware, possibly Japan*

Fig. 518: Cutting board, Wittenburger Steingutfabrik, Germany, c. 1900, earthenware

Fig. 516: Mark on plate in Fig. 515

Fig. 519: Mark on board in Fig. 518

Fig. 520: Plate with Onion Pattern, Johnson Bros. Hanley, England, c. 1980, earthenware

Fig. 523: Rice jar, Porcelain Factory Kolmar, Germany, c. 1882-1900, earthenware

BLUE NORDIC
HAND ENGRAVING
DISHWASHER PROOF
JOHNSON BROTHERS
Made in England
IRONSTONE

Fig. 521: Mark on plate in Fig. 520

Fig. 524: Mark on jar in Fig. 523

Fig. 522: Square bowl, maker unidentified, no mark, earthenware

Fig. 525: Gravy boat with Onion Pattern, maker unidentified, earthenware

Fig. 526: Mark on gravy boat in Fig. 525

254

Fig. 527: Philip Aigner, Vienna, Austria, c. 1900

Fig. 528: Hermann Ohme, Niedersalzbrunn, Germany, c. 1905

Fig. 529: Oscar Schaller Successor, Kirchenlamitz, Bavaria, after 1950

Fig. 530: Count Thun's Porcelain Factory, Klösterle, Bohemia, 1895-c. 1945

Fig. 531: Count Thun's Porcelain Factory, Klösterle, Bohemia, after 1900-c. 1945

Fig. 532: Count Thun's Porcelain Factory, Klösterle, Bohemia, 1918-1945

Fig. 533: Count Thun's Porcelain Factory, Klösterle, Bohemia, 1918-1939 and Duchcovsky Porcelan in Duchcov, Czechoslovakia, 1947-

Fig. 534: Earthenware Factory Amberg, Germany, late 19th century, 1910, on earthenware

Fig. 535: Richard Lichtenstern & Co. Wilhelmsburg, Austria, c. 1920-1938

Fig. 536: Bros. Lichtenstern, Wilhelmsburg, Austria, 1890-1910

There is yet another *Onion Pattern* (Fig. 537). About 1740 the Royal Manufactory in Meissen developed another blue underglaze decoration, the *Strawflower Pattern (Strohblumenmuster)*. Other manufactories copied it even more quickly than the *Onion Pattern*. By 1745, manufactories in Ilmenau produced inexpensive tableware with *Strawflower Pattern*, which soon became known in Germany as "Ilmenau Strawflower Pattern" or "Ilmenau Onion Pattern" or "Middle class Onion Pattern" *(bürgerliches Zwiebelmuster)*.

But it was the Royal Danish Porcelain Factory (Kongelige Danske Porcelains Fabrik) in Copenhagen, Denmark, which made this pattern internationally famous. The modeller Anton Carl Luplau, who created some of the best figurines made by the manufactory in Fürstenberg, Germany, in 1776 was enticed to come to Copenhagen, and among the many things he knew about porcelain was the blue underglaze strawflower pattern.

The first Danish pieces with strawflowers can be dated 1776-1777, though in Copenhagen it was called *Mussel Pattern*. The Royal Danish Porcelain Factory elaborated on it and later called it *"Blue Fluted"* for pieces to be exported. In English speaking countries it is known as *"Immortelle Pattern"* (Fig. 538).

The strawfower pattern has been copied by more than fifty factories in Europe. Since the 1920's it was mass produced in Germany, and there is almost no household there without at least one piece of porcelain with *Strawflower* or "Middle Class Onion Pattern" (Fig. 539). Because the patterns vary on porcelain made by different factories, some antiques dealers have invented special names for the variations as Petersilienmuster ((Parsley Pattern) or Knoblauchmuster (Garlic Pattern). That might be imaginative but is nothing but an unfounded invention.

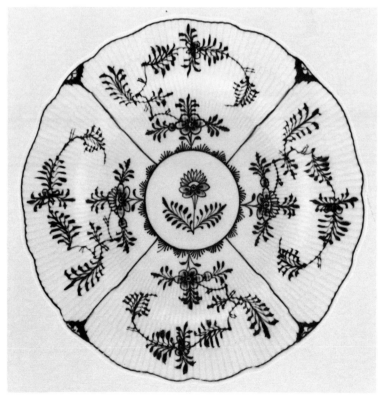

Fig. 537: Plate with Strawflower or Immortelle Pattern, Meissen, 19th century

Fig. 538: Contemporary plate with Strawflower *Pattern by the Royal Danish Porcelain Factory in Copenhagen*

Fig. 539: For mass production the Strawflower *Pattern was reduced to a simplified variation that could be printed easily. This contemporary plate was made by VEB Vereinigte Porzellanwerke Eisenberg, GDR*

Chapter Ten
Marks on Meissen Porcelain

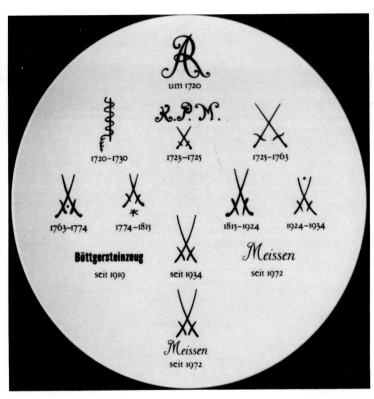

Fig. 540: Modern Meissen plate with marks

On this modern plate (Fig. 540), the Meissen manufactory tries to give a clue to its marks. Everybody - the manufactory included - would be happy if it were possible to identify Meissen porcelain and its age with just twelve marks. But the only useful purpose of this brave attempt is that the plate looks nice hanging on a wall.

For almost 240 years the manufactory had no intelligible and usable marking system that could give information about the year or the period of production the way Sèvres did beginning in 1753. The Meissen Manufactory administrations of the first 64 years had not even contemplated the idea of indicating the production period by the shape of the marks or by additions to them. The marks were the least important subject in the discussions of those years. There were no standards or instructions about the size or the shape of the marks. During the directorship of Count Marcolini, for the first time the marks systematically received additions allowing classification of Meissen porcelain as being made during his thirty-nine year long management. Only in the 1820's did the administration realize that certain marks were considered proof of age, when it was confronted with the request for an earlier mark to be put on newly produced porcelain.

Under these circumstances, most statements about the use of certain marks in certain years are reckless, and have not become more credible because they have been repeated in many books. Supposedly there is a "Long Period", because at one time the swords were very long. Naturally, there also must have been a "Short Period", subsequently a "Dot Period", not withstanding the fact that Meissen had two dot periods. Then there is a "King's Period", which strangely enough, refers to those years when the ruler of Saxony was not a king any more. Famous is the "Star" or "Marcolini Period", and the last one is the "Roman Numeral Period", with which the periodization usually stops for lack of addi-

tions to the marks. The following 160 years are just "Meissen" or frequently "old Meissen".

Most of this is nonsense. No quick and easy classification system can be given. It is necessary to delve deeply into the intricacies of the unorganized Meissen marking habits.

The manufactory itself has difficulties in exactly determining which marks were used when. A plate made about 1918 shows many more marks than the contemporary plate (Fig. 541). Today some of them are no longer considered Meissen marks . In addition the dating of most of the marks on this plate cannot be supported by newer research.

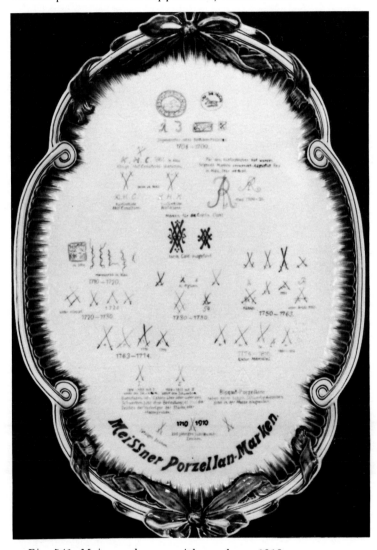

Fig. 541: Meissen charger with marks, c. 1918

Markings and Marks on Red Stoneware

First the markings on red stoneware shall be discussed, since stoneware was the first ceramic product made in Dresden and later in Meissen after the manufactory was established there. Because Oriental porcelain and stoneware were the examples to be recreated, at first Chinese vessels were copied. Chinese-looking teapots from red Meissen Stoneware, formerly in the Dresden Porcelain Collection[1], indicate that moulds were made from the Chinese originals and from these moulds the copies were pulled. These copies are about one sixth smaller than the Chinese tea-pots, which can be considered proof that they were exact copies, because the shrinkage of a piece while drying and being fired is about one sixth of the wet size. Some Chinese marks on early red stoneware could thus be explained, because the plaster moulds taken from the original Chinese vessels also faithfully copied the Chinese marks.

Pseudo-Chinese marks also have been mentioned as signs or marks on red stoneware. In the opinion of an eminent 19th century expert, J.G. Th. Graesse, director of the Royal Porcelain Collection in Dresden, these pieces so perfectly imitated Chinese stoneware, that they could not be distinguished from it. Quite a number of books on porcelain marks repeated this opinion, after it was first published by Graesse in the 19th century in a book which has seen many new editions since then.[2] Graesse's successor, Ernst Zimmermann, in 1908 proved that Graesse had mixed up Chinese and Böttger stoneware.[3] Zimmermann pointed out that the markings on Chinese pieces were erroneously taken for marks on stoneware made in Meissen and corrected this mistake. But even after Zimmermann revised Graesses book in 1915 and omitted these marks, the mistake was not rectified. Several marks books still repeat the attribution of these marks to early red stoneware from the Meissen Manufactory.[4]

In one other case it has been established that Meissen copied vessels produced by foreign makers. The museum in Gotha, Germany, acquired a teapot evidently made in Meissen but bearing the mark of the well-known Dutch potter Ary de Milde (Fig. 542). De Milde, 1634-1708, who called himself a teapot-baker, worked in Delft, Netherlands, and made copies of Chinese pieces from red earthenware, which was rather dense and hard, but not quite stoneware. (Fig. 76) In this case, in Meissen either a plaster mould was taken from a de Milde piece or the piece was copied by hand very meticulously, including the mark of de Milde.

Unexplained are letters and combinations of letters and figures (Fig. 543). They could have been test marks, because Böttger still experimented with different paste combinations and various firing techniques. These signs would have made it possible to identify the results of the experiments. They were incised in the still wet vessels by hand. It is improbable that the letter B, which appears quite often, points to Böttger, as was guessed earlier, because there is no proof that he moulded pieces of red stoneware himself.

Fig. 542: Mark of Ary de Milde

Fig. 543: Signs on early red stoneware

In the early years, moulders and throwers incised or impressed personal signs. They too seem to have been technological markings. A list in the manufactory files (Fig. 544) shows which signs were used in 1711-1712.[5]

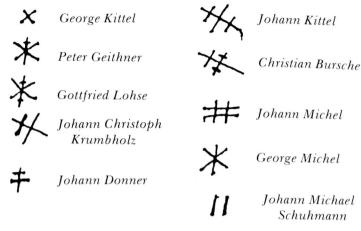

Fig. 544: Signs of throwers and moulders on red stoneware, 1711-1712

George Kittel is listed in the payroll of 1712 as potter and in a file of 1732 as moulder, who also made gypsum plaster forms. Peter Geithner first worked as a potter in Dresden and is mentioned in the manufactory files in 1712 and 1719. Gottfried Lohse in 1708 worked as a potter in Böttger's laboratory, his name appears again in the files of 1712 and 1739. Johann Christoph Krumbholz is listed as a potter in the personnel lists of 1712 and 1719. Johann Donner is characterized as saggar turner in 1712 and 1719. Johann Kittel joined the manufactory about 1710, appears on the payroll of 1712, and was still employed in 1732 as moulder and repairer. Johann Michel and George Michel are mentioned in a personnel list of August 1710. There, their last names are written as "Michael". The other two names, Christian Bursche and Johann Michael Schuhmann have not yet been found in the manufactory archive except in the list shown. They might have been occasional workers, paid by the piece and not regularly employed by the manufactory on a fixed salary as the others. The signs shown above also have been observed within a square or a rectangle (Fig. 545).

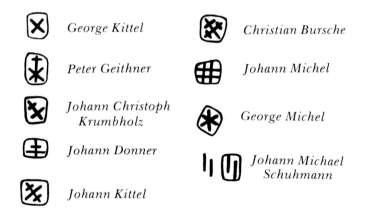

Fig. 545: Signs of throwers and moulders on red stoneware after 1711

A crossed swords mark also has been observed on some pieces of red stoneware (Fig. 546). Since the use of the crossed swords was first recommended in 1722, these pieces were possibly made after that year. The production of red stoneware tapered off in the 1720's and the last pieces were made about 1735. White porcelain had displaced the stoneware in the buyers' favor; and the lack of interest in stoneware was so great that even the recipies for red stoneware were lost in the manufactory.

It was not until 1919 that the red stoneware, now called Böttger stoneware, was reinvented in Meissen as described before. Modern stoneware is marked with the crossed swords either impressed on figurines and groups, or raised in relief on coins or medals (Figs. 547 to 550). Not only standing swords in different sizes can be found, sometimes they are lying and asymmetrical (Fig. 551).

In 1919, the manufactory registered another mark for the red stoneware with the German Patent Office.[6] This mark is impressed into the stoneware and is still in use on certain articles (Fig. 552)

Fig. 546: Crossed swords on red stoneware, probably middle of the 1720s

Figs. 547 to 550: Crossed swords marks on Böttger stoneware after 1919

Fig. 551: Crossed swords on Böttger stoneware medals after 1919

Böttgersteinzeug

Fig. 552: Mark on Böttger stoneware since 1919

Markings and Marks on Porcelain

In the first twelve years of Meissen, red stoneware and porcelain bore no regular manufactory marks. It was not considered necessary to identify the maker, since at least until 1718 there was no competition for Meissen in Europe. And if Meissen products were mistaken for Chinese or Japanese porcelain, it was not to the commercial disadvantage of the manufactory.

The first porcelain pieces, like those made from red stoneware, were influence by Oriental porcelain. It therefore should not be surprising if Chinese-looking marks appeared on those pieces, especially since some of the same plaster moulds were used for red stoneware as well as for porcelain. Quite a number of different Chinese-looking marks on Meissen porcelain have been observed, all of them blue under the glaze (Figs. 553 to 565). They are usually attributed to the very first period of the manufactory. There is one weighty argument against this theory. The blue paint was not usable until 1717 at the earliest and even then it did not always withstand the heat of the kilns. So the Chinese-looking signs blue under the glaze could not have been applied before 1717.

The bulk of pieces with pseudo-Chinese signs was made later, probably after 1720, when blue painting was mastered fairly well. There are indicaions, though, that many of these pieces were produced even much later. In the fourth quarter of the 18th century, the Meissen files register a number of requests for pieces with marks other than the crossed swords marks. They mainly came from Turkish importers of Meissen porcelain.[7] Around 1800, when foreign sales of the manufactory were slow, the administration seem to have been less scrupulous with its mark. Orders from Turkish importers often contained the remark that the pieces were to be signed with Chinese marks, and there is no indication that the manufactory administration denied these requests.

Pseudo-Chinese marks were applied under the directorship of Count Marcolini (1774-1814) and beyond that time. A Turkish cup with a pseudo-Chinese mark in the manufactory collection is decorated with green paint under the glaze. This kind of chromium green for underglaze decoration was developed only in 1817, which means that the cup was not made before that time (Fig. 566). Also, model sketches of Turkish cups (Fig. 567) drawn about 1830 show not only details of new decorations but also a pseudo-Chinese mark on the bottom of one cup.[8] This is more than just circumstantial evidence for the use of these marks even in the first third of the 19th century.

Figs. 553 to 565: Chinese looking marks on Meissen porcelain

Fig. 566: Cup with green underglaze decoration and Chinese looking signs in blue underglaze top right, made after 1817

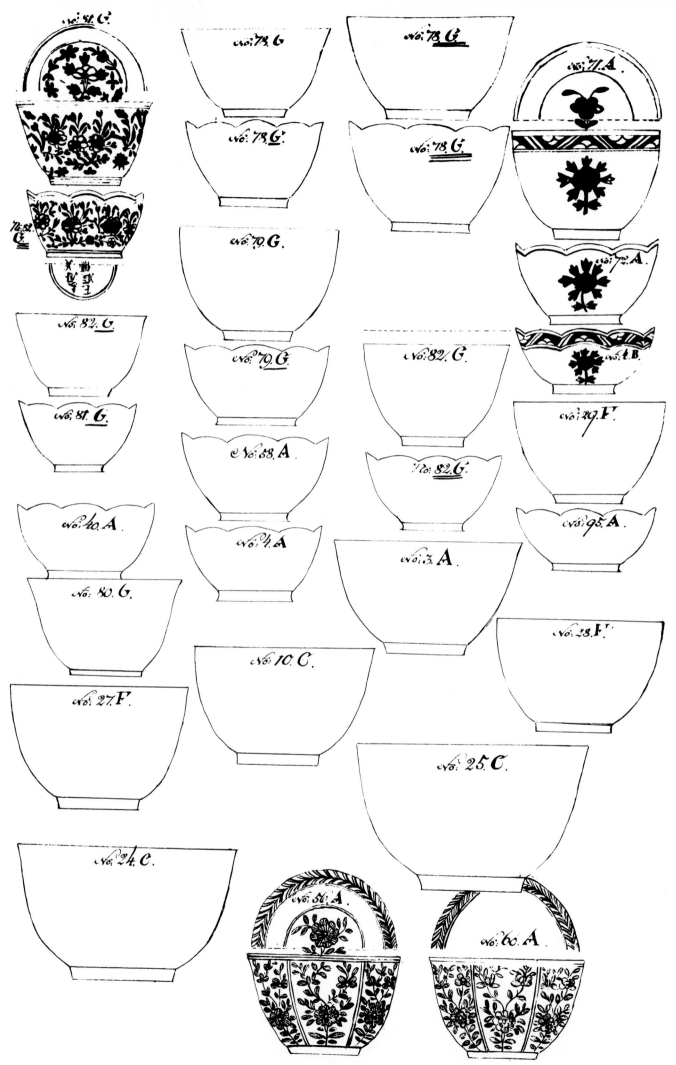

Fig. 567: Page with model sketches of cups, c.1830, bottom of cup on upper left with Chinese looking signs

When in 1718 a porcelain manufactory was established in Vienna, Austria, Meissen and the Royal Court saw no need for a special sign to distinguish the Saxon porcelain from that of Vienna. The foundation of the third European manufactory in Venice, Italy, was no reason either to protect the Meissen products against imitations and copies. This idea was not even contemplated at that time.

When in 1722 the chief painter Höroldt was ordered to sign certain pieces with the letters M.P.M., it was not to identify this porcelain as a Meissen product but rather to show that it was painted in the manufactory itself.

In June of 1722 Höroldt was reminded to mark the tea pots and the sugar bowls of every set with the letters M.P.M.(Fig. 568) They stood for Meissner Porcelaine-Manufactur (Meissen Porcelain Manufactory).[9] A few months later, in October of 1722 a report notes that "the above named painter already has signed a number of tea pots and sugar bowls with M.P.M."[10]

Fig. 568: Mark used in 1722

But less than three weeks after this report, the order was changed. From November of 1722 on the letters K.P.F. for Königliche Porcelaine Fabrique (Royal Porcelain Factory, Figs. 569 and 570) were to be applied.[11] The manufactory inspector Steinbrück opposed this choice of letters. Hinting at David Köhler, one of the arcanists and co-workers of Böttger, he chaffed at the decision, saying that K.P.F. also could be interpreted as "Köhler's Porcelain Factory". He also

Fig. 569: Sugar bowl and cover with Harbour Scenes, Indian Flowers *and landscape, 1722*

Fig. 570: Mark on sugar bowl in Fig. 569, used in 1722

critisized that foreigners would find no meaning in these "German" letters. Steinbrück proposed the use of the crossed swords from the Saxon coat-of-arms instead.[12] He was not listened to at that time.

The letters K.P.F. were shortlived too. A manufactory report of December 1722 shows that they were replaced by K.P.M. for Königliche Porcelaine-Manufactur (Royal Porcelain Manufactory).[13] The report makes clear that not the competion of Vienna and Venice had led to the introduction of manufactory signs. At that time, polychrome decorations already already had been developed in Meissen to high perfection. But outside decorators (Hausmaler) had been procuring white porcelain from the manufactory and painting it at home, selling the decorated pieces as genuine Meissen.

The markings on the tea pots and the sugar bowls were supposed to put an end to this practice. Succedding M.P.M. and K.P.F., the combination K.P.M. was to be used in blue paint under the glaze, something the outside decorators could not copy.

In view of the many outside decorators, the Royal Chamber deemed it necessary to publish this decision and the reason for it in some newspapers. It did so first in Leipzig on April 7th, 1723 [14], when many foreign visitors came to the Easter Fair, and four months later in Prague, which at that time belonged to Austria. The date of the publication of the decision in Leipzig in April of 1723 until now has been considered as the beginning of the K.P.M. period. But actually, the order was issued already in December of 1722 as described here.

The lines of command were very short in those days, and it seems reasonable to assume that the instructions by the manufactory commission were carried out by the painters with all deliberate speed. But there still was a problem. The mark had to be affixed on the unglazed pieces before glazing and high temperature firing. At this stage in the manufacturing process, it was uncertain whether a white piece marked with K.P.M. actually would be painted or not. The manufactory always produced more white ware than the painters could decorate. So it is not totally impossible that even white pieces marked K.P.M. might have been sold or smuggled out of the manufactory, and decorated by outside painters. There is no proof for this suspicion, but neither has proof been found in the archives yet that surplus white ware with the sign K.P.M. was destroyed because it could not be painted within the manufactory.

Lacking definite answers about the time periods in which the different letter combinations were applied, it is only possible to attempt to construct some kind of sequence with the help of the manufactory files.

In June of 1722 chief painter Höroldt was reminded to paint the letters M.P.M. on certain pieces. That means that he had been ordered to do so some time earlier, but evidently had not carried out the order. After Höroldt had been admonished, he reported in October of 1722 that he indeed now had put the letters on a number of tea pots and sugar bowls.

In November of 1722, the combination M.P.M. was replaced by the letters K.P.F. That allows the hypothesis that the sign M.P.M. was applied between June of 1722 and November of 1722.

The letters K.P.F. were in use only in November and December of 1722, when they were replaced by K.P.M. This periodization does not mean that pieces with M.P.M. and K.P.F. necessarily were decorated during these months. They could have been stored in the stockroom. So these pieces could have been painted months or even years later.

Fig. 571: Mark used for painted articles after December 1722

Fig. 572: K.P.M. mark with crossed swords

The same applies to porcelain with the letters K.P.M. They were introduced in December of 1722, but it is not possible to say how long they were employed. There are quite a few pieces showing the crossed swords in addition to the letters K.P.M. (Fig. 572), and this combination is found also on items other than tea pots and sugar bowls. So it is possible that K.P.M. was used as a painting sign even after the crossed swords became the obligatory mark for the products of the Meissen manufactory later in the 1720's. A clockcase at the Ermitage museum in Leningrad, Soviet Union, shows the letters K.P.M. with the crossed swords and an inscription in gold paint overglaze. It is dated 17 May 1727, the day Tsar Peter II ascended to the throne, and the clockcase was probably a present for him. Unfortunately, this inscription is not proof that the letters K.P.M. with the crossed swords were used in 1727, because the clockcase could have been made some years earlier, while the inscription was added later.

When it became possible in Germany to register trademarks, the manufactory in May of 1875 applied for the protection of nine marks, among them the letters K.P.M. with the crossed swords underneath.[15] In its application, the manufactory stated that this combination was used from 1720 to 1730. The same mark was registered in the United States in 1895.[16] In its affidavit to the application the manufactory declared: "The trade mark has been continuously used by the said manufactory since 1720". This statement should not be taken at face value. U.S. and German trademark laws required that a mark for which registration was sought had to be actually used. In order to protect this mark, the manufactory has produced porcelain with the letters K.P.M. and crossed swords from time to time since 1875. It is not known how often such pieces have been made, or how many. But today, the manufactory adds the year of actual production to the old mark in order to avoid confusion.

Kite and "Caduceus"

Other early markings on Meissen porcelain, the kite and the "caduceus" are shrouded in mystery. The kite sign (Figs. 573 to 576) seems to have been influenced by Chinese symbols. Kites indeed play an important part in East and Southeast Asian culture, but an Oriental porcelain piece from which the kite sign could have been copied still has not been found. This mark appears blue under the glaze, which means that it could not have been applied before 1717. But that is all that can be said definitely about the kite mark.

While the fate of the "caduceus" is a bit clearer, its origin is murkier. In some of the kite signs, the tail is wrapped around itself (Fig. 578) and this led to the not unreasonable suggestion that the "caduceus" (or whip, staff, snake mark) was just the kite's tail without the kite.[17] It certainly was easier and quicker to paint, and at that time the markings were not drawn very painstakingly.

  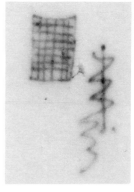

Figs. 573 to 576: Kite marks

This interpretation was too plain for some experts. They set out to find some complicated and more important sounding secret. But meanwhile, they all agreed that the usual name for this sign, namely "caduceus" or Mercury's staff, was wrong. Mercury was the busiest god in Greek mythology, and among his chores was the protection of trade. Besides his winged hat and winged shoes, he carried a winged staff encircled by two snakes. Since the Meissen sign shows only one snake or rather, one circling line, it cannot be a rendition of the caduceus, especially because in those days people still knew their Greek mythology (Fig. 577).

Fig. 577: Mercury with caduceus by Kaendler c. 1774

Getting that out of the way, another interpretation has to be dealt with. Böttger was an apothecary, and the symbol for the medical profession is the staff of Asclepios. This Greek god usually was depicted in European pictorial art as a bearded man leaning on a staff around which a holy snake was coiled. Some authors offer the explanation that the Meissen sign was supposed to represent Asclepios' staff, hinting that the inventor of Meissen porcelain originally had been a member of the healing profession.[18]

Allusions of that kind were quite popular in days past, but in this case they are not likely. Many versions of the mark do not show a snake around the staff at all. The alleged staff and the alleged snake are one uninterrupted line, rather looking like a whip, or - again - like the tail of a kite (Figs. 578 and 579). Later, a straight line and a separate crisscrossing curved line was painted, presumably because it was even easier to apply than one continous line (Figs. 580 to 582).

About the year this mark was used first, many guesses have been offered.[19] The manufactory gave in its German trademark application of 1875 the years 1712 to 1719 as the period for this sign.[15] The years 1712 is also mentioned as first year of use in the U.S. trademark registration.[20] This seems a bit early because, as mentioned before, the earliest time of blue painting under the glaze was 1717.

Figs. 578 and 579: Kite's tail marks

Figs. 580 to 582: Kite's tail marks

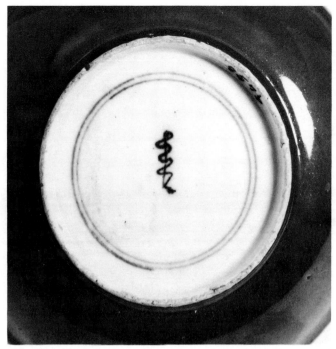

Fig. 584: Kite's tail mark on saucer in Fig. 309

An inventory list of the Royal Porcelain Collection of 1721, with supplements continued until 1727, shows for February of 1722 the arrival of "One half dozen round cups, brown on the outside and on the inside painted blue and white 1 1/2 inches high and 8 in. in diam."[21] These cups, which because of their 8 in. diameter should rather be called flat bowls, were registered under the number N=68=W (Fig. 308). The bowl shown bears the kite's tail in blue paint underglaze, and because the time of production must have been before February of 1722, the bowl proves that this mark was in use before that date (Fig. 583). Since the first successful experiments with blue paint were made in 1717, this year is the earliest possible for the kite's tail mark, which has never been observed other than in blue paint under the glaze. There are samples with a greyish or blackish kite's tail mark, but in these cases the blue paint just did not withstand firing. Blue painting had not been developed to a satisfactory degree of reliability until 1720. The perfect paint on the bowl allows the assumption that it was made between 1720 and February 1722, and this period also could be taken as the probable beginning of the kite's tail mark (Fig. 584).

The Meissen files show that the Turkish importer Manassas Athenas in 1730 refused to accept Meissen porcelain with the crossed swords mark because in the Muslim world they were mistaken for the Christian cross. [22] In 1731 the King permitted the manufactory the application of a different mark on "Turkish articles", the kite's tail. The files give the impression that this sign already had been used erlier to accomodate the Turkish importer.

In 1731 the manufactory commission asked the court which marks should be appied on porcelain
A) for the King himself
B) sold to France
C) sold to other merchants
D) shipped to Turkey[23]

With his answer the King sent back a drawing of the four marks he permitted to be used.[24] If the letters on the drawing (Fig. 585) were supposed to match those in the inquiry, which seems certain, then the kite's tail sign could be painted on wares sold to merchants outside France and in Turkey. But the sign used in the Turkish trade had a little addition, a small dot to the right of the lower end of the staff.

It is remarkable though, that there is a number of matching pieces of which one bears the kite's tail and the matching piece is marked with the crossed swords.[25] This also supports the opinion that the crossed swords and the kite's tail were used simultaneously for a time.

Fig. 583: Kite's tail mark on bowl in Fig. 308, incised inventory mark N=68=W of the Royal Collection in Dresden (P.E. 2192 is the present inventory sign). This particular mark was applied 1720-1722

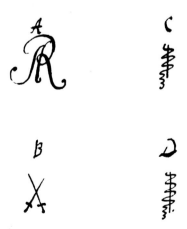

Fig. 585: Drawings accompanying an order by August II about marks to be used, 1731

Fig. 586: Tankard with AR-sign of August II in relief, Böttger porcelain, 1713-1720

AR mark

The Royal order of 1731 (Fig. 585) shows in first place the intertwined letters A and R. They stood for Augustus Rex, the Latin version for King August. Porcelain with this mark was only to be made for the court. That does not mean that it only was used at the court. August II was very generous with the products from his manufactory, and he often lavished porcelain with his AR mark upon his favorites or upon other rulers.

The intertwined letters AR were not especially designed for Meissen porcelain. They appeared long before on milestones, or iron gates or in ornaments, and the King used them to sign documents with his initials. When Böttger invented his red stoneware, the letters were commonly known as the King's symbol. So it was logical to put them on pieces made for the ruler. At first AR was not applied on the bottom, the letters were rather part of the decoration (Fig. 586).[26] As a proprietor's mark, the blue under the glaze AR mark could have been affixed after 1717, when the blue paint became usable. Pieces with this mark in various collections[27] show the early Höroldt painting style. That could indicate the use of the AR mark beginning in 1720 at the earliest (Figs. 587 and 588).

Fig. 587: Hexagonal vase of baluster shape with polychrome chinoiseries, c. 1730-1735

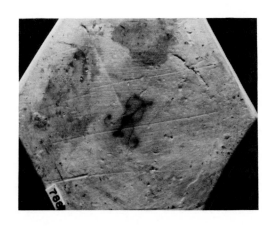

Fig. 588: AR-mark on vase in Fig. 587

It is quite difficult to find a similarly precise date for the termination of this mark. Here the experts differ widely.[28] That the AR mark was still in use in 1731 has been established before. And now history has to be consulted. August II died on February 1, 1733. His son Friedrich August II, did not automatically become King of Poland. The Polish *Sejm* (Diet) first elected Stanislav Lesczynski as the new king, but under Russian and Saxon pressure rescinded the election and chose Friedrich August II of Saxony instead. He ascended to the throne in October of 1733 as August III.

In those days, the rules about titles were very strict. As long as Friedrich August was not yet King, he could not use the AR symbol. On April 28, 1733 the manufactory commission inquired "which mark Your Royal Highness wants to be affixed on porcelain for himself?" Friedrich August II seems to have taken his time with an answer. One year later, in April of 1734 the chancellery of the new King ordered not to use the AR mark for anyone but the King.[29] But which proprietor's mark was used between February and October of 1733? In all probability, the intertwined letters F and A for Friedrich August (Fig. 589). This is the only early Meissen mark that can be dated with sufficient precision as having been used only in 1733, and probably until April of 1734.

The chancellery order of April 1734 strangely enough speaks of an incised AR mark on pieces with Oriental *(Alt-Indischer)* decoration. Incised AR marks have not been reported yet, so it might have been a wrong choice of words by someone who was not too familiar with porcelain technology. But it still has to be noted that the use of the AR mark was restricted to articles with a certain kind of decoration, namely painting after Chinese and Japanese patterns or variations of them. This would include Indian flowers, Chinese scenes, Lion, Dragon, Rock and Bird, Flying Dog and other patterns which even today are called *Indian Painting* at the manufactory. It would exclude harbour, battle and amorous scenes.

Fig. 589: Mark of Prince-Elector Friedrich August II 1733-1734

AR as a mark on porcelain destined for the Royal Court could have been used until 1763. That year August III died and his successor did not become King of Poland. With the Kingship, the Saxon rulers lost the right to the initials AR.[30] But there is evidence that the regular use of this mark was given up some time earlier. A receipt for 703 pieces of porcelain shipped from Meissen to the Royal Court in Warsaw, Poland, in September of 1760 meticulously records how these pieces were marked. Not on a single one of them were the letters AR applied.[31] This would indicate that, at least in 1760, the AR mark was not the rule anymore for porcelain ordered by the King and delivered to him.

So it is not clear how long the AR mark was used. The German trademark registration (Fig. 590) of this sign in 1875 speaks of a period from 1709 to 1726.[15] If the letters AR appearing within a decoration are included, 1709 is close. But the end of this period was certainly much later than 1726. The affidavit of 1895 for the trademark registration in the U.S. says that the mark "has been continously used by the said manufactory since 1709".[32] There is more truth to this than to any other assumption.

Some of the confusion about this mark stems from the fact that there is a large number of pieces with the AR mark around which evidently could not have been made in the first

Fig. 590: AR-mark as shown in the trademark registration of 1875

fifty years of the manufactory, but nevertheless are cherished as priceless early Meissen. On some of these pieces, the mark is crossed by several incisions. This was a quality marking introduced for porcelain sold white in 1852 and for decorated pieces in 1869, as shall be discussed later.

These dates do not match at all any of the propositions about the AR period offered until now. The key to this secret lies in a large number of court files about legal proceedings dragging out over seven years, in which the manufactory was forced to admit an unpleasant fact it rather would have kept hidden.

The Dresden porcelain decorators and antiques dealers Helena Wolfsohn and Leo Meyer in 1876 objected to the registration of the AR mark for the Royal Manufactory, claiming that they themselves had used this mark for over thirty years on their products (Fig. 584) while the Meissen Manufactory had stated in its application for trademark registration that the mark had been used last in 1726, one and a half centuries before.[33] The suit went trough three court hearings, ending at the Imperial Trade Court, which decided against Wolfsohn and Meyer and confirmed the trademark for the Meissen Manufactory.

Not discouraged at all, Helena Wolfsohn in 1877 registered the AR sign as trademark in her own name (Fig. 591). Meyer did too but mainly in tow of Ms. Wolfsohn and her successors, who were the driving force. This time the manufactory sued, demanding that Wolfsohn and Meyer should cease using this mark. At that time, the case became uncomfortable for the manufactory.

Fig. 591: AR-mark used by Helena Wolfsohn in Dresden

One of the conditions for the protection of a trademark was its continuous use at the time of registration and the intention to use it further. The court case concentrated on the question of whether the AR mark had been used only between 1709 and 1726, or if it was still being applied by the manufactory in 1875. Ms. Wolfsohn demanded proof that the manufactory with its AR mark complied with the provisions of the tradmark law. She requested the appearance of six witnesses employed by the manufactory. Fearing that unpleasant facts might come to light the manufactory objected, claiming that trade secrets might be unveiled. It even went so far as to declare that evidence given by these witnesses could be an unintentional betrayal of trade secrets, because they "might not even know what in this case is considered a trade secret and what is not."[34]. The court did not buy this theory of a secret whose owners did not even know that they were keeping a secret.

The witnesses had to appear in court. The clerical employee of the manufactory, Friedrich Rudolf Büttner, testified that in the 1850's porcelain with the AR mark was made for the Royal Court, and those pieces that exceeded the order were sold to the public.[35] The clerk Eduard Winter revealed that he found some pieces with the AR mark in the stockroom of the manufactory and that these pieces had been pulled from moulds first introduced in 1849 or in the 1850's.[36] Friedrich Moritz Fischer, manager of the manufactory-owned store in Leipzig, had seen the AR mark on pieces for which the original models "were created in the third, fourth, fifth and probably also in the sixth decade of the present century".[37]

The director of the manufactory, Moritz Raithel, hedged in his testimony. He restricted it to the time after 1855, the year he became trade representative of the manufactory. Raithel admitted to the repeated production and sale of articles with the AR mark after 1855. Some were produced on orders - on whose orders he refused to say - some at his own discretion. But he added that the manufactory did not sell these pieces just to anyone; he had reserved the decision about who should be allowed to buy AR marked pieces for himself.

Raithel declined to testify about the contemporary meaning of the sign AR and thus evaded an answer to the question whether it was still a proprietor's mark of the King. He also circumvented the question of whether contemporary articles with the AR mark were sold as new or as antique Meissen porcelain.[38]

The trial court felt that there was sufficient evidence for the use of the AR mark by the manufactory in recent times.[39] Ms. Wolfsohn lost her case, the manufactory won but it was a Pyrrhic victory. It had been forced to reveal that the famous and much sought after AR mark was not always proof of the old age of a porcelain piece.

In compliance with the trademark laws, the AR mark after 1875 again was used occasionally, very often on large vases in the style of the first half of the 18th century. After about 1924, the actual year of production was added to the letters AR in order to avoid mistakes and misinterpretations. In the 1950s this practice was abandoned for a number of years, but now the manufactory again identifies pieces with the AR mark as contemporary products.

Crossed Swords

Now finally the best known Meissen mark shall be discussed, the crossed swords. Here too, opinions about the introduction of this mark differ widely.[40] The first proposal to apply a symbol from the coat-of-arms of the Saxon rulers came from the manufactory inspector Steinbrück in 1722. He recommended the crossed swords[12] which identified the Saxon rulers as Imperial Arch Marshalls, one of the highest ranks in the German Empire. There was no reaction from the court of King August, nor did the manufactory decide on Steinbrück's proposal.

Combinations of the crossed swords with the letters K.P.M. are not rare. Similar combinations with the letters M.P.M. or K.P.F. are not known. Since K.P.M. was introduced in December of 1722, replacing K.P.F. which had superseded M.P.M., it stands to reason that the earliest use of the crossed swords was in combination with the letters K.P.M., and that was possible only in December of 1722 at the earliest.

In the second half of the 1720's, the swords became independent from the letters K.P.M. but the actual date that happened is still uncertain. By 1728, they were treated as an established and accepted mark. In December of that year, the manufactory commission asked the King for a decision on the request of the French merchant Lemaire for "Chinese or other signs" on porcelain made for him. In this *Pro Memoria*, the crossed swords were referred to as the "otherwise usual Electoral swords".[41]

That suggests the accepted application of the crossed swords at least in December of 1728. To become a "usual" sign, it must have been introduced some time earlier. The wording of the inquiry addressed to the King leaves the impression that August knew of this mark but had not actually ordered it to be used. That happened shortly before the Leipzig Fair in September of 1729.[42] Since it was only a verbal order without written confirmation it evidently was not followed immediately and completely. Eighteen months later,

in March of 1731, the Royal Chamber felt it necessary to issue another order in the name of the King directing the manufactory to mark all porcelain with the crossed swords.[43] This order was repeated several times in the following month, and with this clearly and definitely expressed Royal demand, the crossed swords in 1731 finally became the general manufactory mark. But there were exceptions, as has been explained in the paragraphs about the kite's tail sign.

Shape and length of the swords were not prescribed, and their application did not demand much skill. While the signs M.P.M., K.P.F. and K.P.M. had been written mainly by the painters, now apprentices and blue painters took over the job of marking. It evidently was not considered very important, and therefore delegated to the youngest and lowest paid employees. Only the painters of blue underglaze decorations drew the marks themselves on the pieces they had decorated.

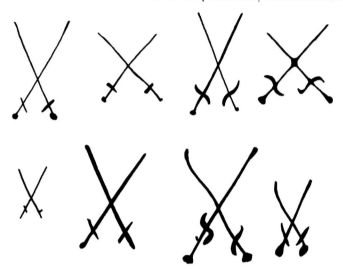

Fig. 592: Different marks used around 1730

The apprentices painted the swords as well as they could but their brushstroke was not yet very sure and every mark came out differently. That is the reason for the many variations in the rendering of the mark during the first 150 years of the manufactory. The marks shown in Fig. 592 are all from the same period around 1730. They not only show a certain insecurity in handling the brush, but also unevenness in the execution, and occasionally running paint and little slips of the brush. Any attempt to date a Meissen piece of these years just by the shape of its mark is futile. A letter from the secretary of Count Hoym to his brother Adam Gottfried Nohr, who was controller at the manufactory, often is cited as proof for the application of very large swords around 1730. Secretary Nohr transmitted to his brother the desire of Count Hoym that the Chief Painter Höroldt or his men should paint the swords in a way "so that at least not so terribly large clubs instead of the swords are applied.[44] It is a little too simple to deduct from this letter that the crossed swords at this time generally were large. Many pieces from this period bear medium-sized or even small marks. And despite the Royal order, quite a number was still not marked with the crossed swords at all.

When this mark was made obligatory for the products of the Meissen manufactory, there was a large stock of unmarked porcelain not only in the stockroom of the manufactory but also at its stores in Leipzig and Dresden. Inventories made in both stores on July 9th of 1729 show 45,373 pieces not yet marked with the crossed swords, 14,103 of them in Liepzig and 31,270 in Dresden.[45] Unknown is how many pieces without marks were still in the stockroom of the manufactory itself.

Except for decorated porcelain and small pieces, all white ware was supposed to be shipped back from Leipzig and Dresden to Meissen.[46] This led some authors to the assumption that these white articles subsequently were marked at the manufactory. Since these wares already were glazed, it was not possible to apply a mark under the glaze. It could only be painted with an enamel paint over the glaze, and indeed, a substantial number of pieces with the crossed swords over the glaze have been reported, not only in blue, but in various colors.[47]

Now it is imaginable that a painter who was ordered to put the crossed swords on the bottom of a piece he just had decorated used any brush handy, regardless of the color. This has been done later with other markings, for instance painters numbers, or numbers that identified a piece as belonging to a certain set.

But there is not proof that the pieces returned from Leipzig and Dresden received crossed swords over the glaze in various colors. It cannot even be ascertained that this white ware was marked with the crossed swords at all. All definite statements about these overglaze marks therefore should be approached with some caution.

Only in one case is the application of blue swords over the glaze certain. The French merchant Lemaire in September of 1729 and in February of 1731 entered into contracts with the manufactory.[48] His business soon developed into a widespread conspiracy to the disadvantage of the manufactory. Even its director general, Count Hoym, was involved, and he lost his job as well as the favor of the King over this affair.

Lemaire wanted the porcelain made for him without the crossed swords mark, instead he asked for a "Chinese or some other sign".[49] The Royal Chamber was rather interested in the first deal with Lemaire, who promised a considerable increase in sales. The chamber respectfully suggested to the King that Lemaire's request should be granted. In his answer, the King agreed to the contract with Lemaire but stayed mute on the marks question.[50] At the time of the first agreement with Lemaire, the King already had made up his mind about the crossed swords as regular mark on Meissen porcelain. His verbal order of that year could be taken as an indirect answer to Lemaire's request, and there is another supporting fact for this assumption.

One month after the second contract was signed with Lemaire, the decree by the Royal Chamber ordered the crossed swords to be affixed on all porcelain exported to France.[23] Despite this clear instruction, Lemaire not only received unmarked porcelain, but even arranged with the help of Count Hoym to have the crossed swords painted over the glaze on many of his orders. According to a later investigation report demanded by the King, Lemaire once explained to the chief painter Höroldt how easy it was to remove the overglaze mark.[51]

At least for Lemaire, some porcelain was marked with the crossed swords blue over the glaze in clear violation of a Royal order. The manufactory commission knew full well Lemaire's intentions to sell unmarked Meissen products for Oriental porcelain. To prevent this it even considered - if the King had agreed to a special mark on Lemaire's orders - publishing this special sign for the benefit of the buying public.[52]

Still, the manufactory wanted to keep track on the porcelain made for Lemaire. Count Hoym's secretary, Nohr, advised the arcanist Stölzel in 1730 to impress an imperceptible marking on all pieces made for the Frenchman, unknown to him and consisting of two or three small indentations near the footring at the bottom made with a fingernail.[53]

When Lemaire was expelled from Saxony after his shenanigans were unveiled, all porcelain in his possession was confisticated and transferred to the Royal porcelain collection. Many of them received the incised "Johanneum" number, an inventory mark[54], but some of them do not show the indentations made by a fingernail. As it was in many other cases, the workers just might have been a bit lax in executing the order. It is also possible that Count Hoym might have rescinded the order his secretary had given. Over the month, relations between Lemaire and Count Hoym had become rather close, and the Count actively supported all of Lemaire's sinister dealings. He then could not have been interested in secret markings by which porcelain made for the French merchant could be traced. This track could only lead directly to him, something he would certainly not be interested in. But this too is - as many other thoughts on the matter of Meissen marks are - only an assumption.

Fig. 593: Mark registered in 1875 with the explanation "Production Period 1720-1730"

Fig. 594: Mark with dot registered in 1875 with the explanation "Production Period 1733-1763"

Fig. 595: Mark with circle registered in 1875 with the explanation "Production Period 1763-1774"

In its trademark application of 1875, the manufactory lists two not very well known marks.[15] According to the application, the mark in Fig. 593 was in use between 1720 and 1730. Occasionally it is called the mark of the Höroldt period. That certainly is a free invention, and in addition there are well founded doubts about any regular application of this mark. It is not a sign that is useful today in determining the age of a piece of Meissen porcelain. Many serious authors do not even mention this mark for lack of its physical confirmation on Meissen products.

Crossed sword with a dot between the hilts (Fig. 594) were supposedly used from 1733 to 1763. It is quite wrong to believe that a mark of this kind was the prevailing or even the only sign on Meissen porcelain during these thirty years. It is not impossible that this mark is the same as the crossed marks with a circle between the hilts, only with the circle drawn as a dot.

Understandable attempts by the manufactory and some porcelain experts to set up some kind of sequential time table for the different marks have proven to be futile. In order to press certain marks into certain periods, facts had to be violated. If the swords with a dot were terminated in 1763, then the swords with a circle between the hilts logically had to begin in 1763. (Fig. 595) This mark and the swords with a dot usually are pigeonholed into a "King's Period", ranging from 1763 to 1774. This "King's Period" starts the same year the rulers of Saxony lost the Polish throne and were not kings anymore. (Only in 1806 the Saxon Prince-Electors were elevated to kings again by Napoleon). There are no understandable reasons why a period without a king should be called the "King's Period". Frequently, this time is also called the "Academic Period" or simply, the "Dot Period". By quiet agreement, these years are supposed to be the ones in which crossed swords with a dot were used in Meissen.[55] Thoughtful and critical authors of late have warned against this far too simple classification of Meissen marks.

A dot between the hilts of the crossed swords has been observed on porcelain dating back to 1740. Why this addition was applied nobody seems to know. It could not have been a painter mark, because it was affixed under the glaze before the sharp firing at a time when no one knew which painter would decorate a particular piece. The assumption that the dots were signs to identify throwers and moulders is unconvincing because these workers never got close to blue paint, and in addition, one dot would not have been sufficient to identify the fairly large number of workers in the throwing and moulding department. Since the arcanists in Meissen always experimented with new pastes and glazes, a dot might have been a technological marking to identify a paste or a glaze of a certain quality.

The beginning of the "Dot Period", if there was a clearly outlined period at all, should be put about 1740, possibly even a bit earlier. The end can be determined fairly well, it was shortly after Count Marcolini became director general of the manufactory in 1774. Eager to leave his personal mark in history, he ordered the addition of two dots (Fig. 596) or a short blue line to the crossed swords. But these marks were in use only a few months, because Count Marcolini reconsidered. He now wanted a different mark to be remembered by.

Fig. 596: Mark used in 1774

In January of 1775 he issued a new order: "I remember to have agreed to have marked all tableware made under my directorship with two dots or one line; but I have changed my mind to the effect that from now on it shall be designated by a star and that directly below the Electoral swords."[56] With this instruction, the beginning of the so-called Marcolini mark (Figs. 597 and 598) can be exactly determined. The Count at first limited the use of this mark to tableware, but it appears also on groups and figurines made during his management. Conventional wisdom let the star disappear with the end of the Marcolini period on January 1st of 1814. That must not have been necessarily so. During almost forty years this mark had become the manufactory mark and the habit of painting it on porcelain did not stop suddenly with Marcolini's resignation. In 1814, very few employees could remember that the star was introduced on Marcolini's instruction, for most of them the swords with the star probably was the regular Meissen mark.

In order to change the mark Marcolini's successor von Oppel would have had to issue a new order deleting the star, but such an order has not been found. So it is not unreasonable to assume that the star mark was used until 1817, when the mark was changed by new additions.

But as with the AR mark, the Marcolini mark too was repeated on Meissen porcelain long after the Marcolini period. In February of 1860 the manufactory asked the Treasury, which was its superior authority at that time, what to do about a request by the Dresden merchant Moritz Meyer to put the old Marcolini mark on porcelain he had ordered.[57] The manufactory pointed out that between 1774 and 1813 all porcelain made in Meissen as as rule - those three words were underlined - were supplemented with a star below the crossed swords. The star is described as consisting of three lines crossing at one point. Meyer, so the letter to the Treasury continued, wanted his buyers to believe that the articles he had ordered in 1860 were from an earlier period. Other merchants had asked for similar changes of the mark, especially importers in England. The manufactory concluded: "Although in previous times, under the directorship of von Oppel, similar request submitted at times have been treated less scrupulously, we now do believe that ... these requests should not be granted under any circumstances."[58]

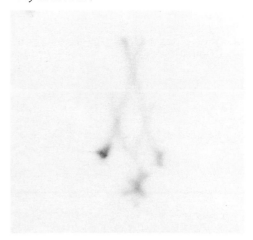

Fig. 597: Mark introduced by Count Marcolini in 1774 and used probably until 1817

Fig. 598: Mark in Fig. 597 on a plate

The Treasury was very quick with its answer. Less than a week after it had received the letter from the manufactory it decreed: "... that until further notice all and any change of the trademark now showing only the Electoral swords has to be stopped."[59] That allows the conclusion that the use of the Marcolini mark did not end in 1814 or in 1817. At least during von Oppel's directorship from 1814 to 1833, but probably even until the final ban in 1860, the star mark still was applied occasionally on Meissen porcelain.

In 1766 the manufactory was able to produce biscuit porcelain. Because this unglazed porcelain looked similar to marble, it was used for figural art. During Marcolini's time a special mark was impressed on biscuit ware, the crossed swords within a triangle, sometimes with a star on top of the triangle (Figs. 599 and 600) It could not be determined whether this mark disappeared with the end of Marcolini's directorship or if impressed swords without the triangle (Fig. 601) were also used during the Marcolini period. But knowing now the generous attitude of his successor towards older marks, it would be inadvisable to take an oath on the disappearance of the crossed swords within a triangle after Marcolini had left Meissen.

Fig. 599: Crossed swords in triangle impressed, crossed swords, star and II blue, on biscuit porcelain

Fig. 600: Mark impressed on biscuit porcelain

Fig. 601: Crossed swords impressed on biscuit porcelain, 19th century

Fig. 602: Crossed swords mark with three dots below hilts, shortly before 1800

Fig. 603: Crossed swords mark with lozenge between tips, shortly before 1800

Unexplained but evidently applied during the Marcolini period are crossed swords with three dots below the hilts (Fig. 602) or a lozenge between the tips (Fig. 603). Plates with these marks owned by U.S. President John Quincy Adams are in the Presidential China Collection of the Smithsonian Institution in Washington, D.C.[60] Adams probably bought them while he was ambassador to the Prussian Court from 1797 until 1800. That would allow the conclusion that these marks were used late in the 18th century during the directorship of Count Marcolini.

At the end of the Marcolini period, the manufactory was technically and financially disorganized. In order to cut production costs a cheaper sort of porcelain was introduced, and apothecary vessels and implements were to be made of an even more inferior kind of paste.[61] Beginning in 1817, wares made from the regular paste had to be identified by the Roman numeral I below the crossed swords (Fig. 604). It was painted blue under the glaze. Articles made from the cheaper paste were to be signed with an additional Roman numeral II (Fig. 605). Apothecary and laboratory utensils were supposed to receive the numeral III. But production of paste III was not taken up until 1822.[62]

In March of 1824 it had become evident that the cheaper quality did not sell satisfactorily, and the paste II was given up.[63] According to the kiln reports, production of pastes II and III continued for a few more months and then tapered off. After that, even laboratory articles were made from paste I which was the only paste used.

Fig. 604: Crossed swords mark with Roman numeral I, 1817-1824

Fig. 605: Crossed swords mark with Roman numeral II, 1817-1824

Porcelain pieces with the Roman numerals I and II are not uncommon, but those with the numeral III still have to be found. They evidently were not produced in large numbers during the years 1822 to 1824. From July to September of 1823, for instance, the value of all articles made from paste III was only 1.8 percent of the combined value of the wares made from pastes I and II. It is imaginable that most of these pieces have been lost, since they easily could have been broken in heavy professional use. In those days, laboratory utensils were not considered collectors or display items which were to be well taken care of.

But that is not the reason why no pieces with the Roman numeral III have been observed. This numeral has never been affixed on Meissen laboratory porcelain. Some authors of porcelain books assumed that pieces made from the third paste were identified with the Roman numeral III in addition to the crossed swords mark, because wares made from paste one bore the numeral I and those made from paste two received the numeral II. But that was a misconception. Articles made from the third paste were signed with the Arabic numeral 3 (Fig. 606) blue under the glaze. Since the manufactory was not proud of its low quality porcelain, it did not mark it with the crossed swords, so that the Arabic numeral 3 is the only marking on Meissen laboratory vessels and implements made between 1822 and 1824.[64]

Fig. 606: Arabic numeral 3 on bottom of a Meissen laboratory vessel made 1822-1824

After 1824, a period began in which the crossed swords often were painted carelessly. Antiques dealers in Germany occasionally call this time the Daub Period *(Schmierzeit)* because of the crude renditions of the mark (Figs. 607 to 610). Under the directorship of von Oppel, many 18th century forms and models were reintroduced. On many pieces made with these forms the crossed swords were just slapped on, and there was not the slightest effort to give the buyer an aid in determining the period of production. On the contrary, much could be said for the suspicion that the marks were painted this way on purpose. Clumsily applied swords could have been taken as signs of an early origin by some buyers.

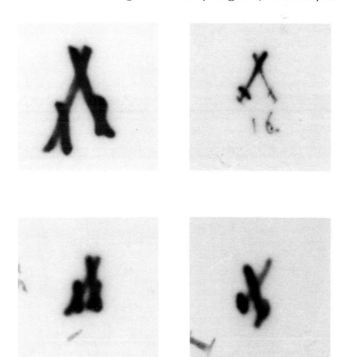

Figs. 607 to 610: Crossed swords marks applied between 1824 and 1850

Figs. 611 to 613: Crossed swords marks with pommels on hilts, applied 1850-1924

Fig. 617: Mark with half circle below the crossed swords, 1945-1946

Fig. 614: "Pommel Sword" of the 18th century

About 1850, the unorganized mark painting was put into some order. From then on the "Pommel Swords" (*Knaufschwerter*) were the usual mark. On the swords, the pommels were emphasized by a little knob (Figs. 611 to 613). Similarly drawn pommels had been used earlier in the 18th century, but at that time the mark painters simply put a dot on the place of the pommels, and the blades were rather straight (Fig. 614). The pommel swords of the 19th and 20th centuries show a distinct curve of the hilts with the pommel knobs on the outside. Occasionally, one blade was a little longer, or the swords did not cross exactly in the middle (Fig. 611).

This led to a rumour among some collectors and dealers. At the beginning of the pommel period, so it was passed on as a trade secret, the crossing point was below the middle, in the middle of the period it was exactly in the middle, and in the last part of the period it went up above the middle. If this was true, then the position of the crossing point could indicate which pieces were made earlier in this period and which later. Unfortunately, it is not only a rumour but bare nonsense. Nobody could have known in 1880 that it was the middle of the period, or in 1920 that the time of the pommel swords was nearing its end.

Only one year can be determined exactly by this mark. On the occasion of its 200th anniversary in 1910, the manufactory affixed a special commemorative mark from June 6th, 1910 until June 5th, 1911 (Fig. 615).

The pommel swords were in common use on Meissen porcelain until 1924. That year, Max Adolf Pfeiffer became general manager of the manufactory, and he introduced a new mark (Fig. 616). It shows slightly curved symmetrical blades with a dot between the tips. In 1933, Pfeiffer was forced to resign by the Nazis, and the dot was eliminated from the "Pfeiffer Mark" the following year. This "Dot Period" therefore can be defined very precisely. It lasted from 1924 until 1934.

After that, the shape of the crossed swords as designed under Pfeiffer was retained, and it is still in use today. Only for two years within this period, in 1945 and in 1946, the swords received an addition. A small arc, sometimes even a half circle, below the hilts of the swords was to symbolize the desire that after the destruction of World War II formerly

antagonistic swords would be joined peacefully in the future (Fig. 617). This mark is not too common, and some collectors do not consider porcelain bearing this mark valuable because they doubt the ability of the manufactory to have achieved its former quality standards so shortly after the war.

From 1946 until 1950, the manufactory was property of the Soviet government. The crossed swords mark was kept during those years. There is no proof for the claim that a new mark, consisting of a hammer and a sickle, had been introduced after the Soviet Union had occupied the part of Germany in which Meissen is located.[65] A piece with a mark like this, or even with hammer and sickle in addition to the crossed swords over the glaze or under it still has not been found. Also proof has to be offered for the application of these signs by the manufactory. Until then the statement by the manufactory stands: that hammer and sickle were never painted on Meissen porcelain after World War II.[66]

After the Soviet Union in 1950 handed over the manufactory to the government of the German Democratic Republic, the new administration for the first time in its history introduced additions to the mark, identifying the period of production (Figs. 618 to 623). These additions are removed from the crossed swords and appear in blue paint under the glaze near the footring.

In England, Meissen porcelain often is called Royal Dresden China, and in France, Vieux Saxe. Mainly in order to prevent other manufactories and factories from using these terms on their imitations of Meissen porcelain, the manufactory in 1938 registered them as trademarks.[67] They were occasionally used on show and dessert plates, on liqueur sets and similar items.[68] These marks (Figs. 624 and 625) were discontinued after 1950.

The misuse of the name Dresden by other porcelain makers urged the manufactory to protect this name in connection with the crossed swords (Figs. 626 and 627). These marks were registered in Germany in 1963.[69] For an English version of the mark (Fig. 628), registration was sought with the U.S. Patent Office in 1966, but it took more than four years before the application was granted.[70]

These marks were only employed occasionally to keep their protection as trademarks. They had to be abandoned, though, after courts in Germany decided on the use of geographical names in trademarks. Only porcelain producers

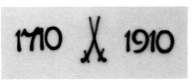

Fig. 615: Anniversaary mark, used from June 6th, 1910 until June 5th 1911

Fig. 616: Crossed swords with dot between the tips (Pfeiffermark) used 1924-1934

Fig. 618: Crossed swords with dot below near footring, 1951-1953

Fig. 619: Crossed swords with vertical line below near footring, 1953-1957

Fig. 620: Crossed swords with horizontal line below near footring, 1957-1972

Fig. 621: Crossed swords with vertical line to the right near footring, 1972-1980

Fig. 622: Crossed swords with horizontal line to the right near footring, 1980

Fig. 623: Crossed swords with horizontal line to the left near footring, since 1980

Royal Dresden China

Fig. 624: Mark used occasionally since 1938

Vieux Saxe

Fig. 625: Mark used occasionally since 1940

Dresden

Fig. 626: Mark used 1963-1973

Dresden China

Fig. 627: Mark used 1963-1973

Dresden Art

Fig. 628: Mark registered in the U.S.A. 1971-1981

actually located in Dresden, so the final judgement said, were entitled to use the name Dresden. But the manufactory at least could save the name Meissen from being misused. In 1972, two marks containing this name were registered (Figs. 629 and 630) and they are applied on select items.[71]

Figs. 629 and 630: Marks used on select items since 1972

Marks with Incisions and Marks on Porcelain Sold Undecorated

Extraordinarily confusing are the crossed swords marks with one or more incisions. Some of the incisions go across the marks, others are found below, above, or at one side of the swords; and recently pieces appeared with the incisions separated from the swords and placed through a short blue line near the footring.

Many pieces of Meissen porcelain now on the market show the crossed swords with incisions. Their meaning has been interpreted differently. Some authors consider them signs for imperfect or even defective porcelain, others identify some of them as markings for porcelain that was sold undecorated in the white. Occasionally, the explanations are very imaginative, but nevertheless wrong.[72] Any attempt to find a logical system for the different kinds of incisions is futile. Some very useful work in this field has been done recently. [73] But whichever explanation is attempted, it greatly taxes the attention, patience, and stamina of the reader.

First, those marks shall be discussed wich indeed indicate that a piece was sold white by the manufactory. The earliest document found in the manufactory archive mentioning this mark is dated November 1764.[74] The Spanish envoy to the Saxon Court, Marquis de Revilla, had ordered a complete dinner set in white porcelain. The manufactory asked for a decision by the regent, referring to an earlier order that forbade the sale of undecorated porcelain without highest permission. In its letter the manufactory pointedly directed the attention of the regent to the fact that the Marquis had offered to pay cash on hand, and that there was a low tide in the manufactory's money box. The regent allowed the sale of the dinner set "but with the proviso that it should be marked - as other completely white porcelain sets - with a horizontal incision through the Electoral swords".[75]

This document allows three conclusions: First, that one incision across the swords at that time was a marking for porcelain sold white. Second, that one incision through the swords was not a sign for porcelain of inferior quality. Third, that the order to mark porcelain sold white with one incision had been issued some time before 1764 (Fig. 631).

It has not been possible yet to precisely ascertain the year when this marking was first introduced. Many documents from the period of the Seven-Years' War (1756-1763) have been lost and they might have contained further enlightenment. Until definite proof can be found, all speculations about the date of introduction of this marking are without foundation.

This method of identifying porcelain sold undecorated continued over the years. A price list of 1814 points out that on porcelain decorated in the manufactory, there never was an incision, while wares sold white were marked by one incision.[76] In the years after 1814, the manufactory for financial reasons sold many white pieces. But it also tried to make

Fig. 631: Crossed swords with one incision across, one incision is a sign that the piece was sold white, before 1764 until 1938

outside decoration of these pieces unprofitable by raising the prices for white porcelain considerably, in certain cases by 50 percent. But in all discussions during those years, one incision across the swords was never mentioned as marking for porcelain of different qualities, it remained a sign for undecorated wares.

This changed after 1850. Between 1850 and 1869, a number of orders were issued about the application of incisions as quality signs. None of these orders identifies on single incision across the swords as a marking for quality. It still was reserved as a characteristic sign for wares sold white. In 1938 the position of this incision was changed.[77] From then on it appeared as a vertical incision next to the crossed swords on porcelain sold undecorated (Fig. 632).

Fig. 632: Crossed swords with one incision next to them as sign that the piece was sold white, 1938 - present

In 1898 the manufactory announced a complete discontinuation of the sale of white porcelain to the public.[78] But there were exceptions. Persons of high rank still could obtain white porcelain with permission of the Treasury. Exceptions almost became a rule, and in 1909 the order was reviewed with the result that white porcelain should only be sold to the Royal Court or to the employees of the manufactory, but in these cases only if the pieces were of the lowest quality grade: Insignificant.[79]

Traders and painters not only had bought white porcelain for outside decoration but also table, coffee and tea sets, as well as plates that were decorated only with narrow plain gilt lines. In 1856 the manufactory subsumed these articles under white wares, and decided that they too should be marked with one incision.[80] Outside decorators had been painting these articles, leaving the gilt rim or the gilt lines but filling the white areas in between with their decorations.

A document of 1914 confirms that the original 18th century order about the marking of porcelain sold white was still in effect.[81] It lists all articles which had to be identified with one incision and also defines those kinds of gilt porcelain which were to be treated as white ware. Pieces with a narrow line around the rim or a thin line around the well got one incision, while pieces with wider gilt bands and more elaborate gilding were not counted as white ware. After World War

I these instructions evidently were extended to gilt decorations consisting of several plain gilt lines (Figs. 633 and 634), and they received the incision occasionally below the swords.

During World War I it became more and more difficult to obtain the necessary ingredients for the paint, and to keep enough decorators from military service for the painting department. The manufactory had to sell more white porcelain, even groups and figurines, and it introduced a new sign for wares it produced with the intention of selling them white. Sometime between 1915 and 1918 it began to impress a special colorless mark into the paste before glazing and sharp firing. (Fig. 635) This mark was in addition to the blue crossed swords, and it is still used today.

Fig. 633: Plate with three narrow gold rings, 1924-1934

Fig. 634: Mark on plate in Fig. 633, incision below swords blackened for better identification

Fig. 635: Mark for articles that are supposed to be sold white, colorless impressed, c. 1915 - present

During World War II (1939-1945) a similar situation arose. Quite a number of pieces, including tableware, was selected to be sold undecorated from the beginning. The articles were marked with a short blue line below the swords, the impressed word *weiss* (white), or both, and the year of production was impressed colorless under the glaze (Fig. 636).

Since the production of white ware exceeds the capacity of the painting department and pieces with visible faults are not decorated at all in most cases, the stock of porcelain of inferior quality at the manufactory increased all the time. Occasionally the manufactory even today sells some of these pieces white, but not without first applying the incision for white ware next to the swords.

From all this it seems possible to offer this thesis: One single incision across the mark is the sign for porcelain of standard quality sold white. This sign has been in use since some time before 1764 until 1938. It also identifies porcelain of standard quality with only modest gilding produced after 1856. One version next to the swords to the right or to the left is a marking for porcelain of standard quality sold white after 1938. This marking is still used today.

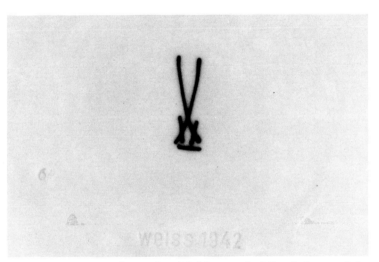

Fig. 636: Crossed swords with blue vertical line below and the colorless impressed identification "weiss 1942" (white 1942) for porcelain produced in 1942 and supposed to be sold white

But since no rule is without exception, when it comes to Meissen porcelain one reservation has to be made. In 1776, the stock of substandard and rejected wares had increased so much that the manufactory opened up a special store for porcelain of inferior quality in Dresden. Manufactory manager Count Marcolini announced in Dresden newspapers that white porcelain of substandard quality available in this store was marked with one incision across the swords.[82] But the manufactory management quickly realized that too many of these white wares were being painted by outside decorators. It had to discontinue the sale of white coffee sets at the Dresden store in 1795.

So the above thesis has to be supplemented by the addition that from 1776 until some time before 1815, one incision across the swords also could indicate that the piece was sold white but was of substandard quality. It is not too difficult to identify these pieces, since they all carry the Marcolini mark, the crossed swords with a star below. During the Marcolini period, another identification for substandard decorated pieces was used for a short while. To prevent outside painting, substandard ware received so-called "Reject Decoration" (*Ausschussmalerei*), which were simplified versions of the usual patterns. Pieces with this kind of decoration were supposed to receive the word "*Ausschuss*" (Reject) on the bottom (Fig. 637). In February of 1779 Count Marcolini issued an order to this effect.[83] Since only a few pieces with this marking are known, it stands to reason that not very many have been designated as such. One problem was that not all painters could write, and the execution of the order was only possible with difficulties. Those painters who could write had to take care of all pieces painted by their

Fig. 637: Crossed swords with star blue under the glaze and the word "Ausschuss" (Reject) purple over the glaze, after 1779 for a few years

illiterate colleagues, and that brought disorder into the painting shop. This difficult method probably was given up soon after it had been ordered.

Except for these two marks, there were no quality markings for porcelain sold white or decorated until 1850. That year, the manufactory administration ordered all English Articles not matching the standard quality grade to be identified by several incisions below the swords.[84] Two years later this order was extended to tableware which received the incisions across the swords. Since one incision already was assigned to white ware of standard quality, the marking system had to start with two incisions across the swords (Figs. 638 to 643).

Figs. 638 and 639: Marks for tableware of Substandard quality, 1852-1869 or later

Figs. 640 to 641: Marks for tableware of the grade Grac, 1852-1869 or later

Figs. 642 to 643: Marks for tableware of the grade Insignificant, 1852-1869 or later

Before the contemplation of incised marks can be continued, some newly-introduced terms for porcelain of inferior quality have to be explained.

One of Böttger's first experiences was that despite all care and caution, most of the porcelain pieces came out of the kilns with imperfections. Small blemishes were ground out carefully, or they were tolerated by everyone because even porcelain from the Orient was not without fault. But the pieces with larger imperfections or even damages had to be sorted out since they would not command the same prices as the other wares.

The number of quality grades that were used first has not been ascertained yet, but by 1712 the manufactory inspector Steinbrück mentioned two grades: *Brac* and *Kaufmanns-Guth* (merchants' goods).[85] The expresion "*Brac*", also called "*Brack*" or "*Brack Goods*" is of North German origin, it means defective, rejected or not as pure as it should be. The word survives in the English language as the word "brackish". It was at that time used for pieces that seemed not salable, which were not Merchants' Goods.

In 1722, a third category is mentioned, called *Mittel-Guth* (Medium Goods)[86] *Brac* at the same time was divided into two classes, "usable Brac" and "bad Brac", the latter to be destroyed.[87] In a report of October 24th, 1722, the broken and completely useless brac was called "*Rommelhux*", an unexplained expression.[88] By the end of 1722, four grades existed:

Merchants' Goods (or Good Goods)
Medium Goods
Brac
Rommelhux

In 1731, the instructions for the new manufactory inspector, David Reinhardt, ordered him to sort all pieces into those four grades, only the term *Rommelhux* was replaced by the classification "ruined pieces".[89]

Merchants Goods were supposed to be without any imperfections, but technology at that time was not able to produce a kilnful of faultless porcelain at any firing. Only a few perfect pieces were among the bulk of Medium Goods and Brac. Medium Goods soon became standard quality, and in 1819, the manufactory commission noted in a report that the Good Goods "existed only in name".[90] *Medium Goods, Rejects (Ausschuss)* and *Brac* were all the stockroom received.

"Rejects" sounds a little harsh, it should be called, substandard in English because the rejects were still marketable wares. In those days, people did not yet suffer from the mania to invent palliative paraphrases for unpleasant facts; they called a spade a spade. But in contrast to Meissen, other manufactories were less critical in their grading systems. Traders and customers complained that they only got Medium Goods and substandard wares from Meissen, while other manufactories offered plenty of Good porcelain.

The Meissen Manufactory did what it should have done long before, and changed the grading system. Beginning in March of 1819 Medium Goods were advanced to Good Goods, Substandard wares became Medium Goods, Brac was promoted to Substandard, and a category not mentioned before, "Insignificant" (*Unscheinbar*), was now called Brac. The few existing Good Goods remained in the class of Good Goods.

The kiln reports show the distribution of the finally fired pieces among these new grades. The average for the month of July to September 1823 showed:

Good Goods	38 %
Medium Goods	36.6%
Substandard	20.2%
Brac	2.4%
Breakage	2.7%

The missing 0.1 percent may be accounted for by breakage. The grade "Insignificant" was not used in these kiln reports, but the number of broken pieces was noted.[91] This is understandable, because only preliminary sorting of the pieces was done in the kiln room. The final grading occured before the white porcelain was stored in the stockroom.

In 1824 the percentage of Good goods dropped suprisingly to less than 4 percent.[92] Since there was no major change in technology that would account for technical difficulties, there must have been another reason. It can be found in the instructions for the new sorting inspector Ernst Friedrich Triebel of December 6th, 1824.[93] These instructions contain the first known detailed and written specifications for the grading of Meissen porcelain, and since they are basically still in use today, the pertinent parts shall be repeated here in a translation from the old-fashioned German version:

The right grading of the porcelains according to their different qualities is the most important part of the duty of the sorting supervisor, to which he has to direct his special attention. According to this specification they are divided in 6 grades, namely

1. Good
2. Medium Good
3. Substandard
4. Brac
5. Insignificant and
6. Breakage

Concerning the different attributes for the classification of the first 5 grades so has

A., tableware considered Good to possess the highest degree... of quality and perfection and must be especially suited for elaborate gold decoration without other painting which makes faults leap to the eye even more. Conditions to be met are a perfect shape, a pure white appearance, a smooth glaze and a faultless surface without specks, dull spots, dimples, pockets and fissures.

B., Medium Goods are porcelains with the above mentioned virtues to a less perfect degree and without showing all of them in one single piece but without faults leaping to the eye. They can show small faults in the glaze, for instance wavy spots or hardly visible spots or dimples or even small deviations in shape as long as the harmonious shape can be restored by a little help in the grinding shop. Medium Good porcelains also can show slightly larger spots of a kind that can be covered with regular painting....

C., Faults of all kinds which are more easily recognizable are allowed the substandard porcelains as long as the proportions of the whole piece are not lost,

D., but everything has to be sorted as Brack that shows evident faults, a color with grey or yellow tint, large fire cracks, many pocks, damaged parts of the glaze, uneven shape, several obvious dark spots etc., but is not unusable and has not completely lost the character of our porcelain.

E., Finally has everything to be placed back as Insignificant that because of the size of its faults is unsalable in the stores or at auctions and

F., it has to be kept separate from the Breakage.

These instructions also show that the old names for the different grades had been changed. The substantive Goods had been eliminated, and the adjectives formerly describing the quality of the goods now became proper names. To distinguish between these names and the grammatical use of adjectives, these grade names shall be written with a capital first letter in the following.

A report of 1852 shows that the grading system was handled generously in certain cases. Dessert plates with plastic relief, fruit bowls, baskets, cups and pierced or reticulated plated were sorted as "Good" even if they were slightly imperfect. They were much in demand, and by grading them "Good" it was possible to get higher prices for them.[94]

These explanations were necessary in order to understand the different marks with more than one incision. Two, three, or four incisions across the swords, or above, below, or next to them were markings for the different qualities introduced in 1850 and 1852.

In November of 1850, the manufactory began identifying quality differences of groups, figurines and vases by one, two or three incisions below (not across) the swords.[95] In this system one incision was used for substandard wares, and two for Brack. But in contrast to the single incision for articles sold white, these incisions did not go through the mark, nor were they applied next to it on the right or on the left side. They were placed below the swords (Figs. 644 to 646).

Fig. 644: Mark on groups, figurines and vases of substandard quality, 1850 - late 19th century

Fig. 645: Mark on groups, figurines and vases of Brac quality, 1850 - late 19th century

Fig. 646: Mark on groups, figurines and vases of Insignificant quality, 1850 - late 19th century

The white ware was graded before it was stored in the stockroom, and at that time inferior pieces received their incisions. From the stockroom, the pieces were taken to be painted. If by painting and decorating flaws and blemishes could be hidden, then these pieces were upgraded. The painters were supposed to add certain letters next to the mark:

A if Insignificant became Substandard
M if Insignificant or Substandard became Medium
G if one of the lower grades could be improved to Good.

This order was in use only for two years, in 1852 it was rescinded. That means that pieces with one of the letters A, M or G painted in color over the glaze on the bottom must have been made between 1850 and 1852.

After 1852, a different method was employed to upgrade pieces which were of inferior quality, as long as they were white and had been improved by painting. On these wares, the incisions were removed completely by grinding them out. These pieces could not be glazed again on the bottom, because the high temperature necessary would have burned away the painting. So the grinding out of the incisions left an unglazed dull spot on the bottom below the swords (Fig. 647).

Fig. 647: Crossed swords with ground out spot below, blackend for better identification, the piece first had received several incisions for a lower quality grade. After it had been improved by garnishing to the grade Good, the incisions were ground out

Fig. 648: Mark on second choice porcelain, 1852-1980

Fig. 649: Mark on third choice porcelain, 1852-1980

Fig. 650: Mark on fourth choice porcelain, 1852-1980

For tableware quality markings were introduced in July of 1852. On Good and Medium wares the swords remained as they were. Substandard received two incisions, Brack three incisions, and Insignificant four incisions through or next to the swords.[96] (Figs. 638-643)

In 1853 porcelain with blue or green underglaze decorations was included in this system. Good and Medium were left untouched, the other grades were marked with incisions above or vertically next to the swords on either side but mostly to the right (Figs. 651 to 656).[97]

Most of these different quality signs were used only until 1869, when the five sorting grades were reduced to four. From this year on the quality incisions had to be made across the swords. Only for the so-called English Articles the old method was continued for a few more years. Decorated 1st choice wares were sold without any incision. 2nd choice porcelain with painting was identified by two incisions across the swords, 3rd choice by three and 4th choice by four incisions. For commercial traffic there were only 1st and 2nd choice officially, but very soon the other quality grades had to be sold too (Figs. 648 to 650).

There is no proof that the placement of the incisions across the swords - through, above or below the crossing point of the swords-has any significance, as has been assumed in some circles. The grinding was done quickly, without much attention to the spot where the wheel hit. Therefore it is not justifiable to draw any particular conclusions from the location of the incisions.

Figs. 651 and 652: Marks on goods of Substandard quality with blue or green painting under the glaze, 1853-1869

Figs. 653 and 654: Marks on goods of Brac quality with blue or green painting under the glaze, 1853-1869

Figs. 655 and 656: Marks on goods of Insignificant quality with blue or green painting under the glaze, 1853-1980

In 1980, the placement of the incisions was changed. Instead of damaging the famous crossed swords any longer, the manufactory decided to grind the incisions through the horizontal blue line to the left of the swords near the footring (Figs. 657 to 659).

Finally, there is another kind of incision but pieces thus marked are not supposed to be seen outside the manufactory. Usable pieces, which were not salable even to the manufactory employees, remain within the manufactory for everyday use. They are marked with two incisions crossing each other (Fig. 660) or with four incisions through the swords and an additional vertical incision next to the swords (Fig. 661). Since these unsalable pieces were supposed to remain white, the vertical line identified them as undecorated articles. The first mention of these marks as being in use "for the last several years" has been found in a document of 1940.[98] Over the years, enough of these wares have been collected to equip the cafeteria of the manufactory with them, and it seems only appropriate that the employees of the manufactory get their lunch on Meissen porcelain, or put the green plants in their offices or workrooms on Meissen saucers.

Another perplexing mark also can be explained now. The famous AR mark has been found with several incisions across the swords. The AR mark was - according to earlier opinions - only used in the 18th century, but two, three, or four incisions across the swords were only applied after 1852. This looks like a contradiction but it is not. Earlier in this chapter, the fate of the AR mark has been discussed, and it has been shown that it still was used in the 19th and 20th centuries. Pieces with an incised AR mark belong to those which were produced after 1852. They are not forgeries, as has been assumed before but reproductions made by the manufactory.[99]

Fig. 657: Mark on second choice porcelain, 1980 -present

Fig. 658: Mark on third choice porcelain, 1980 - present

Fig. 659: Mark on fourth choice porcelain 1980 -present

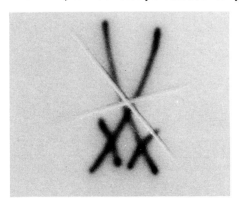

Fig. 660: Crossed swords with two crossing incisions on porcelain to remain in the manufactory

Fig. 661: Crossed swords with four incisions across and one next to the swords on porcelain to remain in the manufactory

Other Markings on Porcelain

The regular manufactory marks are only of limited use in identifying the age of a piece of Meissen porcelain. But in addition to the marks an innumerable variety of different signs and markings can be found, and some of them are helpful for the age classification.

On early pieces of the 1710s and 1720, letters or numbers or combinations of both are written on the bottoms of pieces with an ink made from a mixture of soluble iron salts and tannic acid (*Eisengallustinte*) (Fig. 662). They appear very often on porcelain decorated with "Gold Chinamen" (*Goldchinesen*). Firing in the muffle kilns and the passage of time have given them a special lustre, but most of the markings are only faintly visible.

There is no agreement among the experts about the meaning of these markings. Some of them are supposed to be signatures of outside painters in Augsburg. Some have been identified as coded prices. Others evidently show the initials of the person who ordered the decoration. The letter "F" or the initials "JF" are identified as the initials of Johann Georg Funke, who in Dresden decorated porcelain with "Gold Chinamen" for the manufactory. The letter "G" is supposed to stand for the gold painter Johann Jacob Gäbel. Other markings in lustre have been interpreted as technical notes aiding in assembling sets or services.

It is quite possible that all of these assumptions are true. But each one of them would only apply for a certain piece. A general theory covering all lustre marks still awaits more detailed research. Only one thing can be said for certain: that porcelain with these marks belongs to the very first period of the manufactory.

Fig. 662: Letters and numbers written in ink on early Meissen porcelain

On some pieces of Meissen porcelain, arabesques and ornaments are painted in gold over the glaze (Figs. 663 and 664). In former times they were attributed to Meissen, but in the meantime some of them have been identified. The arabesque in Fig. 663 was painted on the bottom of a piece of Meissen porcelain decorated in Augsburg by Elisabeth Anna Auffenwerth, because the monogram can be read as EA or EAW.

Fig. 663: Arabesque on Meissen porcelain with monogram of Elisabeth Anna Aufenwerth in Augsburg, gold overglaze

The ornament in Fig. 664 used to be called the Cosel mark, after the Countess Cosel who for some time was mistress of Augustus the Strong. The Countess fell out of favor in 1716, and was confined to Castle Stolpe in Saxony, where she was prisoner until August's death in 1733. She stayed at the castle voluntarily, and died there in 1765 at the age of 85. The mark

Fig. 664: So-called "Cosel-mark", gold overglaze

Fig. 665: Contours of "Cosel-Mark" superposed over crossed swords

called the Cosel mark has nothing to do with the Countess at all. In 1716 when she was banished from Dresden, the manufactory was just in its third year of producing porcelain. Polychrome painting had not quite been mastered, and the decorations were rather simple. In her confinement Countess Cosel had neither the money - August II in 1720 had confiscated all her property - nor the incentive to collect Meissen porcelain, and any attribution of this ornament to her should be questioned.

The shape of this ornament suggests a theory that still has to be proven. The gold painting might not have had any other purpose than to hide the crossed swords mark (Fig. 665). Until now no proprietor of a Meissen piece with this mark has been willing to remove at least part of the gold ornament to find out what is hidden beneath. As an argument against this theory, it should be pointed out that there is at least one piece known that carries the blue crossed swords in addition to the gold arabesque.

Throwers, Moulders, and Technological Signs

Some of the throwers' and moulders' markings impressed on red stoneware (Fig. 544) also can be found on early porcelain of the Böttger period. That should not be surprising, since the same workers threw and moulded stoneware and porcelain. Later, new markings were chosen by other workers, not all of them can be identified. Manufactory files of the 1730 show forty-four different markings (Fig. 666) used by throwers, moulders, arcanists, and plaster moulders.[100]

H	Richter Major
V	Hesse
2	Dietrich
X	Pietzsch Major
3	Bormann

Fig. 666a: Workers for the Blue Paste (for porcelain to be painted with blue underglaze decoration)

δδ	Lohse Senior
¡o	Meißner the Middle
‡‡	Moebius
P	Pfitzner
♂	Schubert Junior
♂	Richter Minor
☉	Hoppe
◮	Lange
.∇.	Köhler
◻	Steinbrück

Fig. 666b: In the White Room

∴	Grund Senior
• •	Küttel or Kittel
//	Grutner Junior
#	Herrmann
☿	Schlicke
♀	Meißner Minor

Fig. 666c: In the Blue Front Room

⌗	Schieffer
∵	Müller
⅃	Wolff
♃	Albrecht
н	Haase
♄	Trapschuch Minor

Fig. 666d: In the Blue Back Room

X	Rehschuh
✳	Wildenstein
D	Pietzsch Junior
♀	Richter Medius
:l·	Meißner Senior
∴	Grund Junior

Fig. 666e: In the Red Room, Grund Junior "in the Plaster Moulder's Room"

E	Eckold
✳	Bergmann
✳ ✳	Meinert
₀⁰₀	Seidel
oo	Kühnel
✳	Schuhmann

Fig. 666f: Workers with Bergmann's Paste (named after Bergmann, who developed the paste)

4	Schubert
X ll·	Leibnitz
✚	Günther
O	Hesse
Δ	Fehrmann

Fig. 666g: Workers with Schubert's Paste (named after the arcanist Schubert who developed the paste)

Fig. 666: Throwers' and moulders' signs in the 1730ies

In 1739, Chief modeller Kaendler in a letter proposed a substitution of these signs - he called them whims - by numbers.[101] In his letter, ten of the signs were depicted, some of them are not contained in the list in Fig. 666, and not all of them have been matched with names yet (Fig. 667). Chief painter Höroldt had not much to say against Kaendler's idea. He only wanted the arcanists to continue using their signs for techological reasons.[102] Besides Höroldt, at that time Christian Heinrich Petzsch, Johann Gottlieb Schatter, and Daniel Gottlieb Schertel were arcanists.

Before he had written his letter, Kaendler already had ordered metal number stamps to be made. These numbers from then on were impressed as identification signs for throwers and moulders. The markings that had formerly been used disappeared around 1740 except for the arcanists' symbols. That means that pieces with the throwers' and moulders' signs were made before 1740, and all pieces with numbers for the throwers and moulders were produced after that year.

Unfortunately, the manufactory never has revealed who is hidden behind the impressed numbers, and which numbers were used at what time. A list of numbers and corresponding years of use could give clues as to the time a certain piece was manufactured. These lists have not been compiled yet for one main reason: the reward would not compensate for the investment of time and labor, and independently wealthy scholars with a knack for this kind of pedantic and tiring work are very rare today.

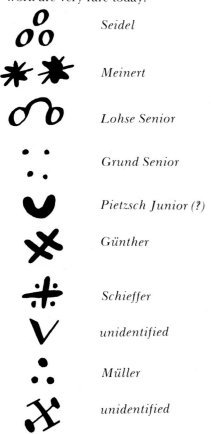

	Seidel
	Meinert
	Lohse Senior
	Grund Senior
	Pietzsch Junior (?)
	Günther
	Schieffer
	unidentified
	Müller
	unidentified

Fig. 667: Throwers' and Moulders' signs sketched by Kaendler in a letter in 1739

Technological signs also can be found on certain pieces of Meissen porcelain. In 1788, the three manufactory arcanists had developed new glazes. For test purposes, the arcanists had to sign the pieces covered with their glazes. These tests were conducted consecutively, and each of the arcanists had to apply the first letter of his family name in blue under the glaze. These letters were used:

B from October 1st, 1788, until December 31st, 1788, for the arcanist Busch (Figs. 668 and 669);

E from January 1st, 1789, until March 31st, 1789, for the arcanist Elsässer, and

W from April 1st, 1789, until June 30th, 1789, for the arcanist Walther.

Fig. 668: Cup made in 1788

Fig. 669: Mark on cup in Fig. 668

On orders of Count Marcolini in 1804, impressed or inscribed signs for different pastes were introduced.[103] It is not known how long they were used. Since in 1817 new markings for pastes of different qualities became common, the signs of 1804 could only have been employed until that year, but they probably were abandoned some time earlier. Marcolini's order of March 14th, 1804, named these signs:

A for tableware subjected to the hottest firing,

B for tableware to be painted blue,

C for "a brown paste for the brown and paille (straw-yellow) glazed tableware",

W for biscuit paste,

II for supports and rests,

O for rings (also supports or dividers).

The last two items are technical aids, used during the firing in the kilns. They will not be encountered today because these auxiliary materials that kept the porcelain pieces straight and separate in the kilns were thrown away after they had served their purpose.

Year Signs

In recent times, the manufactory began marking the year of production on its porcelain., In 1948 it introduced a special sign for every year, to be impressed next to the thrower's or moulder's personal number. In the beginning, these signs had geometrical shapes, but since 1980, capital letters in alphabetical sequence have been impressed (Figs. 670 and 671).

The absence of a year sign does not necessarily mean that a piece was made before 1948. Sometimes a thrower or moulder just neglected to impress a sign, sometimes it was not pressed hard enough into the paste and the glaze covered it. Equally, a year sign is not at the same time an indication for the year of decoration. Frequently, pieces are stored for several years before they are painted.

△	1948	∩	1960	⅄	1972
○	1949	♀	1961	⚥	1973
□	1950	∿	1962	)(	1974
—	1951	=	1963	◡	1975
V	1952	⊏	1964	⊐	1976
⊥	1953	∧	1965	✕	1977
⌐	1954	•	1966	⅀	1978
>	1955	<	1967	X	1979
⋮	1956	⋎	1968		
◇	1957	/	1969		
⊣	1958	⊢	1970		
◖	1959	⚲	1971		

Since 1980 capital letters in alphabetical sequence

A 1980 D 1983
B 1981 E 1984
C 1982

Fig. 670 Year signs since 1948, impressed next to the moulders and throwers numbers under the glaze

Painters' Signs and Numbers

The identification number of polychrome painters, applied on the bottom in one of the colors used in the decoration (Fig. 672), could be another aid in determining the age of a porcelain piece. But as it is with the throwers' and moulders' numbers, there is no complete and concise list of the painters' numbers. The manufactory also never was eager to supply such a list for a certain reason. All employees of the manufactory, even the top designers of patterns and decorations, were supposed to remain unknown. From the beginning, the manufactory itself wanted to be the only originator and creator of its products. To the outside world, its workers, modellers and painters were depersonalized. They were strictly forbidden to sign or to mark any of their work.

Nevertheless, some of them succeeded in leaving their names for posterity. They either put hidden or open initials on the pieces they had decorated, or even signed them with their names. The following painters are known to have signed a few of the pieces they painted. The numbers in brackets are the years of their employment at the manufactory.

Christian Wilhelm Ernst Dietrich (1764-1770)
Johann Georg Funke (1713-1727)
Johann Jakob Gäbel (1724-c.1729)
Johann Georg Heintze (1720-1749)
Christian Friedrich Herold (1725-1778)
Johann Gregorius Höroldt (1720-1765)
Bonaventura Gottlieb Hoyer (1724-1782)
Christoph Conrad Hunger (1715-1717 and 1727-1729)
Johann Gottfried Klinger (1726-1746)
Christian Friedrich Kühnel (1741-c.1786)
Lauch (1724, later outside painter in Dresden)
Johann Georg Loehnig (1763-c.1806)
Adam Friedrich von Löwenfinck (1727-1736)
Johann Carl Mauksch (1775-1821)
Philipp Ernst Schindler (1725-1765)
Johann Ehrenfried Stadler (1723-1741)

Fig. 671: Bottom of a plate with year sign for 1955 near footring

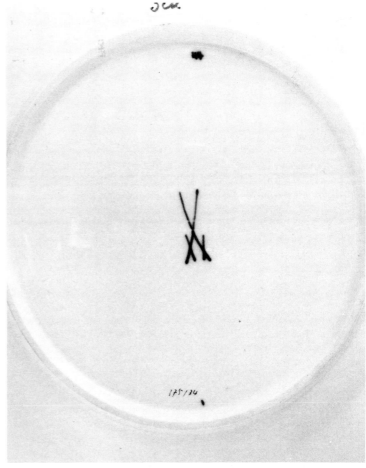

Fig. 672: Painter's number near footring

Unidentified as of now are some other signatures as:
Loehner
L.T.
G.L.
R.

One of the painters gave a fuller description of himself. On a plate with a battle scene he wrote:"C.F. Kühnel, 35 years in service, 57 years old 1776". The manufactory files bear out this statement. Kühnel was born in 1719, joined the manufactory in 1741, and was listed in 1775 as "landscape, architecture, hunt and battle painter 1st class." He died in 1792, six years after his retirement.

Fig. 673: Part of the decortion of a tankard in the British Museum in London, England

Another inscription on a tankard (Fig. 673) has been ascribed to a painter by the name of George Ernst Keil. As far as could be ascertained, there was no painter Keil employed by the manufactory in 1724. That year Höroldt became Court Painter, and this promotion enabled him to marry in 1725. The maiden name of his wife was Rahel Eleonore Keil. Her father, Gottfried Keil, owned the inn *"Zum Hirschen"* in Meissen, and he was a member of the city council. George Ernst Keil was his son, and Höroldt's future brother in law. The inscription was not a painter's signature, but a dedication by Höroldt to a close relative of his wife. In September and December of 1726, Höroldt decorated and dedicated two more tankards for his mother-in-law.

It has been documented that Höroldt took home white porcelain to decorate it at home and to give it away as a gift or sell it.[104] That was illegal, but it neither was allowed to put signatures on porcelain painted at the manufactory. Pieces painted at the manufactory went through inspections before they were delivered, and a signature or openly visible initials would have been discovered. So it could be possible that all or most of all the decorations with clearly identifiable signatures were fruits of homework, because not only Höroldt but also other painters took home porcelain for clandestine decoration. Some of them, like Heintze and Herold, were discovered and reprimanded.

A number of blue painters also put their initials on some pieces. To identify them is not easy, because most of the initials are open to different interpretations. Four theories have been offered in porcelain literature about these initials.

1. They could be test marks used in the 1720's and early 1730's, when the blue paint was very fickle and Höroldt was working on a new recipe for the blue paint.
2. They could be identification markings applied by apprentices. This would have given Chief Painter Höroldt a method of quality control, and he could have picked out those apprentices he wanted to transfer to the more demanding polychrome painting department.
3. They could be signs of the heads of the blue painting department.
4. They were used by blue painters during the Höroldt period. Unfortunately it is not possible to fit all known initials of blue painters and apprentices into these theories, even if all four of them were applied. Only three of the blue painters signs can be explained satisfactorily, and they support theory 3.

HF   stands for Heinrich Förster, head of the blue painting department from 1802 to 1803.

Mö   for Möbius son, head of the blue painting department after 1803 (Fig. 674).

Z   for Zschentsch, head of the blue painting department from 1785 to 1802 (Fig. 675).

Fig. 674: Crossed swords mark with blue painter's sign of Moebius son

Fig. 675: Crossed swords mark with blue painter's sign of Zschentsch

But the other initials are open to interpretation. Here are those observed on blue painted porcelain and the names of the known blue painters and apprentices:

B   Berger, mentioned 1775
Bex, Johan Heinrich Ludwig von (1730-)
Böhme, Johann Tobias (1729-1763)
Büttner, David (-1762)
Bernhardt, Johann Georg (apprentice 1731)
Birkner or Bürkner, Gottlob Siegmund (apprentice 1726 and 1731)
Busch, Cristian Daniel (apprentice 1741)

C   Colmberger, Peter (1745-1779)

E   Eggebrecht, Carl Friedrich (1741-1773)
Engelmann Father, Cristian Friedrich (1729-)
Engelmann Son, Christian Friedrich (1741-1756)
Ehrlich, Carl Gottlob (apprentice 1764)
Erbsmehl, Johann Gottlieb (apprentice 1722-1728)
Eschenbach, Michael Christian August (apprentice 1731)

G   Geissler, mentioned 1775
Gerlach, Johann Benjamin (apprentice 1728 and 1731)
Gotsch, Johann Gottfried (apprentice 1753)
Gottlieb, Johann (apprentice c.1725)

H   Hahnefeld, Johann Gottlieb (c.1750-1785)

h   Hammer, mentioned 1775
Hempel, Johann Georg, mentioned 1775 and 1777
Hermann, Hans Gottlob (1727-after 1756)
Hoffmann, Johann Heinrich (1724-c.1762)
Heintze, Johann Georg (apprentice 1721-1727)
Horn, Johann Christoph (apprentice 1720)

K   Koberwein mentioned 1777
Kolmberger, Peter, see Colmberger, Peter
Krause, Johann Paul (1727-1753)
Kretzschmar, Johann David (1726-1752)
Klinger, Johann Gottfried (apprentice 1726-1731)

L   Lindner, Christian, mentioned 1775
Lanitzsch, Johann Georg (apprentice 1731)
Löwenfinck, Adam Friedrich von (apprentice 1725-1731)
Löwenfinck, Carl Heinrich von (apprentice 1730 and 1735)
Löwenfinck, Christian Wilhelm von (apprentice 1734)

M   Mehlhorn, Johann Gottfried (1720-1722)
Mühlbach, mentioned 1777 and 1780
Müller, Johann Gottfried, mentioned 1758 and 1775

R   Richter, Johann August, mentioned 1720

r   Ripp, Johann Caspar (1721-1723)
Rudolf, mentioned 1775

S   Spittler, Johann Georg (1729-)
Stein, mentioned 1729
Stemmler, mentioned 1775
Schindler Junior, Philipp Ernst (apprentice c. 1734)
Schmidt, Johann Friedrich (apprentice 1742)
Schultze, Johann David (apprentice 1724)

W   Walther, Christian Gotthold (apprentice c.1738)
Wilfig, Johann Christian (apprentice 1731)

Z   Zimmermann, Ferdinand August, mentioned 1731

For the letters "D" and "V", also found on porcelain with blue underglaze decorations, no matching names have been found yet.

This list of blue painters and apprentices in all probability is not complete. A perusal of all the files of the manufactory might turn up more names. But still, the list seems sufficient enough to dispute all theories offered until now about the meaning of blue painters' initials. The question remains unresolved. Only one thing can be stated. The use of initials by painters was by no means restricted to the early periods of the manufactory. The only three identifiable initials range into the 19th century. And one more word about the letter "K". It usually is ascribed to Johann David Kretzschmar with a fierce conviction. It should be treated with less certainty as Kretzschmar's sign, because there were at least three other blue painters who could have used the same initial (Fig. 676)

Fig. 676: Crossed swords mark with blue painter's sign K

The Hollow Triangle

A very curious and still unexplained sign within the painting on certain pieces of Meissen porcelain was discovered by Helmut Joseph a few years ago.[105] He called it the Hollow Triangle, and it has been found mainly on porcelain boxes but also on parts of coffee and tea sets. The triangle, always with one tip pointing downward, and in most cases equilateral, usually is painted in a dark color (Figs. 677 and 678). It is hidden in the decoration, but not so much that a trained eye could not quickly find it.

The pieces it has been observed on were made roughly between 1730 and 1740, and they are distinguished by the excellent quality of the painting. Joseph does not feel that it is the sign of a certain painter, because a comparison of the pieces he has found exclude the possibility of one painter having decorated such large number of boxes. Many of the boxes are gold-mounted, but the triangle could not be a sign for gold-mounting since it also has been found on other boxes, which were not mounted. The variety of different scenes painted, including Chinoiseries, portraits of people, Harbour prospects, Watteau scenes, garden flirtations and frivolous erotic pictures seem to exclude the possibility that one single painter decorated all these pieces.

The guess that the Hollow Triangle might have been some kind of freemason's sign could not be supported either. A hollow triangle in this shape is the alchemistic sign for water, but the possibility of a connection between this alchemistic symbol and the triangles within certain decorations has not yet been explored. The meaning and importance of the Hollow Triangle is still an intriguing subject for scholarly research, because its existence has escaped the attention of experts for more than 225 years. This only proves that Meissen porcelain still holds some surprises.

Another hollow triangle has a different significance. It is applied in a rust-red color over the glaze on the bottom of pieces with light burnished gilding (Fig. 679), that was developed by the technical manager of the manufactory Heinrich Gottlob Kühn in 1827. The new gilding was distinguished from the old heavier gilding by the triangle on the bottom. Since this kind of gilding needed a different method of firing in the kiln, it stands to reason that the triangle was chosen because it is the alchemistic sign for fire. In the Meissen files, this gilding occasionally is called Triangle Gilding. Additional numbers painted on the bottom are the identification numbers of the gilders. Sometimes a line is drawn across the swords mark with the same overglaze paint that was used for the triangle (Fig. 318), and often the triangle is divided by a line.

Fig. 677: Bourdalou, 1730-1740

Fig. 678: Detail of painting on bourdalou, hollow triangle in circle

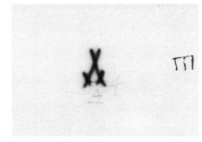

Fig. 679: Crossed swords mark with triangle as sign for Triangle Gilding

The marking for Triangle Gilding was introduced in 1827, but this decoration was not very satisfactory. The gilding did not adhere too well to the glaze and frequent cleaning washed it off. Kühn worked on a better gilding and in 1831 invented the lustre gilding (Glanzgold) which was more durable than the light burnished gilding. In order to keep apart pieces with the two new gildings, the articles with lustre gilding received the Roman numeral I or the Arabic numeral 1, or just a short line in green paint over the glaze. The added numbers in green paint again identified the gilders (Figs. 680 and 681). This marking was used beginning in 1831 but abandoned later in the 19th century, as was the marking for Triangle Gilding.

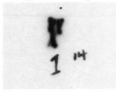

Figs. 680 and 681: Crossed swords with signs for lustre gilding

Proprietor's Marks

On porcelain for everyday use and for display in their Royal households in Warsaw and in and near Dresden, the Saxon rulers understandably used Meissen porcelain. Very many of these pieces bear owner or inventory markings in black or purple or blue paint over the glaze in addition to the manufactory mark. (Figs. 682 to 690)

None of these proprietor's markings have been seen with any other manufactory mark than the crossed swords. In older porcelain literature, some of them are shown by themselves without a manufactory mark. It is not possible today to find out if these markings really appeared on porcelain this way, or if the crossed swords marks were omitted in order to concentrate on the proprietor's marking.

The first of these markings probably were affixed late in the 1720s, their termination can be dated more precisely, it was around 1763. That year August III died, and the Saxon rulers lost the kingship of Poland. As mentioned before, protocol regarding titles was observed carefully in those days. All proprietor's markings beginning with the letter K for *Königlich* (Royal) had to be discontinued, and the markings for the court kitchen and confectionary in Warsaw were superfluous anyway.

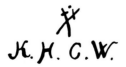

Fig. 682: Königlich-Churfürstliche Pillnitzer Conditorei *(Royal and Prince-Electoral Confectionery in Pillnitz)*

Fig. 683 Königliche Hof-Conditorei *(Royal Court Confectionery)*

Fig. 684: Königliche Hof-Conditorei Warschau *(Royal Court Confectionery in Warsaw)*

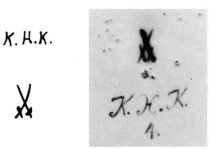

Figs. 685 and 686: Königliche Hof-Küche *(Royal Court Kitchen)*

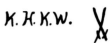

Fig. 687: Königliche Hof-Küche Warschau *(Royal Court Kitchen in Warsaw)*

Fig. 688: Königliche Pillnitzer Konditorei *(Royal Confectionery in Pillnitz)*

Fig. 689: Königliche Pillnitzer Küche *(Royal Kitchen in Pillnitz)*

Fig. 690: Königliche Silber-Kammer *(Royal Silver Chamber)*

After 1763, the Saxon Prince-Electors, or as their title then was written in German, the *Churfürsten*, had different proprietor's signs painted on their porcelain (Figs. 691 to 693). In 1806, the Prince Elector Friedrich August III signed an alliance treaty with Napoleon I who as a reward elevated Saxony to the status of kingdom. That lets it appear probable that the Prince-Electoral proprietor's markings were affixed from 1763 until 1806, possibly not even that long, because there are very few pieces around with these markings. After Saxony had become kingdom, the old proprietor's markings beginning with the letter K were not reintroduced, which might be taken as circumstantial evidence that these proprietor's markings were not even thought of anymore because they had been given up long before. Instead another proprietor's mark was introduced but it is not certain when that happened. Tableware for the Royal Court was signed on the bottom with "Königl. Hofwirtschaft" (Royal Court Household) in black paint over the glaze. Often a year was added. The small number of pieces observed with this inscription would suggest that there was no strict order or rule to apply this proprietor's mark on all tableware delivered to the Royal Household. This marking was terminated in 1918, when the Saxon King abdicated and Saxony became a republic.

Another proprietor's mark is known. Porcelain in the Royal Russian Collection in St. Petersburg, Russia, in the 18th century were signed with the Cyrillic letters P and K (Fig.694). It was possible for private buyers to order proprietor's marks on porcelain to be applied in the manufactory. Private marks also could be applied later outside the manufactory. Since these pieces are spread all over the world, it seems impossible to give a reliable survey of these private proprietors' marks.

C.H.K.

Ⓧ

Fig. 691: Churfürstliche Hof-Küche *(Prince-Electoral Court Kitchen)*

ĊHĊ

Ⓧ
✳

Fig. 692: Churfürstliche Hof-Conditorei *(Prince-Electoral Court Confectionery)*

C.P.C.

Ⓧ

Fig. 693: Churfürstliche Pillnitzer Conditorei *(Prince-Electoral Confectionery in Pillnitz)*

Fig. 694: Proprietor's mark of the Royal Russian Court in St. Petersburg

Model Numbers

The multitude of figurines, groups, decorative, and other porcelain made it necessary very early to register and number the different models. The first register was made in 1731, it has not been preserved. In 1749 Christian Heinrich Kaendler, head of the throwing and moulding department and brother of the chief modeller J.J. Kaendler, was charged with compiling a new list of the existing models.

The Seven-Years'-War brought quite some disorder and disarray to the manufactory. After the war had ended the keeper of the moulds, Johann Jacob Petri, was directed to review and renew the old lists. Today it is impossible to reconstruct his system of numbering the models. He did not arrange them in the sequence they were designed. In September of 1764 the number 3089 was reached. Attempts to match numbers and corresponding years or periods are moving like a ghost through porcelain literature. One frequently published list is based on handwritten notes by Erich Hösel[106] and repeated uncritically in a number of publications. Whoever copied Hösel's notes evidently got only a part of them, because the list stops in 1833, while Hösel continued it into the 20th century.

Since this list is around, a corrected version shall be given here, but only with the urgent recommendation to take into account the qualifications and reservations accompanying it.

Numbers	Period
Until c.1280	until 1749
1281-1470	1750
1471-1660	1751
1661-1850	1752
1851-2040	1753
2041-2220	1754
2221-2400	1755
2401-2480	1756
2481-2560	1757
2561-2620	1758
2621-2700	1759
2701-2780	1760
2781-2860	1761
2861-2940	1762
2941-3020	1763
3020-3051	until June of 1764

Here, the list must be interrupted for some explanations. It continued with combinations of letters and numbers but actually the number 3051 was not the last one. The counting continued until number 3089 (nos. 3064 to 3068 were not assigned to models), and the files in Meissen not only show a few numbers in the 4,000s (for instance no. 4291 *Boy with dog* by Ehder) but also no. 10,012 (One Figurine with Dolphin).

There are some more objections to this list. First of all, it is by no means even in an approximate time sequence. A few examples:

No.		was made c.
1	was made	c.1730
20	in	1741
50	in	1734
72	in	1728
127	in	1769
142	in	1732
1301	in	1755
2927	in	1736
2996	in	1769
4291	in	1743

It can not even be said that all models up to no. 3089 were designed before September of 1764, as no. 2996 of the above mentioned examples shows. Only one thing seems certain, none of the pulls made before September of 1764 bears an inscribed or impressed model number. The manufactory began putting the model numbers on the bottom of pieces pulled from the old moulds only after that date but sometimes they were simply left off. These numbers and all later numbers are by no means proof that a piece was made in the year that matches with the number. They merely indicate the year the original model was created, and not the year subsequent pulls were made. The numbers belong to the models, and a pull of a model made in the 20th century bears the same number as the 18th century original.

The numbering system was pierced by the habit of starting again with no. 1 when registering the members of a set, for instance the *Evangelists, the Monkey-Band, the Deeds of Hercules, the Dutch Village,* and others. The numbers 1 to 10, as one example, were assigned at least eighteen times.

To make the matter even worse, certain numbers were given to different objects, sometimes much later. No. 5 can serve as an example; under this number are listed:

5 Chinese Lion
5 Shepherd with Sheet Music
5 Goose
5 Mouse
5x Shepherdess with Sheep
5x Goose

So any list with model numbers and corresponding years is of very limited value. In the meantime, some of the old numbers have disappeared completely. When moulds became dull from frequent use, they were renewed, and often they received new numbers. A Tom Turkey made by Kaendler in 1733 was renumbered B 145 in the 1850s and a *Hen Turkey* made by Eberlein in 1735 later was registered as B 146.

A new numbering system was introduced in 1764, a combination of letters and numbers. With the proviso that this system is not foolproof either, the approximate times of the creation of the models shall be given.

Numbers	Period
A 1 to A 99	1764 to 1766
B 1 to B 100	1766 to 1768
C 1 to C 100	1768 to 1770
D 1 to D 100	1770 to 1775
E 1 to E 100	1772 to 1775
F 1 to F 100	1775 to 1779
G 1 to G 100	1779 to 1782

H 1 to H 100	1782 to 1785
J 1 to J 100	1785 to 1790
K 1 to K 100	1789 to 1795
L 1 to L 100	1796 to 1801
M 1 to M 22	1802
M 23 to M 33	1803
M 34 to M 49	1804
M 50 to M 67	1805
M 68 to M 99	1806
N 1 to N 100	1810 to 1815
O 1 to O 100	1814 to 1817
P 1 to P 100	1816 to 1818
Q 1 to Q 100	1818 to 1819
R 1 to R 100	1820 to 1832
S 1 to S 100	1827 to after 1831
T 1 to T 193	1831 to 1841
U 1 to U 100	1832 to 1836
V 1 to V 100	1837 to 1842
W 1 to W 100	1836 to 1843
X 1 to X 24	1842 to 1844
X 25 to X 100	1844 to 1847
Y 1 to Y 57	1846 to 1848
Y 58 to Y 100	1848 to 1850
Z 1 to Z 100	1849 to 1851
A 100 to A 200	1851 to 1855
B 100 to B 200	1853 to 1855
C 100 to C 200	1855 to 1863
D 100 to D 200	1855 to 1863
E 100 to E 200	1855 to 1863
F 100 to F 200	1863 to 1865
G 100 to G 200	1863 to 1866
H 100 to H 200	1863 to 1875
I 100 to I 200	1863 to 1876
K 100 to K 200	1876 to ?
L 100 to L 200	1877 to 1880
M 100 to M 200	1880 to 1882 (Fig. 647)
N 100 to N 200	1882 to 1885
O 102 to O 140	1886
O 141 to O 193	1889 to 1890
O 194 to P 105	1892
P 106 to P 121	1893
P 122 to P 162	1894
P 163 to Q 141	1895 to 1896
Q 142 to Q 200	1897 to 1905
R 101 to R 182	1898 to 1904
R 183 to S 134	1899 to 1904
S 135 to S 182	1900 to 1904
S 183 to S 200	1901 to 1905
T 1 to T 200	1901 to 1904

Beginning in 1909, letters and numbers in the 200s were used. The exact time periods for these designations could not be identified in all cases.

A 201 to A 300	1909 to
B 201 to B 300	1911 to
C 201 to C 300	1912 to
D 201 to D 300	1913 to
E 201 to E 300	1914 to 1916
F 201 to F 300	1914 to 1939
G 201 to G 300	to 1939
H 201 to H 300	to 1961
I 201 to I 300	to 1958
K 201 to K 300	
L 201 to L 300	
M 201 to M 300	
N 201 to N 300	to 1948
O 201 to O 300	1912 to 1951
P 201 to P 300	to 1952
Q 201 to Q 300	to 1955
R 201 to R 300	to 1954
S 201 to S 300	to 1956
T 201 to T 300	to 1961
U 201 to U 300	to 1970
V 201 to V 300	to 1970
W 201 to W 300	to 1973
X 201 to X 300	to 1973

This list too has to be taken with caution. Some of the models and designs with fascistic and militaristic motifs were stricken from the list after 1945, and their numbers assigned to new creations. Model no. O 276 for instance was a bust of the Nazi leader Hitler. In 1946 this number was given to a group: *The Seven Swabians* by Alexander Struck. The same thing happened to other models.

Beginning in 1923, some figurines and groups, that first received numbers between 200 and 300 in the D to G series were changed to a new system consisting of the letter A and a four-digit-number. The first five models by Paul Scheurich in 1913 were numbered D 283 to D 287. After 1923, they were renumbered A 1001 to A 1005. The A-plus-four-digits-numbers probably were issued until 1940 to models of free-lancers, for reasons of keeping an exact account of the royalties due.

A complete list containing each single model number and its corresponding year of creation or first pull would require years of research.[107] And even then, a synoptical presentation would only show the year of first production. For those antique pieces not yet identified completely as to the time of their creation, it would be of help. But still, any number only says that the piece bearing it was not produced before a certain year. It does not reveal, when this particular piece was actually made.

There is one definite break in the numbering system, though. In 1974 the burdensome and difficult to handle combination of letters and numbers method was changed completely to a five-digit numbering system suited for electronic data processing. The first two digits always indicate the article group, whose names still follow the 18th century arrangement.

Series (Monkey Band, Paris Peddlers etc.)

clockcases, busts	60 ...
Gardeners, Shepherds, Vintagers, Seasons	61 ...
Hunters	63 ...
Italian Comedy	64 ...
Japanese, Chinese	65 ...
Exotic and Foreign people, Pagodas	67 ...
Soldiers, Miners	69 ...
Mythological and allegorical subjects	79 ...
Saints and Evangelists	72 ...
Miscellaneous	73 ...
Birds	77 ...
Animals	78 ...
Candleholders	79 ...
Table decorations	80 ...
Böttger stoneware, figurines, groups and busts	85 ...
Animals from Böttger stoneware	86 ...

Here the list has to be interrupted again. The model numbers T 1 to T 193 and some of the U to Y series had been assigned between 1831 to 1851 to designs made after pressed or cut glass. Most of these articles were discontinued in 1851, others at the end of the 19th century and their numbers given to new models. But some of them were kept in production under their old numbers, so that the numbering of the T to Y series is rather confusing. The following numbers were taken out of production in November of 1851:

T. 1 to 7, 9 to 46, 48, 49, 52 to 69, 71 to 84, 86 to 98, 101, 102, 105 to 107, 109 to 111, 113 to 116, 118 to 121, 125 to 127, 129, 130, 133 to 136, 139 to 145, 147 to 153, 156 to 159, 161 to 163, 165, 167, 170, 172, 173, 175, 176, 179, 181, 182, 184, 185, 186 to 191

U 11, 28, 42 44b, 70, 73, 74, 79, 80, 83, 89, 90, 92, 98

V 11, 14, 15, 17, 18, 25, 28, 34b to 36, 49 to 52, 55, 59, 61, 66, 72b, 74b, 75, 76, 83, 93

W 7a, 7b, 7c, 8a, 8b, 8c, 14, 17 to 20, 26, 28, 44a, 44b, 47, 48, 52, 57a, 57b, 57c, 60, 62, 64 to 66, 68, 69, 72, 74, 78, 79, 82, 83a, 83b, 84, 85, 87, 91, 94, 100

X 1, 2a, 2b, 2c, 4, 13, 14, 16, 25, 26, 31, 40, 41, 43, 39, 61, 72, 76, 89a, 89b, 91 to 93

Y 4, 5a, 5b, 14, 16, 37, 70

Numbers on Tableware

Tableware also received special article numbers in the 18th century. These numbers were alike for all the different forms, they did not distinguish for instance between the form. Old *Ozier* for example, was not distinct from *the Swan Service*. In every set, the plates were counted from 0 to 6, each number standing for a certain diameter, the lowest identifying the largest diameter.

Number	Diameter	
0	25 cm	9 27/32 in.
1	25 cm	9 27/32 in
2	23.5 cm	9 1/4 in.
3	21.5 cm	8 1/2 in.
4	20 cm	7 7/8 in.
5	18 cm	7 1/8 in.
6	17.5 cm	6 15/16 in.

When a new piece of the set with a different size was developed, the new part had to be squeezed in with a new number, for instance Plate V 54 with 16 cm (6 9/32 in.) With every other article of a set, the counting again began at 1. Soup plates were counted from 1 to 5, gravy boats from 1 to 4, and for gravy boats designed later, the designations N 131, A 2, B 116, N 56 in two sizes, P 199 and no. 1132 in two sizes were chosen.

After World War I, this confusing system was reorganized. From 1919 only consecutive numbers were used; for plates 1 to 7, for soup plates 8 to 12, for tureens 13 to 23 and so on. Later, the numbering method was refined by putting two digits in front of the item numbers. These first two digits identified the form of the tableware; the last two described the particular part of the set. The form *New Cutout (Neuer Ausschnitt)* was an exception, its parts were numbered consecutively beginning with no. 1.

After 1974, the tableware also was included in the five digit numbering system. At that time, the sequence that had been used before was reversed. The lowest number then identified the smallest size.

Form	Old numbering system	New numbering system
Neuer Ausschnitt (New Cutout)	1 -	00 ...
Altozier (Old Ozier)	29.. to 32..	01 ...
Neubrandenstein (New Brandenstein)	20.. to 22..	02 ...
Neumarseille (New Marseille)	37.. and 38..	03 ...
Sulkowski	40.. and 41..	04 ...
Schwanen-Dessin (Swan design)	39..	05 ...
Doulong	34..	06
Glatte Form (Smooth Form)	10.. to 12..	10 ...
I-Form	11.. and 12..	11 ...
Biedermeier Form with border decoration	Letters N and U with numbers and numbers between 725 and 750	12 ...
Biedermeier Form without border decoration		13 ...
Schwanenhenkel (Swan Handle)	Letters N and U with numbers and numbers between 700 and 725	14 ...
B-Form with ornament	Letters B, C, L, N and P with numbers	15 ...
B-Form with lines	Letters B, C, I and L with numbers	16 ...
X-Form	Letters K, N, and X with numbers	17 ...
Börner-Form	Letters M and N with numbers	18 ...
Michel/Grosser Form	63..	19 ...
Collective Form	6..	20 ...
Zepner Form	63..	21 ...
Blütenrelief (Flower Relief)	63..	22 ...

These numbers, the old and the new, appear impressed in the paste. The old form numbers on a piece indicate that it was made before 1974; the five-digit-number is proof of a production after 1974.

The same applies to decorative porcelain like vases, flower pots, etageres, jugs, tankards, candle snuffers, knife handles, paperweights, footed bowls, reticulated pieces and similar articles, which formerly also had been identified by an unimaginable variety of numbers and letters plus numbers. For them, the digits 50 ... to 59 ... in the five-digit-system are now reserved.

Johanneum Numbers

A special kind of markings on Meissen porcelain was not applied by the manufactory. The so-called Johanneum numbers are considered proof for 18th century provenience of the pieces bearing them. These letters and numbers, incised or written in black, were the inventory markings of the Royal Porcelain Collection in Dresden. It was first kept in the "Green Vaults", a secret depository for documents and very valuable items, and in the "Dutch Palace" *(Holländisches Palais)*.

This palace was built by Count Flemming near the bank of the river Elbe in 1715. Since he immediately leased it to the Dutch ambassador, it was called the "Dutch Palace". In 1717, King August bought the building, and 12 years later he had it remodelled and extended, because he wanted it to become his "Porcelain Castle", a bit of one upmanship because other rulers only had "Porcelain Cabinets". August's idea was never realized. The Dutch Palace was renamed "Japanese Palace", and the largest part of the porcelain collection was kept there. The other part consisting of about 500 pieces, was brought to the tower room of the Royal Castle in Dresden. In 1875, most of the porcelain was removed to the upper story of the old picture gallery building, called Johanneum. Ceramic research began at about that time, and the incised or written inventory markings on the porcelain pieces in the Royal Collection, which now were studied at the Johanneum, became "Johanneum Numbers".

In 1721, the first inventory of the porcelain collection was made, and pieces acquired in the following years were added until 1727. This inventory had disappeared until shortly after 1900, but even after it was discovered, it was not evaluated for many years. It took until 1969 before the parts concerning Meissen products were published for the first time.[21]

All pieces in the collection were listed consecutively, and marked with the letter N and the list number. The introductory remarks explain the inventory system. "White Saxon Porcelain" received an added letter W to the inventory marking. Red stoneware, called "Brown Saxon Porcelain" was identified by the additional letter R. On black oriental pieces and Meissen stoneware with black glaze, the letter P was inscribed.

White Porcelain was divided into three groups:

Chapter I: "Gilt, neatly painted also enameled Saxon porcelain, consisting mainly of chocolate and coffee cups, small bowls, and copgen."

Chapter II: "Plain white Saxon porcelain, bottles, mugs, figurines, and docken." (docken is an unexplained expression)

Chapter III: "Bowls, milk pots, butter dishes, jugs, salt basins, writing utensils, tea and coffee things."

In 1770, a new inventory was made, because during the Seven-Years'-War "many of the pieces were ruined or stolen and the former inventory had become inaccurate" according to the major-domo of the court, Peter August von Schönberg [108]. That was not the only reason. A number of pieces had been removed for use in the Royal or Prince-Electoral household, or given away as gifts.

The inventory of 1770 repeats all of the items from the list of 1721 that were still in stock with the same numbers, but the chapter definition was changed to:
a) the former chapter II, added to the items were epergnes,
b) the former chapter I
c) the former chapter III
d) a new chapter "table sets as tureens, bowls, plates and butter dishes".
Since the complete inventories can not be repeated here, a short summary shall be given:

Inventory of 1721	Inventory of 1770
Chapter I: 64 positions registered until 1721 nos. 65-67 added in 1722 nos. 68-70 added in 1723 no. 71 added in 1727	Chaper b) counts to no. 503
Chapter II: 92 positions registered until 1721 no. 93 added in 1722 nos. 94-96 added in 1723 nos. 97-99 added in 1724 nos. 100-102 added in 1727	Chapter a) counts to no. 461
Chapter III: 62 positions registered until 1721 nos. 63-73 added in 1722 nos. 74-92 added in 1723 nos. 93 and 94 added in 1724 nos. 95-97 added in 1725	Chapter c) counts to no. 111
	Chapter d) counts to no. 401
Brown Saxon Stoneware (red stoneware) 87 positions registered until 1721 no. 88 added in 1722	counts to no. 244
Black Porcelain 40 positions registered until 1721 nos. 41 and 42 added in 1722	counts to no. 74

In the inventory of 1770, a number of positions is missing. In 1727 chapter I ended at no. 71; in 1770 the same chapter, now called b), ended at no. 503. But between no. 71 and no. 503, one hundred and twenty five positions are left out. The major-domo evidently compared the remaining pieces with a former inventory and he had to stick to the old numbering system because the numbers were incised or written on the pieces. The inventory used as basis for the list of 1770 has not been found yet. It is possible that the inventory list of 1721 was just continued after 1727 by adding new acquisitions as had been done between 1721 and 1727. At the end of chapter I in the inventory of 1721, a remark says "See page 961", but this page is missing in the files.

The Johanneum numbers at least say that a certain piece was made before the date it was registered in the inventory and received the inventory marking. Fig. 695 appears on the plate in Fig. 300, Fig. 696 on the plate in Fig. 299. The marking in Fig. 697 appears on a cup with cherry blossom painting.[109] The inventory of 1770 describes the position N=349-W in chapter b) as: "five pieces ditto (meaning cups) with little flowers 2 1/2 inches high, 3 1/4 inches in Diam."

This position contains not only five cups, but also five saucers. All ten of them received the same inventory marking. This is true for many other positions, so that the same Johanneum number appears on several pieces.

Some Johanneum numbers on porcelain cannot be found in the inventories. The highest number reached was N=503-W, but a waste bowl decorated in the Kakiemon style bears the number N=507-W. [110] Two explanations seem possible. Either the number was incised in order to pretend that this piece came from the Royal collection and the forger did not know that the inventory ended at no. 503, or the inventory was continued later, and that this continuation has not been found yet.

Fig. 695 to 697: Incised and blackened proprietor's marks of the Royal Saxon Court, so-called Johanneum Numbers

Chapter Eleven
Imitations of Meissen Marks

The first Meissen marks were intended as a protection against the decoration of Meissen porcelain by outside painters. The crossed swords, introduced a few years later, already had the character of a trademark, an identification sign for porcelain made by the Meissen manufactory. This turned out to be necessary very soon, because the number of porcelain manufactories in Europe grew very fast. Within fifty years after the Meissen manufactory had been established more than thirty manufactories had sprung up. On the European continent most of them were encouraged, furthered, and privileged by local or regional rulers and sovereigns.

Vienna, Austria	1717
Venice, Italy	1723
Chantilly, France	1725
Copenhagen, Denmark	1731
Mennecy-Villeroy, France	1734
Doccia, Italy	1737
Vincennes-Sèvres, France	1738
Rauenstein, Germany	1738
Buen Retiro, Spain	1739
Capo di Monte, Italy	1743
Chelsea, England	1743
St. Petersburg, Russia	1744
Höchst, Germany	1746
Fürstenberg, Germany	1747
Neudeck-Nymphenburg, Germany	1747
Bow, England	1748
Longton Hall, England	1750
Bristol, England	1750
Berlin, Germany	1751
Baden-Baden, Germany	1751
Worcester, England	1751
Lowestoft, England	1752
Frankenthal, Germany	1755
Derby, England	1756
Ansbach, Germany	1757
Gotha, Germany	1757
Ludwigsburg, Germany	1758
Ellwangen, Germany	1758
Sitzerode, Germany	1759
Kloster Veilsdorf, Germany	1760
Sitzendorf-Volkstedt, Germany	1760

Except for the French manufactories, most of the continental manufactories not only got some of the secrets of porcelain making illegitimately from Meissen - often by runaway workers or painters - they also copied and imitated Meissen designs and decorations. Meissen was the pacesetter, and a shining example the other manufactories wanted to reach. That was not easy, and because many of these porcelain producers could not match Meissen in the quality of their products, they tried to elevate their wares by passing them off as Meissen.

One of the early Meissen marks, the kite's tail, has been reported [1] to be on a basin made during the first years of the Worcester factory (Fig. 698). But despite the fact that Worcester copied the crossed swords of Meissen, this one is doubtful. Except for this single piece, no other Worcester product with a kite's tail mark has been seen or mentioned in porcelain literature.

Fig. 698: Kite's tail mark ascribed to Worcester

The factory of Edmé Samson in Paris, France, produced pieces with a mark similar to the kite's tail (Fig. 699), but evidently not very many. This mark was not too well known as a Meissen mark, and therefore pieces with the kite's tail did not appear desirable to the regular buying public. That might have been one reason why the Samson factory did not apply this mark more often. It is known that the Samson factory affixed any mark a customer ordered, and the pieces with the kite's tail could have been made on special order.

Fig. 699: Kite's tail mark used by Samson in Paris, France

An imitation of the Meissen pseudo-Chinese marks has not been proven. It is very questionable whether they were copied at all, because they were copies themselves and did not identify a piece as Meissen porcelain at first sign, on the contrary, this mark was supposed to hide the Meissen provenience.

The marks M.P.M., K.P.F., and K.P.M. were too shortlived to become really established. By the time other companies started copying Meissen marks, the crossed swords already were considered the regular mark on Meissen products. The Royal Prussian Porcelain Manufactory in Berlin, Germany, in the 19th century introduced some marks with the letters KPM for its German name *Königliche Porzellan Manufaktur*. These letters were always accompanied by other symbols the Berlin manufactory used (Fig. 700 to 702).

Figs. 700 to 702: Marks of the Royal Porcelain Manufactory in Berlin

Figs. 703 to 706 Marks of the Krister Porcelain Factory in Waldenburg, Silesia, 1855-1927

Figs. 707 and 708: Marks of the Krister Porcelain Factory in Waldenburg, Silesia, 1885-1945

The mark in Fig. 701 was imitated extensively by other factories, killing two birds with one stone. It could be taken for a Meissen mark or for a Berlin mark. In the second half of the 19th century, the letters KPM more and more became the identification for porcelain from Berlin, and even today the Berlin manufactory in everyday usage is referred to as "KPM". Copies and variations of the KPM marks first appeared in the 1880s. The Krister Porcelain Manufactory in Waldenburg, Silesia, in 1885 registered four trade-marks, all containing the letters KPM (Figs. 703 to 706). Later, other marks with KPM were introduced (Figs. 707 and 708) and the factory always argued that these letters stood for Krister Porcelain Manufactory. To support this claim the name of the factory, which originally was *"Carl Krister Porzellanfabrik"* (Carl Krister Porcelain Factory) and then *"Krister Porzellanindustrie"* (Krister Porcelain Industry), finally was changed to *"Krister Porzellan Manufaktur"* (Krister Porcelain Manufactory) despite the fact that it was not a manufactory at all, but a mass-producing factory.

The factory of A.W.Fr. Kister in Scheibe-Alsbach, Thuringia, offered a similar reason for using the letters KPM. Its trademark also contained the letters KPM plus two crossed lines (Fig. 709). The crossed lines certainly were intended to suggest the crossed swords to uninitiated buyers.

Fig. 709: Mark of the factory of A.W. Fr. Kister in Scheibe-Alsbach, after 1887

A factory in Kranichfeld, Saxony, justified the letters KPM in its mark with its name *"Kranichfelder Porzellanmanufaktur"* (Kranichfeld Porcelain Manufactory) (Figs. 710 and 711).

Figs. 710 and 711: Marks of the Kranichfeld Porcelain Manufactory in Kranichfeld, after 1903

The factory of Krautzberger, Mayer and Purkert in Wistritz, Bohemia, used the initials of the three proprietors which correctly would read KMP (Fig. 712), but with a little imagination could be arranged in the desired sequence (Fig. 713).

Figs. 712 and 713: Marks of the factory of Krautzberger, Mayer & Purkert in Wistritz, Bohemia, 1911-1945

The Kerafina Porcelain Factory in Marktredwitz, Bavaria also employed the letter combination KPM in some of its marks (Fig. 714 and 715). In this case, the letters seem to be an abbreviation of the factory name and its location.

Figs. 714 and 715: Marks of Kerafina Porcelain Factory in Marktredwitz, Bavaria, after 1950

Another one of the early marks, the letters KPF, were used by the company of A.W.Fr. Kister in Scheibe-Alsbach (Fig 716) also, as well as by the Krister porcelain factory in Waldenburg, (Fig. 717 and 718).

Fig. 716: Mark of A.W.Fr. Kister in Scheibe-Alsbach

          (K)(P)(F)

Figs. 717 and 718: Marks of the Krister Porcelain Factory in Waldenburg, Silesia, second half 19th century to 1927

Fig. 719: Mark of the Porcelain and Brick Factory Mosa, Netherlands

Fig. 720: Mark of C. Müller, Steinwiesen, after 1905

M. P. M.

Fig. 721: Mark of E. & A. Müller Schönwald, Bavaria, 1904-1927

The letters MPM have been found on products of the Dutch *Porselain- en Muurtegelfabrick Mosa* (Porcelain and Brick Factory Mosa) in Maastricht, Netherlands (Fig. 719). Here a confusion with Meissen porcelain is rather improbable. The company of C. Müller in Steinwiesen, Bavaria, which produced fayence and decorated porcelain, enclosed the letters MPM in a triangle and added the letter S for Steinwiesen (Fig. 720). This mark usually is applied over the glaze. The factory of E. & A. Müller in Schönwald, Bavaria, founded in 1904, used the letters M.P.M. without any additions on its porcelain (Figs. 470 and 721). It also copied Meissen decorating motifs, among them the *Onion Pattern*.

While a careful scrutiny of all these marks would show that they are not Meissen marks, and the porcelain on which they are affixed are not by far Meissen products, the intertwined letters AR (Fig. 722) create real problems. For a long time, porcelain with this sign was considered very valuable because the manufactory itself had declared that this mark was only used in the years 1709 until 1726.[2] In the second half of the 19th century, a large number of Meissen imitations with the AR mark appeared on the market. The first company to copy this mark was the antiques dealer Helena Wolfsohn in Dresden (Fig. 723 to 726). She also operated a porcelain decorating shop, but kept quiet about it. The AR mark was not protected as a trademark in 1848 when she started using it. The mark was convincing only when it was applied under the glaze before the sharp firing. That Ms. Wolfsohn could not do. She operated muffle kilns to fix the painting on porcelain, but these kilns reached only 800 to 900 degrees Celsius (1500 to 1650 degrees Fahrenheit). That is about 600 to 500 degrees Celsius (1100 to 900 degrees Fahrenheit) below the heat necessary for sharp firing and glazing. She therefore could not have produced the white porcelain with the blue underglaze AR mark she decorated in her shop. That porcelain must have been made by other factories. For a long time, the *"Wiener Porzellanfabrik"* (Viennese Porcelain Factory) in Elbogen, Bohemia, founded by the Bros. Haidinger was suspected of having produced white porcelain with the AR mark for Helena Wolfsohn. This suspicion has no foundation any more.

In 1875 the Royal Manufactory registered AR as its trademark. One year later the company of Helena Wolfsohn and the Dresden antiques dealer Leo Meyer applied for the cancellation of the mark.[3] They argued that the manufactory had claimed to have used this mark from 1709 until 1726, in a period 150 years ago. The Trademark Act required that a mark for which protection was sought was in use at the time of the application for a trademark registration. Since this was not the case - the two plaintiffs argued - the Royal Manufactory had no right to the AR mark, while they themselves had used this mark without interruption for thirty years. For this they offered proof, and they named the porcelain factories of Christian Fischer in Zwickau, Saxony, and of C.M. Hutschenreuther in Hohenberg, Bavaria, as witnesses. They were supposed to testify that they had produced white porcelain with the AR mark for Wolfsohn and Meyer.

Fig. 722: Meissen AR-mark

Figs. 723 to 726: AR-marks by Helena Wolfsohn, Dresden, c. 1850-1881

Answering an inquiry by the Royal Manufactory, Christian Fischer admitted that he had applied any letters requested by his customers and it was quite clear that the letters AR were among them.[4] The C.M. Hutschenreuther factory did not answer an inquiry by the Meissen manufactory. It could not even be forced to answer by a Saxon court, because the factory was located in Bavaria, where Saxony had no jurisdiction. Wolfsohn and Meyer expected from the C.M. Hutschenreuther factory testimony that it had made white porcelain with the AR mark blue under the glaze for them. The plaintiffs would not have called this witness if they were not absolutely sure that he would support their claim. It therefore seems reasonable to assume that C.M. Hutschenreuther produced white porcelain with the AR mark for Wolfsohn and Meyer just as Christian Fischer did.

In the meantime, two World Wars and many changes have gone through Germany and today the Hutschenreuther company says that the old files concerning this matter have vanished. Only some old model books show that white porcelain was delivered to the companies of Wolfsohn and Meyer, unfortunately without any indication which marks had been applied.[5]

After lengthy litigation from 1876 to 1881 the final court judgement said that Wolfsohn and Meyer were "not entitled to use the sign AR on porcelain products".[6] But that was not the end of it. The case was pending in England too. There Wolfsohn and Meyer had applied for the cancellation of the Royal Manufactory's AR trademark registration in England. In 1883, the successors of Helena Wolfsohn her daughter Emilie Elb and her grandson Leopold Ludwig Elb, who continued the business under the name of Helena Wolfsohn, finally gave up. They signed an agreement promising to withdraw their suit in London, to have their AR mark cancelled in England, to pay $2,500 for every violation of the agreement, and never to sue abroad again.[7]

But before this agreement was signed, the Elbs conducted a protracted retreat. They tried to save the AR mark for their company and changed it after 1881 (Fig. 727 to 728). The Meissen manufactory was determined not to let them get away with anything that even faintly resembled the AR mark and it was in a good position. Emilie and Leopold Elb were well aware that their court case in London did not look good, and the Meissen Manufactory any day could send the marshals to close down their shop in Dresden. They had to give in, but they did it one slow step after the other.

Figs. 727 and 728: Variations of Wolfsohn Mark, 1881-1882

The Royal Manufactory objected to the new marks too. To be on the safe side it insisted on grinding out the AR mark on all pieces still in stock at the Wolfsohn decorating shop and in the Wolfsohn stores. It not only offered to do it free of charge, it also was willing to glaze over the ground out spot

and to fire the pieces again. It even went so far as to pay for the shipment of 7,000 pieces of white porcelain from Dresden to Meissen.

When the Elbs asked if instead of the AR mark the letter D "with some little ornament" could be applied by the Meissen manufactory, its manager was quite willing to conform, but he first wanted to know what they meant by "some little ornament". It later turned out to be a crown, and this mark (Fig. 729) with many variations (Figs. 730 to 732) was used by the company of Helena Wolfsohn after 1883.

Fig. 729: Mark registered by the company of Helena Wolfsohn in 1881

Figs. 730 to 732: Variations of Mark in Fig. 729

Fig. 733: AR-mark of the Wolfsohn company with its new mark added over the glaze, after 1881

One more problem had to be solved. Ms. Elb and her son had a large number of decorated pieces in stock. The marks could be ground out, but the rough spot left could not be glazed over and fired again. The intense heat of the sharp fire would have burned off the decoration. After prolonged negotiations, Ms. Elb agreed to add a crown and the capital letter D to her AR mark (Fig. 733) on all pieces in her warehouses and stores in Dresden, Paris, France, and Karlsbad, Bohemia. Leo Meyer, who had joined the legal actions of the Wolfsohn company, submitted to similar conditions and also ceased using the AR mark.

The company of Wolfsohn was not the only one that used the AR mark, but it certainly was the biggest. Its products were mainly exported to England and the United States of America. While it is impossible to distinguish between the real AR mark and a Wolfsohn copy, it is easy to identify the decoration on a Wolfsohn piece. Compared to Meissen it is rather crude and lacks the accuracy and precision of the Meissen painters, as described in Chapter VIII.

Another company that used an intertwined AR was the decorating shop of Armin Richter in Plaue, Thuringia. Richter signed the pieces painted by him with his initials blue over the glaze (Fig. 734 and 735). The Meissen Manufactory sued him in 1912, and sent the police to confiscate all porcelain with Richter's AR mark. They found 281 pieces, some with an additional crown on top of the letters and some with the added name "Plaue".

Richter defended himself by claiming the sign AR as his monogram, and he insisted on not even knowing the Meissen AR mark. The Superior Court in Erfurt dismissed the action of the Royal Manufactory and the Imperial Court confirmed the decision. Richter was allowed the further use of his mark.[9]

Figs. 734 and 735: AR-marks by Armin Richter in Plaue, after 1900

Fig. 736: AR-mark of Anton Richter, Dresden

Another Richter, Anton Richter in Dresden, also applied his initials on porcelain he had decorated. This mark was painted in blue color over the glaze (Fig. 736). Since it seemed removed far enough from the Meissen original, the Royal Manufactory waived legal actions against Anton Richter.

The factory of Muth & Metzger in Tirschenreuth, Bavaria, also had used the AR mark since 1868, but the Meissen Manufactory became aware of it only in 1882. Muth & Metzger had answered a circular letter the Meissen Manufactory had sent to other porcelain producers notifying them of its intention to strictly protect the Meissen trademarks. The company in Tirschenreuth wrote back that it had discontinued the use of the AR mark the same day it had learned about the court decision against the company of Helena Wolfsohn in 1881.[10]

Prince Friedrich Christian of Saxony, living at Castle Altshausen in Württemberg, FRG in 1950 applied for the trademark registration of the intertwined letters AR with a crown above them (Fig. 737). The mark was supposed to be applied on porcelain and ceramic products.[11] The Patent Office in the Federal Republic of Germany did not grant the application.

Fig. 737: AR-mark for which Prince Friedrich Christian of Saxony unsuccessfully sought a trademark registration

Fig. 738: Mark of Albin Rosenlöcher in Küps, Bavaria, 1887 -c.1906

A mark similar to that of Meissen was registered in 1887 for the porcelain factory of Albin Rosenlöcher in Küps, Bavaria (Fig. 738). Its use was abandoned about 1906.

A number of other AR marks cannot be attributed with certainty. It only can be said that the pieces on which they have been observed were not made by the Meissen Manufactory (Figs. 739 to 743). Some of them might have been made for Wolfsohn and Meyer by the factories of Fischer and C.M. Hutschenreuther or they were produced by Muth & Metzger. Since most of the marks evidently were painted by hand, variations in shape and size would not be uncommon.

The Royal Manufactory not only took action against straight imitations of the AR mark, it also wanted to do away with marks that looked similar and could be mistaken for the Meissen sign. In answering the circular letter mentioned before, the porcelain factory of August Bauscher in Weiden, Bavaria, asked if the Meissen Manufactory had any objections against the intertwined initials AB (Fig. 744). Carried

away by the successful litigation against Wolfsohn and Meyer, the manager of the manufactory in his answer first admitted that this mark not really infringed on Meissen rights but then continued "I beg your pardon for my frankness but I consider it dangerous for the reputation of a conscious manufacturer when he tries to deceive the public with a speculative mark".[12] Mr. Bauscher did not like this insinuation and contemplated legal action. He only refrained from it because - as he wrote back - "my lawyer has advised me against suing you for the remarks you called 'frankness' because the law does not consider them libel".[13] The company of Bauscher continued using the mark for some time, but shortly after 1900 replaced it with other marks.

The host of copies and imitations of the crossed swords mark of the Meissen manufactory is countless and incalculable. But in most cases quality of the paste, the shape, and the decoration of the pieces with the copied crossed swords give them away as imitations. It is necessary, though, to become familiar with the characteristic features of Meissen porcelain and painting, some of which this book tries to describe. To depend solely on the crossed swords mark is not advisable when it comes to porcelain that is supposed to be antique or old. After 1900 the famous crossed swords mark was imitated less often than in the 19th century.

The very first imitations of the crossed swords have been observed on British porcelain. By the middle of the 18th century, some factories in England tried to pass off their products as Meissen porcelain, or as it was called, as "Dresden China". It is impossible to exactly date those pieces with an imitation of the crossed swords, so the dates given encompass the probable period of production.

One of the first factories to imitate the crossed swords mark seems to have been the shop of Nicholas Sprimont in Chelsea (Figs. 745 to 748). William Lowdin in Bristol, at least for a short time, used the crossed swords, in some cases in brown paint over the glaze (Figs. 749 and 750). Cookworthy & Champion in Bristol evidently made generous use of the Meissen mark (Figs. 751 to 755). On their porcelain it appears blue under the glaze. Some of the crossed swords marks of Bristol show added numbers painted in gold over the glaze (Figs. 756 to 758). Others have been found with two additional crossed lines painted blue over the glaze, either next to the crossed swords or superimposed (Figs. 759 to 762).

William Duesbury in Derby is known to have advertised his porcelain as made "after the finest Dresden models".[14] It is not surprising to learn that he also applied the well-known crossed swords on his porcelain designed after Meissen models (Figs. 763 to 765).

Figs. 745 to 748: Marks of Nicholas Sprimont, Chelsea, England

Figs. 749 and 750: Marks of William Lowdin, Bristol, England

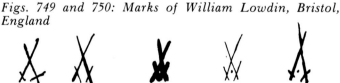

Figs. 751 to 755: Marks of Cookworthy & Champion, Bristol, England

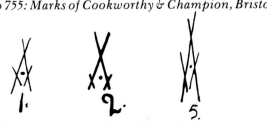

Figs. 756 to 758: Marks of Cookworthy & Champion, Bristol, England

Figs. 739 to 743: Undentified AR-marks

Fig. 744: Mark of August Bauscher in Weiden, Bavaria, 1881 -shortly after 1900

Figs. 759 to 762: Marks of Cookworthy & Champion, Bristol, England

Figs. 763 to 765: Marks of William Duesbury, Derby, England

Figs. 766 and 767: Marks of Dr. John Wall, Worcester, England

Figs. 768 to 770: Marks of Dr. John Wall, Worcester, England

Fig. 771: Mark of Weatherby & Crowther Bow, England

Figs. 772 to 774: Marks of Walker, Browne, Aldred & Richman, Lowestoft, England

Figs. 775 and 776: Marks of Thomas Turner, Caughley, England

Figs. 777 to 779: Marks of Thomas Turner, Caughley, England

Fig. 780: Mark of Thomas Turner, Caughley, England

Figs. 781 to 783: Marks of William Littler, Longton Hall, England

Figs. 784 to 786: Later marks of Derby, England

While Dr. John Wall was proprietor, the factory in Worcester quite extensively used the crossed swords (Figs. 766 and 767). They appear in many variations and often numbers are added, mainly 9 and 91 (Figs. 768 to 770). From a dot next to some of the numbers, it can be deducted that the Worcester crossed swords were supposed to be looked at upside down, but that certainly would not be convincing proof that Dr. Wall's mark were not really imitations of the Meissen mark.

From Weatherby & Crowther in Bow, very few pieces with crossed swords have been observed (Fig. 771). The company of Walker, Browne, Aldred and Richman in Lowestoft also seems to have used the crossed swords only sparingly (Figs. 772 to 774). Thomas Turner in Caughley added the capital letter S to the swords (Figs. 775 and 776), or a star plus the letter S (Figs. 777 to 779), or just a star on top between the tips of the swords. (Fig. 780)

William Littler in Longton Hall marked his porcelain with a sign that could be interpreted as crossed letters L (Figs. 781 to 783). They usually have a number of dots below them.

Later marks of Derby, late in the 18th century and in the 19th century, combine the crossed swords with the Derby crown mark. They are painted over the glaze (Figs. 784 to 786). To the 19th century also belongs an imitation of the Meissen swords by John Rose & Co. in Coalport (Fig. 787).

Factories on the European continent very often added something to the crossed swords or they varied the Meissen mark. The factory of Count Gronsveldt-Diepenbroek in Weesp, Netherlands, put several dots into the vectors created by the crossing lines (Figs. 788 to 790). In 1771, Johannes de Mol took over the factory and moved it from Weesp to Oude Loosdrecht. During the first years he impressed a sign on his porcelain that looked similar to the Meissen swords (Fig. 791).

F.J. Peterinck in Tournay, Belgium, put little crossed lines into the vectors made by the crossed swords (Figs 792 and 793). In Paris, France, Pierre Antoine Hannong signed his porcelain with something resembling crossed pipes (Figs. 794 to 796), despite his public announcement to be using the letter H on his products.

Fig. 787: Mark of John Rose, Coalport, England

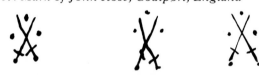

Figs. 788 to 790: Marks of Count Groonsveldt-Diepenbroek, Weesp, Netherlands

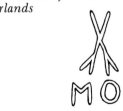

Fig. 791: Mark of Johannes de Mol, Weesp, Netherlands

Figs. 792 and 793: Marks of F.J. Peterinck, Tournay, Belgium

Figs. 794 to 796: Marks of Pierre Antoine Hannong, Paris, France

Figs. 797 to 799 Marks of manufactory La Courtille, Paris, France

Another factory in Paris, La Courtille at the rue Fontaine-au-Roi used marks that looked like torches or arrows (Figs. 797 to 799). It was founded in 1771 by Guilleaume Locré de Roissy, who had learned porcelain making in Germany. His products were called *"Porceleine Allemande"* (German Porcelain).

In Sceaux, department Seine, Richard Glot in 1772 bought a fayence manufactory and converted it for porcelain production, at the same time continuing to make fayence. For both, he used the same marks (Figs. 800 to 802). Porcelain had to be made almost clandestinely, because the manufactory was not officially allowed to produce it since the manufactory in Sèvres had a monopoly on porcelain making.

The factory of Tinet in Montreuil-sous-Bois, department Seine, from 1815 to 1875 produced porcelain with Oriental decorations. Its mark (Fig. 803) occasionally is accompanied by the addition "29 *Rue du Bac*" or "32 *Rue du Bac*". In this Paris street, Tinet had his own store.

In Poland, the manufactory Belvedere in Warsaw is supposed to have employed the crossed swords with dots, and with dot and star (Figs. 804 and 805). It has not been definitely proven, though, that these marks really belong to Belvedere.

In Russia, Francis Gardner, an Englishman who operated a manufactory near Moscow, occasionally signed with the crossed swords and an added star (Fig. 806 and 807).

In Germany, several early porcelain manufactories had their signs inspired by the crossed swords. The short-lived Princely Fulda Fine Porcelain Factory (1784-1789) used two crossed lines (Figs. 808 and 809) which could be justified by the fact that its founder, the Prince Abbot of Fulda wanted a Christian sign on his porcelain.

Figs. 800 to 802: Marks of Richard Glot, Sceaux, France

Fig. 803: Mark of Tinet, Montreuil-sous-Bois, France

Figs. 804 and 805: Marks ascribed to porcelain manufactory Belvedere, Warsaw, Poland

Figs. 806 and 807: Marks of Francis Gardner, Moscow, Russia

Figs. 808 and 809: Marks of the Princely Porcelain Factory in Fulda, Germany

Fig. 810: Mark of the Ducal Brunswick Procelain Factory in Fürstenberg, Germany

The Ducal Brunswick Porcelain Manufactory in Fürstenberg (Fig. 810) occasionally copied the crossed swords during the Marcolini period of Meissen (1774-1814).

Not identified satisfactorily are some other marks. Figs. 811 and 812 are attributed in ceramic literature to a manufactory in Anspach, but there was no city of that name in Germany. The name "Anspach" does appear on some pieces of the fayence manufactory in Ansbach, Bavaria (1710-1806). Porcelain literature also mentions a manufactory in Arnstadt, Thuringia, that supposedly was founded in 1790, and the marks in Figs. 813 and 814 usually are attributed to it. The Anspach marks await further proof, while it is certain that there never was a porcelain manufactory in Arnstadt.

Most of the problems for the Meissen Manufactory were created by the manufactories in neighboring Thuringia. Within the relatively short period between 1760 and 1783, eleven manufactories were founded, not quite of the same importance as Meissen, but noticeable as competitors. Porcelain history now considers them as outstanding because of their originality, their natural style, and their portrayal of burghers, merchants, artisans, and peasants of the late 18th and early 19th centuries.

At first, these manufactories tried to copy Meissen styles and decorations, and most of them imitated the crossed swords mark one way or the other. Georg Heinrich Macheleid on his own developed a manufacturing process for hard paste porcelain, and in 1760 he founded a manufactory in Sitzendorf that was moved to Volkstedt-Rudolstadt two years later. The company, of which the ruler of the territory of Schwarzburg-Rudolstadt was a stockholder, did not do too well, and in 1767 it was leased to Christian Nonne. Macheleid already had put the fork from the Princely coat-of-arms as sign on his products together with his initial "M" (Fig. 815). Christian Nonne at first continued using it without the letter M, but before long decided to cross two forks, and with a few alterations he made them look similar to the crossed swords (Figs. 816 and 817).

The Closter Veilsdorf manufactory, founded in 1760 and privileged in 1765, tried to arrange the initials C and V in a manner similar to the crossed swords (Fig. 818). That was not easy and sometimes just a copy of the crossed swords was painted on the pieces.

Figs. 811 and 812: Marks ascribed to a manufactory in Ansbach, Germany, questionable

Figs. 813 and 814: Marks ascribed to a manufactory in Arnstadt, Germany, very questionable

Fig. 815: Mark of Georg Heinrich Macheleid, Sitzendorf and Volkstedt, 1760-1767

Figs. 816 and 817: Marks of Christian Nonne in Volkstedt

Fig. 818: Marks of the porcelain manufactory in Closter Veilsdorf, Germany

For the manufactory in Wallendorf it was easier to vary the initial W to be confused with the crossed swords (Figs. 819 to 821). Most of the Wallendorf marks tried to keep at least a faint resemblance to the letter W, which remained the mark of the manufactory until today.

Gotthelf Greiner, the founder of the manufactory in Limbach and the most important personality of the Thuringian porcelain industry, designed one of his first marks in the shape of two crossed capital "LL's" Figs. 822 to 825). They looked close enough to be taken for the Meissen mark. In 1782, Greiner bought the manufactory in Grossbreitenbach, Thuringi, which had been founded in 1777. Here, he applied the same marks as in Limbch and it is impossible to distinguish Limbach products from those of Grossbreitenbach by the marks alone. A third manufactory operated by Gotthelf Greiner was located in Ilmenau. Founded in 1777, it was leased to Greiner in 1786. Seven years later, Christian None from Volkstedt bought the manufactory. During the time of Greiner's leasehold, the manufactory had two crossed capital "II's" with a line through them as its mark (Figs. 826 to 828). The manufactory in Schney, now Bavaria, was established in 1781 by workers from Wallendorf. Among its early marks are two crossed lines with the capital letter S (Fig. 868 and 869). These marks easily can be confused with marks used much later in the 19th century by the factory of A.W. Fr. Kister in Scheibe-Alsbach (Fig. 866) now VEB Porcelain Factory Scheibe-Alsbach (Fig. 867) and by the factory of L. Schleich in Buschbad, Saxony (Fig. 865).

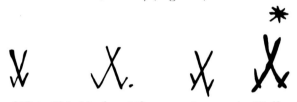

Figs. 819 to 821: Marks of the manufactory in Wallendorf

Figs. 822 to 825: Marks of Gotthelf Greiner in Limbach, Germany

Figs. 826 to 828: Marks of Gotthelf Greiner in Ilmenau

Three other members of the large Greiner clan in Thuringia, Johann Friedrich, Johann Georg, and his son Christian Daniel, in 1783 founded the manufactory in Rauenstein. They imitated the crossed swords of Meissen (Fig. 848), but soon added the letters R or R-n (Figs. 845 to 847).

The Meissen Manufactory did not like these imitations at all, and neither did its owner, the Prince-Elector of Saxony. On October 3rd, 1775, he issued a General Order prohibiting import and sale of porcelain with marks that looked like the crossed swords of Meissen.[15] But the Thuringian manufactories did not care much about this order. In May of 1776 the Saxon Prince-Elector, Friedrich August, wrote to the Prince at Schwarzburg-Rudolstadt recommending the use of a distinguishable sign by the manufactory in Volkstedt-Rudolstadt. The reason was that the proprietor Christian Nonne had begun to eliminate his sign of the two crossed forks altogether. The Saxon Prince-Elector suspected him of trying to sell his now unmarked products as Meissen porcelain outside Saxony.

In October of 1777, the Prince at Schwarzburg-Rudolstadt complained to his Saxon neighbor about the confiscation of four boxes with unmarked porcelain from the Volkstedt manufactory in the Saxon city of Leipzig. In an appeal for mercy, Christian Nonne explained that these boxes were only in transit through Saxony, and a shipping clerk mistakenly had written in the bill of lading that the porcelain pieces had been produced in Nuremberg, Bavaria. In his pleas for the release of his shipment, Nonne protested his innocene, and declared that he had not applied the crossed forks for a long time.[16] The Saxon authorities knew better because in the years before Nonne adamantly had refused to change his sign.[17] The matter went hence and forth, and in 1779 the Prince at Schwarzburg-Rudolstadt advised his noble cousin in Dresden that he had instructed Nonne to obey the General Order of 1775.

That was six weeks after the Saxon Prince-Elector in 1778 had issued another stern order threatening severe penalties for import and sale of foreign porcelain without a mark or with a sign similar to the crossed swords. A penalty of double the market value of the porcelain was laid down, of which informers was promised one third as reward. [18]

Even this order was not sufficient. In 1782, the Mayor of the city of Leipzig, Carl Wilhelm Müller, reported to the Prince-Elector about porcelain from the manufactory at Closter Veilsdorf, which in former times had applied obscure marks but at that time put on its porcelain "even the Prince-Electoral swords clearly and unabashedly".[19] When the owner of the manufactory at Closter Veilsdorf, Prince Fr. W. Eugen of Saxony-Hildburghausen, asked his manager about the marking habits, the manager was not impressed by this inquiry. He coolly pointed out that many other manufactories employed similar marks.

The pressure from the Saxon court on the neighboring little principalities increased further. The Duke of Saxony-Meiningen sternly demanded that the proprietor of the manufactory in Limbach, Gotthelf Greiner, was not to use misleading marks any more. In an advertisement on January 8th, 1788, Greiner made a clean sweep of the matter. He admitted that "traders frequently had sold my porcelain for Meissen" and announced the introduction of a new sign, the clover-leaf from his coat-of-arms (Fig. 829) for his three manufactories in Limbach, Ilmenau and Grossbreitenbach. [20]

Slowly, the other manufactories followed suit, and around the turn of the 19th century, the Thuringian manufactories had stopped the blatant imitations of the crossed swords mark.

Porcelain with imitated marks described above are not quite of Meissen quality, but they are antiques in their own right. With the imitations of the 19th and 20th centuries, it is quite differenct. In the first half of the 19th century, the porcelain industry in central Europe began to develop only slowly. An imitation of the Meissen crossed swords did not seem worthwhile at that time, because the fame of Meissen had suffered from the artistic decline after the Napoleonic Wars. By 1850, not only had the Meissen manufactory regained the esteem of the buying public, but the number of porcelain factories increased rapidly in Germany. Both developments gave new incentives for imitations of the crossed swords. This time imitators avoided copying the mark directly, but they tried to get as close as possible without giving the Royal Manufactory cause for legal actions.

But litigation was not always easy, especially not outside Saxony. In 1870, the Meissen manufactory learned about the use of the crossed swords by a manufactory in Austria-Hungary. The company of Wahliss in Vienna, dealer in Meissen and other porcelains, wrote to the Royal Manufactory in March of 1870 that the porcelain manufactory of

Fig. 829: Mark of Gotthelf Greiner for his manufactories in Limbach, Ilmenau and Grossbreitenbach after 1788

Moritz Fischer in Herend, Hungary, had repeatedly offered to deliver pieces with old Meissen marks.[21] The Meissen manufactury obtained two little baskets and one small box showing the crossed swords with a star below, which supposedly were made in Herend. The Saxon Treasury instructed the Saxon legation in Vienna to investigate the case, and to ask the authorities in Austria-Hungary to take measures against the use of the crossed swords by Moritz Fischer.

Fischer denied the allegation, and a search in his manufactury turned up no wares with the crossed swords. In a statement Fischer only admitted that he had copied Meissen designs, which was not illegal. His manufactory in 1844 indeed had received an order by the Countess Esterhazy for replacement parts for her Meissen dinner service. Fischer had delivered the parts to the satisfaction of the very influential Countess, and that had given him the idea to copy Meissen designs and those of other famous manufactories, even those on old Chinese and Japanese porcelain.

In his statement Fischer bluntly accused the Meissen manufactory of having abandoned the old styles and allowed its porcelain to artistically deteriorate. He, on the other hand (so he declared), had upheld the old perfection for which once Meissen was famous. Many persons of high birth needed replacement parts for their Meissen sets, but the Royal Manufactory had not been able to provide them, Fischer continued, so these persons had turned to him, because he could produce exact copies of old Meissen porcelain. Foreign dealers, even a purveyor to the Saxon court in Dresden, had asked him for copies of old Meissen pieces and requested Meissen marks on them. But Fischer emphatically denied ever having applied a Meissen mark on his porcelain.[22]

The German embassy in Vienna believed Fischer, and suggested that some other manufacturer was the producer of the three pieces. The Meissen Manufactory was not convinced, but the Saxon Treasury in 1872 decided to drop the case. Even today, the Herend manufactory maintains never in its history to have applied Meissen marks on its products.[23] This attitude is understandable, because the Herend manufactory has acquired a worldwide reputation and does not want to cloud it by possible transgressions of former proprietors. Nevertheless, the statement of the Herend manufactory now is refutable. The Museum of Arts and Crafts in Budapest, Hungary, has in its depot a large cup and a saucer (Fig. 830) with proof of the use of the Meissen crossed swords by the Herend manufactory. Impressed at the bottom of the cup in colorless letters is "FM-HEREND-847". The letters FM stand for Fisher, Moritz, HEREND speaks for itself, and the number could be a model number. It is also possible that 847 stands for the year 1847.

In addition to this impressed mark, the crossed swords are painted blue under the glaze (Fig. 831). This is remarkable, because the impressed inscription gives the producer away despite the imitated Meissen mark.[24] Reports by the Wahliss store in Vienna suggest that the Herend manufactory produced porcelain with the crossed swords and without Fischer's impressed initials or the name Herend. Since the Hungarian manufactory almost perfectly copied old Meissen porcelain it is very difficult to definitely identify a Herend copy of old Meissen. In 1876, the Royal Manufactory registered its trademarks in Hungary too, and that made it more difficult for the Herend manufactory to copy the crossed swords.

In Germany, the Meissen Manufactory did not tolerate any infringement on its rights after the enactment of the Trademark Law in 1875. It brought one of the first suits against the *Schlesische Porzellanfabrik Paul Donath* (Silesian Porcelain Factory Paul Donath) in Tiefenfurt, Silesia. Louis Lövinsohn, the founder of the factory, in 1886 had registered a trademark (Fig. 832) consisting of two crossed sabres with the letter S between the hilts.[25] He produced coffee and tea sets as well as decorative porcelain in the Meissen style. In 1891 he sold his factory to Paul Donath including the rights to his trademark. Donath made the letter S on his porcelain much smaller, and that annoyed the Meissen Manufactory. Customers began to order replacement parts for Donath sets in Meissen, believing their porcelain had been made by the Royal Manufactory (Fig. 833).

Fig. 830: Cup and saucer made by the manufactory of Moritz Fischer in Herend, Hungary, about 1850

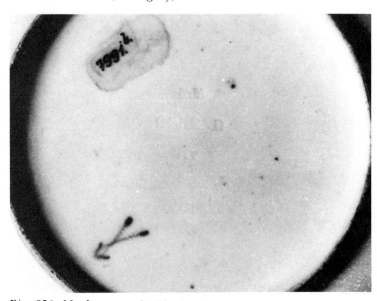

Fig. 831: Mark on cup in Fig. 830

Fig. 832: Mark registered by Louis Lövinsohn, Tiefenfurth, Silesia, in 1886

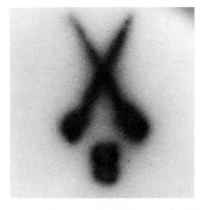

Fig. 833: Mark of Paul Donath in Tiefenfurth, Silesia, after 1891

The manufactory sued Donath, and called the general manager of the Royal Porcelain Manufactory in Berlin, Dr. Heinecke, as an expert witness. Heinecke testified that he had shown a number of Donath pieces to some of his employees, and that they at first sight had identified them as Meissen products. Only closer scrutiny had revealed the pieces as Donath porcelain.

The court was not convinced. It dismissed the suit, stating that "the average buyer would notice the difference immediately."[26] An appeal to the Imperial Court was to no avail. In those years of rapid economic expansion and industrial growth, the courts felt it was their duty to encourage industrial development, and to protect it from infringing restrictions. Private enterprise was allowed almost anything short of blatant crime.

The Donath factory in 1895 registered the trademark again. Immediately the Meissen Manufactory applied for its cancellation at the Imperial Patent Office, and this time it succeeded. In 1896 the Donath mark was cancelled.

The attitude of the courts made it difficult for the Royal Manufactory to protect its marks. But despite the many disappointments, it kept after the most ruthless imitators. One of them, a longtime pain in the neck of the Royal Manufactory, was a porcelain factory founded by Carl Thieme in Potschappel near Dresden. The Chapter "Dresden China" describes the problems the Meissen Manufactory had with Thieme. From the beginning, his Saxonian Porcelain Factory tried to copy the crossed swords of Meissen. At first it was careful, introducing in 1867 a mark not too close to the crossed swords (Fig. 834). At that time, the company only decorated porcelain it bought white from the factory of C.G. Schierholz in Plaue, Saxony. The Thieme mark had to be applied by the Schierholz factory and it is possible that it hesitated to affix a mark too close to that of Meissen.

When the Thieme factory in 1872 began producing its own porcelain, it continued using this mark for a while. In 1875 it asked the Royal Manufactory whether it had any objections to a mark showing two crossed mattocks with the letter T (Fig. 835). The Meissen Manufactory thought this mark too close to the crossed swords, and the Thieme factory promised not to use it. Instead, it declared its intention to mark its porcelain with the letters S.P.F. (for Saxon Porcelain Factory). To its chagrin, the Royal Manufactory found out that the Thieme factory nevertheless signed its porcelain with something that faintly resembled crossed mattocks. It sternly pointed out to the Thieme factory that it would not hesitate to legally proceed against the factory in Potschappel if it did not abandon this mark.[27]

The Thieme factory gave in, and in 1882 it advised the Royal Manufactory of its intention to introduce a new mark (Fig. 837). After it got no answer from Meissen, it had the mark registered with the Inferior Court in Döhlen in 1888.[28]

Fig. 834: Mark registered in 1876 by Carl Thieme in Potschappel near Dresden

Fig. 835: Mark of Carl Thieme in 1875

Fig. 836: Mark of Carl Thieme after 1875

Fig. 837: Mark of Carl Thieme in 1882

In 1895 it extended the registration for the entire German Empire. This time the Meissen Manufactory did not stay idle, because it had encountered several variations of the new Thieme mark abroad, especially in France (Fig. 838). It applied for cancellation of the mark, and after five years of litigation the Saxonian Porcelain Factory Carl Thieme on January 31st, 1901, wrote to its customers: "Dear Sir: We beg to inform you that, in consequence of a decision of the law courts we are forced to abandon our well known trademark after having it used for over 30 years. The action was brought against us by the Royal Saxon Porcelain Works at Meissen, who have now finally succeeded in what they have been aiming at for a long time."[29] In this circular letter the factory also announced its new mark (Fig. 839), which is still in use today.

Fig. 838: Variations of Thieme mark in Fig. 837

Fig. 839: Mark of Carl Thieme factory after 1901, often without crown

Another lengthy controversy with the porcelain factory of Ernst Teichert in Meissen is described in the chapter "Onion Pattern".

The fierce competition among the porcelain producers in the second half of the 19th century and the often reckless business practices urged the Saxon Treasury as proprietor of the Meissen manufactory to energetically protect its trademarks. In a promotional leaflet of about 1894, the manufactory showed seventeen "Trade-marks of other China-manufactories resembling the trade-marks" of the Meissen Manufactory, and advised buyers "Pay attention to the resemblance of the foreign trade-marks with the Meissen marks and examine the exact execution."[30] Handwritten remarks on the copy of this leaflet in the manufactory archive say that the manufactory successfully fought against ten of these marks.

One company that caused considerable trouble was the factory of Triebner, Ens & Eckert in Volkstedt, Thuringia, successors of the Macheleid/Nonne manufactory. When the Royal Manufactory learned about imitations of the crossed swords in Volkstedt, its general manager Raithel in 1883 asked a business friend to procure two pieces with the Volkstedt mark. And in true fiscal frugality common at that time he set a price limit of $2.50 to $7.50 for both pieces, but not more.[31]

The Volkstedt mark (Fig. 840) indeed was close to the crossed swords. Triebner, Ens & Eckert had it registered in 1880. Under legal pressure, the factory in 1884 signed an agreement giving up its mark and promising to add the letter V twice on all its porcelain still in stock (Fig. 841). On the unglazed pieces, the letters had to be affixed under the glaze in blue, on already decorated articles in blue paint over the glaze. After their old mark was cancelled, Triebner, Ens & Eckert registered a new one (Fig. 842).

Fig. 840: Marks of Triebner, Ens & Eckert, Volkstedt, 1880-1884

Fig. 841: Mark of Triebner, Ens & Eckert, Volkstedt, 1884-1886

Fig. 842: Mark of Triebner, Ens & Eckert, Volkstedt, 1884-1894

But that was not the end of the matter. In 1894 the company of Triebner, Ens & Eckert was liquidated. One year later, the Royal Manufactory found out that a *Volkstedter Porzellanfabrik Richard Eckert* (Volkstedt Porcelain Factory Richard Eckert) employed a mark similar to both the Triebner, Ens & Eckert mark and the Meissen crossed swords (Fig. 843). The left part of the mark resembling crossed swords was applied in blue under the glaze, the right part, star and number 4, was painted in red over the glaze. Richard Eckert explained the overglaze part - which could be removed without too much difficulty - as a sign showing that the piece was decorated at his factory. The Imperial Patent Office followed the argumentation of the Royal Meissen Manufactory about an infringement of its rights and cancelled Eckert's mark.[32] As soon as it had lost its case, the Eckert factory registered a new mark, consisting of two crossed forks (Fig. 844), a sign that already had been used by the manufactory of Christian Nonne in Volkstedt in the 18th century (Fig. 816). For ten years the Royal Manufactory could not do anything against the mark, until variations appeared which in the opinion of the Meissen administration looked more like crossed swords than like crossed forks. Since it was too late for an application for cancellation of the mark-the Eckert factory had renewed it in 1904 without objections by the Meissen Manufactory - the Saxon Treasury started a criminal case. But the District Attorney refused to open legal proceedings against Richard Eckert, stating that "some attention would prevent a confusion" of the Volkstedt and the Meissen marks.

Fig. 843: Mark of Richard Eckert, Volkstedt, 1894-1895

Fig. 844: Marks of Richard Eckert, Volkstedt, after 1895

The factory of Fr. Chr. Greiner & Sons in Rauenstein in the 1890s wanted to register its signs (Figs. 845 to 847), which were introduced about 1850 as a trademark. The Royal Manufactory intervened as it had done more than a hundred years ago against other Rauenstein marks (Fig. 848). The Greiner factory in 1898 withdrew its application. Objections by the Meissen Manufactory also prevented the registration of marks by the Friedrich Kästner factory in Oberhohndorf (Fig. 849) in 1897 and of Bros. Schoenau in Hüttensteinach in 1897 (Fig. 850).

But the Meissen Manufactory's brave fight against imitators of its crossed sword mark was a tilt against windmills. Dozens of porcelain factories borrowed the idea of crossed lines, and designed their own marks as close to the Meissen swords as was legally possible. The porcelain decorators in Dresden, always a source of irritation for the Royal Manufactory, led the pack.

The files of the Inferior Court in Dresden show how the leading porcelain painting shops tried to register trademarks similar to the crossed swords, and how the manufactory had to fight them. The first one was Helena Wolfsohn with the AR mark in 1877. She tried another mark in 1882 (Fig. 851). Oswald Lorenz in May of 1881 registered a mark (Fig. 852) to which the Meissen Manufactory objected, Lorenz withdrew his mark after 18 months. Adolf Hamann's trademark (Fig. 853) lasted thirteen months, from October 1881 until November of 1882. Helena Wolfsohn tried it again in January of 1882 (Fig. 854) but after ten months the trademark was cancelled. Donath & Co. registered a mark in March of 1882 (Fig. 855), but lost it sixteen months later. During the proceedings against Donath & Co., it was revealed that the porcelain

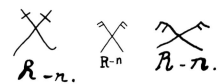

Figs. 845 to 847: Marks of Fr. Chr. Greiner and successors, Rauenstein, Thuringia. 1850 - c.1898

Fig. 848: Mark of Rauenstein manufactory, 18th century

Fig. 849: Mark of Friedrich Kästner, Oberhohndorf until 1897

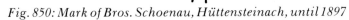

Fig. 850: Mark of Bros. Schoenau, Hüttensteinach, until 1897

Fig. 851: Helena Wolfsohn, Dresden, 1882

Fig. 852: Oswald Lorenz, Dresden, 1881-1882

Fig. 853: Adolf Hamann, Dresden, 1881-1882

Fig. 854: Helena Wolfsohn, Dresden, 1882-1883

Fig. 855: Donath & Co., Dresden, 1882-1883

Fig. 856: Grossbaum & Sons, Dresden, after 1892

Fig. 857: Franziska Hirsch, Dresden, after 1893

factory C.M. Hutschenreuther in Hohenberg, Bavaria, already known from the case Royal Manufactory versus Helena Wolfsohn, had made for Donath & Co. a number of cups and saucers with the incriminated mark.

B. Grossbaum & Sons were not molested for their mark (Fig. 856), but Franziska Hirsch angered the Royal Manufactory in 1893 with her mark (Fig. 857). The manufactory objected on the grounds that the mark was too similar to one of its own marks. The Meissen Manufactory lost. Ms. Hirsch was allowed uninhibited use of the mark by the Imperial Patent Office.

The company of Meyer & Sons in Dresden, that together with Helena Wolfsohn had fought the Royal Manufactory because of the AR mark, also used a variation of the crossed swords (Figs. 858 and 859). The white porcelain with this mark probably was made by the factory of C.M. Hutschenreuther too, because in 1876 C.M. Hutschenreuther registered this sign as its own trademark (Fig. 860). The Imperial Patent Office cancelled this mark in 1887.

Many other German porcelain factories used marks that could be taken for the crossed swords of Meissen by someone who is not too familiar with porcelain, its styles, and its history. These factories probably speculated on their buyer's lack of knowledge, and even today there are some antiques dealers around who sell these pieces as genuine Meissen, not always in an attempt to cheat, sometimes only because they do not know better. Marks of other German factories that could be mistaken for Meissen marks are shown in Figs. 861 to 879).[33]

Figs. 858 and 859: Meyer & Sons, Dresden, c.1850-1887

Fig. 860: C.M. Hutschenreuther, Hohenberg, Bavaria, after 1876-1887

Fig. 861: F.A. Reinicke, Eisenberg, after 1900

Figs. 862 and 863: Dornheim, Koch & Fischer, Gräfenroda, 1887 - c.1938

Fig. 864: Porcelain Factory Günthersfeld, Gehren, Germany, 1886-1902

Fig. 865: L. Schleich, Buschbad, 1886-1927

Fig. 866: A.W.Fr. Kister, Scheibe-Alsbach, Germany, before 1900-1972

Fig. 867: VEB Porcelain Manufactory Scheibe-Alsbach, 1972 - present

Figs. 868 and 869: Bremer & Liebmann, Schney, 1882 -c.1923

Fig. 870: Joseph Schachtel, Charlottenbrunn, Germany, after 1866

Fig. 871: Bros. Voigt, Alfred Voigt and VEB Sitzendorfer Porcelain Manufactory, Sitzendorfer, 1887 -present

Figs. 872 to 875: Bros. Voigt and Alfred Voigt, Sitzendorf, c.1887 - c.1900

Figs. 876 to 878: C.G. Schierholz, Plaue, Germany, c.1880 - c.1906

Fig. 879: Ernst Teichert, Meissen, 19th century

Imitations of the crossed swords mark were by no means restricted to Germany. In France, several factories during the 19th century used marks similar to the crossed swords. The manufactory of Tinet in Montreuil very early combined four crossed swords (Fig. 803), an idea that was adopted by Jacob Petit in Fontainebleau, department Seine-et-Marne about 1830. Petit only added his initials to the mark (Fig. 880). He also used the crossed swords (Fig. 881). E. Jaquemin was sucessor of Petit and he too used the double-crossed swords with his initials (Fig. 882); he also applied variations of a mark he had deposited in 1863 (Figs. 882 to 884).

J. Vialatte's marks are similar to some of Jaquemin's (Figs. 885 and 886). He registered them in 1876, when his address was Paris, rue de la Boule-Rouge.

Figs. 880 and 881: Jacob Petit, Fontainebleau, France

Figs. 882 to 884: E. Jaquemin, Fontainebleau, France

Figs. 885 and 886: J. Vialatte, Paris, France, after 1876

Gabriel Legrand, a porcelain decorator in Paris, after 1890 painted a mark overglaze (Fig. 887) that also could be confused with the marks of William Littler & Co. in Longton Hall, England (Figs. 781 to 783).

The company of Levy & Cie. in Charenton after 1875 employed two marks (Figs. 888 and 889) with crossing lines.

The porcelain decorator Renaud in Paris introduced an overglaze mark (Fig. 890) for his decorating shop in 1895.

Arrow-shaped marks were used by Bloch & Cie. (Fig. 891) in Paris, rue de la Pierre Levée since 1887, and by its successor, the company Porcelaine de Paris since 1936.

Daudin & Laner in Paris, rue de Paradis, in 1911 registered a mark (Fig. 892) that with some imagination could be considered as two crossed forks.

Crossed swords with added letters were employed by three companies: by Achille Bloch, and his successors Bourdois & Bloch in Paris, rue de la Pierre Levée after 1887 (Fig. 893). They had taken it over from their predecessor Marx Eugene Clauss (Figs. 894 to 896), who had used it since 1868.

Fig. 887: *Gabriel Legrand, Paris, France, after 1890*

Figs. 888 and 889: *Levy & Cie., Charenton, France*

Fig. 890: *Renaud, Paris, France*

Fig. 891: *Bloch & Cie, Paris, France*

Fig. 892: *Daudin & Laner, Paris, France, after 1911*

Fig. 893: *Achille Bloch and Bourdois & Bloch, Paris, France*

Figs. 894 to 896: *Marx Eugene Clauss, Paris, France*

Fig. 897: Desjardin, Choisy-le-Roi, *France*

The factory of Desjardins in Choisy-le-Roi put the initials E and D to the crossed swords (Fig. 897). The marks of Bourdois & Bloch and of Desjardins finally were too much for the Meissen Manufactory. In 1890 it sued four porcelain factories and four porcelain dealers in France, who had sold

porcelain with marks the Meissen Manufactory considered imitations of its trademarks, which were registered in France too. The French courts were not very friendly toward the Meissen Manufactory. The Appeals Court in Paris declared that the addition of initials showed the buyer that he purchased a copy, and copying a porcelain piece was not illegal as long as the public was not deceived about the maker.

After five years of litigation, all cases were decided. These were the marks and the factories or dealers using them:

Fig. 898: *Sluizer in Fontainebleau, porcelain factory, sentenced to remove the mark*

Fig. 899: *Bourdois & Bloch in Paris, porcelain factory, suit dismissed*

Fig. 900: *Desjardins in Choisy-le-Roi, porcelain factory, suit dismissed*

Fig. 901: *Samson & Sons in Paris, porcelain factory and Ledentu, Paris, dealer, sentenced to remove the mark*

Fig. 902: *Fournier in Paris, dealer, suit dismissed*

Fig. 903: *Herzog in Paris, dealer, suit dismissed*

Fig. 904: *Herzog in Paris, dealer, sentenced to remove the mark*

Figs. 905 and 906: *Bon Marché in Paris, dealer for porcelain painted by Franziska Hirsch in Dresden, suit dismissed*

Fig. 907: *Bon Marché in Paris, dealer for porcelain by Carl Thieme in Potschappel, suit dismissed*

Edmé Samson and his successor company Samson & Fils (Samson & Sons) were the scourge of porcelain collectors all over the world, honored by the title "Samson the Imitator". Until about 1870, the company seemed only to have decorated porcelain made by other factories. Probably in 1873 the Samsons acquired the porcelain factory of Tinet in Montreuil-sous-Bois and began producing their own porcelain. Headquarters of the Samson company was in Paris, rue Béranger. In a catalogue for the Paris Fair in 1889, the Samsons offered copies of porcelain from famous manufactories, among them, Meissen. A law of 1803 made it illegal in France to copy marks or signs of other companies and producers, and officially, the Samson company obeyed the law. But there is proof that they clandestinely copied marks of famous porcelain manufactories if the customers wanted it done, and then kept quiet about it. (Fig. 908). The Samsons always maintained that the added letter S to the crossed swords of Meissen (Fig. 909) was sufficient to identify this porcelain as having been made by them.

The first Samson mark close to the crossed swords was registered in 1873 (Figs. 910 and 911), the next one in 1885 (Fig. 912). In 1927 Samson & Cie. again registered a mark it had been forced to give up in 1895 (Fig. 913), this time with the explanation *"pour les reproductions de Saxe"* (for reproductions of Meissen porcelain). The last mark similar to the crossed swords was registered in 1957 (Fig. 914). In the 1970s the company closed down its office in Paris and moved to Montreuil-sous-Bois. The auction house of Christie's in London in 1971 sold figurines after old English originals from the Samson factory "used as working models in the factory". Since then, not much has been heard from the Samson company.

In addition to Franziska Hirsch and the factory of Carl Thieme, another Dresden porcelain decorator, Karl Hamann, had a French connection. He worked with the company of Arnold Rub-Leprince in Paris. Rub-Leprince in 1895 applied for registration of a trademark (Fig. 915) at the German Imperial Patent Office. The Meissen Manufactory objected, and in 1896 Rub-Leprince withdrew his application. Nevertheless, in the following years this mark appeared on porcelain sold in France. In 1913 the Royal Manufactory found out that the Dresdeen porcelain decorator Karl Hamann had decorated porcelain for Rub-Leprince. The white ware he had bought from the Rosenthal factory in Selb, Bavaria, which had put its own trademark on all pieces sold to him. Hamann covered the original Rosenthal mark with a rose painted in gold (Fig. 916) and then applied the Rub-Leprince mark next to it.[34] This practice of hiding manufacturers marks under a golden flower or a blob of gold paint was employed by other Dresden porcelain decorators too.

Fig. 908: Samson company, Paris, France, 19th century

Fig. 909: Samson company, Paris, France, 19th and 20th century

Figs. 910 and 911: Samson company, Paris, France, after 1873

Fig. 912: Samson company, Paris, France, after 1885

Fig. 913: Samson company, Paris, France, after 1927

Fig. 914: Samson company, Paris, France, after 1957

Fig. 915: Arnold Rub-Leprince, Paris, France, after 1895

Fig. 916: Karl Hamann in Dresden for Rub-Leprince in Paris, Frnce, after 1896

In England, imitations of the crossed swords in the 19th century were rare. In 1898 a figurine with this mark was subject of a suit the Royal Manufactory brought against the store of Hampton & Sons in London (Fig. 917). The manufactory won. Hampton & Sons were prohibited from selling porcelain with the crossed swords mark not made in Meissen but it was never revealed who had produced the incriminated porcelain piece. It probably had been made in France, and Hampton & Sons maintained that they had bought the figurine at an auction.

Only one British company is known to have copied the crossed swords on its wares. James & John Bevington in Hanley registered this mark (Fig. 918), in 1872 and applied it on its products until 1892.

In 20th century Germany, the crossed swords had prevailed as the Meissen mark. But after World War II, some businessmen tried to take advantage of the changed political situation. Germany had been separated into two parts. Western Germany, which since 1949 had been the Federal Republic of Germany, became part of the Western political and military alliance. Its economic system was based on the idea of free enterprise.

In East Germany, which since 1949 had been the German Democratic Republic, a different system was established, with the goal to erect a socialistic state with a planned economy. The Soviet Union, which in 1945 after the end of World War II had occupied East Germany, ordered the confiscation of all enterprises that belonged to active followers of the Nazi ideology, or that had produced products used for the German war effort. Because the whole German industry had worked for the war effort in one way or the other, all big companies, banks, mines, and important privately owned factories were expropriated, as well as all farms larger than 150 acres.

That created strong animosity against the later to be GDR as new proprietor of the now nationalized enterprises, especially from those people who had begun living in Wes Germany and had lost their property in East Germany. Theii number was not small, and their political influence in the FRG considerable.

In those days, the prevalent opinion in the West was that the political and economic system in the GDR soon would collapse; and the more it could be hurt, the faster it would disintegrate. This feeling was shared by the western allies of the FRG. One of the battlegrounds - not the most important by far - was the field of trademarks. Taking away an old trademark with a worldwide reputation from a nationalized company in the GDR meant to put it at a serious disadvantage in international commerce. The Meissen marks were among the many trademarks under attack.

In 1950, Prince Friedrich Christian, Duke at Saxony, who lived in Altshausen, West Germany, applied for the registra-

Fig. 917: Mark on a group sold by Hampton & Sons, London, England, 1898, group probably made in France

Fig. 918: James & John Bevington, Hanley, England, 1872-1892

Figs. 919 to 921: Marks for which trade-mark registration was sought unsuccessfully in 1950 by Prince Fr. Chr. of Saxony

tion of three trademarks with the crossed swords in them (Figs. 919 to 921). He declared his intention of using them for porcelain and ceramic products. The Prince was a member of the Wettin family that had ruled Saxony until 1918, and after 1945 had lost all of its property in East Germany. Among his many titles was "Margrave of Meissen".

Despite the political enmities, the Patent Office in the Federal Republic of Germany refused to register these marks. The crossed swords were still considered the mark of the Meissen Manufactory, and the West German Patent Office protected them without hesitation.

Another Prince of Saxony, Ernst Heinrich, who gave his address as Post Liscmacoffrey, County Westmeath, Ireland, tried the same thing in the U.S. The Prince in 1953 filed an application for a trademark (Fig. 922) that was granted in 1957.[35] In the United States, all German trademarks had been confiscated as enemy property, among them the marks of the Meissen Manufactory. Prince Ernst Heinrich tried to step into a void and to obtain the crossed swords for himself. The U.S. trademark register contains his statement that this mark was first used in 1952 for tea and dinner sets, including plates, cups and saucers, vases and decorative serving tea tiles. If these wares were ever made, they must have been produced in very small numbers, because they have not been found on the market, not even today's antiques market.

In 1962, the Royal Saxe Corporation in New York, N.Y. applied for the registration of the same mark in its name. It had acquired the rights to the mark from Prince Ernst Heinrich. The mark was registered in 1964.[36] The register this time showed a significant difference in the description of the wares on which the mark should be applied. It listed the same items as in the first application, but added "made of porcelain or China".

In 1962, the Royal Saxe Corporation very quickly got a registration for another mark (Fig. 923). This mark first was published upside down by the U.S. Patent Office, which had to issue a certificate of correction four months later.[37] The Royal Saxe Corporation evidently never had any serious intention of producing porcelain, but it was very busy in another field. Already in 1957 it had obtained a decision by the U.S. Patent Office declaring that the Meissen Manufactory had no rights to its previously used marks. In 1962, the Treasury Department in Washington granted an application by the Royal Saxe Corporation for a ban on all imports of Meissen porcelain, be it new, old, or antique by anyone but the Royal Saxe Corporation. The corporation from then on

claimed the exclusive right to sell Meissen porcelain in the United States, or to import it into the country.[38]

Since the corporation had no connections with the Meissen Manufactory, this claim was without any justifiable or practical foundation. The Royal Saxe Corporation was partly in West German hands, and its aim might have been to affect adversely the sale of new Meissen porcelain in the United States, and in so doing, hurt the owner of the manufactory: the government of the GDR. But some of its further activities point more to the suspicion that it wanted to force itself on the manufactory as a sole importer and agent for Meissen porcelain in the U.S. The D.M. and Antique Import Company in New York, N.Y., at that time legal importer and agent of the Meissen Manufactory, reported to Meissen that the Royal Saxe Corporation tried to drive a wedge between itself and the manufactory.[39] Through a New York law firm, the American importer and the manufactory applied for cancellation of the marks of the Royal Saxe Corporation, and these applications were finally granted in 1970. Five months later the U.S. Patent Office registered the old Meissen marks again for the manufactory, after its applications had been in limbo for five years.

In the Federal Republic of Germany, several porcelain producers and decorators had assumed that the Meissen Manufactory politically and financially was in no position to protect its rights. During the first postwar years until the late 1950s, the manufactory had considerable problems defending its marks. In 1953 it even lacked sufficient foreign currency to pay for the renewal of all the Meissen marks abroad, and decided not to keep up the registration of crossed swords with additions like dot or star.[40] After 1960, forgeries and imitations forced the manufactory to again energetically protect its interests. At that time, the sales abroad brought in more than enough foreign currency for the registration fees.

In 1963, the porcelain decorating shop of Martha Budich in Kronach, Bavaria, FRG, escaped a court judgement only by signing an "amicable agreement". Ms. Budich agreed to change her mark (Fig. 924) by eliminating the upper part (Fig. 925). She also submitted to the demand of the manufactory not to use the expressions "Dresden Form", "Dresden Style", "Dresden Decoration", "Dresden Art", "Handpainted Dresden" or any other combination that included the name Dresden[41].

The Meissen Manufactory had to continue its fight against imitators, who even up to recent times not only forged the marks, but even Meissen figurines. In 1980 the Superior Court in Fürth, Bavaria, FRG, decided once and for all that it was illegal to apply marks looking similar to the crossed swords, and to sell pieces with these marks as Meissen porcelain.[42]

The legal side seems to be clear, but there is little doubt that once in a while someone will try again to benefit financially from the fame of the Meissen Manufactory, and come up with another forged Meissen mark. Close scrutiny will give away these forgeries. That will require a little more knowledge and effort, but Meissen porcelain is worth it.

Fig. 922: Prince Ernst Heinrich of Saxony and Royal Saxe Corp. New York, N.Y., 1953-1970

Fig. 923: Royal Saxe Corp. New York, N.Y., 1962-1970

Fig. 924: Martha Budich, Kronach, Bavaria, after 1948-1963

Fig. 925: Proposal by the Meissen manufactory for a change of the Budich mark in Fig. 924

Chapter Twelve

Dresden China

There is an ineradicable and dangerous confusion about the term "Dresden China". Ineradicable because the name "Dresden China" for Meissen porcelain is more than 250 years old. Dangerous because of ignorance or in an attempt to cheat, other porcelain is sold under the name Dresden China, leading the unaware buyer to the assumption that he has purchased porcelain made by the famous manufactory in Meissen.

The problem started in England, where Meissen porcelain was collected immediately after it appeared on the market in 1715. It was mainly sold in Dresden; the manufactory did not operate a store in Meissen itself.[1] Dresden was well known in Europe as the residence of the splendor-loving Augustus the Strong. All foreign legations were located there and visitors lodged in Dresden, especially porcelain buyers from abroad.

The old city of Meissen, some 25km (15 miles) away from Dresden, was the place where the porcelain was actually manufactured, but since most business transactions were conducted in Dresden, the name of this city accompanied the porcelain shipped to England. In 1736, the British traveller Richard Pococke journeyed through Europe, where he also visited Saxony. His report about Meissen begins:

> "Meissen: the only manufacture of Dresden porcelain is at Meissen. It belongs to the King, and is sold only in one place in Dresden and Leipzig, and the cheapest of it is dearer than China-ware of the same quality in England."[2]

Pococke's use of the term "Dresden porcelain" shows that this expression already was firmly established in England, if not in 1736, the year of his journey, but certainly in 1745, the year his report was published. The first manufactory-owned store for the sale of Meissen porcelain to the public was established at the Dresden New Market in 1715. In Leipzig, Meissen porcelain first was only exhibited and sold at the Leipzig Fairs, which then were held thrice a year (twice a year today). Later, a second permanent sales shop was opened up in Leipzig, and a third one in Warsaw, Poland.

The porcelain manufactory in Derby, England, in 1756 and 1758 advertised its figurines and groups as being "the nearest to Dresden" as possible, or as "second Dresden", admitting by the choice of these comparisons that Meissen porcelain was something desirable, but also proving that the term "Dresden" for Meissen porcelain was in common use. From England, the name "Dresden porcelain" or "Dresden China" migrated to the colonies in North America, and since then it has become a household word. Later, this term was reinforced in the English-language porcelain literature. W.B. Honey, then Assistant Keeper in the Department of Ceramics at the Victoria and Albert Museum in London, in 1934 gave his book about Meissen porcelain the title "Dresden China" and the subtitle "An introduction to the study of Meissen Porcelain".[3]

In his preface, Honey defended the term "Dresden China" by arguing that it was in familiar use, that the French, the Italians and the Spaniards also avoided the name Meissen "so that we are not alone in having our own word for the china, which only a tiresome pedantry would wish to ban in favour of the more accurate name of Meissen".

When Honey wrote his book, the name Dresden had been misused for more than eighty years to glorify a vast number of Meissen imitations and copies. A few were not altogether bad but most of them were crude and cheap. Either Honey was not aware of it or he choose to ignore it, as did other British and American authors, who thus contributed to the general confusion.[4]

It is not just a matter of linguistic purity to call Meissen "Meissen" and Dresden "Dresden". Until about 1850, the term "Dresden China" was acceptable for Meissen porcelain, even though it was inaccurate. And until that time, any attempt to change this term in England and in the United States indeed would have been superfluous. But in the second half of the 19th century, its meaning deliberately was expanded to cover a vast number of imitations of Meissen porcelain.

There was never a porcelain factory or manufactory in the city of Dresden, but between 1850 and 1914 quite a number of porcelain decorators busily worked on creating a Dresden style. This style, a mixture of Meissen and Vienna flower painting and copies of other Meissen painting motifs, was not necessarily improved by their efforts to produce as much "Dresden China" as possible (Plate 257)

Through their activities, the term "Dresden China" acquired a completely new meaning. The porcelain decorators took advantage of the fact that Meissen porcelain for a long time was know as Dresden China in England, the United States, Canada, and other English-speaking countries. They succeeded beyond expectation by creating complete confusion.

Even some reputable auction houses in the United States today indiscriminately use the terms "Dresden" and "Meissen" interchangeably, as do a number of antique shops or dealers in antique shows.

With the intention of fighting the misuse of the name Dresden, the manufactory in 1938 registered a new trademark (Fig. 624). This mark is occasionally used today for certain items, described by the manufactory as dessert bowls, liqueur sets, show plates and similar pieces. Since this mark evidently was not sufficient, three more marks were registered in 1963 (Figs. 626 to 628). These marks were used from 1963 until about 1973, and then given up.[5] Except for these four marks, the manufactory never has used Dresden in its marks, especially not before 1938. Whenever the name Dresden is written or stamped on the bottom of a piece of porcelain in any other way, one can be dead sure that this piece has never seen the inside of the Meissen Manufactory.

There is one exception. On very few pieces, the marking in (Fig. 926) can be seen. The meaning of the letters B.P.T. has not been found out yet. It is curious, though, that all but one marking of this kind shown in ceramic literature are dated 1739. Only in one case no year is given.[6]

The bulk of the "Dresden China" came from the porcelain decorators in or near Dresden. Some of them easily could match the Meissen painters in the quality of their work. Occasionally, they were even better than the average Meissen painter. They did not participate in the mass production of "Dresden China", and even members of the Royal Academy of Arts considered them superior to Meissen. They arranged a competition between the best Meissen and the best Dresden painters which ended inconclusively. Nobody was declared the winner, but on the other hand, nobody had lost either,

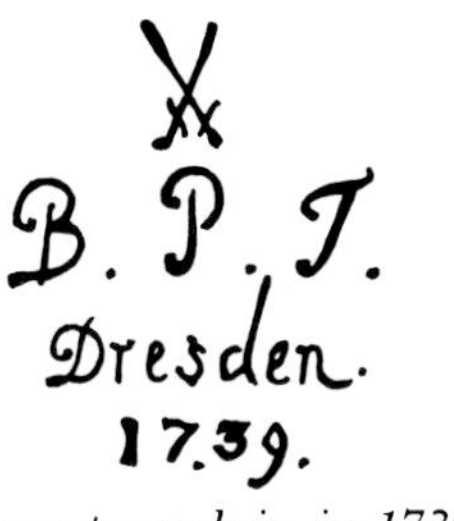

Fig. 926: Mark on Meissen porcelain in 1739

which meant that the painters from Dresden were at least equal to their Meissen collegues.

As long as they did not sell their products as Meissen, all painters could use the decoration patterns of the manufactory. Most of them belonged to porcelain history, and there was nothing the manufactory could or would do against it. It had borrowed ideas from East Asia itself, which it could not copyright. One of the most popular motifs was the Red Dragon. There was almost no porcelain decorator who did not paint the dragon but they came out in different degrees of quality (Plates 258 to 262).

Today only one porcelain painting shop is left that continues the tradition of the good porcelain painters. Several formerly private porcelain painters have joined in a co-operative PGH *Meissner Porzellanmalerei* (Production Co-Operative Meissen Porcelain Painting). Founded in 1958, it produces high quality painting that is so much in demand that the co-operative is not able to fill all orders (Plates 263 and 264)

But unfortunately, most of the "Dresden" painters were in the business to make a quick buck. The most important - and most notorious - of them - was Helena Wolfsohn, who first appeared in the Dresden business directory in 1848 as an antiques dealer. Very soon other porcelain decorators opened up shops in Dresden. The directories from 1855 to 1944 show more than two hundred names of porcelain painting shops in Dresden alone. Most of them employed several painters. During the years between 1875 and 1915, the most productive for the Dresden decorating shops, the company of Helena Wolfsohn had thirty painters working for it. It alone must have produced millions of pieces of "Dresden-China" (Plates 265 and 266). Other large shops were not unproductive either. Besides the painters they employed directly, they had decorators on hand, who worked at home and were paid by the piece.

Many of the large shops had their own stores near the Dresden Main-Railway-Station, at the Prager and Zinzendorfer Streets. They mostly dealt in antiques also, carried genuine Meissen porcelain and cleverly mixed Meissen pieces with imitations and copies in their displays. The company of Helena Wolfsohn for half a century was listed in the directories only as antiques dealership. In 1898 it finally decided to show its true colors, and from then on the firm called itself a porcelain decorating shop. At that time the proprietor was Leopold Elb, the grandson of Helena Wolfsohn.

Some of the painting shops in Dresden evidently even entered into an agreement to promote their "Dresden China" enterprise. On February 7th, 1883, the porcelain painters Oswald Lorenz, Richard Klemm, Adolph Hamann, and Karl Hermann Donath entered simultanously the registrars office at the Inferior Court in Dresden, and exactly at half past five in the afternoon they registered the same trademark for all four of them (Fig. 927).

But that doesn't seem to have worked out well. Since they all painted in the same style, not even they could distinguish who had made what. So ten years later, when the trademark had to be renewed, they each changed their common mark slightly (Figs. 928 to 930).

Fig. 927: Common mark of O. Lorenz, R. Klemm, A. Hamann and K.H. Donath all in Dresden, registered in 1883

Fig. 928: Adolph Hamann, after 1893

302

Fig. 929: Richard Klemm, after 1893

Fig. 930: Karl Hermann Donath and Donath & Co., after 1893

Fig. 931: Oswald Lorenz, after 1893

Aldolph (or Adolf) Hamann evidently very early saw the possibilities of selling his wares in the United States, and he registered his marks with the U.S. Patent Office.[7] Since the end of the previous century, porcelain with these marks and that of Helena Wolfsohn frequently were called "Crown Dresden", with the the implied meaning that it was of even higher quality than the other "Dresden-China".

Oswald Lorenz in 1893 dropped out of the cartel and registered a mark that looked similar to one the Royal Porcelain Manufactory in Vienna had used (Fig. 931) Since this manufactory had been closed in 1864, there was no danger of a complaint from Vienna.

Oswald had a good reason to avoid any confrontation about marks. In 1882 he had a heavy bout with the Meissen Manufactory, which had not liked one of his marks (see Chapter on Imitations of Meissen Marks). After he had learned that the manufactory was determined to take him to the Imperial Court, he gave in. Knowing that the manufactory closely watched the dealings of Messrs. Klemm, Hamann and Donath, he decided to part company with them.

Relatively few of the marks are known which were used by the Dresden porcelain decorators. Research in this field is very difficult, because most files were destroyed during the Allied bombing raids on Dresden on February 13th and 14th, 1945. After World War II, the porcelain painting business never recovered. Today only three painting shops are working in Dresden. Since many painters used the initials of their names in their marks, a list of the names known of Dresden porcelain painters is provided in the back of this book. It might be of help in identifying hitherto unknown marks on Dresden-China. It also includes shops, which were not called painting shops, but porcelain or antiques dealerships, but actually decorated porcelain.

For the following porcelain decorating shops their marks could be ascertained:

BRAM
MER
MALER

Fig. 932: E. Brammer & Co.

KRON   CROWN

Figs. 933 and 934: Donath & Co. see also 855, 927, 930

Fig. 935: R. Eckert

G·S

Fig. 936: Julius Greiner Son

Fig. 937: Josef Günter

Figs. 938 and 939: Adolph Hamann, see also 853, 927, 928

Fig. 940: Karl Eduard Hamann

Fig. 941: Heufel & Co.

Figs. 942 to 946: Franziska Hirsch, see also 857, 905, 906

Figs. 947 to 949: Franz Junckersdorf

Figs. 950 to 953: Richard Klemm, see also 927, 929

Fig. 954: Louis Knöller

Fig. 955: Wilhelm Koch

Figs. 956 to 958: Ambrosius Lamm

Fig. 959: Adolf Leube

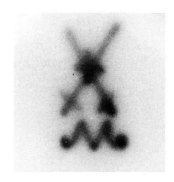

Fig. 960: Meyer & Sons

Fig. 961: Anton Ott

Fig. 962: Max Robra

Figs. 963 and 964: Oskar Gustav Schade

S. u. P.
Dresden.

Fig. 965: Strobel & Petschk

Fig. 966: Ella Strobel and Johann Strobel

Fig. 967: Franz Till

UFER
MEISSEN

Fig. 968 R. Ufer

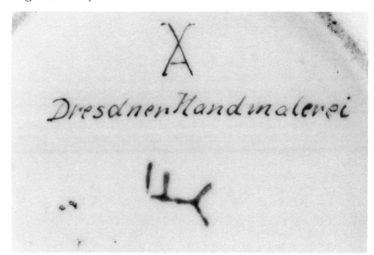

Fig. 969: Arthur Voigtmann

Figs. 970 and 971: Adolf Wache

Wagner

Fig. 972: Carl and Anna Wagner

Figs. 973 to 975: Richard and Gerhard Wehsener

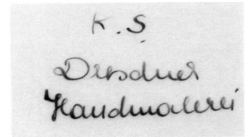

Fig. 976: Unidentified

Fig. 977: Arthur Rohleder in Meissen

The shops of Richard Klemm and Donath & Co. in 1916 merged to form *"Vereinigte Dresdner Porzellanmalereien"* (United Dresden Porcelain Painting Shops). Two years later, the Porcelain Factory of C.M. Hutschenreuther in Hohenberg, Bavaria, took over this company, and also the shop of Richard Wehsener, establishing the "Art-Department of C.M. Hutschenreuther" in Dresden. All marks used by C.M. Hutschenreuther in Dresden contained the original symbol of the factory. (Figs. 978 to 980) But the Hutschenreuther company also used the confusion about the name Dresden to its advantage. In a 1931 advertising booklet the factory wrote: "The famous 'Dresden China' is the world-wide known description of those Dresden handpaintings which have found friends and admirers among all connoisseurs of art far beyond the boundaries of Germany...Dresden China is, and this applies particularly to Americans and the English, what is implied since many years by porcelain handpainted in Dresden."[8]

Here, the C.M. Hutschenreuther factory completely ignored the fact that the Americans and the English first of all considered Meissen porcelain to be Dresden China. Meissen now was pushed out of the "Dresden China" business by the decorating shops, which sold their products much cheaper than genuine Meissen.

Figs. 978 to 980: Painting shop of C.M. Hutschenreuther, Hohenberg, in Dresden

While the Art Department of C.M. Hutschenreuther only decorated porcelain made by the Hutschenreuther factories, the other shops bought white ware from porcelain factories, which was expressly ordered without a factory mark. But some other factories had chosen marks which were close enough to the crossed swords to be mistaken. Their products were preferred by some of the Dresden painters (Plates 267 to 269).

But the demand forced them also to use otherwise marked porcelain. Since a factory mark would have given away the pieces as not being "Dresden China", the decorators hid them under a blob of gold paint or under a golden blossom on the bottom. A few could be identified:

Fig. 981: Donath & Co.

Fig. 982: Grossbaum & Sons

Fig. 983: Franziska Hirsch

Fig. 984: Richard Wehsener

Fig. 985: Helena Wolfsohn

Fig. 986: Saxonian Porcelain Factory Carl Thieme

These sample do not mean that the shops used only these shapes. Size and shape of a blossom always depended on the size and shape of the original porcelain manufacturer's mark. These golden blossoms could be verified, because in addition to them, the mark of the painting shop was applied.

The last company in the list above played a remarkable part in the business of "Dresden China". The *"Sächsische Porzellanfabrik zu Potschappel von Carl Thieme"*(Saxonian Porcelain Factory at Potschappel of Carl Thieme) was located in Potschappel outside Dresden. Later Potschappel actually was incorporated into the city of Dresden, but at that time it had nothing to do with Dresden.

The factory was founded in 1867, but the title "factory" was an exaggeration. For the first five years, it was nothing but a porcelain decorating shop (Plate 270). White porcelain was bought from the porcelain factory of C.G. Schierholz & Sohn in Plaue, which applied its own marks (Figs. 876 to 878) or a Thieme mark (Fig. 834) under the glaze. Beginning in 1872, porcelain production began in Potschappel and in 1884 the company advertised: "Fancy articles in Dresden Style, such as: Vases, Epergnes, Candelabras, Statuettes, Flower Pots, Cups, Cups and Saucers, Perforated Plates etc. Dinner Services painted a la Watteau and Wouverman in Ground Colour or Stripes with Birds, Flowers, Landscapes or Wreaths."[9]

The factory unbashedly copied Meissen forms, figures, and decorations, which were not copyrighted. These pieces, although not matching Meissen porcelain by far, were fairly well-executed, and sold under the flag of "Dresden China". There were many quarrels between Meissen and Potschappel, some of them were taken to the courts.

The Thieme factory was later continued by Karl August Kuntzsch, who had married Thieme's daughter, and subsequently by Carl A. Kuntzsch and Emil A. Kuntzsch. But the fights with the Meissen Manufactory were taken up by each generation anew.

The first Thieme mark (Fig. 834) became a matter for prolonged litigation. First, the German Patent Office refused the registration of this mark. The factory in Potschappel appealed against this decision and won. The Appeals Chamber of the Patent Office was of the opinion that many marks using crossed lines were registered already, and it concluded: "it must be assumed that the public has become familiar with the fine differences and does not consider the motif of crossed lines characteristic for the Royal Saxonian mark."[10]

This opinion was remarkable and wrong; not only the public was unfamiliar with the differences, even collectors fell prey to Thieme's subterfuge. The Amercan antiques author Yates reported: "A famous collector woke up to find himself in possession of some two hundred fifty thousand dollars worth of forgeries, Meissen, all of it. Here to be found were cleverly executed flacons, bonbonnieres, and other little flippancies so reminiscent of the early days of Meissen and all now eagerly sought by modern connoisseurs. The German expert, Dr. Brinckmann and the English expert, Frederick Litchfield, pointed them out for what they were: cheap little once-white pieces which were once sold at Potschappel, and beautifully decorated in the fine manner of the original."[11]

Litchfield himself recalled the incident that in 1909 led to a law-suit against some unscrupulous London dealers, who had sold Thieme porcelain as "Old Dresden" and demanded $2,500 to $6,000 for Thieme's copies of old Kaendler figurines.[12] He noted that the "Dresden" groups and figurines made by the Thieme factory were likely to deceive the careless amateur. The mark Litchfield showed as Thieme mark (Fig. 987) proves that the Meissen manufactory was justified in its suspicion that Thieme's factory was not satisfied with just crossed lines, but varied its registered mark to more closely resemble the crossed swords of Meissen. The Danish ceramic expert, Hannover, also was of the opinion that: "Of the works in Saxony at present imitating old Meissen Porcelain, the cleverest and most dangerous is probably a continuation of this same Thieme factory, namely the *Sächsische Porzellanfabrik Carl Thieme* (proprietor C. Kutsch at Potschappel near Dresden)."[13]

Fig. 987: Variation of Thieme mark

Figs. 988 to 991: Thieme marks after 1901

The names "Dresden" and "Dresden China" were not protected. After the Thieme factory had to give up its contested mark, it quickly adopted some new ones, all with the name "Dresden" in them (Figs. 988 to 991). In the "Chatty Letters", which the Dresden Hotel Bellevue provided to its lady customers as a courtesy, and which were paid for by the Dresden merchants, the factory had written about itself in 1931, that a visit to the *Sächsische Porzellanfabrik zu Potschappel* would show "what 'Dresden China' means...What you will find here, I wish to emphasize expressly, is really genuine 'Dresden China' of pure style." And the letter then chatted about an American lady, who had a passion for china: "People have repeatedly sold her pieces as 'real Dresden' which had nothing of the 'real' Dresden china about them except the name." The letterwriter directed the American lady to the Thieme factory and "when she came back she was most grateful to me and kept on repeating that she would explain things to her fellow countrymen and point out how disgraceful it is for them that any clever salesman can palm off copies on them as 'real Dresden' ".[14]

The cheat was complaining about the cheaters. They all preyed upon American ladies and those from other parts of the globe. Whatever they wrote on the bottom of their porcelain pieces in combination with the name Dresden, it always was in English. It is not hard to understand why. In Germany nobody would call Meissen porcelain Dresden. The expression Dresden China was not used at all. But especially in England, the main market place for American visitors, dealers went on a rampage with the term "Dresden China". In the meantime, some porcelain factories in Thuringia and Bavaria had realized that there was money to be made with the name Dresden in England and the U.S. So did French manufacturers, and even some English and American factories included the name Dresden in their marks (Figs. 992 to 1000).

Fig. 992: Bates, Walker & Co. Burslem, England, 1875-1878 on earthenware

Fig. 993: Schumann China Corporation, New York, N.Y., 1931-c.1941

305

  DRESDEN HOTEL CHINA DRESDEN HOTEL CHINA.

Figs. 994 to 1000: Potters Cooperative Co. East Liverpool, Ohio, U.S.A. after 1892

In 1898, the Meissen Manufactory reported to the Treasury that its sales to England had declined. As the main reason, it mentioned the competition by other factories, which exploited the confusion about the name Dresden China. One of the more important merchants in London who sold Meissen porcelain, W. Oppenheim of Farringdon Street, wrote to the manufactory in December of 1897; "As when I have had the pleasure of being in Meissen, you have more than once asked me if I could explain why your goods do not sell in England as they used to."[15] Oppenheim sent the explanation with his letter: a Christmas Catalogue of the famous Harrod's Stores, offering cheap "Dresden China". He had gone to the stores himself, and asked a salesman if real Dresden was not supposed to bear the crossed swords mark. The answer by the salesman was that there were dozens of china factories in Dresden.

Oppenheim identified some of the pieces; they came from Thuringia "the very commonest rubbish made at Volkstedt" and from Potschappel. "The goods from the latter are particularly hurtful for most of them are copies of your models and bear a mark so near that the uninitiated easily mistake it for that of the Royal Manufactory."

The Trade Marks Protection Society in London, (with or without Mr. Openheim's prodding is not known) sent a buyer to Harrod's Stores. She bought a candelabra and insisted that the bill of sale should show the candelabra as "Dresden", as it was advertised in the catalogue.[16]

With that candelabra and the bill, the society took Harrod's Stores to court for "exposing for sale, selling, and having in their possession for sale, china to which the false trade description of "Dresden" was applied." The attorney for Harrod's Stores argued that "Dresden" was a generic name, but to no avail, the stores were fined $150.

They appealed and tried to prove that the term "Dresden China" had outgrown the Meissen Manufactory, that it only designated a certain style, similar to Stilton Cheese, which was not always produced in Stilton. Harrod's Stores lost again. But the confusion continued.

In another court case in London, the explanation was offered by an expert witness that there was a difference between "Old Dresden China" and "Dresden China". "Old Dresden China" was only porcelain made by the Royal Manufactory in Meissen in the 18th century, he said, while "Dresden China", in his opinion, was the name for a certain decoration style, mainly executed in or near Dresden.

The matter was not only of concern for the Meissen Manufactory, it even went into diplomatic channels. In 1907, the British envoy to the Saxon Court, Lord Gough, discreetly pointed out to the Ministry of Foreign Affairs that the misuse of the name "Dresden China" should be stopped. He recommended, in the interest of the English buyers and in the interest of the manufactory, an "appropriate enlightenment" of the public.[17] The Treasury ordered the manufactory to insert advertisements in the English-language newspaper "Daily Record" published in Dresden, and to enclose the same statement in all letters and catalogues going to England for one year.[18]

The manufactory did this only half heartedly. It almost had resigned to the feeling that fighting the misuse of "Dresden China" was a fight against Hydra. In a letter to the Treasury, the manufactory director Paul Gesell wrote: "From our own experience, based on careful observations at home and abroad over a period of tens of years, we have only a faint hope that any attempt to prevent the misuse of the name "Dresden China" would be succesful".[19]

In a rather highbrow manner Gesell continued, that it could be taken for granted that those buyers, who were not able to form a critical opinion about porcelain would not be cheated by "Dresden China". They would get what they paid for, and those buyers would not necessarily identify "Dresden China" with Meissen porcelain. They just would think that they had bought something valuable. Gesell admitted that those buyers were in the majority.

But the discriminating purchaser "well educated in history, with sufficient knowledge of the arts and alert about the trademark" would be able to protect himself against the misuse of "Dresden China". And he touched on another ticklish problem when he pointed out that the manufactory would rather avoid the courts in this matter, because the manufactory being located in Meissen actually could not legally claim the word "Dresden" for itself. It even could happen, Gesell speculated, that porcelain from the manufactory would not be allowed to be sold as Dresden China any more in England, because it came from Meissen.

Some years later, the manufactory regretted not having defended the name "Dresden China" for Meissen porcelain more energetically. But by then it was too late. In 1930, the C.M. Hutschenreuther porcelain factory in Hohenberg, Bavaria, which had its Art Department in Dresden, tried to get some order into the "Dresden" confusion with the goal of preventing factories and painters outside of Dresden from selling their wares as "Dresden China". In a letter to the Meissen Manufactory, it asked if the Dresden porcelain painting shops could call themselves "producers of the real

Dresden handpainting", and if the Thieme factory was allowed to call its porcelain "Dresden".[20] Manufactory director Max Adolf Pfeiffer, a trifle resigned, answered that the manufactory unfortunately had neglected to legally proceed against the use of "Dresden China" by the Dresden porcelain painters.

In December of 1930, Pfeiffer, representatives of C.M. Hutschenreuther, of the Thieme factory, and several Dresden porcelain painters met and came to an agreement: The manufactory declared that it would not object to the use of "Dresden China" or to an inscription "really handpainted in Dresden" by the others. The others also were allowed to call themselves "producers of Dresden China". All of them promised to enforce the agreement against anyone outside of their group. The only consolation for the Meissen manufactory was that the inscription "real Dresden handpainted" was reserved for Meissen advertising and catalogues.

The battles, the Meissen Manufactory should have fought, had been won by others. In 1931, the Thieme factory sued the Porcelain Factory Tirschenreuth in Bavaria because it had used "Dresden" and "Dresden Decoration" on its porcelain. The Tirschenreuth factory, a subsidiary of the other Hutschenreuther company, Lorenz Hutschenreuther in Selb, Bavaria, argued that the Thieme factory had no legal standing, since it was not located in Dresden either, and that Hutschenreuther porcelain marked "Dresden" was solely to be exported to the United States. And the factory lawyer pointed out that several other German porcelain factories used the name Dresden or any combination with it for their exports to the U.S.

The court felt that the Thieme factory was closer to Dresden than the Tirschenreuth factory, and therefore had a right to sue. The Tirschenreuth factory was ordered to cease using "Dresden" or "Dresden Decoration" on its porcelain.[21]

But the misuse of the name Dresden continued. After World War II, a number of porcelain factories and sales companies tried to take advantage of the political and legal uncertainties arising from the existence of two separate states on German soil. Expecting that the Meissen Manufactory in the German Democratic Republic would not sue in the Federal Republic of Germany, they unabashedly put the name Dresden on their porcelain. While contemplating legal actions, the Meissen Manufactory encountered the same problem its director Gesell had mentioned in 1907: How could it explain convincingly to a court that "Dresden" actually included Meissen?

The manufactory people for a long time racked their brains for a convincing explanation. But this pondering was to no avail. The manufactory could not protect the name Dresden for itself, as the West German Patent Office made clear, when it tersely asked the manufactory for proof that its official place of business actually was in the city of Dresden.

It was discomforting for the manufactory to have to watch others misuse the name Dresden for porcelain that had never been even near the city. In an attempt to establish its claims, the manufactory considered opening up its own shop in Dresden again which had been closed many years earlier. But before the preparations could be completed, the disputes and suits had been settled, and the shop in Dresden was given up.

A court decision ruled on the Dresden matter once and for all - at least in Germany. The court decreed that only a person or a company physically doing business in a certain city could use the name of this city in its trademark or its advertising. For the Meissen Manufactory, this judgement meant the end of the use of the name Dresden or Dresden China for its products. It relinquished all trademarks containing the name Dresden (Figs. 626 to 628, see beginning of this chapter) with the exception of "Royal Dresden China" (Fig. 624). Since the number of porcelain painting shops in Dresden had dwindled to three, the name Dresden China seemed to become extinct. But not really, because there was still the former Thieme factory around. After World War II, it first had been put into government trusteeship, and in 1972 it was nationalized and continued, under the name *VEB Sächsische Porzellanmanufaktur Dresden* (Peoples Own Enterprise Saxonian Porcelain Manufactory Dresden). By

that time it could legally include Dresden in its name because Potschappel had been incorporated in the city of Dresden. Today, the company is still using the 1901 mark (Fig. 997), and its products - mainly for export - are now of considerable quality. It has developed its own style, different from that of Meissen, and is now the only producer of Dresden China in Germany.

With a sense of compassion for the many proud owners of "Dresden China" it has to be stated that only pieces with marks which combine "Dresden Art", "Dresden China" or "Dresden" with the crossed swords or bear the inscription "Royal Dresden China" on the bottom are genuine Meissen porcelain. Everything else is just porcelain. That is a sorry fact. In English-speaking countries, the term "Dresden China" will continue to put collectors on the wrong track, and many of them will pay dearly for the failure of Honey and other authors to use the accurate name for Meissen porcelain. When it comes to antique or even newer porcelain, precision should not be called pedantry, and precision pays off, even if it might appear tiresome.

Fig. 1001: Miner breaking kaolin in the manufactory-owned
pit near Seilitz

Chapter Thirteen

Technology

On a beautiful day in the year 1700 the wealthy mine owner Veit Hans Schnorr rode along the road between the city of Aue and the hamlet of Lauter in the Saxon Ore Mountains (Erzgebirge). Suddenly his horse stumbled, and Schnorr barely could keep his balance in the saddle. He dismounted to check for the reason for his horse's missing its footing. It was not the horse's fault, it had stepped onto a soft spot in the ground, which looked like white paste. Schnorr took some of the substance home, found out that it could be dried and ground to a fine white powder, and he marketed it in handy packages as a new toilet item for powdering the elaborate full bottom wigs worn by distinguished people.

A few years later, in 1708, Johann Friedrich Böttger was curious about the white powder his servant used. He took some of it to his laboratory, mixed it with other minerals and water to a paste, threw a little vessel from the paste on a potter's wheel, baked it in a kiln, and -Eureka! - he had invented European hard paste porcelain.

That is a nice story, traded in a number of books and articles about porcelain, making the invention a matter of accidents and luck. That it was not, it was the result of systematic experiments, empirical science and ingenuity. Man had made pottery for more than 10,000 years before Böttger invented hard paste porcelain. The basic ingredients and the process of making pottery were known, and by changing them the various kinds of pottery were developed. Most of them were non-vitrified wares. The different ingredients were baked together, not fused, and the vessels remained porous. Colored opaque glazes were invented not only to enhance the appearance of earthenware vessels but mainly to cover the porous surface. There are many possibilites to classify ceramic products, here they shall be separated into porous and non-porous or dense ceramics.

To the porous ceramics belong all kinds of earthenware, including terracotta, maiolica and fayence. Stoneware, vitreous china, soft paste and hard paste porcelains are dense ceramics, but only soft and hard paste porcelains are true porcelains. Their main ingredients are kaolin, felspar and quartz.

Besides the composition of the paste, the firing temperature divides the various kinds of ceramic products. High vitrification can only be achieved at temperatures above 1300°C (2370°F).

Felspar is a mineral that softens in temperatures above 1150°C (2100°F) but does not run. The Chinese called kaolin the flesh and felspar the bones of porcelain. Felspar contributes to the density and stability of a porcelain piece. Quartz is a non-plastic mineral that decreases the plasticity of a porcelain paste and the shrinkage of drying or fired paste. It also aids in the vitrification of porcelain in the fire.

Clay is a fine grained product of the decomposition of rocks containing felspar, like granite, gneiss or basalt. If the originally white clay is washed away from its forming ground and deposited at some other location, it picks up metal-oxides and organic matter on its way, which give clays in secondary deposits different colors. Clay that remains in its place retains the white color. The Chinese called it Kao-Ling, and in Europe this name was changed to kaolin. It was also used for the white clay that at first was called white earth in Saxony.

Among the many clays Böttger and his collaborators tested, the kaolin from the vicinity of the city of Colditz in Saxony and from Schnorr's mine were suited best for porcelain-making. Colditz clay had been used by potters in Dresden already in the 17th century, but it was mined only in limited quantities. When Böttger experimented with different clays, King August II ordered all clay pits in Saxony to deliver sixty-five pounds to ninety pounds of clay to Böttger's laboratory for test purposes.[1] At first Colditz clay was the main ingredient of Böttger's porcelain but it was increasingly replaced by kaolin from Aue.

There the mine owner Veit Hans Schnorr indeed about 1700 had encountered white earth. He found it while mining an iron ore vein. Schnorr called the pit "White St. Andreas" mine. At first he used the white earth as fluxing medium in his cobalt factory. In 1708 Pabst von Ohain sent a small sample of Aue kaolin to Böttger, who immediately recognized its superior quality and in 1711 asked the King to reserve "Schnorr's Earth" solely for the Meissen manufactory.

Aue kaolin excells because of its high plasticity and purity. It was probably created by heat under the influence of steam or water and not by simple decomposition of granite. A kaolin of similar properties has been found nowhere in the world. Already in 1712 Stölzel noted in a test protocol that he worked with a paste consisting of ten parts of Aue kaolin, five parts of Colditz clay and three parts of alabaster.[2] This mixture was probably the basic paste used for porcelain until 1724. Its result was a calcareous porcelain (*Kalkporzellan*) that posed considerable problems. The fluxing action of calcium compounds like alabaster occurs withing a small temperature range very vehemently, and in the early years it was not possible to precisely control the temperature in the kilns. Inspector Steinbrück called the kiln in the Albrechtsburg a "Pot of Chance" (*Glückstopf*).

Böttger and his assistants continued their search for a better paste, testing other clays, adding chalk, quartz or "stone", which might have been felspar. The notes of Köhler and Stölzel show that a number of different pastes not only were tested but also used for porcelain wares. If porcelain made during Böttger's time is called Böttger Porcelain today then this designation does not mean that Böttger Porcelain always was made from the same paste. It differs from later porcelain mainly because alabaster was used instead of felspar.

The first tests with felspar were made in 1721 but only in 1724 in some pastes alabaster was substituted by felspar. About 1735 Meissen porcelain had been completely changed from a calcareous to a felspar porcelain. The manufactory

	kaolin	felspar	quartz	clay	firing temperature
					Table 1
Earthenware		3%-12%	35%-55%	40%-55%	1200°C/2190°F
Stoneware		50%	10%	35%-45%	1300°C/2370°F
Vitreous China	5%-15%	20%-30%	20%-30%	20%-30%	1300°C/2370°F
Soft paste porcelain	20%-30%	30%-50%	30%-40%		1300°C/2370°F
Hard paste porcelain	40%-60%	30%-50%	30%-40%		1450°C/2640°F

Table 1
Average technological parameters of certain kinds of pottery

continuously experimented with other kaolins especially after the pit near Aue neared exhaustion at the end of the 18th century. In the vicinity of Meissen some kaolin deposits had been found in the course of a systematic geological exploration of Saxony that had started in 1789. One kaolin deposit near Seilitz, not far from Meissen, had been discovered by the father of a Meissen porcelain painter and was offered to the manufactory. In 1764 the first kaolin was mined in Seilitz and from then on it was used regularly for the Meissen porcelain paste. The quality of Seilitz kaolin was close to the quality of the kaolin from Aue. It too contained very few impurities coming from iron and titanium oxides, and it gave the porcelain paste an even greater stability. Its only disadvantage was that porcelain with Seilitz kaolin did not come out of the kilns as purely white as porcelain made with Aue kaolin. That problem was solved in Meissen only four years after the first tests with Seilitz kaolin had been made, and since 1768 it has been an important ingredient of the Meissen porcelain paste (Fig. 1002). This paste has, because of its ingredients, not been matched by any other porcelain producer. It is, besides the sculptural art and the decorations and painting, a main factor that distinguishes Meissen porcelain from all other porcelains.

When it became obvious that the deposits of good and pure kaolin in Aue were running out, a kaolin from Schletta near Meissen was introduced. Its quality was inferior to the kaolins from Aue and Seilitz. Schletta kaolin was not suited for figurines or dinnerware, so beginning in 1822 it was used for apothecary and laboratory vessels and later from 1849 until 1951 for lithopanes.

After 1842 kaolin from Sornzig became one of the ingredients of some Meissen pastes but only in small quantities, because it was not white enough. In 1970 the pit in Sornzig was closed. Figure 1002 shows which kinds of kaolin were used by the manufactory between 1710 and 1900. [3] Today the

Fig. 1002: Kaolins used in Meissen for porcelain paste between 1710 and 1900

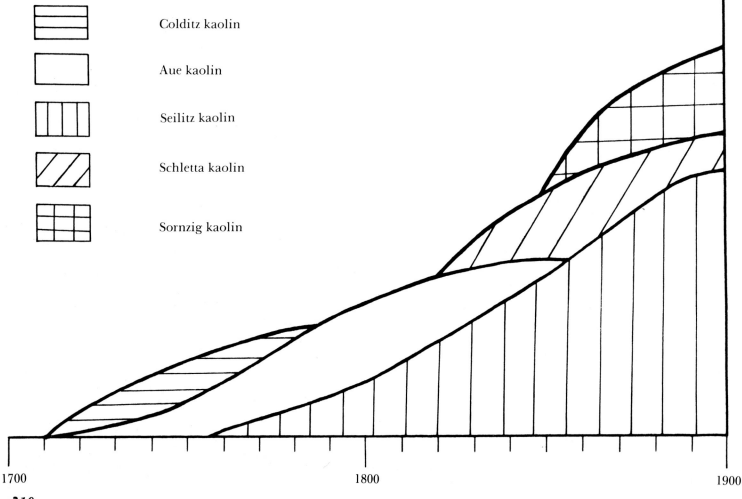

	Colditz kaolin
	Aue kaolin
	Seilitz kaolin
	Schletta kaolin
	Sornzig kaolin

1700   1800   1900

Meissen manufactory uses industrially prepared Bohemian kaolin and Seilitz kaolin. The proportions of the mixtures vary, depending on the use of the different pastes, but for the highest quality paste the ratio is almost one to one Bohemian and Seilitz kaolin.

Quartz is the least expensive ingredient of porcelain. Industrially produced porcelain usually contains a substantial portion of quartz, while to the paste presently used in Meissen no quartz is added. The quartz naturally found in kaolin is sufficient to make a porcelain piece refractory during firing. The manufactory still keeps its paste mixtures secret, but it can be said that they consist of about 68% kaolin and 32% felspar.

Chemical analysis of early Meissen porcelain show a distinct difference to Chinese and Japanese porcelain of about the same time period as can be seen in Table II. For comparison two analyses from the 20th century are added. But it has to be considered that these figures only apply to the analyzed pieces. Other vessels or figurines made during the years mentioned, could show different proportions.

or with a more or less distinct yellowish tint. Very early Böttger's collaborators had found out that a "hot" fire resulted in a yellowish color. Hot fire meant a flame and a kiln atmosphere saturated with oxygen. Porcelain pastes and porcelain glazes always contain extremely small parts of iron compounds. In the presence of an oxygen surplus above about 1000°C (1830°F) these iron compounds oxydize and give the porcelain piece a yellowish color.

If at temperatures above 1000°C (1830°F) a lack of oxygen and a surplus of carbondioxide is created in the kiln, or - in a technical term a reducing atmosphere is present - porcelain will be finished with a white color.

Meissen has experimented with colored pastes too but -with one exception - never produced colored porcelain for regular sale. The exception was a pink paste made after 1945 for a few years. It was only used for toilet sets and small bowls with plastic decoration in low relief.

There are no records about the kiln Böttger used first. The manufactory files only indicate that he designed a new kiln different from those potters used. Potters' kilns were made

Table II
Chemical composition of Chinese, Japanese and Meissen porcelain samples

percentages	SiO2	Al2O3	K2O	CaO	Na2O	MgO	Rest
Chinese vessel, last quarter 17th century[4]	72	20	5.7	0.7	0.5	.	1.1
Japanese Plate c. 1700[4]	74	19	5.0	0.3	0.4	.	1.3
Böttger porcelain covered vase c. 1715[4]	61	33	0.1	4.8	0.2	.	0.9
Meissen vase, felspar porcelain, c. 1731[4]	59	35	4.0	0.3	0.8	.	0.9
Meissen porcelain figurine 1904[5]	62.2	32.48	3.27	0.39	0.98	0.49	0.1
Meissen porcelain unknown object 1965[6]	57.72	29.94	2.75	0.56	0.6	0.23	8.48

The low CaO content in the vase of 1731 proves that this vase, which was modelled by Kirchner, already was made from a paste in which alabaster had been substituted by felspar. The figures for SiO_2 in the table show how much of the paste has been changed to a glassy substance in the fire. A high Al_2O_3 content is an indication that less quartz was used. The Chinese and Japanese porcelains contain about 20% Al_2O_3, a sign for a high quartz addition. Böttger did not use quartz as an ingredient for his paste, only later quartz was added occasionally to some Meissen pastes in small amounts. Today - as mentioned before - Meissen paste does not contain additional quartz.

Porcelain glazes were changed even more often than porcelain pastes. Glazes not only have to match the physical properties of the pastes to which they are applied, they also have to fuse with the pastes during the firing in the kiln and cool down at the same speed without creating tensions between shard and glaze. Too much tension results in fine fissures in the glaze during the cooling period. Occasionally this tension is desired to achieve a decorative network of fine fissures in the glaze, called craquelure.

Glaze is prepared as a liquid with basically the same ingredients as can be found in porcelain paste. But glaze liquid has to melt in the kiln, and therefore a higher proportion of a fluxing agent is necessary. Used as fluxing agents are felspar and several kinds of calcium compounds. They induce the glaze to melting while the paste is vitrifying. The melting glaze covers the surface of a porcelain piece evenly and changes to a hard glassy cover that is solidly fused to the shard. To find the right glazes has been a problem since European hard paste porcelain was invented. Even today ceramic research in all porcelain producing countries is still trying to find the secret of the right glaze.

The color of a porcelain piece depends not only on the ingredients of the paste and the glaze, the method of firing in the kiln decides too whether the piece comes out purely white

from regular bricks which could not withstand high heat. Böttger developed fire proof bricks of a kind that today is called chamotte. In kilns built with these bricks the manufactory could reach temperatures up to 1500°C (2730°F). They were fired with logs of wood. The flame first was drawn downwards through a short channel and then upwards into the kiln itself. On the opposite side of the firegrate the smoke left through a chimney.

The first know Meissen kilns were small. They had the shape of a lying half cylinder, about 60 centimeters (c. 2 feet) long and about 30 centimeters (c. 1 foot) wide on the outside. Inside the kiln the pieces to be fired were enclosed in saggars, fireproof chamotte containers intended to protect the porcelain pieces from direct flames and flying ash particles.

Böttger introduced a new firing technique into porcelain making. Chinese and Japanese porcelains were fired once at temperatures of about 1300°C (2370°F) or below. Decorations and glazes were applied before the firing. Böttger fired his porcelain in two steps. At first the air-dried "green ware" was subjected to 900°C (1650°F). At this temperature the mechanically and chemically bound water is driven out, and the paste turns into a hard shard that is still porous but does not soften in water any more. After this "biscuit-firing" the pieces are glazed and again fired at 1450°C (2640°F). During this sharp fire the paste vitrifies, and the glaze melts and becomes transparent.

Kilns after Böttger's design, although considerably improved over the years, were used in Meissen for more than a century. In 1815 newly developed round or multiple story kilns (Rund- oder Etagenöfen) were introduced (Fig. 1003). They reached from the ground floor through several stories up to the roof. Inside they were divided into several firing levels and heated from five firegrates which were evenly distributed around the kilns. The flames were channelled from the firegrates to a duct in the center of the kiln, from where the heat rose to the different firing levels.

Fig. 1003: Lower level of a Multiple Story Kiln in Meissen about 1900

The bottom level was layed out for sharp firing. In the second level the temperature had cooled down from 1450°C (2640°F) to the biscuit firing temperature of 900°C (1650°F), and in the upper level 600°C (1110°F) were reached for baking saggars. The saggar paste, withstanding even higher temperatures than porcelain, was mixed with coarse sawdust. In the heat of the upper firing level the sawdust burned away, the saggars became porous and allowed the heat to better penetrate them. Originally the round-kilns used to have four stories, but it turned out that the fourth levels were of no use, and they were closed off.

In 1829 Kühn had developed a method of firing the kilns with coal instead of wood. Similar attempts in 1798 had failed as had experiments of using gas. Black lignite imported from Bohemia proved to be a cleaner and more efficient heat source than wood and gas.

Only in 1972, when new kilns were installed, gas firing became common for the Meissen porcelain kilns. That year six new electronically controlled truck chamber kilns *(Herdwagenöfen)* were installed. Their advantages are manifold. Since the flames from the eight gas burners in each kiln are clean, saggars are no longer necessary. Only plates are still put in saggars, but only because three plates instead of one plate can be stacked on the racks of the wagons if they are enclosed in saggars that separate them from each other.

For the truck chamber kilns the wares to be fired are loaded on open wagons with several shelves. The wagons run on rails from the loading platform (Fig. 1004), into the kilns. For sharp firing they remain there for about thirty-six hours. The first sixteen hours a kiln is gradually heated up to 1450°C (2640°F) and during the following twenty hours the kiln slowly cools down.

For smelting enamel paints onto the glaze the manufactory presently employs four muffle kilns and one tunnel kiln. In a muffle kiln the wares are not subject to direct fire. The flames are led around a fireproof inner box that allows the heat to penetrate. Today mostly electrically heated kilns that do not need a "muffle" or inner box are used. Nevertheless these kilns still are called muffle kilns. In a tunnel kiln small carts with porcelain pieces continuously roll through a long heated tunnel that is open in the front and in the back. The temperature necessary for fixing enamel paint to the porcelain glaze lies between 750°C and 850°C (1380°F and 1560°F).

In Meissen three kinds of decoration techniques are used: underglaze painting, sharpfire painting and overglaze painting. For underglaze decorations two colors are preferred, blue and green. The blue paint, first developed in 1717, is made from cobaltoxides. These are insoluble in water and they have to be made into a paint by mixing them with a sugar solution, a syrup or glycerine. Blue underglaze decorations (Figs. 308, 310, and 312) are painted on the still porous surface, and no corrections are possible. Utmost cleanliness is necessary, because dust would clog to form little balls on the tip of a brush. A trace of paint on a finger that touches a piece of biscuit fired porcelain will leave an indelible spot.

The best known blue underglaze decoration is the Onion Pattern (Plates 251 and 252). The painters prepare an unglazed piece by copying on it the outlines of the pattern. They use stripes of tinfoil into which each painter has punched the outlines of the pattern with a pin before. Through the little holes he powders carbon dust onto the porcelain piece (Fig. 1005). The general idea of this method is to get the proportions of the pattern right on the piece and to put each element on its proper place. The painters by no means slavishly follow the dotted lines. Small deviations are unavoidable. The brush has to be led in long, swift and steady movements and that does not always permit the painter to exactly follow the dots (Fig. 1006). It also is not expected from him, and so each piece with Onion Pattern bears the characteristic brushstroke of the painter. Some of the older painters in Meissen can, just by looking at a decoration, identify the painter.

Fig. 1004: Loaded wagon ready to be rolled into a Truck Chamber Kiln

Fig. 1005: Plate prepared to be decorated with Onion Pattern, carbon dust has been powdered onto the shard through perforated tinfoil

Fig. 1006: Half finished Onion Pattern decoration

Fig. 1007: Application of the crossed swords mark with a brush that is cut to a fine point

After the Onion Pattern has been painted, the piece is dipped into the glaze and the decoration disappears completely under the glaze liquid. In the sharp fire the originally greyish-black cobaltoxide paint reacts chemically with the glaze and changes to blue cobaltsilicate. Carbon dust and sugar solution, syrup or glycerine used as painting aids burn completely without trace. The blue decoration is now protected by the glaze against abrasion and wear. The Meissen trademarks are applied the same way, safe from inconspicuous tampering (Fig. 1007).

Blue underglaze painting has its difficulties. On a hard biscuit piece not enough paint is absorbed and the decoration appears pale. On a soft and thin shard the paint can sink too deep and glimmer through from the underside. Firing blue underglaze decorations poses a number of dangers too. In areas with a thicker layer of paint the glaze tends to "boil up", it rises in bubbles, and when these bubbles burst, the glaze does not run again to cover the damaged areas. If the liquid glaze is applied too thickly, the cobalt paint that reacts with the glaze flows slightly and the decoration looks washed out. Under these circumstances it should not be surprising that only about 55% of the finished pieces with blue underglaze decoration are considered completely faultless (Table III).

Underglaze decorations with green paint are similarly sensitive. For them a chromiumoxide is used that neither is absorbed by the porous piece nor reacts with the glaze. It sits as a covering pigment between shard and glaze. While cobaltoxides can be applied in varying shades of blue, chromium green decorations are evencolored. The decoration is painted through templates which are temporarily fixed to the unglazed porcelain pieces by oil or varnish in which they have been soaked. Chromiumoxides have to be laid on twice, otherwise the porcelain areas underneath would shine through the paint.

The most popular green underglaze decoration is the Vineleaf Pattern (Plate 179). Here only the leaves are painted with the aid of templates. The tendrils between the leaves are painted off-hand with a chromium-green paint that has been darkened by iridium- or rutheniumoxides.

If the green paint is applied in a thick layer, the decoration appears as a relief under the glaze after firing. It is also possible that the weight of the paint can bend the border of a plate downwards. Sometimes the painted areas separate from the shard while a piece is dipped into the glaze and slide off to some other spot of the piece during sharp firing. These faults can not always be avoided because in many cases ceramic technology is still a matter of trial and error. The number of substandard pieces with green underglaze decorations is even higher than the number for wares with blue underglaze painting (Table III).

Table III Quality sorting of porcelain with blue or green underglaze decorations 1965[7]		
	blue	green
1. Choice wares	55.1%	36.8%
2. Choice wares	28.6%	38.4%
3. Choice wares	8.8%	14.5%
4. Choice wares	2.6%	4.5%
Breakage	4.9%	5.8%

Sharpfire painting was developed in the second half of the 19th century. It is a special kind of overglaze decoration. The paints tolerate high temperatures and are applied on the glazed piece. While the decorated porcelain is subjected to the sharp fire the glaze softens, and the paint sinks into the glaze, partly dissolving it. Today sharp fire paints are mainly used for ground colors, especially for the royal blue decoration (Plates 182, 183 and 185).

Enamel painting is not only the most impressive decoration technique, it also permits a wide range of possibilities. At present 160 stock colors are used in Meissen, which can be mixed to more than one-thousand varieties (Plate 271). All paints are made in the manufactory and their ingredients are a secret. A considerable number of Meissen paints have not been matched by other paint or porcelain producers, and Meissen aims to keep it that way.

The main ingredients of enamel paints are metals or metal compounds, most of which will not melt at temperatures between 750°C and 850°C. It is therefore necessary to lower their melting points. This is done by adding alkaline, lead or boron compounds. Most of these compounds are hygroscopic, some of them even dissolve after absorbing humidity from the air. To make them stable they are fritted. Kaolin, quartz, alumina or tin oxide are added and the batch is heated until it reaches a glassy consistency. This frit is mixed with the metal oxides or with pigments (*Farbkörper*). Pigments are made from a mixture of metals or metal oxides with refractory compounds like kaolin, quartz or alumina which is chemically combined at a high temperature.

The solid pieces of raw paint material first are finely ground. On a roughened glass plate, water, turpentine or spirit are added and the paste is rubbed with a pestle to extreme fineness (Fig. 1008). Afterwards the paint is dried to a powder. These powders are used as they are or mixed to achieve the required color (Fig. 1009) before they go to the painting shop.

But overglaze paints prepared with the same adhesive agents as underglaze paints would not stick to the smooth and non-absorbent glaze. They have to be mixed with an agent that adheres to the glaze. Oily liquids with a high resin content are suited best. They dry quickly and permit the painter to apply differently colored paints on top of each other. Oil of turpentine has proven to be the best agent for overglaze painting, but it has to be prepared first.

The painter fills a small vessel with oil full to the brim. The oil slowly creeps over the brim into a slighly larger vessel. Since the first vessel is topped up all the time, the second vessel fills up, and the oil creeps into an even larger third vessel and from there into a fourth (Fig. 1010). During this process volatile ingredients of the oil vaporize, and the resin content increases. This concentrated oil (*Dicköl*) is combined with the paint powder and thoroughly mixed with a spatula to the necessary smoothness for painting.

The painter's working table has on one side a raised platform with a semi-circular cutout. On this platform the painting hand of the painter rests while the fingers of the other

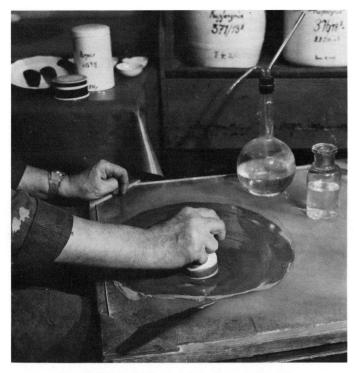

Fig. 1008: Rubbing of paint on a glassplate

Fig. 1010: Vessels for preparing concontrated oil of turpentine on a painter's working table

Fig. 1009: Preparation of paint powder in the paint laboratory

Fig. 1011: Painter's working table

hand lead the piece to be painted through the cutout (Fig. 1011). To mark the right proportions and the distribution of the elements of the decoration the painter can sketch lines with a soft pencil. These marks burn away in the fire as does the oil of turpentine.

If a painter makes a mistake he can wipe off the paint with a lint free rag moistened with fresh oil of turpentine or spirit. Dried paint which has been applied in the wrong spots or dried-in specks of dust or foreign particles can be removed with a sharp erasing knife.

Painted porcelain pieces are fired again in a muffle kiln or in an enamel-melting tunnel kiln. In the kilns the decorated porcelain is heated up to the required temperature for five to six hours, and then it has to cool down for at least the same time. During the firing the paint superficially melts onto the glaze. It is not protected by the glaze, and heavy wear, careless cleaning, scratching, even organic acids and alcaline cleaning agents in hot water can damage overglaze decorations.

The higher the temperature at which an overglaze paint is fired the more resistant it is. Meissen overglaze decorations are fired to about 820°C (1510°F) and withstand all but the most reckless treatments. After coming out of the muffle kiln a decorated piece is finished. Although the process of porcelain making is not uninteresting, the Meissen manufactory rarely has depicted it in its porcelain. Only Theodor Eichler in 1919 made a series showing the stages of porcelain making

from the preparation of the paste to the finished product ready for sale (Plates 274 to 282).

But it is a long way from the kaolin pit to the showroom. First the raw kaolin is washed in plenty of water and poured through several meshes which remove larger lumps and foreign matters. Then the slurry is elutriated. In earlier times a series of large basins connected by channels was used for separating finely grained kaolin from coarser particles. The slurry was continuously running from one basin to the next. The finest kaolin particles remained in the suspension and flowed with the stream from basin to basin. Larger particles like sand, felspar and quartz sank to the bottom of the basins. At the end felspar and quartz contents were reduced and the slurry enriched with kaolin. Today this process is abbreviated by the use of hydraulic cyclone separators, which utilize the centrifugal force for separation.

Felspar, which is mined in lumps, first is broken down in mills to particles of about 3 mm (1/8 of an inch) diameter. These particles are ground to a diameter size below 0.004 mm (0.00016 in.). During the grinding process iron oxides, quartz

Fig. 1012: Filter press in the Meissen manufactory

Fig. 1013: Cakes of porcelain paste from the filter press

Fig. 1014: Workable porcelain paste coming out of the vacuum extrusion press

and mica are removed as far as possible. Then kaolin and felspar are mixed with water to a viscous liquid and homogenized. After that most of the water is extracted in a filter press (Fig. 1012). Because the round and flat cakes coming out of the press (Fig. 1013) still do not have the necessary homogeneity, they are fed into a vacuum extrusion press, in which the paste is thoroughly kneaded and the air is sucked out. The paste coming out of the vacuum press (Fig. 1014) is usable for further processing to porcelain plates, vessels, figurines or any other item that can be made from porcelain paste.

Figurines and groups are formed in parts with plaster moulds (Fig. 3). The plaster absorbs part of the water contained in the paste, and after a short while a part can easily be removed from the mould. A repairer (*Bossierer*) puts the parts together with liquidified paste as glue and carefully removes all burrs and uneven spots. The green ware air-dries to a leathery consistency and shrinks about 3% to 6% in all directions during the drying process. Another 10% to 13% of the size are lost while a piece undergoes the biscuit firing. After having cooled down the piece is dipped into the glaze and then subjected to the sharp firing. Afterwards a white piece can be garnished or painted with overglaze paints. In the model stockroom of the manufactory (Fig. 1015) many finished pieces are stored to serve as samples for repairers and painters.

For groups often figurines or parts of other groups were composed after the already mentioned modular-design principle. Plates 272 and 273 and Figures 1016 to 1019 give an impression of the variety of models that could be chosen, for instance for the Clemens-August-Goblet (Plate 1).

Smaller vessels and vases can be slip-cast. The porcelain slip is poured into plaster moulds consisting of two or three parts which join closely. After a sufficiently thick layer of paste has adhered to the inside of the mould the remaining slip is poured out. The mould is taken apart, the vessel is removed and subsequently treated like a piece made from paste. Casting is preferred for vessels which are difficult to throw on a potter's wheel. Small pieces like handles for cups, bowls or pots usually are cast.

The larger hollow ware is thrown on a potter's wheel by hand (Fig. 1020) For bulgy vessels templates are used inside and out to give them a perfect shape and the required thick-

Fig. 1015: Part of the model stockroom

ness. Plates are turned on the wheel over blanks (*Hubel*) that shape the inside or the outside of a plate. The other side is shaped with the help of templates (Fig. 1021) which also determine the thickness of the piece. Reliefs to be impressed on a plate first are engraved negatively into the blank (Fig. 1022).

On plates and bowls with relief basketweave decoration the weave is impressed by a blank. After the paste has dried to leather-hardness, a worker cuts out the spaces between the seemingly interwoven strands of the relief decoration with a small knife (Fig. 1023). It takes more than an hour to cut a pierced plate, one of the reasons why Meissen porcelain is more expensive than porcelain made by machines.

Another reason for the expensiveness of Meissen porcelain are the strict quality standards. As an example, the figures for 1965 shall be quoted (Table IV). That year of 900,679 pieces of porcelain that were made in Meissen, only 264,800 of them were deemed worth the highest grade.

Table IV
Quality Sorting of Porcelain 1965[7]
In percent of Total

	Subtotal	Tableware	Figurines and Groups
1. Choice	29.4	23.5	81.2
2. Choice	42.2	45.4	12.2
3. Choice	1.6	-	2.4
4. Choice	9.6	11.3	0.5
Breakage	17.2	19.8	3.7

Most people would not even notice the tiny faults on porcelain graded as "2. Choice", but the Meissen sorters rarely miss them. Almost invisible holes in the glaze, looking as if they were made with a pin, black spots from iron oxide particles, unevenness or little dull spots in the glaze, slight deviations in the tint compared to the desired color, they all relegate a piece to a lower grade. Often these faults can be remedied by grinding and then glazing and firing the piece again but that does not lower the cost of Meissen porcelain.

Fig. 1017: Hunter with bugle, felled stag and hounds by Eberlein, model no. 216. The hunter with bugle was also modelled without stages and hounds (model no. 1647), with one dog (model no. 2261), or with several hounds (model no. 217)

Fig. 1016: Running stag by Kaendler, model no. 875

Fig. 1018: Hunter with felled stag and hounds by Kaendler, model no. 2706

317

Pieces with a slightly different color can be sold separately if they were intended as single pieces, like showplates. In a table, coffee or any other set, though, each piece has to match the next perfectly. Substandard porcelain is sold at discounted prices, which still are high compared to other porcelain.

In the present times almost everything can be made from practical plastics, dishwashers wash the dishes, and "art" can be bought in drugstores. The question arises, why porcelain shoud be made as tediously, laboriously and perfectly as in Meissen. Is there still a place in this world for these precious and delicate creations of man's skills and artistic talents?

That decision has to be made individually, and it seems that there are enough people around who appreciate the beauty of Meissen porcelain, its exquisitness and possibly even feel that not an insensible machine has made it but the careful hand of an engaged worker or artist. As long as these qualities are held in esteem, Meissen porcelain will continue to be desirable.

Fig. 1021: *Shaping the underside of a plate with a template*

Fig. 1019: *Hounds hunting down a stag by Kaendler, model no. 2709*

Fig. 1022: *Engraving of the negative of a relief decoration on a plaster blank*

Fig. 1020: *Throwing of a vase on a potter's wheel*

Fig. 1023: *Cutting out of the spaces in a basketweave relief decoration*

318

List of Lithopanes

Compilation after a price list of before 1840[1], a price list of 1846[2], a later schedule continued until 1925[3] and a price list of 1970[4]. Those lithopanes marked with an asterisk were taken out of current production in 1851. Differences between the lists are noted in brackets. Also in brackets are the years mentioned in which new copies were made.

1. St. John, oval*
2. Maria Magdalena after Corregio*
3. St. John, round*
4. Moonlit Landscape by Habenicht
5. Vesuvius with Landscape
6a. Inside of a Church*
6b. Winter Landscape with Church*
6c. English Hunt*
6d. Landscape with Farmhouse*
6e. Two Cows in Landscape*
6f. Dutch Windmill*
6g. Seascape with House*
6h. Seascape with Castle*
7. Day*
8. Night*
9. Pleasure Castle Pillnitz
10. Russian Mail
11. Landscape with Farmhouse
12. Shepherd with Flock (1846: Shepherd with Flock in Storm)
13. Girl at Drawwell (in production in 1970)
14. Tilting at the Rings*
15. Landscape with Girl at Well
16. St. John, large round
17. Royal Saxon Family, round
18. Night after Thorwaldsen, round
19. Turkish Landscape
20. Gothic Lattice Door
21. Swiss Landscape
22. Landscape with Ruin
23. Old German Head*
24. Bivouac
25. Head of French Chevalier, round*
26. Amor and Satyr, round*
27. Meissen, Staircase of Castle
28. Moonlit Gothic Building
29. Woman with Lamp
30. King of Prussia, small
31. Inside of a Gothic Hall*
32. Outside of a Gothic Hall*
33. Head of Zephyrus, round
34. Woman and Child at Window
35. Venus in Clouds
36. Seascape at Sunrise*
37. Outside of a Gothic Cathedral*
38. Gate with Gothic Ornaments*
39. Cavalier with Lady in Moonlit Landscape*
40. Bower in a Castle*
41. Dutch Family with Distaff*
42. Apollo* (1846: Apollo standing)
43. Girl with Headdress, round*
44. Hunting Dog, standing*
45. Dutch Farmer's Living Room*
46. Inside of a Cathedral*
47. Cupid after Mengs
48. Belisarius (1846: The Blind Belisarius)

49. Christ at the Cross
50. Storm at Sea
51. Slave Trade in the Middle East
52. Martin Luther
53. Madonna della Sedia after Raffhael, round
54. St. Stephen's Church in Vienna, small
55. St. Stephen's Church in Vienna, larger
56. Inside of a Cathedral*
57. Philip Melanchthon
58. Angel of the Spanish Madonna, round
59. Group of Cats (1846: Cat Family)
60. Cathedral at Meissen
61. Dresden
62. King Anton of Saxony, round*
63. Winter Landscape (later: Landscape with Water)*
64. Landscape with Water and Rider on Horseback (later: Winter Landscape with Rider on Horseback)*
65. Madonna Della Sedia, small (copy made in 1925)
66. Russian Sleighride
67. Dutch Motif after Hogarth*
68. Dutch Farmer at a Barrel*
69. Old Woman Reading a Book*
70. Landscape with Church and Bridge*
71. Pope Pius VIII, oval*
72. Prince Metternich, oval*
73. Angel after Raffhael
74. Child and Woman in Thunderstorm (in production in 1970)
75. A Politician*
76. Woman and Child in a Room*
77. Dutch Spinning Room*
78. Ancient Building in Winter Landscape*
79. Head of St. John, small*
80. Christ after Dolce (1846: Christ with Chalice)
81. Old Woman
82. Landscape with Water Mill
83. Sistine Madonna
84. Bethrosal
85. Girl with Dog in Room* (in production in 1970)
86. Hagar in the Desert
87. Youth Carrying Girl Across Creek
88. Woman with Goat* (1846: Woman with Goat and Tub on her Head)
89. Angel's Head after Raffhael*
90. King Friedrich August of Saxony

(1846: Prince Friedrich August, Co-Regent of Saxony)
91. Castle Albrechtsburg at Meissen
92. Church at Prietitz (1846: Church in Sunrise)
93. Countess Hatzfeld prostrating before Napoleon*
94. Sistine Madonna, small
95. Napoleon in Front of a Hospital
96. Maria Magdalena after Battoni
97. Figure symbolizing Time*
98. Poachers
99. Angel's Head
100. Head of Zephyrus (copy made in 1922)
101. Holy Night after Corregio
102. Missing in lists of before 1840 and of 1846. Later: Venus, large
103. Girl in Front of Dresser
104. Missing in lists of before 1840 and of 1846. Later: Venus, large
105. Moonlit Seascape*
106. Landscape*
107. Landscape*
108. Church*
109. Chapel*
110. Napoleon
111. Cossack Raid after Peter Hess, designed in 1834
112. Ascension of Christ after Meng's Altar Piece in the Catholic Church in Dresden, designed in 1834
113. Boy and Girl in a Boat
114. Napoleon next to a Cannon*
115. The Kiss, scene from Goethe's "Faust" after Retzsch
116. Girl in Front of Mirror
117. King of Prussia*
118. Prospect of Dresden as seen from the Brühl Terrace (later: Square in Front of the Royal Castle in Dresden, in production in 1970)
119. Faust and Gretchen in Garden, scene from Goethe's "Faust"
120. Inside of a Hall* (later: Entrance Hall of Castle Ehrenberg)
121. Landscape (later: Prospect of Mückenburg)
122. Cooper sitting at Barrel, large
123. Cooper standing at Barrel, small
124. Scene on Board of a Ship with three Figures (1846: Proposal of marriage on the Island of Heligoland), designed in 1836
125. Tsar Nicolaus of Russia with Family in a Boat (1846: Rus-

List of Lithopanic Lampshades and Hanging Lamps

according to a list of 1851[5]

S 28.1   1 bellshaped lampshade

S 28.2   1 ditto with round motifs from lithopanes nos. 4, 5, 9 and 11

S 28.3   1 ditto with elaborate motifs from lithopanes nos. 80, 89, 61 and 6c

S 28.4   1 hanging lamp with figures

S 28.5   1 bellshaped lampshade, small, with round motifs from lithopanes nos. 4, 36, 89 and 100

S 28.6   1 bellshaped lampshade with round motifs from lithopanes nos. 3, 20, 27 and 58

S 28.6   1 bellshaped lampshade with round motifs from lithopanes nos. 5, 22 and 78

S 28   1 bellshaped lampshade, elaborate, with round motifs from lithopanes nos. 9, 10, 22 and 66

S 28.7   1 bellshaped lampshade with motifs from lithopanes nos. 6e, 6g, 21 and 24

S 28.8   1 bellshaped lampshade with round motifs from lithopanes nos. 3, 58, 89 and 100

S 28.8   1 bellshaped lampshade new sort

S 28.9   1 bellshaped lampshade

S 29.10   1 bellshaped lampshade, elaborate, largest sort with round motifs from lithopanes nos. 4, 5, 36 and 82

S 28.11   1 bellshaped lampshade (unidentifiable word, probably: finsiedelsche) sort

S 28.12   hanging lamp with landscapes

S 28.13   1 bellshaped lampshade, largest sort with round motifs from lithopanes nos. 9, 10, 22 and 66

S 28.14   1 bellshaped lampshade for hurricane lamps with round motifs from lithopanes nos. 4, 5 and 121

S 28.15   1 nightlamp with bellshaped lampshade and base

P 35a   1 lithopanic vase with Napoleon and storm at sea

P 35b   1 ditto with castle Pillnitz

P 35c   1 ditto with prospect of Dresden

S 28.15   1 nightlamp with bellshaped lampshade without base

Y 65   1 bellshaped lampshade for gaslight

Y 66   1 ditto

Y 67   1 ditto

Z 68   1 ditto

List of Pieces Executed in Marble Porcelain

(Marmorphan, Marmoroit)[6]

1. Bust of Danae after Rauch on white pedestal
1b. Ditto on marble pedestal
2. Bust Piety
3. Figure Ganymed
4. Butterfly Catcher after Drake
5. Figure Fanny Elsler
6. Vase
7. Figure of Christ without Cross with appurtenances
8. Cross for no. 7
9. Bust of H.M. the King of Saxony
10. Figure Pandora
11. Group Ariadne, 2nd quality
11b. Ditto 3rd quality
12. Amorous Figure male
13. Amorous Figure female
14. Bust of H.M. the King of Saxony, 2nd quality
15. Bust of Liebig, 2nd quality
15b. Ditto 3rd quality
16. Greek Child
17. Ditto
18. Gardener's Child
19. -25. Ditto
26. Bust of Homer
27. Bust of Socrates
28. Bust of Christ
29. Bust of Maria
30. Bust of Martin Luther
31. Bust of Melanchthon
32. Bust of Goethe
33. Bust of Schiller
34. Bust of Napoleon
35. Bust of Schiller, small
36. Bust of Goethe, small
37. Figure of Christ without Cross, with apurtenances
38. Fisher Boy after Metri, defect

Further:
in soft marblelike material one bas relief: The Genius after Thorwaldsen and the same: Madame Schröder-Devrient

List of Independent Porcelain Painting Shops and Porcelain Painters in Dresden

between 1855 and 1944 [7]

1. Ander, Richard
2. Artelt
3. Baerschneider
4. Balleke, name later was changed to Balcke and then to Balque, Alfred
5. Barthol, Valeska
6. Berthold, Hugo
7. Beuchelt, Max
8. Biery, Helene
9. Böhm, Eduard
10. Böhme
11. Böhmer, Moritz
12. Brammer & Co.
13. Bräuer
14. Bretschneider
15. Bucker, Heinrich
16. Buschbeck, Carl
17. Butter
18. Büttner
19. Christiansen, Carl
20. Colditz
21. Correvon
22. Delly
23. Dittrich, Rudolph
24. Donath & Co.
25. Dorn, Curt
26. Dresdner Kunstverlag Richard Eckert
27. Drobisch

28. Eckardt, Georg A. Louis
29. Eckardt, Louis
30. Eckelmann, Martha
31. Eckelmann, Max
32. Eimert, Otto
33. Ens, Emil
34. Ens, Wilhelmine
35. Fehrmann, Carl
36. Fischer, C.E.
37. Fischer, C. Gottlieb
38. Fischer, C. Robert
39. Forbriger, Georg
40. Flack
41. Franz, Gustav
42. Friedrich
43. Fritzsche, called Hartmann
44. Führ, Christoph
45. Fuhrmeister, Wilhelm
46. Gaunitz, Carl
47. Gerstmann & Klemm
48. Glaser, Johann
49. Götze, Julius
50. Görner
51. Graf
52. Greiner-Sohn, Julius
53. Gretzschel, Carl
54. Gretzschel & Götz
55. Grossbaum & Söhne, B.
56. Grosser
57. Günter, Josef
58. Günter, Raimund
59. Gürtler, Eduard
60. Gutkaes, also Gutkäs
61. Hamann, Adolph also Adolf
62. Hamann, Gustav
63. Hamann, Konrad
64. Hamann, Max
65. Hammer
66. Hausen
67. Häring, Josef
68. Hässlich, later Hesslich, Clemens
69. Haushälter, Louis
70. Helbig
71. Hendler
72. Hertel, Carl
73. Hertel, Carl (not identical with 72)
74. Hetschel
75. Hetzschel
76. Heufel, later Heufel & Co.
77. Hiller
78. Hirsch, Franziska
79. Hoffmann
80. Jäger, Hermann
81. John, Bernhard
82. Junkersdorf, Franz
83. Kalich, Amalie
84. Kästner & Jaques
85. Kämpf
86. Kirms
87. Klemm, Ernst
88. Klemm, Richard
89. Knöbel, Theodor
90. Knöller, Louis
91. Koban, Franz
92. Koch, Wilhelm
93. Koch, Hermann
94. Köhler, C. Gottlieb
95. Köhler, Max
96. Kölbel, Arthur

97. Körner
98. Kotte, Ernst
99. Krause
100. Krebs, Bruno
101. Kreiser, Gertrud
102. Kretzschmar
103. Kretzschmar, Ernst
104. Kubich, later Kubig, Ernst
105. Kühn, Friedrich
106. Kunath
107. Lamm, Ambrosius
108. Lantzsch
109. Lanzendorf
110. Lehmann
111. Leinert, Hugo
112. Lengefelder
113. Leube, Adolf
114. Liebert, William
115. Lippold
116. Lorenz, Franz
117. Lorenz, Oswald
118. Löwe
119. Ludemia, Alfred
120. März, Bernhard
121. März, E. Julius
122. Matheus, Emil
123. Matthesius
124. Metzner, Johannes
125. Meyer & Sohn, Leo
126. Miersch, Felix
127. Miersch, Oswald
128. Mollwitz
129. Müller, Max
130. Müller, Herbert
131. Münch, Max
132. Naacke, called Hermersdorf
133. Naumann, Paul
134. Naumann, R.
135. Neubert, Alfred
136. Nonnenprediger
137. Oehme
138. Oppitz
139. Ott, Anton
140. Ott, Franz
141. Pauli, Julius
142. Pertsch, Curt
143. Petschel, August
144. Petschk, Georg
145. Pfohl, Julius
146. Pietsch
147. Pönitz, Reinhold
148. Prager
149. Püschel, Eduard
150. Reibisch
151. Reichel, Oskar Arno
152. Reissig, Arthur
153. Reissig, Clara
154. Richter, Anton
155. Richter, C.A.H.
156. Richter, Carl Gottlob
157. Richter, C.M.
158. Richter, M.
159. Rieth
160. Röbiger, Paul
161. Robra, Max
162. Rühl
163. Schade, Oskar Gustav
164. Schaller
165. Schellenberg
166. **Schellhase, Friedrich**

167. Schettler, Emil
168. Schindhelm
169. Schmidt, Friedrich
170. Schmidt, Hermann
171. Schneidenbach, Camillo
172. Schönherr
173. Schubarth, Johannes
174. Schuhmann
175. Schulz
176. Schulze, Carl
177. Schütz
178. Sembdner, Eduard
179. Simon
180. Stede, called Hansen
181. Stefan
182. Stein, Dorothea
183. Stein, Max
184. Stephan, Walter
185. Stöckel, Paul
186. Strobel, Ella
187. Strobel, Johann
188. Strobel & Petschk
189. Strohbach, Paul
190. Sturm, L.
191. Stürmer
192. Tannert, Ernst
193. Tanz
194. Thiele, Gustav
195. Thiele, Julius
196. Thiele, Moritz Adolf
197. Thiem
198. Thieme
199. Thieme, Julius
200. Till, Franz
201. Till, Marie
202. Tschorn, Curt
203. Tschorn, Max
204. Ungethüm, Rudolf "Porzellan-Malerei Alt-Dresden"
205. Ufer, R.
206. Versandhaus Erato
207. Voigt, Arthur
208. Voigtmann, Arthur
209. Wache, Adolf
210. Wagner, Anna
211. Wagner, Carl
212. Warnick
213. Wedekind
214. Wehsener, Gerhard
215. Wehsener, Richard
216. Weidner, Ernst
217. Wiedemuth
218. Wiegand, Wilhelm
219. Wolf
220. Wölfel, Johann
221. Wollf
222. Wolfsohn, Helena, successor Elb, Leopold, successor Stephan, W.E.
223. Zapf
224. Zeiler
225. Zwierzina, Otto

Conversion Table
Saxon Currency to U.S. Dollar

A straight conversion of the two currencies would not give much enlightenment. Therefore the denominations are compared on the basis of their silver contents. The U.S. Dollar is valued at 24.1 grams or 371.25 grains or 0.77 ounce of fine silver according to the former price of 1.29 U.S. Dollar per ounce of fine silver which used to be the standard of the U.S. currency.

A look at the silver notations in the business section of a newspaper will show, what the old Saxon coins - or the silver dollar for that matter - would buy today.

For gilding of porcelain the gold from Dukat-coins was used. The Ducat was the main gold coin in all states of the German Empire until 1874 but was treated separately and not included in conventions about currencies. It contained 3.44 grams of gold at a coin weight of 3.49 grams (53.09 grains troy to 53.86 grains troy) meaning that it was 98.57 percent pure.

Saxon currency	U.S. currency
1690 - 1763	
One Thaler =	
24 Groschen	0.81$
1763 - 1838	
One Speciesthaler =	
32 Groschen	0.97$
One Thaler =	
24 Groschen	0.73$
One Gulden =	
16 Groschen	0.49$
but for bills and payrolls:	
One Accounting Gulden	
(fl) =21 Groschen	0.61$
1838 - 1873	
One Thaler =	
30 Neugroschen	0.69$
1873 - 1907	
One Thaler =	
30 Neugroschen	0.62$
1873 - 1918	
One Mark =	
100 Pfennig	0.21$
1924 - 1937	
One Mark =	
100 Pfennig	0.105$

Notes

The notes are grouped by chapters.
(bibliography no. 1...) refers to literature listed in the bibliography of this book.
WA means files in the Werkarchiv (Work Archive) of VEB State's Porcelain Manufactory Meissen.
St. A. means files in the Staatsarchiv (State's Archive) in Dresden.

In old files only the front side of a folio is numbered. In this book the backside is indicated by the letter b behind the folio number.

Chapter One

(1)Eckard Wagner (bibliography no. 238) found a wooden memorial tablet from 1739 describing the event.
(2)Rapports 1741, WA I Ab, pp. 16, 113 and 192.
(3)Erich Köllmann (bibliography no. 113) p. 329.
(4)Hildegard Westhoff-Krummacher (bibliography no. 260) p. 28 pointed out that the goblet was not included in an auction of the Clemens-August estate in 1764 and might already have been badly damaged before that time.
(5)In his work report of May 29th, 1741, Ehder noted that he embossed two escutcheons on the goblet and also modelled the foot with a huntsman, a stag and a tree. WA AAI Ab, p. 115.
(6)R.J. Charleston (bibliography n. 32) p. 90.
(7)Yvonne Hackenbroch (bibliography no. 78) p. 115, advances the assumption that the goblet might have been painted blue and white in the family colors of the Prince-Elector. Erich Köllman (bibliography no. 113) p. 329 writes that the small pieces left from the goblet bear no traces of paint. He deducts from this fact that the goblet remained white and unpainted. In the meantime it has been shown that the pieces did not belong to the Clemens-August-Goblet. Jürgen Schärer (bibliography no. 205) p. 30 states: "Kaendler's modelling work then satisfied the orderer, he got it white."
(8)Yvonne Hackenbroch (bibliography no. 78) p. 73 proposes the theory that August III might have seen the goblet and ordered Kaendler to repeat the model for him. A slight doubt might be permitted. If Kaendler had to make a new pull, he probably would have changed the cup and replaced the prince-electoral hat by the royal crown. August was not only very proud of his kingship, in those times protocol and proper insignia were taken very seriously and strictly. Therefore it seems that the goblet in New York is one of several pulls made at the same time as spares.
(9)Hildegard Westhoff-Krummacher (bibliography no. 260) p. 27ff points out a number of shortcomings of the pulls made after 1924.
(10)Heinz Werner in interview with author, January 11, 1982.
(11)Ludwig Zepner in interview with author, January 11, 1982.
(12)Günter Meier (bibliography no. 129) p. 84.
(13)The author is grateful to Mr. Jürgen Schärer for this information.
(14)*Perspektivplan* 1957, Meissen manufactory archive NAS 237, pp. 36-77.
(15)WA S S I.
(16)Program for the Artistical Development, Meissen manufactory archive NAS 122, pp. 44-47.
(17)Peter Strang in interview with author, January 11, 1982.
(18)Böttger in his answer to a Royal Commission, November 17, 1709, St.A. Loc. 41910, Rep. IXb, Blatt 218b, No. 205c, pp. 5b-9.

Chapter Two

(1)Engelhardt (bibliography no. 60) p. 1.
(2)Stemper, A. (bibliography no. 231) pp. 225-227.
(3)A new theory about these discussion groups and their importance for the invention of porcelain was offered at the occasion of the celebrations of Böttger's 300th birthday in February of 1982. Goder (bibliography no. 183) advanced the idea that European hard-paste porcelain actually was invented by a team consisting of Tschirnhaus, Böttger, Pabst von Ohain and five workers sent from Freiberg. He called this collective team a contubernium, based on Reinhardt (bibliography no. 191), who used this expression several times. A *contubernium* in the original sense of the word is a unit of Roman soldiers sleeping together in one tent. Here it is used as the name of a research team that collectively works on one project. This theory still lacks confirmation by historic sources and leaves room for many doubts.
(4)WA, Pretiosa No. 44, IAf4, p.5.
(5)Mields (bibliography no. 163) first translated, deciphered and interpreted the Lab protocol.
(6)Böttger's collaborator Paul Wildenstein wrote in 1736 (WA I Aa pp. 312, 312b): "In 1706 I came to Baron Böttger in Meissen, into the secret laboratory, ...and the Baron and Tschirnhaus also made experiments in Red Porcelain of Plates and marbled Tiles." These recollections were written down thirty years later and they often are cited as proof that Böttger already in 1706 had experimented with porcelain. In another entry Wildenstein wrote that Tschirnhaus made samples of red porcelain and brought them to Böttger in Meissen. Red porcelain at that time was the name for red stoneware. Rückert (bibography no. 200) p. 11 cites from two letters by Böttger of 1706 1707, in which he declared that working on porcelain was Tschirnhaus' business and he would not meddle in it.
(7)St. A. Loc. 1339, Vol. I, 1707-1709, p. 58a.
(8)File "Boettgeriana", Porcelain Collection Dresden, p. 20.
(9)City of Dresden archive, C XXVI.9 "*Acta die Porcellin- und andere Manufacturen betr.* 1710.
(10)Engelhardt (bibliography no. 60) pp. 485, 486.
(11)Shakespeare, Hamlet I, ii.
(12)Steinbrück (bibliography no. 228).
(13)WA Af3 p. 162ff.
(14)WA I Aa5, pp. 238-240.
(15)St. A. Loc. 1341, Vol. IV, p. 5.
(16)WA I Aa1f, pp. 136-156.
(17)St. A. Loc. 1342, Vol. VII, pp. 26, 26b.
(18)St. A. Loc. 1342, Vol. VII, p. 19.
(19)WA Af3, pp. 269-270.
(20)WA I Aa1, p. 149.
(21)St. A. Loc. 1341, Vol. IV, p. 113.
(22)St. A. Loc. 1341, Vol. IV, pp. 160, 160b.
(23)St. A. Loc. 1341, Vol. V, p. 66b.
(24)St. A. Loc. 1341, Vol. V, p. 439.
(25)St. A. Loc. 41910, Sect. IV, Lit. E, No. 1, p. 1.
(26)WA I Aa1, pp. 144-145.

(27)St. A. Loc. 1344, Vol. XVIIIb, p. 11.
(28)Boltz (bibliography no. 21) describes in detail the dealings of Count Hoym and Lemaire.
(29)St. A. Loc. 955, Vol. I, p. 48.
(30)St. A. Loc. 32,562, Vol. IV, Nr. 120 a, p. 187ff.
(31)Boltz (bibliography no. 21) p. 66ff shows a list of a number of the Hoym Lemaire pieces with the crossed swords mark over the glaze. Ten of them are at the Cummer Gallery in Jacksonville, Florida, in the Wark Collection.
(32)St. A. Loc. 1342, Vol. XV, pp. 10, 10b.
(33)St. A. *Finanzministerium* No. 2478, Sect. IV, Lit. A, No. 15, p. 22.
(34)St. A. Loc. 1342, Vol. VII.
(35)WA I Aa 32, p. 152ff.
(36)St. A. Loc. 1344, Vol. XVIII a, p. 470ff.
(37)St. A. Loc. 1344, Vol. XVIII a, p. 283ff.
(38)WA Aa 41, pp. 40-42.
(39)St. A. Loc. 1344, Vol. XIX, pp. 229-238.
(40)St. A. Loc. 1344, Vol XXI, p. 59ff.
(41)St. A. Loc. 1345, Vol. XIV, no pagination.
(42)St. A. Loc. 1345, Vol. XIV, no pagination.
(43)St. A. Loc. 11,114, Vol. I, p. 198.
(44)Wa I Af 9, *Geschichte der Kgl. Sächs. Porzellanmanufactur* 26.6.1828.
(45)St. A. *Finanzministerium* Loc. 2478, Sect. IV, Lit. A. No. 15, p. 9.
(46)WA AA I Bb, pp. 27-30b.
(47)See appendix for explanation of Saxon and German currency.
(48)Manufactory catalogue No. 379, about 1938.

Chapter Three

(1)See note 6, Chapter 2.
(2)St. A. Loc. 41,910, p. 14ff.
(3)WA Aa1, pp. 53-57b.
(4)At the Böttger Symposium in February of 1982 in Dresden Leif Lautrup-Larsen of the Porcelain Manufactory Copenhagen said, refering to the old papers of the founders of the Copenhagen manufactory of two hundred years ago: "These papers also report of those problems we ceramists still encounter today - as for instance crooked plates, bad glaze and wrong colors. Mankind can send a man to the moon but we are still not able to make shape-retaining porcelain plates with a certainty. I say this to comfort all future ceramic engineers - there are still problems to be solved."
(5)Steinbrück (bibliography no. 228) pp. 63, 64.
(6)Boltz (bibliography no. 19) points out that most of the vessels of the first years were made with moulds.
(7)St. A. Loc. 41,910, pp. 31, 31b.
(8)Boltz (bibliography no. 19) meritoriously has analyzed the inventories of 1711 and thus contributed to a clearer understanding of the first years of the manufactory.
(9)Zimmermann (bibliography no. 269) pp. 77, 78 is of the opinion that the facetted decoration was cut. Menzhausen (bibliography no. 150) p. 15 shares this opinion. The manufactory inventory of August 1711 mentions Form 1 "gadrooned or facetted Tea Pot", Form 2 "ditto, a little smaller" and "53 low facetted Beer Mugs (unfired)". The existence of moulds for facetted vessels strongly points to the possibility that not all facetted pieces got their decoration by cutting. The moulds impressed the facettes which were later highlighted by polishing.
(10)St. A. Loc. 41,910, p. 27b.
(11)St. A. Loc. 41,910, Rep. IXb, Blatt 218b, No. 205c, p. 213.
(12)St. A. Loc. 1340, Vol. I, p. 117.
(13)Steinbrück (bibliography no. 228) p. 67.
(14)H. Walter in a paper delivered to the participants of the Böttger symposium in Dresden on February 5th, 1982, author's notes.
(15)Menzhausen (bibliography no. 151), p. 23 proposes the French sculptor Francois Coudray as the creator of the medal. Coudray came to Dresden in 1715.
(16)Steinbrück (bibliography no. 228).
(17)Steinbrück (bibliography no. 229).
(18)According to Kramer (bibliography no. 118) who cites the archives in Vienna, Dresden, Warsaw, Ludwigsburg and Merseburg.
(19)The director of the Albrechtsburg in November of 1981 stated to the author that he considered the theory of red paste having been stored in the cellars of the castle for seventy-five years or more as very dubious.

Chapter Four

(1)WA If, p. 84 and p. 102.
(2)St. A. Loc. 1340, Convolut II, p. 253.
(3)Steinbrück (bibliography no. 228), p. 23.
(4)see note 3, p. 32.
(5)WA I Aaf, p. 136ff.
(6)*Mater Dolorosa* = mourning mother of Jesus Christ.
(7)Hofmann (bibliography no. 90) ascribes "Monsieur Piperouk" to Fritzsche; Morley-Fletcher (bibliography no. 168) feels that a musician in miner's uniform might have been made by Fritzsche; Walcha (bibliography no. 250), attributes a pagoda to Fritzsche.
(8)St. A. Loc. 1341, Vol. VI, p. 203.
(9)St. A. Loc. 1342, Vol. II, p. 95b.
(10)In the U.S.A. variations can be found in the Untermyer Collection at the Metropolitan Museum of Arts in New York, at the Wadsworth Atheneum in Hartford, Connecticut and in the Morgan Collection.
(11)R. Rückert has thoroughly investigated the ridicule tailors were subjected to and its expression in porcelain and stoneware in an article "*Meissen und der Schneiderspott*" (bibliography no. 201).

(12)St. A. Loc. 1344, Vol. XVIIIa p. 339.
(13)St. A. Loc. 1344, Vol;. XVIIIa, p. 342.
(14)Biscuit from the Italian *biscotto*, meaning fired twice.
(15)WA III H 168, p. 2.
(16)Unfiled typewritten note of September 10th, 1908, in the manufactory archive; the author is grateful to Mr. Manfred Haude, archivist of the manufactory, for his assistance in tracing the fate of this group.
(17)WA III K 25 B, pp. 456 and 459.

Chapter Five

(1)St. A. Loc. 41,910, pp. 239-311; Loc. 1340, Conv. I, pp. 118-127b.
(2)Menzhausen (bibliography no. 150) pp. 36-60.
(3)WA III H 106; WA III H 115; WA AA V, 9,45.
(4)WA III D 35, pp. 98-100b and pp. 123 and 123b.

Chapter Six

(1) WA I Af 2, p. 78 .
(2) J. Horschick (bibliography no. 96).
(3) Steinbrück (bibliography no. 228) p. 73.
(4) WA I Aa 1a, p. 166.
(5) Ducret (bibliography no. 55) p. 12-14.
(6) This information and the following ones according to Seyffarth (bibliography no. 222) p. 33ff. Seyffarth and Ducret had a very polite running battle over the Gold Chinamen in which Seyffarth finally came up with better proof for his contentions.
(7)In a complaint against Höroldt the manufactory inspector Reinhardt and Kaendler wrote about 1734 that Höroldt knew nothing about enamel paints when he came to Meissen.
(8)In 1979 the publishing house Edition Leipzig in Leipzig, GDR, published a facsimile edition of the more than 130 plates of the Schulz-Codex, each plate containing several sketches.
(9)Kakiemon porcelain originally was export porcelain made by the family enterprise of Kakiemon Sakaida near the city of Sarita on the Japanese island of Kyushu. Today all polychrome painted porcelain from the vicinity of Sarita usually is called Kakiemon.
(10)T.H. Clarke (bibliography no. 35)
(11)St. A. Loc. 1342, Vol. XI, p. 10.
(12)WA Pretiosa No. 3, Köhler's recipe book.
(13)WA I Aa 10, p. 323 of 1727; WA I Aa 12, p. 334 of 1729; St. A. Loc. 1341, Vol. II, pp. 281b-284b.
(14)St. A. Loc. 1342, Vol. VI, p. 106 b; Vol. VIII, pp. 129, 129b; Vol. IX, p. 45.
(15)Burwell (bibliography no. 29), pp. 103-108.
(16)St. A. Loc. 1342, Vol. X, p. 493ff.
(17)St. A. Loc. 33 298, Vol. I, p. 214.
(18)WA I Ac 2, pp. 268-269.
(19)WA III G 1, pp. 157 and 160.
(20)WA III G 1, pp. 156, 156b.
(21)Hematite, a fine grained mineral basically consisting of Fe_2O_3 with a dark to brick red color.
(22)St. A. Loc. 36 345, Vol. II, p. 57ff.
(23)Oil of Lavendula spica, in German *Grosser Speik*, in English Great or Broadleaved Lavender an aromatic plant of South European origin.

Chapter Seven

(1)WA III H 28.
(2)Law about the Issuance and Redemption of Emergency Money *(Gesetz über die Ausgabe und Einlösung von Notgeld, 17 Juli 1922, Reichsgesetzblatt Teil I, 1922*, Nr. 58, p. 693-695).
(3)Price list of 1923.
(4)WA III K 45, p. 1.
(5)WA III K 47, p. 1.
(6)WA III K 45, pp. 420, 420b.
(7)WA III K 48, p. 9.
(8)WA III G 1, p. 162.
(9)WA III G 1, p. 163b.
(10)WA III G 1, p. 165.
(11)Because the bulk of lithopanes first came from the Royal Porcelain Manufactory in Berlin in English-speaking countries they often were called "Berlin Transparencies".
(1)According to Kunze *"Lithopanien der Meissner Porzellanmanufaktur"* (bibliography no. 123).
(13)St. A. Loc. 36 355, Vol. XII, p. 132.
(14)WA III H 64, p. 224ff.
(15)*Grundpreisliste Figuren*, January 1970.
(16)WA AA I Bb 12, pp. 7-17.
(17)For instance at the hotel Newa and the coffee houses *Altmarkt* and *Rosengarten* in Dresden, at the hotel *Stadt Halle* in Halle, GDR, at the milkbar, the mochabar and the restaurant of the Palace of the Republic in Berlin, GDR.
(18)The most comprehensive survey about babies in swaddling clothes is given by Ernst Meyer-Heilemann in *Keramos* (bibliography no. 158).
(19)First described by Kunze in *Keramos* (bibliography no. 125).
(20)In 1852 the manufactory got an order for 15,800 porcelain insulators for the Saxon telegraph system. St. A. Loc. 41,843, Vol. V, Sect. IV, Lit. A, No. 8, p. 192.

Chapter Eight

(1)WA I Af 3, pp. 266-267.
(2)In the churchbooks of the late 17th century the name Aufenwerth is written in two words as Aufm Werth (see Ducret, bibliography no. 55 p. 87). The letters JAW can probably be explained as an abbreviation of Johannes Aufm Werth.
(3)Anna Elisabeth Aufenwerth was married to Jakob Wald. Her signature EAW could be read as Elisabeth Anna Wald and her other signature AW could be interpreted as Anna Wald. But that would mean use of these signatures only after her marriage in 1722. A more probable thesis is that EAW stands for Elisabeth Aufm Werth and AW simply for Aufm Werth. This thesis is supported by the signature of her sister Sabina. She was married to Isaac Hosennestel but signed with the letters SAW which only can be interpreted as Sabina Aufm Werth.
(4)St. A. Loc. 1341, Vol. V, pp. 464, 464b.
(5)St. A. Loc. 1341, Vol. IV, p. 5.
(6)St. A. Loc. 1342, Vol. VIII, p. 72b.
(7)St. A. Loc. 32 561, Vol. I, Nr. 118, p. 266b.
(8)St. A. Loc. 32 561, Vol. I, Nr. 117, p. 111.
(9)St. A. Loc. 1341, Vol. V, p. 307.
(10)St. A. Loc. 1344, Vol. XVII, p. 237.
(11)*Codicis Augustei, Special Verordnungen IV, Buch I, Cap. Von Cammer- und Rent-Sachen*, columns 1325-1328.
(12)*Zweyte Fortsetzung des Codicis Augustei Zweyter Teil*, columns 15 and 16.
(13)St. A. Loc. 1345, Vol. XXIII, p. 284.
(14)St. A. Loc. 41,911, p. 5.
(15)WA I Ak 4, pp. 35-40b.
(16)WA I Bl 56, pp. 193-196.
(17)WA I Bl 56, pp. 42-44.
(18)*Leipziger Tageblatt*, March 25th, 1909.

(19)Copies of the dealer's files are in the possession of the author. Since the dealer is still in business his identity should be protected.
(20)The Nelson Rockefeller Collection, sales catalogue 1980-1981.

Chapter Nine

(1)Numbers 13:23, Deuteronomy 8:8, Song of Solomon 4:3, 6:7, 8:2.
(2)According to Berling (bibliography no. 12) p. 150, a blue painter earned 122 to 150 Thalers annually, while polychrome painters made 176 to 338 Thalers per year.
(3)Smithsonian Institution, Washington, D.C., Adams-Clement Acc. 187 487, Cat. 54 060.
(4)Berling (bibliography no. 12) p. 84.
(5)Berling (bibliography no. 12) p. 134.
(6)The booklet *Informationen der Meissner Porzellanmanufaktur*, published in 1963, states that the crossed swords were added to the decoration in 1886.
The booklet *Meissner Porzellan, Weisses Gold mit den Blauen Schwertern*, published by the manufactory in 1981 says on p. 37 that the swords were added in 1893.
At the occasion of an exhibition of porcelain with Onion Pattern, arranged by the manufactory in 1934 in all leading porcelain stores, the trade journal *Sprechsaal für Keramik Glas Email* wrote (1934, p. 163) that the manufactory applied the swords within the decoration since 1900.
(7)In *Deutsche Töpfer-Zeitung*, 1887.
(8)WA Ab 31, p. 130.
(9)*Sprechsaal* 1896, p. 161.
(10)*Adressbuch der Exportindustrie* 1884, III, p. 36.
(11)Commemorative publication *50 Jahre Meissner Ofen- und Porzellanfabrik, vorm. C. Teichert*, Meissen, 18.8.1922, no pagination.
(12)Archive of VEB Plattenwerk Max Dietel in Meissen.
(13)The author himself has mistakenly repeated this assumption in his book "Marks on German, Bohemian and Austrian Porcelain" (bibliography no. 198) p. 563.
(14)*Porzellan- und Glashandlung*, 30th year, no. 24, June 14th, 1930.
(15)*Gesellschaftsvertrag des Verbandes der Porzellangeschirrfabriken*, § 37.
(16)WA I Bl, p. 39.
(17)Letter by Roland Dorschner, Chairman of the Board of Hutschenreuther AG to author, July 8, 1982.
(18)Promotional leaflet *Hutschenreuther Blau Zwiebelmuster* by Hutschenreuther AG, 1980.
(19)WA I Bl, p. 56.
(20)Judgement by the District Court in Reichenberg, Bohemia, Case 4-0-19/42, Sept. 21, 1942.
(21)The other two factories were *Duxer Porzellanmanufaktur* (Dux Porcelain Manufactory) in Dux (presently Duchcov) and *Gräflich Thun'sche Porzellanfabrik* (Count Thun's Porcelain Factory) in Klösterle (presently Klasterec).
(22)This mark was registered in the United States on May 29th, 1962 under no. 125,205. The accompanying affidavit by 'Duchcovsky Porcelan' states a trifle daringly that the company is the owner of a Czechoslovakian trademark registration no. 110,726 of Sept. 2, 1913 for the same mark. (In 1913 the state of Czechoslovakia did not exist at all and the registration no. for this mark of B. Bloch in 1913 was 7,834.
(23)*Juristische Wochenschrift* 1926, p. 1984, no. 10.

Chapter Ten

(1)Shown in Zimmermann, (bibliography no. 269) p. 122.
(2)Graesse (bibliography no. 72).
(3)Zimmermann (bibliography no. 269) p. 297.
(4)Hartmann (bibliography no. 86) pp. 62-63.
Kovel (bibliography no. 115) nos. 187, 188.
Poche (bibliography no. 185) no. 2033. He even writes that Chinese marks were applied in blue paint on red stoneware.
Unitt (bibliography no. 237) p. 117.
(5)WA I Af 3, p. 161b.
(6)German Patent Office, registration no. 281 494.
(7)WA III J, p. 10.
(8)WA V 9, p. 26.
(9)WA I Aa 5, p. 195.
(10)WA I Aa 5, p. 214b.
(11)WA I Aa 5, p. 248.
(12)WA I Aa 5, p. 299.
(13)WA I Aa 2, pp. 181-183.
(14)*Leipziger Post-Zeitungen*, April 7, 1723.
(15)*Dritte Beilage zum Deutschen Reichs-Anzeiger und Königlich Preussischen Staats-Anzeiger*, Nr. 132, June 9, 1875.
(16)U.S. Patent Office, registration no. 26,482, April 30, 1895.
(17)Hofmann (bibliography no. 90) p. 302.
(18)Doenges (bibliography no. 49) p. 215.
Walcha (bibliography no. 250) p. 497.
(19)Chaffers (bibliography no. 31) Vol. 1, p. 475: 1712-1720.
Cushion (bibliography no. 44) p. 100: from c. 1723.
Danckert (bibliography no. 47) p. 276: 1722-1780.
Doenges (bibliography no. 49) p. 192: pieces with kite-mark must have been made in Meissen at least until 1725.
Hannover (bibliography no. 85) Vol. 3 p. 106: found for the most part on so-called Türkencopgen of the period 1727-1735.
Hofmann (bibliography no. 91) p. 141: 1721/1722/1731/1732.
Honey (bibliography no. 92) p. 162-163: kite mark about 1720-1725 and later; Caduceus first about 1723 but continued in use for some time longer.
Mickenhagen (bibliography no. 159) p. 33: 1720-1730.
Savage (bibliography no. 204) p. 221: 1723 onwards.
Weiss (bibliography no. 259) p. 275: 1723-1724.
(20)U.S. Patent Office, registration no. 26, 481, April 30th, 1895.
(21)Menzhausen (bibliography no. 150) pp. 36-60.
(22)St. A. Loc. 1341, Vol. V, p. 252b.
(23)St. A. Loc. 1341, Vol. V, p. 464b.
(24)St. A. Loc. 1341, Vol. V, p. 469.
(25)For instance, nos. 124 and 143 in the catalogue of the Hans-Syz-Collection at the Smithsonian Institution in Washington, D.C.
(26)For instance, on a tea-pot in the Wark Collection at the Cummer Gallery of Art in Jacksonville, Florida.
(27)Part tea set at the Museum of Arts and Crafts, Berlin, Germany, dated c. 1723-1725; bowl at Castle Lustheim, Bavaria, Germany, collection of Ernst Schneider, dated 1725; baluster vase at the Dresden Porcelain Collection signed "J.G. Höroldt fec. Meissen, 17 *Augusti* 1726".
(28)Chaffers (bibliography no. 31) Vol. 2, p. 473: from about 1710-1712.
Cushion (bibliography no. 44) p. 102: generally 1725-1730.
Danckert (bibliography no. 47) p. 276: 1725-1740.
Graesse (bibliography no. 73) p. 484: 1723-1736.
Honey (bibliography no. 92) p. 170: much more common on porcelain of 1725-1730 than later.
Jedding (bibliography no. 98) p. 22: about 1723-1736.
Kovel (bibliography no. 115) p. 6: c. 1725.
Litchfield (bibliography no. 127) P. 188: 1709-1726.

Meissen 1975 (bibliography no. 205) p. 28: around 1725 to around 1740.
Mickenhagen (bibliography no. 159) p. 33: 1710-1725.
Newman (bibliography no. 177) p. 35: supposedly about 1723 until 1736.
Savage (bibliography no. 204) p. 221: 1725 onwards, cessation doubtful but prior to 1763.
Ware (bibliography no. 254) p. 106: until 1733.
Weiss (bibliography no. 259) p. 275: until 1733.

(29)WA I Aa 21, p. 66

(30)One example for the strict observation of protocol and ceremonial rules are the trade treaties between Saxony and the Republic of Venice in Italy. In the treaty of 1756 the Saxon Prince-Elector was named first because of his rank of King of Poland. In 1763 he had lost the title of King. But in the ratification document of a new trade agreement in 1769 the Saxon Prince-Elector again was named in first place. The Republic of Venice refused to accept the document because it considered itself of higher rank than a German Prince-Elector. The agreement was never ratified, but after some negotiations both sides acted as if it were in force.
St. A. Loc. 2817, Bd. 1, 1750-1768; Bd. 2, 1769-1776.

(31)St. A. files *Oberhofmarschallamt* T XI, No. 61 (enclosure).

(32)U.S. Patent Office registration no. 26,,480, April 30th, 1895.

(33)St. A. Loc. 41 724, Sect. IV, Lit. E, No. 6, Vol. I, p. 86b.

(34)St. A. Loc. 41 724, Sect. IV, Lit. E, No. 6, Vol. II, pp. 60 and 60b.

(35)St. A. Loc. 41 724, Sect. IV, Lit. E, No. 6, Vol. II, p. 68.

(36)St. A. Loc. 41 724, Sect. IV, Lit. E, No. 6, Vol. II, p. 77.

(37)St. A. Loc. 41 724, Sect. IV, Lit. E, No. 6, Vol. II, p. 83.

(38)St. A. Loc. 41 724, Sect. IV, Lit. E, No. 6, Vol. II, pp. 72b-74b.

(39)St. A. Loc. 41 724, Sect. IV, Lit. E, No. 6 , Vol. II, p. 162.

(40)A Meissen card with marks, published by the manufactory in 1981: crossed swords with letters K.P.M. 1723-1725, crossed swords alone 1725.
A Meissen porcelain plate of 1980, Fig. 540: 1730.
A Meissen Porcelain plate of about 1918, Fig. 541: 1720.
German trademark registration of 1875: 1720.
U.S. Patent Office registration of 1895: 1720.
Auscher (bibliography no. 6) p. 54: 1725.
Chaffers (bibliography no. 31) Vol. I p. 475: 1716.
Cushion (bibliography no. 44) p. 100: 1723.
Danckert (bibliography no. 47): 1722.
Graesse (bibliography no. 73) p. 480: 1723.
Hartman (bibliography no. 86) p. 63: 1719.
Hofmann (bibliography no. 90) p. 141: 1723/1724-
Honey (bibliography no. 92) p. 164: about 1724.
Jedding (bibliography no. 98) p. 22: 1723/1724.
Köllmann (bibliography no. 114) p. 31: about 1723.
Kovel (bibliography no. 115) p. 219: 1723.
Meissen 75 (bibliography no. 205) p. 28: around 1723.
Newman (bibliography no. 177) p. 33: 1723.
Poche (bibliography no. 185) no. 193: 1723.
Rückert (bibliography no. 200) p. 38: 1723-
Savage (bibliography no. 204) p. 222: about 1724.
Seyffarth (bibliography no. 223) p. 73: beginning in 1723 on every piece.
Thorn (bibliography no. 234) p. 30: 1724.
Walcha (bibliography no. 250) p. 499: 1725.
Ware (bibliography no. 254) p. 106: about 1723.
Weiss (bibliography no. 259) p. 275: 1725.

(41)*Pro Memoria* to King August II, Dec. 1728, saying that it depends on a Royal decision whether porcelain for the French trader Lemaire "should receive a Chinese letter or a different sign instead of the otherwise usual two Electoral swords?"
St. A. Loc. 1341, Vol. IV, pp. 158, 158b.

(42)St. A. Loc. 32 561, Vol. I, No. 117, p. 111b-112.
"...because the marking of this white porcelain with the Electoral swords has been done only after His Majesty's oral high order (and not been observed previously)..."

(43)St. A. Loc. 32 562, Vol. IV, No. 120a, pp. 140-141.

(44)St. A. Loc. 1341, Varia concerning the Porcelain Manufactory p. 59b.

(45)*Amtsgericht* Meissen, A No. 1133.

(46)St. A. Loc. 32 561, Vol. II, No. 118, pp. 311b-312b.

(47)Doenges (bibliography no. 49) p. 201: blue.
Graesse (bibliography no. 73) p. 489: blue, violet, ironred, black, gold.
Honey (bibliography no. 92) p. 164: states that overglaze marks in black, red, blue etc. occured earlier than underglaze marks, "sometimes on porcelain apparently dating back to Böttger's time".
Jedding (bibliography no. 98) p. 22: rarely in blue over the glaze.
Newman (bibliography no. 177) p. 34: blue, rarely red or purple.
Rückert (bibliography no. 200) p. 38: blue.
Schnorr von Carolsfeld (bibliography no. 215) p. 156: mostly in light blue.
Seyffarth (bibliography no. 223) p. 441: blue, ironred, purple, gold.
Wynter (bibliography no. 263) p. 44: for a certain shape of the mark "usually blue or black enamel".

(48)St. A. Loc. 32 561, Vol. I, No. 117, pp. 68-71 and 136-137.

(49)St. A. Loc. 1341, Vol. IV, pp. 189b, 190.

(50)St. A. Loc. 1341, Vol. IV, pp. 206b, 207.

(51)St. A. Loc. 955, Vol. I, p. 359b.

(52)St. A. Loc. 1341, Vol. IV, p. 158b.

(53)Berling (bibliography no. 12) p. 176, note 382.

(54)Boltz, (bibliography no. 21) p. 70ff.

(55)Chaffers (bibliography no. 31) p. 479: after 1763, "*Saxe au point*, and it is also known as King's Period".
Litchfield (bibliography no. 127) p. 189: 1770.
Thorn (bibliography no. 234) p. 30: 1763-1774.

(56)WA I Ac 1, p. 27.

(57)St. A. Loc. 41 724, Sect. IV, Lit. E, No. 6, Vol. I, p. 1.

(58)St. A. Loc. 41 724, Sect. IV, Lit. E, No. 6, Vol. I, p. 1b.

(59)St. A. Loc. 41 724, Sect. IV, Lit. E, No. 6, Vol I, p. 3.

(60)Smithsonian Institution, Washington, D.C. plates from the household of President John Quincy Adams, Adams-Clement Acc. 187 487, cat. 54060 and 54061.

(61)St. A. Loc. 41 911, p. 218b; WA IV 9-13, p. 20.
Actually there were two kinds of pastes I and II each and one kind of paste III. A report of 1823 describes them (WA I Bb 3, no pagination);

Paste I	Auer Paste	81 lbs. earth from Aue, 29 lbs. felspar
	Paste GR	40 1 2 lbs. earth from Aue, 40 1/2 lbs. earth from Seilitz, 29 lbs. felspar
Paste II	Ordinary Paste II	42 4 13 lbs. clay from Kascha. 42 4/13 lbs. earth trom Seilitz, 23 2 26 lbs. felspar, 2 3 26 lbs. limestone
	Paste AG	40 1 2 lbs. earth from Aue, 40 1/2 lbs. clay from Kascha, 29 lbs. felspar
Paste 3		90 lbs. earth from Seilitz, 45 lbs. clay from Kascha, 45 lbs. earth from Schletta, 10 lbs. lime

(62)WA IV 9-13, p. 143.

(63)WA III D 35, p. 39.

(64)WA III D 17a, p. 47.

(65)Warman (bibliography no. 257) p. 286: "It has been reported that a new mark has been instituted since the Russian occupation — that of a hammer and sickle". Newman (bibliography no. 177) p. 37: "After World War 2 for a short time hammer and sickle were painted next to the swords over the glaze".

(66)Letter by the manufactory to author, August 24, 1978.

(67)German Patent Office, trademark roll, nos. 523 830 and 523 831.

(68)Letter by the manufactory to author, July 5, 1979.

(69)Registered in the GDR under nos. 631 321 and 631 506, in the FRG under nos. 816 234 and 816 235 of the trademark rolls.

(70)U.S. Patent Office, trademark registration no. 906,708, Jan. 26, 1971.

(71)Registered in the GDR under nos. 638 766 and 638 767, in the FRG under nos. 949 873 and 917 631 of the trademark rolls.

(72)Chaffers (bibliography no. 31) Vol. 1, p. 482 feels that one "nick in the paste" is a sign "on white porcelain vessels without defect", one or more nicks above or below the crossed swords and more than one nick across the swords he considers indications for defective porcelain.
Cushion (bibliography no. 44) p. 104 states: "factory cancellation marks on wares sold in the white or as imperfect specimens".
Danckert (bibliography no. 47) p. 277 about one incision: "until 1850 brush strokes across the point where the swords cross for white porcelain of all qualities" and about two incisions: "From 16 November 1850 two brush strokes, at first only for decorative porcelain, later as a mark to indicate imperfections". The expression "brush strokes" is probably a mistake by the translator. The German edition correctly says "incisions".
Kovel (bibliography no. 115) p. 217, in their opinion all crossed swords with "scratched" lines are marks for defect or imperfect pieces.
Poche (bibliography no. 185) nos. 212-218 defines:
one incision across the mark = medium quality
one incision below the mark = medium quality, unpainted
one incision above the mark = medium quality, painted
two incisions across the mark = 2nd quality, painted
two incisions below the mark = discarded, painted
two incisions above the mark = discarded, unpainted
three incisions across the mark = discarded
four incisions across the mark = 3rd quality.

(73)Just (bibliography no. 103) and Kunze (bibliography no. 122).

(74)Until now a document of 1766 found by Berling in the Dresden State's Archive, Loc. 1346, Vol. III, p. 98 was considered the earliest known source.

(75)WA I Bl 41, p. 154.

(76)WA IV, 9-13.

(77)The author is grateful to Mr. Heinz Brandes of VEB State's Porcelain Manufactory for the explanation of this mark.

(78)WA I Bl 56, p. 226.

(79)WA I Bl 56, pp. 229, 229b.

(80)St. A. Loc. 41, 843, Vol. VI, § 145.

(81)WA I Bl 56, p. 208.

(82)WA I Ag 13a, p. 1.

(83)St. A. Loc. 1345. Vol. XXIII, p. 252.

(84)St. A. Loc. 41,843, Vol. V, § 85.

(85)Steinbrück in a report, WA I Af 2, p. 23, grades the Brac ware:
"1. in usable shards,
2. vessels which are broken in a way that they are impossible to be used.
3. defective ones which could be used if need be,
4. rather usable ones, but still no merchant's goods because of some imperfections, as
1. that they are crooked or out of shape
2. covered with bubbles
3. chipped somewhere or blemished."

(86)WA I Aa5, p. 197, an inquiry what to do with "so-called brac" and "too bad medium goods".

(87)WA I Aa 2, p. 169.

(88)WA I Aa 5, p. 216.

(89)St. A. Loc. 1341, Vol. V, p. 108b.

(90)WA I Ak 4, p. 40.

(91)WA III D 34, pp. 138-141.

(92)WA III D 35, p. 166.

(93)WA II Ab 7a.

(94)Quoted in Kunze (bibliography no. 122) p. 28 from St. A. Loc. 41,911, M, pp. 53 and 57.

(95)WA IV 21 § 141.

(96)WA IV 21 § 99.

(97)St. A. Loc. 41,843, Vol. V, § 40.

(98)Compilation by the manufactory administration of the usual signs "for strict observation", 1940.

(99)William Funk, chemist at the manufactory, (bibliography no. 66) p. 493. Neuwirth (bibliography no. 173) p. 25 agrees with Funk's opinion that pieces with the AR mark and incisions are forgeries.

(100)The late archivist of the manufactory, Otto Walcha, matched most of the signs with names (bibliography no. 252) p. 24.

(101)WA I Aa 25a, p. 146b.

(102)WA I 25, p. 285.

(103)WA I Ac8, pp. 361-368.

(104)Seyffarth (bibliography no. 222) p. 162.

(105)Joseph first described his discovery in *Keramos* (bibliography no. 101).

(106)WA III H 119.

(107)Mr. Manfred Haude, archivist of the Meissen manufactory presently is working on a list of model numbers and corresponding dates to be published at an as yet uncertain date.

(108)St. A. *Hausmarschallamt* R XVI, Ns. 55 to 58, Vol. I to V.

(109)Cup in Bayerisches National Museum in Munich, Germany, Inv. no. 73/61.

(110)In the Hans-Syz-Collection at the Smithsonian Institution in Washington, D.C., catalogue no. 102.

Chapter Eleven

(1)Chaffers (bibliography no. 31), Vol. 2 p. 156, shows this mark. Exactly the same mark appears in Doenges (bibliography no. 49) p. 216 and in Litchfield (bibliography no. 127) p. 453, here with the remark that this mark occurs "in great variety on early Worcester specimens".
Graesse (bibliography no. 73) p. 561 shows a very similar looking mark. Thorn (bibliography no. 234) p. 77 calls the kite's tail mark an early Worcester mark, and the Kovels (bibliography no. 115) p. 227 attribute the mark both to Meissen and Worcester.

(2)Kratze (bibliography no. 119) p. 2.

(3)St. A. Loc. 41724, Sect. IV, Lit. E, No. 6, Vol. I, p. 86b

(4)St. A. Loc. 41724, Sect. IV, Lit E, No. 6, Vol. I, p. 93.

(5)Letter by Roland Dorschner, Chairman of the Board of Hutschenreuther AG to author, July 8th, 1982.

(6)St. A. Loc. 41 724, Sect. IV, Lit. E, No. 6, Vol. II, p. 133.

(7)WA I Bl 71, pp. 2-5.

(8)WA I Bl 60, p. 332-338b and pp. 349-350.

(9)WA I Bl 39, p. 3.

(10)WA I Bl 55, p. 54b.

(11)Warenzeichenblatt I, 1951, p. 561.

(12)WA I Bl 55, p. 36.

(13)WA I Bl 55, p. 60.

(14)Brayshaw Gilhespy (bibliography no. 26) p. 26.

(15)St. A. Loc. 11 114, Vol. I, pp. 6-7.

(16)St. A. Loc. 1345, Vol. XXII, p. 325.

(17)St. A. Loc. 1345, Vol. XXII, p. 337.
(18)St. A. Loc. 1345, Vol. XXII, pp. 8-9.
(19)St. A. Loc. 11114, Vol. I, p. 21
(20)St. A. Loc. 11 114, Vol. I, p. 154.
(21)St. A. Loc. 41 724, Vol. I, Sect. IV, Lit. E, No. 6, p. 15b.
(22)St. A. Loc. 41 724, Vol. IX, D 4, Bd. 7, p. 151ff.
(23)Information given to author by Dr. Margit Eisenbart, public relations spokeswoman of the Herend manufactory, on May 24th, 1982.
(24)Imre Katona, keeper of the ceramics department at the Museum of Arts and Crafts in Budapest, Hungary, advanced the explanation that the Herend manufactory in the 1870s still had old porcelain in stock that was fired once but not glazed and fired for the second time. These pieces might have been spares from earlier orders by the Hungarian nobility for copies of Meissen porcelain. In the 1870s — Katona assumes — these pieces were signed with the crossed swords and then glazed. Katona is of the opinion that the Herend manufactory was justified in doing this, because he feels that the Meissen manufactory competed with unfair business practices against Herend in Hungary. To defend itself against what Katona considers a fierce attack by Meissen, the Herend manufactory in his opinion probably also imitated other Meissen marks.
(25)Nachweisung I (bibliography no.272).
(26)WA I Bl 27, p. 886.
(27)WA I Bl 55, p. 32.
(28)St. A. Loc. 41 724, Abt. IX, Abschn. D, No. 4, Vol. III, pp. 108, 108b.
(29)WA I Bl 28, p. 261.
(30)WA I Bl 29, p. 115.
(31)WA I Bl 55, p. 59.
(32)WA I Bm 5, p. 6.
(33)Röntgen (bibliography no. 198) pp. 510-573 shows more than 400 marks that could be mistaken for marks of the Meissen manufactory.
(34)St. A. Loc. 39 201, no pagination.
(35)U.S. Patent Office, Trademark no. 655,242.
(36)U.S. Patent Office, Trademark no. 772,301.
(37)U.S. Patent Office, Trademark no. 740,005.
(38)WA AR 867.
(39)WA AR 867.
(40)WA-NA 591.
(41)WA AR 867.
(42)Judgement by the Landgericht Fürth against the company of Pepelas Stavros, Dec. 19th, 1980.

Chapter Twelve

(1)Today the manufactory operates one store in Meissen and a second one in Berlin GDR.
(2)Pococke, R. (bibliography no. 186) pp. 234-235.
(3)Honey (bibliography no. 92.
(4)Angus-Butterworth (bibliography no. 4) p. 75.
Chaffers (bibliography no. 31) Vol. 1, p. 466
Eberlein and Ramsdell (bibliography no. 58) pp. 179-180
Kovel (bibliography no. 116) p. 160 state "Dresden China is any china made in the town of Dresden, Germany. The most famous factory in Dresden is the Meissen factory". On page 307: "Meissen is a town in Germany where porcelain has been made since 1710. Any china made in that town can be called Meissen, although the famous Meissen Factory made the finest porcelains of this area."
Litchfield (bibliography no. 127) p. 503 "Meissen, see Dresden". He should have known better because he appeared in several court cases in London as an expert witness in matters concerning porcelain forgeries.
Ray (bibliography no. 187) p. 60 feels that Meissen porcelain is "correctly called both Dresden and Meissen".

Warman (bibliography no. 257) p. 286.
(5)The marks with crossed swords and *Dresden Art* was registered with the U.S. Patent Office on January 26, 1971, no. 906,708, after the application had been filed on September 8, 1966. The accompanying affidavit by the manufactory states that this mark was first used in commerce in July of 1966.
(6)Chaffers (bibliography no. 31) Vol. 1, p. 478 mentions four examples.
Doenges (bibliography no. 49) p. 213.
Graesse (bibliography no. 73) p. 486.
Grollier (bibliography no. 76) p. 174.
Honey (bibliography no. 92) p. 172.
Cushion and Honey (bibliography no. 43) p. 186, without years, described as "unidentified palace mark".
(7)U.S. Patent Office Trademark Register no. 10,282 in 1883; no. 52,719 in 1906.
(8)Booklet *Dresden China Illustrated* by C.M. Hutschenreuther Art Department, Dresden 1931.
(9)*Adressbuch der Exportindustrie* 1884, Leipzig, p. 70.
(10)*Kaiserliches Patentamt*, p95/20 Wz, Berlin 2 January 1896.
(11)Yates (bibliography no. 264) p. 152.
(12)Litchfield (bibliography no. 127) p. 73.
(13)Hannover (bibliography no. 85) Vol. III, p. 110. The correct name of the proprietor was Kuntzsch.
(14)*Chatty Letters about Dresden's Smart Shops*, distributed by Hotel Bellevue, Dresden, April 12th, 1931, pp. 22-23.
(15)Letter by W. Oppenheim, London, to the manufactory, WA I Bl 34, pp. 1-2.
(16)*The Times*, London, January 28th, 1898, p. 2.
(17)St. A. Loc. 41 724, p. 127.
(18)St. A. Loc. 41 724, p. 134.
(19)St. A. Loc. 41 724, p. 129ff.
(20)WA I Bl 62, pp. 49-53.
(21)WA I Bl 62, pp. 202-204.

Chapter Thirteen

(1)St. A. Loc. 1340, Vol. I, p. 44.
(2)WA Pretiosa No. 13, p. 13.
(3)Graph after Goder (bibliography no. 71) p. 112.
(4)Schulle and Ullrich (bibliography no. 216).
(5)WA I Bl 29, p. 28.
(6)NA 632, p. 183.
(7)NA 523, no pagination.

Lists

(1)St. A. Loc. 41 846, p. 6ff.
(2)WA III H 64, p. 331-343.
(3)WA III H 64, p. 224ff.
(4)*Grundpreisliste Figuren*, January 1970.
(5)WA III H 28.
(6)WA AAI Bb 12, p. 19.
(7)Compiled from the business sections of the directories for the city of Dresden from 1855 until 1943/1944. Before 1855 porcelain painters were not listed separately. The directory for 1943/1944 was the last one published. The telephone book for 1981 lists three porcelain painting shops. Added to the lists were also porcelain painters which were not listed in the directories but of which published advertisements could be found.

Bibliography

Abbreviations: *Keramos - Zeitschrift der Gesellschaft der Keramikfreunde (Journal of the Society of Friends of Ceramics)* Düsseldorf, FRG
KFS - Mitteilungsblatt Keramik-Freunde der Schweiz (Bulletin of Friends of Ceramics in Switzerland) Zurich, Switzerland

1. Ade Boger, L., *The Dictionary of World Pottery and Porcelain*, New York: 1961.
2. Albiker, C., *Die Meissner Porzellantiere im 18. Jahrhundert*, Berlin: 1935.
3. Albrecht, H., *Böttger und seine Zeit* in: *KFS* 40.
4. Angus-Butterworth, L.M., *Pottery and Porcelain*, London and Glasgow: 1964.
5. Asche, S., *Die Dresdner Künstler des frühen 18. Jahrhunderts als Meister des Böttgersteinzeugs* in: *Keramos* 50.
6. Auscher, E.S., *Comment Reconnaître Les Porcelaines et Les Faiences*, Paris: no date.
7. Bachmann, Petermann e.a., *Johann Friedrich Böttger zu Ehren - Meissen Frühzeit und Gegenwart*, Dresden: 1982.
8. Baer, I., *Glas und Steinzeug, Original Kopie oder Fälschung*, Hannover: 1979.
9. Bangert, A. editor, *Antiquitäten Porzellan*, München: 1977.
10. Behrends, R., *Das Meissner Musterbuch für Höroldt-Chinoiserien (Schulz-Codex)*, Leipzig: 1978.
11. Berling, K., *Das Meissner Porzellan und seine Geschichte*, Leipzig: 1900.
12. Berling, K., *Meissen China, an Illustrated History*, New York: 1972, reprint.
13. Biedrzynski, E., *Bruckmann's Porzellan Lexikon*, München: 1979.
14. Biehn, H., *Deutsche Porzellanfiguren des 18. Jahrhunderts*, Königsberg: 1943.
15. Blunt, A., *Meissen and Oriental Porcelain - The James A. de Rothschild Collection at Waddesdon Manor*, Fribourg: 1971.
16. Böhmert, V., *Urkundliche Geschichte und Statistik der Meissner Porzellanmanufactur von 1710 bis 1800.* in: *Zeitschrift des K. Sächsischen Statistischen Bureaus, XXVI Jahrgang, Heft I und II*, Dresden: 1880.
17. Boltz, C., *Ein Beitrag zum grünen Watteau-Service für Neapel* in: *Keramos* 79.
18. Boltz, C., *Ein "Present vor die Königin von Frankreich"* in: *KFS* 94.
19. Boltz, C., *Formen des Böttgersteinzeugs im Jahr 1711* in: *KFS* 96.
20. Boltz, C. and Chojnacka, H., *Fata des Meissner Porzellanservices mit blauen Blumen und AR für die "Königliche Hof Conditorey Warschau"* in: *Bulletin Du Musée National de Varsovie Vol. XIX, 3/1978.*
21. Boltz, C., *Hoym, Lemaire und Meissen* in: *Keramos* 88.
22. Boltz, C., *Zu einem Meissner Tafelservice* in: *Dresdener Kunstblätter* IV/1975.
23. Bott, G. editor, *Böttgersteinzeug und frühes Meissner Porzellan* catalogue Germanisches Nationalmuseum, Nürnberg: 1982.
24. Brandes, H. e.a., *Meissner Porzellan von 1710 bis zur Gegenwart* exhibition catalogue, Wien: 1983
25. Brandes, H. e.a., *Meissner Porzellan von 1710 bis zur Gegenwart* exhibition catalogue, Köln: 1983.
26. Brayshaw Gilhespy, F., *Derby Porcelain*, London: 1965.
27. Brüning, A., *Porzellan*, Berlin: 1914.
28. Buckendahl, W. *Zu einer Meissner Tasse mit Goldchinesen von Abraham Seuter* in: *Keramos* 86.
29. Burwell, R.L. Jr., *LES JEAUX ET PLAISIERS DE L'ENFANCE VON JAQUES STELLA als Quelle für das Meissen Service "Kinder a la Raphael"* in: *Keramos* 88.
30. Bursche, S., *Meissen*, Berlin: 1980.
31. Chaffers, W., *Marks and Monograms on European and Oriental Pottery and Porcelain*, London: 1974.
32. Charleston, J.R., *World Ceramics*, London, New York: 1979.
33. Clarke, T.H., *An important early Meissen tankard painted by J.G. Herold* in: *KFS* 45.
34. Clarke, T.H., *August der Starke in Chatsworth* in: *Keramos* 95.
35. Clarke, T.H., *Böttger-Wappenporzellan* in: *Keramos* 95.
36. Clarke, T.H., *Die "Römische Bestellung", Die Meissner Altar-Garnitur, die August III dem Cardinal Annibale Albani im Jahre 1736 schenkte* in: *Keramos* 86.
37. Clarke, T.H., *Eine Meissen-Entdeckung - Sabina Auffenwerth in Augsburg* in: *Keramos* 60.
38. Clarke, T.H., *Ein Kruzifix aus Böttgerporzellan im Palazzo Pitti: Ein Zwischenbericht* in: *Keramos* 95.
39. Clarke, T.H., *Sabina Auffenwerth, The Augsburg Hausmalerin - another documentary discovery* in: *Keramos* 61.
40. Clarke, T.H. *The Northumberland Service of Meissen Porcelain* in: *Keramos* 70.
41. Cox, W.E., *The Book of Pottery and Porcelain*, New York: 1973.
42. Cummer Gallery of Art, *The Constance I. and Ralph H. Wark Collection of Meissen Porcelain*, Jacksonville, Florida: 1965.
43. Cushion, J.P. and Honey, W.B., *Handbook of Pottery and Porcelain Marks*, New York: no date.
44. Cushion, J.P., *Pocket Book of German Ceramic Marks and those of other Central European Countries*, London: 1961.
45. Cushion, J.P., *Porcelain*, London: 1975.
46. Danckert, L., *Handbuch des Europäischen Porzellans*, München: 1978.
47. Danckert, L., *Directory of European Porcelain*, London: 1981.
48. Demel, E., *Porzellanmalerei, Vorbilder und Arbeitsanlage*, Zürich: 1979.
49. Doenges, W., *Meissner Porzellan, Seine Geschichte und künstlerische Entwicklung*, Berlin: 1907.
50. Donhof, M., *Böttgersteinzeug, Böttgerporzellan*, inventory catalogue of Schlossmuseum Arnstadt: 1982.
51. Doussy, M., *Antiques, Professional Secrets for the Amateur, The Art of Restoration*, New York: 1971.

52. Ducret, S., *Einige Hinweise für Junge Sammler* in: *Keramos* 24.
53. Ducret, S., *German Porcelain and Faience*, New York: 1962.
54. Ducret, S., *Meissner Porzellan*, Bern: 1974.
55. Ducret, S., *Meissner Porzellan bemalt in Augusburg*, Braunschweig: 1971-1972.
56. Ducret, S. and Wolgensinger, M., *The Colour Treasury of 18th Century Porcelain*, Zürich: 1971.
57. Dürr, H. editor, *Antiquitäten und ihre Preise*, München: 1973.
58. Eberlein, H.D. and Ramsdell, R.W., *The Practical Book of Chinaware*, Philadelphia and New York: 1948.
59. Ehret, G., *Battenberg Antiquitäten-Kataloge Porzellan*, München: 1979.
60. Engelhardt, C.A., *J.F. Böttger*, Leipzig: 1981, reprint.
61. Erichsen-Firle, U., *Figürliches Porzellan*, Köln: 1975.
62. Falke, O. von, *Deutsche Porzellanfiguren*, Berlin: 1919.
63. Falke, O. von, *Majolika*, Berlin, 1907.
64. Fillmann, A., *Die Kartelle und Konzerne in der deutschen Porzellanindustrie* in: *Weltwirtschaftliches Archiv, 21. Band, Jena:* 1925.
65. Fry, P.S., *The World of Antiques*, London: 1970.
66. Funk, W., *Über Porzellanschutzmarken und Porzellanfälschungen* in: *Der Kunstwanderer, 1. Juniheft 1922 und 1.-2. Juliheft 1922.*
67. Gardner, P.V., *Meissen and other German Porcelain in the Alfred Duane Pell Collection*, Washington, D.C.: 1956.
68. Gibb, W. and Rackham, B., *A Book of Porcelain*, London: 1910.
69. Goder, W., *Johann Kunckel und Johann Friedrich Böttger - zwei Erfinder - ein Glas - und ein Porzellanmacher* in: *Silikattechnik* 2/1982.
70. Goder, W. and Walter, H., *Johann Friedrich Böttger - Erfinder des Europäischen Porzellans* in: *Silikattechnik* 2/1982.
71. Goder, W., *Zum Zusammenhang zwischen dem Entwicklungsstand der Produktivkräfte im sächsischen Berg- und Hüttenwesen und der Erfindung des ersten europäischen Porzellans sowie zwischen der Entwicklung der Montanwissenschaften insbesondere durch die Gründung der Bergakademie Freiberg und der Weiterentwicklung des ersten deutschen Porzellans zum Meissner Porzellan*, doctoral thesis, manuscript, Freiberg: 1979.
72. Graesse, J.G. Th., *Guide de l'Amateur de Porcelaines et de Faiences*, Dresden: 1869.
73. Graesse, J.G. Th. and Jaennicke, E., *Führer für Sammler von Porzellan und Fayence Steinzeug, Steingut usw.*, Braunschweig: 1974.
74. Graul, R. and Kurzwelly, A., *Altthüringer Porzellan*, Leipzig: 1909.
75. Gröger, H., *Johann Joachim Kaendler*, Dresden: 1956.
76. Grollier, Ch. de, *Manuel de l'amateur des Porcelaines Manufactures Francaises*, Paris: 1922.
77. Hackenbroch, Y., *Der Jagdpokal des Kurfürsten Clemens August* in: *Keramos* 73.
78. Hackenbroch, Y., *Der Jagdpokal des Kurfürsten Clemens August* in: *Keramos* 88.
79. Hackenbroch, Y. and Parker, J., *The Lesley and Emma Sheafer Collection. A Selective Presentation.* The Metropolitan Museum of Arts, New York: 1975.
80. Haedeke, H.-U., *Bestecke und Griffe aus Meissner Porzellan im Deutschen Klingenmuseum Solingen* in: *Keramos* 50.
81. Haedeke, H.-U., *Die Dresdner Porzellansammlung* in: *Keramos* 5.
82. Haggar, R.G., *The Concise Encyclopedia of Continental Pottery and Porcelain*, New York: 1960.
83. Hamer, F., *The Potter's Dictionary of Materials and Techniques*, London-New York: 1975.
84. Handt, I. and Rakebrand, H., *Meissner Porzellan des Achtzehnten Jahrhunderts 1710-1750.* Dresden: 1956.
85. Hannover, E., *Pottery and Porcelain, Europe & The Near East, Earthenware & Stoneware*, London: 1925.
86. Hartmann, H., *Porcelain & Pottery Marks*, New York: 1943.
87. Hayward, F.J., *Viennese Porcelain of the Du Paquier Period*, London: 1952.
88. Heintze, J., *Beitrag zur Geschichte der europäischen Porzellanfabrikation* in: *Zeitschrift für Architektur und Ingenieurwesen 5/1898*, pp. 387-398.
89. Heuschkel, H. and Muche, K., *ABC Keramik*, Leipzig: 1975.
90. Hofmann, F., *Das Porzellan der europäischen Manufakturen*, Oldenburg: 1980.
91. Hofmann, F., *Das Europäische Porzellan des Bayer. Nationalmuseums*, München: 1908.
92. Honey, W.B., *Dresden China*, London: 1934.
93. Honey, W.B., *German Porcelain*, London: 1954.
94. Honey, W.B., *A Porcelain Tankard painted by C.W.E. Dietrich* in: *The Burlington Magazine* August 1931.
95. Hornig-Sutter, M., *Kritische Betrachtungen zur Ausstellung "Fälschung und Forschung"* in: *Keramos* 75.
96. Horschick, J., *Die vergessene Bemalung der grossen Meissner Porzellantiere* in: *Keramos* 78.
97. Jedding, H., *Europäisches Porzellan*, München: 1974.
98. Jedding, H., *Meissner Porzellan des 18. Jahrhunderts*, München: 1979.
99. Jedding, H., *Meissner Porzellan des 19. und 20. Jahrhunderts*, München: 1981.
100. Jedding, H., *Porzellan aus der Sammlung Blohm*, Hamburg: 1968.
101. Joseph, H., *Das "Hohle Dreieck" auf Meissen-Dosen* in: *Keramos* 77.
102. Just, J., *Der künstlerische Erneuerungsprozess der Porzellanmanufaktur Meissen um 1900*, doctoral thesis, Martin-Luther-Universität Halle-Wittenberg: 1972.
103. Just, J., *Geschnittene Marken auf Meissner Porzellan, Güteklassen und Weissverkauf* in: *Jahrbuch der Staatlichen Kunstsammlungen* Dresden: 1970/1971, pp. 209-216.
104. Just, J., *Kaendlers letzte Porträtdarstellung*, in: *KFS* 77.
105. Just, J., *Marken und Markierungen auf Meissner Porzellan ab 1775* in: *Keramos* 53/54.
106. Just, R., *Neue Forschungen über die Pressnitzer Porzellan-Hausmaler* in: *KFS* 46.

107.Kalnein, W. von, *Die Porzellan- und Fayencesammlung des Zähringer Museums in Baden-Baden*
in: *Keramos* 32.
108.Katona, I., *Ismeretlen Adatok A Herendi Porcelán-gyárról*
in: *Informations by the Museums of the Comitat Veszprem*, Vol. 10, Veszprem: 1971.
109.Katona, I., *Korai Meisseni Márkautánzatok Magyarországon A XIX. Század Második Felében*, Budapest: no date.
110.Katzander, H.L., *Antiques and Art*, Garden City, New York: 1977.
111.Klamkin, M., *White House China*, New York: 1972.
112.Köllmann, E., *Der Mopsorden*
in: *Keramos* 50.
113.Köllmann, E., *Kurfürst Clemens August von Köln - Ein Porzellansammler des 18. Jahrhunderts*
in: *Keramos* 13.
114.Köllmann, E., *Meissner Porzellan*, Braunschweig: 1975.
115.Kovel, R.M. and T.H., *Dictionary of Marks - Pottery and Porcelain*, New York: 1974.
116.Kovel, R.M. and T.H., *The Kovel's Complete Antiques Price List*, New York: 1979.
117.Kovel, R.M. and T.H., *Know Your Antiques*, New York: 1972.
118.Kramer, E., *Ein Porträt Johann Friedrich Böttgers*
in: *Keramos* 30.
119.Kratze, W., *Meissner Porzellanmarken VIEUX SAXE*, Klotzsche-Königswald: no date.
120.Kunze, J., *Beitrag zur Geschichte der Porzellanmanufaktur Meissen in der Biedermeierzeit*
in: *Keramos* 86.
121.Kunze, J., *Die Bedeutung des "Englischen Handels" mit Porzellanen im "Altfranzösischen Geschmack" der Meissner Manufaktur in der ersten Hälfte des 19. Jahrhunderts*
in: *Keramos* 95.
122.Kunze, J., *Die Schwertermarken der Porzellanmanufaktur Meissen mach 1813 bis 1860*
in: *Keramos* 96.
123.Kunze, J., *Lithopanien der Meissen Porzellanmanufaktur*
in: *Keramos* 92.
124.Kunze, J., *Mitteilungen über Georg Friedrich Kerstings Tätigkeit an der Porzellanmanufaktur Meissen von 1818 bis 1847*
in: *Keramos* 95.
125.Kunze, J., *Nebenproduktionen der Meissner Porzellanmanufaktur in der ersten Hälfte des 19. Jahrhunderts*
in: *Keramos* 98.
126.Kunze, J., *Vergoldungsarten für Porzellane der Meissner Manufaktur in der ersten Hälfte des 19. Jahrhunderts*
in: *Keramos* 99.
127.Litchfield, F., *Pottery and Porcelain*, London: 1912.
128.Loesch, P., *Johann Friedrich Böttger von 1706 bis 1707 Arrestant auf der Festung Königstein*, published by Museum Festung Königstein: 1981.
129.Meier, G., *Künstlerisches Porzellan aus der Meissner Manufaktur*, doctoral thesis, Humboldt-Universität Berlin: 1980.
130.Meier, G., *Porzellan aus der Meissner Manufaktur*, Berlin: 1981.
131.Marik, K.T., *Zwei Walzenkrüge von J.G. Höroldt*
in: *KFS* 67.
132.McClinton, K.M., *Antiques Past and Present*, New York: 1971.
133.Mediger, P., *Arbeiten von William Baring für die Meissner Manufaktur*
in: *Keramos* 90.
134.Mediger, P., *Ein Böttger-Porzellan mit Auffenwerth-Bemalung*
in: *Keramos* 71.
135.Mediger, P., *Ein Meissner Leuchtermodell zum Andreas-Service des russischen Hofes nach Meissonier-Vorbild*
in: *KFS* 77.
136.Mediger, P., *Johann-Joachim Kaendler und Paul Scheurich - vergleichende Betrachtungen*
in: *KFS* 78.
137.Mediger, P., *Kupferstich- und Architekturvorbilder zu Meissner Porzellanstücken*
in: *KFS* 75.
138.Mediger, P., *Scheurichs Verhältnis zu Ballet und Oper*
in: *KFS* 70.
139.Mediger, P., *Zur Entstehungsgeschichte des Schwanenservices*
in: *KFS* 78.
140.Meinert, G., *Handelsbeziehungen zwischen Sachsen und Italien 1740-1814*, Weimar: 1974.
141.Meinz, M., *Neuentdeckungen zum "Hohlen Dreieck" auf Meissner Porzellan*
in: *Keramos* 86.
142.Meissen Manufactory, publisher, *250 Jahre Staatliche Porzellan-Manufaktur Meissen*, Meissen: 1960.
143.Meissen Manufactory, publisher, *VEB Staatliche Porzellan-Manufaktur Meissen, aus ihrer Geschichte und ihrem Schaffen*, Meissen: 1961.
144.Meissen Manufactory, publisher, *Meissner Porzellan, Weisses Gold mit den blauen Schwertern*, Meissen: 1981.
145.Meissen Manufactory, publisher, *Informationen der Meissner Porzellanmanufaktur*, Meissen: 1963.
146.Meissen Manufactory, publisher, *VEB Staatliche Porzellan Manufaktur Meissen, Deutsche Demokratische Republik, Aus ihrer Geschichte und ihrem Schaffen*, Meissen: 1973.
147.Menzhausen-Handt, I., *Böttgersteinzeug mit Emailmalerei und Edelsteinen*
in: *Keramos* 24.
148.Menzhausen, I., *Das Älteste aus Meissen: Böttgers "rothes und weisses Porzellan"*
in: *Dresdener Kunstblätter: 1/1982.*
149.*Menzhausen-Handt, I., Das erste Inventar der Dresdener Porzellansammlung*
in: *Keramos* 12.
150.Menzhausen, I., *Böttgersteinzeug - Böttgerporzellan aus der Dresdener Porzellansammlung*, Dresden: 1969.
151.Menzhausen, I., *Das Bildnis Johann Friedrich Böttgers*
in: *Dresdener Kunstblätter:* 1/1982.
152.Menzhausen, I., *Eine neue kryptische Signatur von Höroldt*
in: *KFS* 67.
153.Menzhausen, I., *Kritische Bemerkungen zu einer Gruppe von Meissner Walzenkrügen*
in: *Keramos* 47.
154.Menzhausen, I., *Porzellansammlung im Zwinger (A Guide to the Dresden Porcelain Collection)*, Dresden: 1980.
155.Menzhausen, I., *Porzellansammlung im Zwinger (A Guide to the Dresden Porcelain Collection)*, Dresden: 1982.
156.Menzhausen, I., *Zur Eröffnung der Porzellansammlung im Zwinger*
in: *Jahrbuch der Staatlichen Kunstsammlungen* Dresden: 1961/1962.
157.Menzhausen, I., *Das Neueste aus Meissen*
in: *Dresdener Kunstblätter*, 1/1982.
158.Meyer-Heilemann, M., *Das Wickelkind*
in: *Keramos* 80.
159.Mickenhagen, R., *Europäisches Porzellan*, München: no date.
160.Mields, M. and Lauschke, R.. *Praxis der Porzellanmalerei*, München: 1965.
161.Mields, M., *Aus der Jugendzeit des europäischen Porzellans*
in: *Sprechsaal*, 10/1960.
162.Mields, M., *Die Entwicklung der Aufglasurpalette des europäischen Hartporzellans bis 1731 mit besonderer Berücksichtigung der Arbeiten von J.G. Höroldt*
in: *Keramische Zeitschrift*, 8/1963.
163.Mields, M., *Eine Versuchsaufzeichnung von Johann Friedrich Böttger zur Porzellanerfindung aus dem Jahr 1708*
in: *Berichte der Deutschen Keramischen Gesellschaft, Band 44* (1967), *Heft* 10, pp. 513-517.
164.Milly, Graf von, *Die Kunst das aechte Porcellaen zu verfertigen*, Leipzig: 1977, reprint of the edition of 1774.
165.Mischell, H.H., *Eine Meissner Kaffeekanne mit Malerei von Abraham Seuter*
in: *Keramos* 71.
166.Molnar, L., *Die Herender Porzellanfabrik Aktiengesellschaft*
in: *Annales Universitatis Scientiarum Budapestinensis de Rolande Eötvös Nominate, Separatum Sectio Historica, Tomus XX*, Budapest: 1980.
167.Molnar, L., *Die Porzellanmanufaktur Herend*
in: *Keramos* 89.
168.Morley-Fletcher, H., *Porzellan aus Meissen*, Wiesbaden: 1971.
169.Müller-Fraureuth, K., *Wörterbuch der obersächsischen und erzgebirgischen Mundarten*,
170.*Museum Folkwang Essen and Staatl. Museen Preussischer Kulturbessitz, Berlin, Fälschung und Forschung*, Essen/Berlin: 1976.
171.Nekam, L., *Meissen Porcelain in the Budapest Museum of Applied Arts*, Budapest: 1980.
172.Neuwirth, W., *Meissener Marken und Wiener Bindenschild, Original, Imitation, Verfälschung, Fälschung*, Wien: 1977.
173.Neuwirth, W., *Meissener Marken, Original, Imitation, Verfälschung, Fälschung*, Wien: 1980.
174.Neuwirth, W., *Böttgersteinzeug, YIXING und andere rote Ware, Band II*, Wien: 1982.
175.Neuwirth, W., *Porzellanmaler - Lexikon*, Braunschweig: 1977.
176.Neuwirth, W., *Das AR-Monogramm. Neue Erkenntnisse zur Datierung der Meissener AR-Marke sowie zur Provenienz der AR-Fälschungen*
in: *Keramos* 100.
177.Newman, M., *Die deutschen Porzellan-Manufakturen im 18. Jahrhundert*, Braunschweig: 1977.
178.N.N., *Dresden China, The Royal Saxon Porcelain Works at Meissen circa 1878*, Texas: 1970.
179.N.N., *Verzeichnis der Sammlungen im Herzogl. Schlosse zu Altenburg*, Altenburg: 1912.
180.Patterson, J.E., *Porcelain*, Washington, D.C., 1979.
181.Pazaurek, G.E., *Meissner Porzellanmalerei des 18. Jahrhunderts*, Stuttgart: 1929.
182.Penkala, M., *European Porcelain*, Amsterdam: 1947.
183.Petermann, K. e.a., *Internationales Symposium anlässlich der Johann-Friedrich-Böttger-Ehrung Dresden-Meissen 1982*, Freiberg: 1983.
184.Peters, R., *Eine Meissner Kaffeekanne und ihre graphischen Vorlagen*
in: *Keramos* 71.
185.Poche, E., *Porcelain Marks of the World*, New York: 1974.
186.Pococke, R., *A description of the East and some other countries, vol. 2, book* 5, London: 1745.
187.Ray, M., *Collectible Ceramics*, New York: 1974.
188.Reichel, F., *Bemaltes Porzellan*, Leipzig: 1976.
189.Reineking von Bock, G., *Paul Scheurich in Meissen*
in: *Kunst und Antiquitäten IV*/1983, pp. 67-73.
190.Reinhardt, C., *Beiträge zur Lebensgeschichte von Ehrenfried Walter von Tschirnhaus*
in: *Wissenschaftliche Beilage zum Jahresbericht der Fürsten- und Landesschule St. Afra zu Meissen*, Meissen: 1903.
191.Reinhardt, C., *Tschirnhaus oder Böttger. Eine urkundliche Geschichte der Erfindung des Meissner Porzellans*
in: *Neues Lausitzisches Magazin, Band 88*, Görlitz: 1912.
192.Reinheckel, G., *Die erste Folge der Pariser Ausrufer in Meissner Porzellan*
in: *Keramos* 50.
193.Reinheckel, G., *Leplat und Meissen*
in: *Keramos* 23.
194.Reinheckel, G., *Nachrichten über eingeschickte Vorbilder und Modelle aus den Akten des Meissner Werkarchivs von 1720 bis 1745*
in: *KFS* 56.
195.Reinheckel, G., *Plastische Dekorationsformen im Meissner Porzellan des 18. Jahrhunderts*, doctoral thesis, Martin-Luther-Universität, Halle-Wittenberg: 1964.
196.Renard, E., *Clemens August, Kurfürst von Köln*, Bielefeld und Leipzig: 1927.
197.Roemer, C.H. von, *Staatsrecht und Statistik des Churfürstenthums Sachsen und der dabey befindlichen Lande;* Erster Theil, Halle 1787; Zweyter Theil, Halle 1788; Dritter Theil, Wittenberg 1792.
198.Röntgen, R., *Marks on German, Bohemian and Austrian Porcelain 1710 to the Present*, Exton, Pennsylvania: 1981.
199.Rosenfeld, D., *Porcelain Figures of the Eighteenth Century*, New York & London: 1949.
200.Rückert, R., *Meissner Porzellan 1710-1815*, München: 1966.
201.Rückert, R., *Meissen und der Schneiderspott*
in: *Kunst und Antiquitäten III*/1979.
202.Rückert, R. and Willsberger, J., *Meissen, Porzellan des 18. Jahrhunderts*, Wien: 1977.
203.Savage, G. and Newman, H., *An Illustrated Dictionary of Ceramics*, London: 1974.
204.Savage, G., *18th-century German Porcelain*, London: 1958.
205.Schärer, J., *Meissen '75*, Meissen: 1975.
206.Scherf, H., *Blaue Schwerter auf Thüringer Porzellan*
in: *Jahrbuch der Staatlichen Kunstsammlungen* Dresden: 1978/1979.
207.Scherf, H., *Thüringer Porzellan*, Seitenroda: 1978.
208.Scherf, H. and Karpinski, J., *Thüringer Porzellan*, Leipzig: 1980.
209.Scheuch, K., *Medaillen aus Porzellan und Ton Band I-IV*, Krumbach: 1967-1970.
210.Scheuch, K., *Münzen aus Porzellan und Ton*, Biebertal: 1971.
211.Scheuch, K., *Spenden-Medaillen aus Porzellan und Ton*, Ober-Eschbach: 1966.
212.Schmidt-Heidelberg, W., *Johann Eleazar Zeissig gen. Schenau*
in: *Der Kunstwanderer 2. Februarheft*, 1922.
213.Schneider-Aschaffenburg, E., *Ein Meissner Musikerkrug der Höroldtzeit*
in: *Keramos*, 35.
214.Schneider, E., *Eine versteckte Signatur auf Meissner Porcelain*
in: *Keramos* 34.
215.Schnorr von Carolsfeld L./Köllmann E., *Porzellan*, Braunschweig: 1974.
216.Schulle, W. and Ullrich, B., *Ergebnisse gefügeanalytischer Untersuchungen an Böttgerporzellan*
in: *Silikattechnik* 2/1982.
217.Scott, G.R., *Herold at DuPaquier and Herold at Meissen 1720 until 1723*
in: *KFS* 45.
218.Seidlitz, W. von, *Die Meissner Porzellanmanufaktur unter Böttger*
in: *Neues Archiv für Sächsiscne Geschichte und Altertumskunde*, Vol. 9, Dresden: 1888, pp. 115-136.
219.Seyffarth, R., *Die Porzellanmalerei*
in: *Keramos* 13.
220.Seyffarth, R., *Generalbefehle, das "Weisse Gut" betreffend*
in: *Keramos* 15.
221.Seyffarth, R., *Eine Fälschung und ihr Vorbild*
in: *KFS* 45.
222.Seyffarth, R., *Johann Gregorius Höroldt*, Dresden: 1981.
223.Seyffarth, R., *Marken der "Königlichen-Porzellan-Manufaktur" zu Meissen von 1721-1750*
in: *KFS* 50.
224.Seyffarth, R., *Von Pfuschern und Fälschern*
in: *Keramos* 34.
225.Shono, M., *Japanisches Aritaporzellan im sogenannten "Kakiemonstil" als Vorbild für die Meissener Porzellanmanufaktur*, München: 1973.
226.Slotta, R., *Das Herder-Service*, Bochum: 1981.
227.Spiegl, W., *Meissner Porzellan*, München: 1978.
228.Steinbrück, J.M., *Bericht über die Porzellanmanufaktur Meissen von den Anfängen bis zum*

Jahr 1717, Facsimile edition of the original handwritten report, Leipzig: 1982.

229. Steinbrück, J.M., *Jesus Mea Salus, Geschichtskalender derer Königl. Pohln. und Churfürstl. Sächs. neuen Manufacturen* Historic Calender of the Royal Polish and Prince-Electoral Saxon new Manufactories
in: *Staatliche Porzellan Manufaktur Meissen Bericht über das Jahr* 1919).

230. Stieda, W., *Die Anfänge der Porzellanfabrikation auf dem Thüringerwalde*, Jena: 1902.

231. Stemper, A., *Ein zeitgenössisches Urteil über den "Stein der Weisen" Johann Friedrich Böttgers*
in: *Deutsche Apotheker-Zeitung*, No. 98/1958.

232. Syz, H. e.a., *Catalogue of the Hans Syz Collection*, Washington, D.C.: 1979.

233. Tardy, *Les Porcelaines Francaises*, Paris: 1975.

234. Thorn, C.J., *Handbook of old Pottery and Porcelain Marks*, New York: 1947.

235. Trömel, W., *Kartell und Preisbildung in der deutschen Geschirr-und Luxusporzellanindustrie*
in: *Abhandlungen des wirtschaftswissenschaftlichen Seminars zu Jena, 17. Band, Drittes Heft*, Jena: 1926.

236. Ungar, S., *Early DuPaquier Porcelain*
in: *KFS* 43.

237. Unitt, D. & P., *Book of Marks*, Peterborough: 1973.

238. Wagner, E., *Der Meissner Jagdpokal des Kurfürsten Clemens August*
in: *Keramos* 71.

239. Walcha, O., *Der Meissner Porzellanmaler Christian Gottlieb Hottewitzsch*
in: *Keramos* 15.

240. Walcha, O., *Die Marcolini-Zeit der Meissner Manufaktur*
in: *Keramos* 40.

241. Walcha, O., *Die Meissner Porzellanlieferungen an Friedrich II. während der Schlesischen Kriege*
in: *Keramos* 7.

242. Walcha, O., *Die zweifigurigen Jahreszeitengruppen Kaendlers*
in: *Keramos* 24.

243. Walcha, O., *Ein Skizzenbuch Kaendlers*
in: *Keramos* 21.

244. Walcha, O., *Formerzeichen auf Böttger-Steinzeug*
in: *KFS* 43.

245. Walcha, O., *Friedrichs II. letzte bedeutende Porzellanbestellung in Meissen*
in: *Keramos* 12.

246. Walcha, O., *Fröhlich und Schmiedel im Meissner Porzellan*
in: *Keramos* 32.

247. Walcha, O., *Höroldts Propositionen vom 24. Februar 1731*
in: *KFS* 43.

248. Walcha, O., *Incunabeln aus dem Meissner Werkarchiv; Die Geburtsstunde des Europäischen Porzellans*
in: *KFS* 46.

249. Walcha, O., *Kleine Chronik der frühen Meissner Blaumalerei*
in: *Keramos* 47.

250. Walcha, O., *Meissner Porzellan*, Dresden: 1973.

251. Walcha, O., *Rivalen*, Berlin: 1963.

252. Walcha, O., *Zur Quellengeschichte des Meissner Porzellans*
in: *KFS* 42.

253. Walter, H. and Goder, W., *Die Erfindung des europäischen Porzellans*
in: *Dresdener Kunstblätter* 1/1982.

254. Ware, G.W., *German and Austrian Porcelain*, New York: 1963.

255. Wark, R., *Adam Friedrich von Löwenfinck, einer der bedeutendsten deutschen Porzellan- und Fayencemaler des 18. Jahrhunderts*
in: *KFS* 34.

256. Wark, R., *Neu bekanntgewordene Porzellane Adam Friedrich von Löwenfincks*
in: *KFS* 43.

257. Warman, G.E., *Twelfth Antiques and their Current Prices*, Uniontown, Pennsylvania: 1975.

258. Weber, F.J., *Die Kunst das Achte Porzellain zu verfertigen*, Hildesheim: 1977, reprint of the edition of 1798.

259. Weiss, G., *The Book of Porcelain*, New York/Washington: 1971.

260. Westhoff-Krummacher, H., *Jagdreportage in Porzellan - Der Jagdpokal des Kurfürsten Clemens August. - Ein Exemplar im Westfälischen Landesmuseum Münster*
in: *Keramos* 95.

261. Wills, G., *Practical Guide to Antiques Collecting*, New York: 1961.

262. Winter, E., *Der Bahnbrecher der deutschen Frühaufklärung E.W.v. Tschirnhaus und die Frühaufklärung in Mittel- und Osteuropa*, Berlin: 1960.

263. Wynter, H., *An Introduction to European Porcelain*, New York: 1972.

264. Yates, R.F., *Antique Fakes and their Detection*, New York: 1950.

265. Zaunick, R., *Ehrenfried Walther von Tschirnhaus*, Acta Historica Leopoldina, Leipzig: 1/1963.

266. Zick, G., *Kaendler und Lafontaine*
in: *Keramos* 53-54.

267. Zimmermann, E., *Egermann oder Tschirnhaus?*
in: *Der Kunstwanderer*, 2. Juliheft: 1921.

268. Zimmermann, E., *Die Anfänge der Blaumalerei in Meissner Porzellan*
in: *Mitteilungen aus den Sächsischen Kunstsammlungen*, 2. Jg. 1911.

269. Zimmermann, E., *Die Erfindung und Frühzeit des Meissner Porzellans*, Berlin: 1908.

270. Zimmermann, E., *In welchem Jahr wurde das Meissner Porzellan erfunden?*
in: *Neues Archiv für Sächsische Geschichte und Altertumskunde*, vol. 27, Dresden: 1906.

271. Zimmermann, E., *Wer war der Erfinder des Meissner Porzellans?*
in: *Neues Archiv für Sächsische Geschichte und Altertumskunde*, vol. 28, Dresden: 1907.

272. *Nachweisung der im Deutschen Reiche gesetzlich geschützten Warenzeichen*, Berlin: 1866 ff, 3 main volumes, 8 supplement volumes.

273. *Warenzeichenblatt*, Berlin: 1884-1945, München: 1949-current.

274. Warenzeichen- und Musterblatt, later Warenzeichenblatt, Berlin, GDR: 1954-current.

275. *Zentralmarkenanzeiger*, Wien: 1905-current.

276. Autorenkollektiv (Collective of Writers) Medaillen aus Meissner Porzellan, Vol. 1962-1969, Berlin 1981. Vol. 1970-1974, Berlin 1979.

Index of Persons